Effective Leadership
in Adventure Programming

Simon Priest, PhD

Michael A. Gass, PhD

University of New Hampshire

Human Kinetics

Library of Congress Cataloging-in-Publication Data

Priest, Simon
    Effective leadership in adventure programming / Simon Priest,
Michael A. Gass.
      p.   cm.
    Includes bibliographical references and index.
    ISBN 0-87322-637-2
    1. Recreation leadership.   2. Outdoor recreation--Management.
3. Leisure--Management.   4. Recreational therapy.   I. Gass, Michael
A. II. Title.
GV181.43.P75   1997
790'.06'9--dc21   97-7791
                                         CIP

ISBN: 0-87322-637-2

Acquisitions Editors: Richard D. Frey and Scott Wikgren; **Developmental Editor:** Kirby Mittelmeier; **Assistant Editor:** Jennifer Stallard; **Editorial Assistants:** Jennifer Hemphill and Amy Carnes; **Copyeditor:** Bonnie Pettifor; **Proofreader:** Pam Johnson; **Graphic Designer:** Robert Reuther; **Graphic Artist:** Kathleen Boudreau-Fuoss; **Photo Editor:** Boyd Lafoon; **Cover Designer:** Jack Davis; **Photographer (cover):** New England Stock Photo/Peter Cole; **Printer:** Braun-Brumfield

Printed in the United States of America   10 9 8 7 6 5

Human Kinetics
Web site: www.humankinetics.com

United States: Human Kinetics, P.O. Box 5076, Champaign, IL 61825-5076
800-747-4457
e-mail: humank@hkusa.com

Canada: Human Kinetics, 475 Devonshire Road, Unit 100, Windsor, ON N8Y 2L5
800-465-7301 (in Canada only)
e-mail: orders@hkcanada.com

Europe: Human Kinetics, Units C2/C3 Wira Business Park, West Park Ring Road
Leeds LS16 6EB, United Kingdom
+44 (0) 113 278 1708
e-mail: hk@hkeurope.com

Australia: Human Kinetics, 57A Price Avenue, Lower Mitcham, South Australia 5062
08 8277 1555
e-mail: liahka@senet.com.au

New Zealand: Human Kinetics, P.O. Box 105-231, Auckland Central
09-523-3462
e-mail: hkp@ihug.co.nz

To the gardeners in our lives for all they sow, nurture, and reap

Contents

PART II: PRACTICAL AND ORGANIZATIONAL SKILLS FOR OUTDOOR LEADERS   73

PART III: INSTRUCTION IN ADVENTURE PROGRAMMING   133

PART IV: FACILITATION IN ADVENTURE PROGRAMMING   171

Acknowledgments

We would like to thank the following individuals who have raised the standards of our writing by challenging our thinking and co-authoring articles with us. Many of the ideas and concepts found in this book are due to their hard work: Aram Attarian, Rusty Baillie, Camille Bunting, Gaylene Carpenter, Bob Chase, Carina Dolcino (Ziemek), Kathy Doherty, Phyllis Ford, Dan Garvey, Lee Gillis, Don Hammerman, Jasper Hunt, Christian Itin, Kim Klint, Chris Loynes, Alistair McArthur, Pam McPhee (Kerr), Peter Martin, John Miles, Todd Miner, Denise Mitten, Sabine Schubert, Jed Williamson, and Scott Wurdinger.

Three people deserve special mention: Betty van der Smissen for her critical analysis and suggestions for the risk management chapter; Karl Rohnke for unselfishly sharing and having fun doing it; and Craig Dobkin for leading us in play for the most noble of causes—peace, love, and compassion.

Credits

Figure 7.2 is adapted, by permission, from S. Priest and R. Baillie, 1987, "Justifying the risk to others: The real razor's edge," *Journal of Experiential Education* 10(1): 16-22.

Figures 11.7 and 20.1 are adapted, by permission, from S. Priest, 1990, "Everything you always wanted to know about judgment, but were afraid to ask," *The Journal of Adventure Education and Outdoor Leadership* 7(3), 5-12.

Figure 12.1 is adapted, by permission, from D. Hammerman and S. Priest, 1989, "The inquire/discovery approach to learning in adventure," *The Journal of Adventure Education and Outdoor Leadership* 6(2), 29-32.

Figure 12.2 is adapted, by permission, from S. Priest and D. Hammerman, 1990, "Teaching outdoor adventure skills," *The Journal of Adventure Education and Outdoor Leadership* 6(4), 16-18.

Figure 21.1 is adapted, by permission, from S. Priest, 1988, "The role of judgment, decision making, and problem solving for outdoor leaders," *Journal of Experiential Education* 11(3), 19-26.

Figure 22.1 is adapted, by permission, from S. Priest, 1988, "AVALANCHE! Decision analysis: one way to solve problems," *Journal of Adventure Education and Outdoor Leadership* 5(3), 14-16.

PHOTOS

Photos on pages 1, 5, 27, 41, 61, 68, 75, 87, 109, 121, 149, 161, 173, 189, 207, 223, 237, 247, 255, 263, 273, and 283 © Simon Priest.

Photos on pages 18, 103, 135, 155, and 293 © Richard Etchberger.

Photo on page 31 courtesy of North Carolina Outward Bound School.

Preface

Outdoor leadership professionals are finding an increasing number and wide range of exciting opportunities in the field of adventure programming. Often quite different than other professional vocations, the field requires you to work in challenging learning environments with a variety of mediums, clients, and professional practices. To demonstrate the range of these opportunities, the following situations portray possible roles you could fill as an outdoor leader when properly trained.

RECREATION: THE OUTDOOR INSTRUCTOR

You are teaching a whitewater paddling course to a public group, focusing on eddy turns in a series of class II rapids. In preparing for this session, you implement a variety of proactive safety measures, including site reconnaissance of the river for any recent changes before the adventure; use of appropriate safety gear such as PFDs and helmets; and possession and positioning of rescue gear such as throw bags, Z-pulley rope systems, and rescue boaters. Having previously taught your students appropriate skills through lectures, demonstrations, and actual experience (e.g., practical swim tests, rescue procedures, exit procedures and Eskimo rolls, and paddle strokes in calm water), you are confident that they are ready for the real thing. During the experience, one boater overturns and becomes separated from her boat on a rock in the middle of the river channel. Before you intercede, the class immediately reacts by setting up a "Tyrolean system" to successfully evacuate the stranded boater to the river bank, as well as a system to retrieve her kayak downstream.

EDUCATION: THE SCHOOL TEACHER

In working with a high school physical education class, you are teaching a rock climbing course using the indoor climbing wall of the gymnasium. The class consists of students with a variety of capabilities, and you work on adapting the curriculum to fit their individual needs. At the same time, you focus on the group dynamics that exist when students place themselves in positions requiring trust and risk taking. While students are involved in actual climbing activities, you use appropriate learning progressions and safety procedures, yet facilitate students' climbing and belaying one another. You coach students on using appropriate verbal techniques and considerations, like using the "full value contract" (a contract emphasizing fully valuing yourself and others), particularly when students are in positions that are especially difficult for them. Several times in this class students become overwhelmed and physically "frozen" with fear. In these situations, you employ a variety of self-efficacy building techniques, such as verbally linking the student to past successes and informing them of the group's support, explaining the options available to them, and helping them focus on those areas proving most difficult. After the activity is completed, you reinforce students' learning through debriefing their successes and setbacks through a discussion of feelings, events, and new learning, emphasizing how they might apply their new-found confidence to school and home situations in the future.

DEVELOPMENT: THE CORPORATE TRAINER

You are working with managers of a health care company to help them with several troublesome issues. The corporation is experiencing a contradiction between quality and expediency and is looking for your corporate adventure program to provide strategies for how these concepts could work synergistically rather than in opposition to one another. In working with these clients, you design a series of adventure activities related to their identified needs. You focus special attention on this relationship, creating a metaphorical connection through which the energies, focuses, and outcomes of producing a successful method in adventure experiences result in the successful resolution of the company's specific issues.

Because of its strong relationship to the needs of the company, one of the key activities you select to use is the "Spider's Web" initiative, which involves passing members of a group through openings in a giant web of rope without touching the strands. You design the initiative for further relevance by presenting it as a task where the employees must demonstrate a model delivery and transfer service by passing employees through a complex network of resources in a caring and efficient manner. The web initiative becomes analogous to the complex interactive system they are working through where each opening becomes a manager's personal area of responsibility to address during the interactive resolution process. Only one person may pass through each delegated area, since to send someone through that opening again would be a replication of services. You also add a time limit (a common constraint facing this company) of 25 minutes, with a 25% bonus if they complete the task in under 20 minutes and a consequence for every minute it takes over 25 to complete the task. With this metaphorical framework in place, you begin the activity.

THERAPY:
THE FAMILY COUNSELOR

As an adventure professional with a therapeutic training background, you work in a substance abuse program for youth, focusing on enhancing communication between adolescents with drug addictions and their parents. Your program uses adventure experiences as adjunctive therapy to established treatment plans. Your focus for this session is to redirect interaction between a 14-year-old son and his mother who have become emotionally separated in their single-parent family. Current symptoms of the son's behavior include substance abuse, low self-esteem, and a strong fear that his mother will also abandon him. As you begin to work with the mother and son, you select the "Trust Lean" initiative, an activity where one person falls into the supporting arms of another, providing a "mirror image" of what is happening in their relationship and how this influences them. This particular exercise highlights the issues of kids growing up to be adults,

figuring out what they will be able to accomplish, and testing personal limits. You implement actions as well as verbal techniques that build on these issues, replacing old dysfunctional behaviors with relevant functional ones. During the Trust Lean experience, the mother sees the parallel between her successful interaction with her son and the need for her to have a "hands-on" relationship with him in order to help him maintain appropriate balance in his life. Simultaneously, the son recognizes that "staying straight" in the Trust Lean has a positive effect on both his success as well as his relationship with his mother. Following the activity, you facilitate a discussion about the issues of interaction and relationship. Each represents a key feature in providing a solution to the various concerns they have.

PURPOSE OF THE BOOK

These scenarios are actual examples of current applications of the adventure programming profession: recreational, educational, developmental, and therapeutic. While complex, they portray a variety of principles and practices forming the body of outdoor leadership knowledge. In writing this book, we intend to provide guidelines for you as an outdoor leader to enhance your understanding of this rapidly emerging profession. We have organized this book as a course text for the preparation of undergraduate and graduate students in outdoor leadership, but if you are a professional already working in the field of adventure learning, you can use it as a reference manual. In other words, this book provides a comprehensive source for entry-level outdoor leaders, but advanced practitioners may also find sections that are valuable for their ongoing professional development. In approaching the material, we assume that you are interested in being an outdoor leader and have some personal experience in at least one adventure activity.

HOW THE BOOK
IS ARRANGED

The first chapter of this book identifies 12 components that are important for effective outdoor leadership. We can divide 6 of these 12 into the "hard" skills, that is, those that are solid, tangible, measurable, and easier to train and assess, and "soft" skills, that is, those that are more amorphous, intangible, more difficult to measure, and tougher to train or assess, of an effective outdoor leader. We can consider the other 6 components "metaskills," those higher-order core abilities that integrate other skills in a workable, systematic manner.

Figure 1 portrays these skills as building bricks, mortar, and a rock foundation used to construct a wall, analogous to the training you need to become an effective leader. Specifically, we can view the "wall" of outdoor leadership as being built of soft skill "bricks" on top of hard skill "bricks." Metaskills serve as the "mortar" holding these bricks together and allowing them to form a solid and cohesive wall. This entire arrangement of outdoor adventure leadership preparation is built on a rock-solid theoretical "foundation" of philosophy, history, and individual and group behaviors. We have written at least one chapter to cover the body of knowledge concerning each of the skills listed here.

The capabilities to perform technical skills, do them safely, and make them environmentally sound—the so-called hard skills—are quite common among outdoor leaders. The abilities of leaders to climb, paddle, or peddle; to find their way from origin to destination without getting lost or injured; and to camp along the way without leaving a mess are relatively easier to learn and assess. Since a great many how-to-do-it books exist on these hard skills, we will devote only three chapters (6-8) to reviewing critical information. We refer you to other how-to-do-it books in the reference section of each chapter.

Unfortunately, the abilities to instruct, organize, and facilitate people involved in adventure experiences—the so-called soft skills—are less common in the preparation of outdoor leaders. In an effort to fill this gap, we will devote a number of chapters to these topics. In chapters 9 and 10, we'll outline how to plan trips and manage risks in adventure programs. Collectively, in these chapters, we'll review the base of knowledge regarding the role of the outdoor leader as an organizer of adventure experiences. Then in chapters 11, 12, and 13, we'll discuss educational theories and models relevant to teaching in adventure programs and review the existing knowledge related to the role of the outdoor leader as an instructor of adventure experiences. In chapters 14 through 17, we'll explain the underlying roles of facilitation and detail techniques for working with groups and individuals in the outdoors, thereby reviewing the base of knowledge pertaining to the role of the outdoor leader as facilitator of adventure experiences.

Keeping in mind that the hard and soft skills of effective outdoor adventure leadership are interwoven and bound together by metaskills, we'll devote the next six chapters (18-23) to detailing the importance of flexible leadership style, problem-solving and decision-making skills, experience-based judgment, effective communication, and ethical behaviors. We define metaskills as highly specialized skills that if correctly executed, permit the most effective expression of all the other skills. Acting like "glue," they bind everything together. They permit the repertoire of hard and soft skills to be synergistic, for which your combined competence is greater than the sum of your individual skills. Indeed, with metaskills, you will be the most effective you can be. Finally,

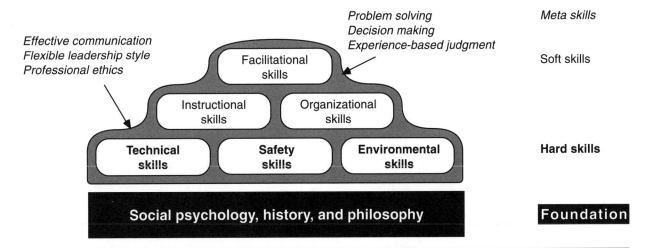

Figure 1   The effective outdoor leadership wall (with skills listing).

in chapter 24, we'll deal with the current trends and issues in the outdoor leadership field. In all, the knowledge contained in this book will hopefully build you a solid wall of skills to be an effective outdoor adventure leader. However, as with all construction, the most important feature is the constant attention to maintain a solid consistency.

Simon Priest
Michael Gass
Durham, N.H.

Introduction to Effective
Outdoor Leadership

> Leadership is one of the most observed and least understood phenomena on earth.
>
> —Burns, 1978
>
> ___
>
> Since the beginning of recorded history, scientists called alchemists have attempted to change a variety of common minerals, such as lead and iron, into precious metals, such as gold and silver. Some alchemists spent their entire lives searching in vain for a magical element that might make such a change, calling the elusive element the "Philosopher's Stone." They believed the addition of this special stone to a collection of minerals, subjected to key processes, would result in pure gold! It was also believed that the alchemist who found the stone would not only acquire vast riches, but also spiritual perfection, everlasting life, and the secrets of the universe. But no one ever found the secret formula for such "transmutation."

We can compare the process of preparing effective outdoor leaders for the adventure programming profession to the process of alchemy. The purpose of preparing outdoor leaders is often focused on transmuting motivated, outdoorsy people into "golden" outdoor leaders. Like the key processes of alchemy, outdoor leadership preparation involves the processes of selecting, training, and assessing leadership candidates. While alchemists never succeeded, outdoor leadership preparation sometimes does. But too often, something has been missing: either the base elements have been incomplete or in the wrong proportions or the processes have been incorrectly applied. Whatever the case, preparing outdoor leaders has proven far from easy. In this chapter, we'll examine the elements and processes of preparing outdoor leaders, then present an overview of the materials we'll cover in subsequent chapters. But first, to understand the relevance of these elements and processes, let's consider why outdoor leaders are even necessary.

NEED FOR EFFECTIVE OUTDOOR LEADERS

More and more people are discovering benefits related to participating in outdoor experiences. Leisure service agencies report a growing interest in participating in "risk-related" recreational activities. Social services and health agencies note greater use of adventure therapy with clients.

Increasing public participation in outdoor pursuits and adventure activities appears to be a trend for the future (Ewert, 1989). People are becoming more interested in and knowledgeable about the outdoors. Thus, educational opportunities devised to enjoy the outdoor experience are plentiful. Moreover, today, ultralight equipment and space-age clothing make "roughing it" considerably more comfortable than it was decades ago. And superhighways lead to the edge of wilderness, providing easy access to pristine areas.

Unfortunately, this growth in outdoor use has brought with it increases in participant injuries and environmental damage. Careless treatment of natural hazards has often led poorly prepared enthusiasts to injure themselves. Furthermore, many participants are slowly loving the outdoors to death, ignorantly destroying the very beauty they seek to enjoy. Some people approach the outdoors as a survival challenge in a sort of "no-win competition" of Humans against Nature. In "beating" Nature, Humans leave the scars of conquest behind: extinct species, trodden vegetation, soil erosion, and litter. In losing to Nature, Humans may also receive a share of injuries, such as negative memories, social embarrassment, physical damage, and, occasionally, fatalities. The time is long overdue to promote a new attitude of Humans *with* Nature, in which the two coexist in harmony and neither suffers at the expense of the other.

To achieve a mutually beneficial coexistence, a different approach is necessary. The approach, portrayed through the elements and processes we'll outline in this text, will give you the knowledge and processes necessary to enhance elements of safety, increase client satisfaction, and provide greater protection of the environment through increasing client knowledge of conservation.

EMERGING AND DESIGNATED LEADERS

Before discussing the elements and processes for creating effective outdoor adventure leaders, we must clarify two processes on how people become leaders. **Leadership** is a process of influence. In most informal group settings, people who become group leaders influence other group members to create, identify, work toward, achieve, and share mutually acceptable goals. Often in such situations, more than one group member emerges to fulfill different leadership responsibilities.

In outdoor organizations, the sponsoring agency designates leaders as being "in charge" of the group. As a designated outdoor leader, you'll have the legal and moral responsibility to learn how to adequately supervise your groups as well as how to protect the environment. Differentiating between informal and designated leaders is important, because designated leaders can often conflict with emerging ones.

RESEARCH ON OUTDOOR LEADERSHIP

What does it take to be a good outdoor leader? Several studies have been done on outdoor leadership competency, outdoor leadership curricula, and on what the qualities of an effective outdoor leader are.

Green (1981) surveyed 61 outdoor leaders in the Pacific Northwest and, based on their responses, developed a college course curriculum for land-based outdoor pursuit leaders. Among his conclusions, he reported that knowledge of emergency medical techniques and outdoor living skills are critical to outdoor leaders of land-based outdoor pursuits, but should be obtained prior to their involvement in an outdoor leadership course. Swiderski (1981) concentrated on surveying 148 outdoor leaders in the western United States and found important differences between regions on some outdoor leadership competencies. Specifically, he noted regional dif-

ferences among respondents regarding topics related to snow or ice travel and off-trail navigation. Buell (1981) surveyed 120 supervisors, educators, and leaders of outdoor programs in the United States and some parts of Canada regarding a list of approximately 200 important competencies for outdoor leaders. Priest (1984) surveyed 189 administrators and leaders in attendance at the 11th annual conference of the Association of Experiential Education. Confirming some earlier works, Raiola (1986) developed his own curriculum for an outdoor leadership preparation program. In an international study, Priest (1986) surveyed 169 out of 250 experts from the five nations of Australia, Canada, Great Britain, New Zealand, and the United States. The top 10 items from each researcher's response list are presented in figure 1.1.

A metanalysis of these studies (Priest, 1987) suggests that determining the key elements of an effective outdoor leader might be possible. The 12 elements that arose from these studies as the critical core competencies of effective outdoor leaders include the following:

1. **Technical skills** are competencies in the actual adventure activities or outdoor pursuits being led. Two examples include being able to climb at a certain level or standard and being able to paddle a particular grade or class of whitewater. If, as an outdoor leader, you are able to perform at a proficiency higher than that of the group members, you will probably have a much easier time in maintaining group control during these activities, giving you a greater margin of safety by providing a "cushion of competence."

2. **Safety skills** are those competencies necessary to enjoy the adventure activity in a safe and prudent manner. Examples of safety skills include navigation, survival, weather interpretation, body temperature regulation, first aid, accident response, search and rescue, and water safety.

3. **Environmental skills** are those competencies necessary to prevent damage to the natural surroundings. Examples of these skills include practicing and encouraging minimum-impact travel and no-trace camping, and modeling behaviors such as carrying out the garbage and not crosscutting switchback trails.

Green (1981)

Risk management plans
Small-group dynamics
Liability considerations
Outdoor leadership methods
Judgment
Minimum-impact practices
Decision making
Assessment of group capabilities
Assessment of individual capabilities
Outdoor leadership objectives

Swiderski (1981)

Exercise good judgment
Handle safety problems
Prepare for accidents
Prevent illness and injury
Teach environmental injuries
Follow a wilderness ethic
Model positive attitudes
Demonstrate minimum impact
Recognize own limitations
Recognize problem indicators

Buell (1981)

Design and use a first aid kit
Have knowledge of group safety
Possess physical fitness
Limit activities to capabilities
Anticipate problems
Provide standard of care
Apply physical and emotional care
Develop safety procedures
Select and implement logistics
Carry out staff preplanning

Priest (1984)

Ability to anticipate accidents
Wilderness first aid skills
Awareness of group dynamics
Ability to clearly identify problems
Ability to evaluate natural hazards
Ability to foster teamwork
Ability to provide personal growth
Proficiency in land-based activities
Proficiency in water-based activities
Ability to prepare accident responses

Raiola (1986)

Leadership style
Judgment (objective & subjective)
Trip planning and organization
Environmental issues
Risk management
Instructional principles
Navigation
Group dynamics
Nutrition
Field experience

Priest (1986)

Safety skills
Judgment based on experience
Awareness and empathy
Group management skills
Problem-solving skills
Instructional skills
Technical activity skills
Flexible leadership style
Motivational philosophy
Environmental skills

Figure 1.1 Summary of top 10 items from past outdoor leadership research.

4. **Organizational skills** are those competencies permitting you to plan, prepare, execute, and evaluate experiences for the specific needs of particular client groups. For example, you must manage risks, arrange transportation, coordinate group food and lodging needs, schedule activities, select routes, plan contingencies, and secure necessary permits, equipment, and clothing to increase the likelihood of successful experiences.

5. **Instructional skills** are those competencies required to teach participants appropriate technical skills related to the activity, environment, and safety. For example, teaching skiing technique in a series of progressions, teaching safety through the inquiry or discovery approach, and using effective instructional aids to teach environmental concepts are all important instructional skills.

6. **Facilitation skills** are those competencies fostering productive group dynamics, enabling clients to work toward completing tasks while developing appropriate interpersonal relationships. For example, as an outdoor adventure leader, you will often need to resolve conflicts, communicate ef-

fectively, and foster personal trust and group cooperation. You also need to know how to debrief and guide reflection on adventure experiences to generate conditions for optimal learning.

7. **Flexible leadership style** means knowing how, why, and when to utilize differing leadership approaches. For example, under most conditions, group decision making is generally a democratic or shared process. At other times, such as an emergency, you must be autocratic—giving directions and expecting them to be carried out. When an experience is progressing well, however, you may go beyond democratic and be abdicratic—abdicating or delegating responsibility to the group. These diverse examples highlight the need for you to learn to adapt your leadership style to suit the circumstances.

8. **Experience-based judgment** is a required skill since you will often confront situations in the outdoors in which pertinent information is missing or vague. By considering past experiences and using sound judgment, you can appropriately substitute predictions for the missing or vague information. This type of judg-

ment becomes extremely important when the act of delaying a decision in the hope that new information will become available might result in further problems. Sound judgment comes from surviving past judgment calls, whether good or bad, analyzing those successes and failures, and applying learning from the analysis to future situations. This generally requires that you gain plenty of intensive and extensive field experience as a leader. While wide experience does not ensure sound judgment, the lack of experience will inhibit your ability to create sound predictions as to what to do when presented with uncertain information.

9. **Problem-solving skills** can be creative or analytical, and a combination of both might be best. Follow analytical processes to recognize problems, define difficulties, anticipate outcomes, identify several possible solutions, select the most probable one, put it into action, and evaluate its effectiveness. However, you also need to be able to use creative techniques, such as brainstorming, extended effort, attribute listing, forced relationships, and deferred prejudice.

10. **Decision-making skills** enable you to make choices. Specifically, you must be capable of discovering and assessing multiple options as well as selecting the "best" choice for the participant. Some useful methods include gathering, screening, organizing, prioritizing, and choosing.

11. **Effective communication** is a process of two or more people exchanging information, resulting in behavioral change. The information in the form of ideas, actions, or emotions is transmitted along a pathway of audio, visual, or tactile channels. You must be able to generate, encode, link, send, transmit, receive, decode, and interpret such messages. Moreover, you should be able to use feedback to confirm that the message received was indeed the same as the message sent.

12. **Professional ethics** refer to the moral standards and value systems that you may have and that adventure programming demands. For example, "challenge

by choice" (e.g., Schoel, Prouty, & Radcliffe, 1988) is an ethic that defines and often guides adventure programming. This ethic asserts that people have the right to choose the level of participation in activities they feel comfortable with; you should not coerce them into doing any action they are uncomfortable performing. Similarly, you hold enormous power over clients; thus, it is primarily ethics that must guide you away from possible abuses of this power, including, but not limited to, deception and sexual contact with clients.

CREATING THE APPROPRIATE MIXTURE IN THE RIGHT SETTINGS

Even if outdoor leaders could agree on what ingredients constitute a good outdoor leader, like alchemists, they would face a dilemma in

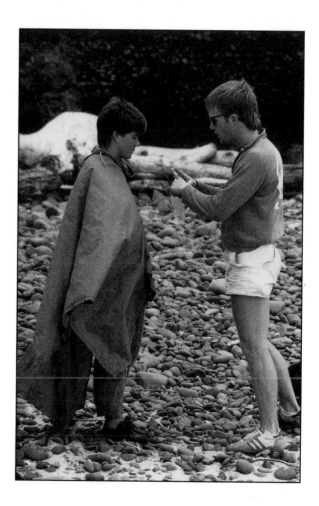

utilizing these elements in the proper mixture and conditions—which is equally important in making "golden" outdoor leaders. Currently, no consensus exists in the profession as to how to best prepare outdoor leaders. While we'll discuss this issue in greater detail later on, three examples of how the field currently addresses the creation of outdoor leaders include the following:

1. Individual certification—a process guaranteeing that certain minimum standards of competency have been met or exceeded by an outdoor leadership candidate, as evaluated by a certifying agency

2. Program accreditation—a process recognizing that a program or institution has met certain predetermined standards of operation and that the individuals operating under the program's guidelines are able to conduct outdoor experiences appropriately

3. Outdoor leadership preparation—a process in which an organization provides one or more training experiences to train professionals to be outdoor leaders, often including steps such as screening and testing, assessment, skill development, leadership field experience under the guidance of a mentor, and required practicum experiences

Note that within each of these examples of how the profession prepares leaders, a great deal of variation takes place. This becomes particularly true when you consider the wide variety of activities, geographic locations, and populations served by outdoor programs. It is also important to note that such processes are not mutually exclusive and some overlapping principles exist.

In short, the process of preparing effective outdoors leaders is still far from an exact science. There is no question that the profession needs to train competent outdoor leaders and that this task is becoming increasingly complex. But the discovery of a magical "Philosopher's Stone" of outdoor leadership able to provide the remaining answers continues to be a mystery.

In the chapters that follow, we'll compile the body of knowledge associated with the field of outdoor leadership. In each chapter, we'll address one whole or part of the 12 elements of outdoor leadership competence. It is our hope that this book will help you become a successful professional outdoor leader.

EFFECTIVE OUTDOOR LEADERS SHOULD

☞ Have a thorough understanding of the 12 elements needed to prepare effective outdoor leaders and know their level of competence in each element.

☞ Strive to be proficient in all 12 elements and seek to enhance their competence in any weak areas.

SUMMARY

Extensive use of the outdoors for recreation, education, development, and therapy is increasing. Accompanying this increased usage are greater numbers of accidents and damage to the natural environment, and despite suggestions for change toward a less competitive and conquering attitude, the problems continue. One solution is to prepare outdoor leaders to educate users as to proper and safe conduct.

Preparing effective outdoor leaders is a lot like the practice of alchemy. Alchemists failed in their transmutation of common minerals like lead and iron into precious metals such as gold and silver, because they were unable to find the magical agent known as the "Philosopher's Stone." Outdoor leadership experts are aware of the necessary elements, but the correct processes are still a mystery.

Current examples of processes used to prepare effective outdoor leaders include individual certification, program accreditation, and outdoor leadership preparation. But as of yet, the best combination of proportions and sequences of these remains unknown. The adventure programming profession is still seeking its "Philosopher's Stone."

QUESTIONS TO THINK ABOUT

1. Define "leadership" in your own words.
2. Give three good reasons why outdoor leaders are necessary in adventure programming.
3. Assess yourself on each of the 12 outdoor leadership elements listed. Write a sentence for each one detailing what you will do to improve your shortcomings in this component.

4. Differentiate between outdoor leadership certification and outdoor leadership preparation.

5. Do you think the elusive "Philosopher's Stone" exists in the outdoor leadership field? If so, what is it? If not, why not?

REFERENCES

Buell, L.H. (1981). *The identification of outdoor adventure leadership competencies for entry-level and experience-level personnel*. Unpublished doctoral dissertation, University of Massachusetts.

Burns, J.M. (1978). *Leadership*. New York, NY: Harper and Row.

Ewert, A. (1989). *Outdoor adventure pursuits*. Worthington, OH: Publishing Horizons.

Green, P.J. (1981). *The content of a college-level outdoor leadership course for land-based outdoor pursuits in the Pacific Northwest: A Delphi consensus*. Unpublished doctoral dissertation, University of Oregon.

Priest, S. (1984). Effective outdoor leadership: A survey. *Journal of Experiential Education* 7(3), 34-36.

Priest, S. (1986). *Outdoor leadership in five nations*. Unpublished doctoral dissertation, University of Oregon.

Priest, S. (1987). *Preparing effective outdoor pursuit leaders*. Eugene, OR: Institute of Recreation Research and Service.

Raiola, E.O. (1986). *Outdoor wilderness education—A leadership curriculum*. Unpublished doctoral dissertation, Antioch, OH: Union Graduate School.

Schoel, J., Prouty, D., & Radcliffe, P. (1988). *Islands of healing: A guide to adventure based counseling*. Hamilton, MA: Project Adventure.

Swiderski, M.J. (1981). *Outdoor leadership competencies identified by outdoor leaders in five western regions*. Unpublished doctoral dissertation, University of Oregon.

PART

I

Foundations of Adventure Programming

Philosophy of Adventure
Programming

"Would you tell me please which way I ought to go from here?" asked Alice.

"That depends a good deal on where you want to get to," said the Cat.

"I don't much care where," said Alice.

"Then it doesn't matter which way you go," said the Cat.

"—so long as I get somewhere," Alice added as an explanation.

"Oh you're sure to do that," said the Cat, "if you only walk long enough."

—Carroll, 1916

"The act of learning is the result of reflection upon experience. . . . Having an experience does not [necessarily] result in learning; you have to reflect on it. The purpose of learning is to gain something new and to put that new skill or information to the test of usefulness. In order to learn, one must be willing to risk exposing oneself to new things, [be] willing to test the validity of old things in relation to the new, and be willing to form new conclusions. I believe that to adventure is to risk exposing oneself to an unknown outcome. Therefore, to learn is to venture into the unknown: to learn is to adventure!

Learning and adventure are both delving into the unknown. . . . Everyone should have the opportunity to achieve self-fulfillment by engaging in learning that involves stress, striving, self-direction, sacrifice, goal-setting, perfecting skills, and working cooperatively with others to achieve goals. That is experiential learning. . . .

The intensity of getting lost in the work of learning contributes in a unique way to the quality of one's life. This occurs during the concentrated activity of perfecting a skill or serving others or protecting oneself from [risk]. This type of experiential learning and its outcomes should be available to each person."

—King, 1988

In the preface, which outlined the structure of this book, one of the cornerstones we identified as a critical piece in the "wallstructure" of outdoor leadership preparation was "philosophy." The term "philosophy" is probably quite distant from the conscious thoughts of clients actively engaged in adventure experiences. Or even from the thoughts of leaders immersed in preparing for a trip, who are too busy ensuring that all the equipment, food, and clients are accounted for and nothing has been forgotten.

But as seen in the dialogue between Alice in Wonderland and the Cat in the first vignette,

without a strong sense of the philosophical and other theoretical concepts that serve as a foundation for what happens in adventure programming, clients, students, and professionals run the risk of "running around in circles" and not achieving the true potential of adventure experiences.

Philosophy, in the manner we are using it in this book, addresses the concepts of epistemology, a cornerstone of how and what we know, and metaphysics, the way the world is: how one's reality is created and viewed (Crosby, 1981). In the second vignette, Keith King passionately leads readers through his philosophical beliefs on what adventure programming professionals should stress, why it is important, the direction you should take, as well as how you should get there.

How and what we know about adventure programming allows us as professionals to develop a stronger practice. A "practice" can be defined as a set of rules that provide a professional activity with its structure of what we should be accomplished as well as how this should be done. When outdoor leaders fail to have a solid philosophical underpinning on what clients are doing or how clients are led, we run the risk of acting like Alice. When this occurs, we may lack the proper direction and the ability to match experiences to meet particular client needs, the ability to know how to select one technique over another as more appropriate, and the ability to communicate why one procedure is better than others or even important to use at all. (Gass, 1992).

In this chapter, we'll present one overview of how you can apply the philosophical tenets of adventure programming as a "practice" through six mediums. We'll

1. present a brief overview of philosophical tenets and how past philosophers and educators have presented statements supporting adventure programming,

2. define various terms used in adventure education to help frame the context, or the way the *profession* is currently viewed, in the adventure programming field,

3. outline common products, or outcomes, that generally occur for adventure programming participants. We will break these outcomes down into the two interacting categories of intrapersonal, that is, individual and emotional, and interpersonal, that is, group and social, development,

4. highlight one process for how you can achieve such products or outcomes,

5. differentiate among the types of adventure programs commonly used in the current field, and

6. summarize the hallmarks of good adventure programming.

PHILOSOPHY: AN INTRODUCTION

Philosophy comes from the Greek words for liking or seeking wisdom. As a field of study, it considers the underlying principles and the ultimate real truth—versus the ideal truth—of the human condition. As we stated in the preface, philosophy has several aspects that are relevant to adventure programming. Let's define the following aspects of philosophy: esthetics, ethics, logic, politics, epistemology, and metaphysics.

Esthetics is the study of form or artistic beauty, such as the inherent attraction of nature. **Ethics** is the study of conduct or moral living (see chapter 3). **Logic** is the study of thinking or reasoning methods, such as the metaskills of judgment, problem solving, and decision making (see chapters 20, 21, and 22). **Politics** is the study of society or social order theories, such as how people interact in groups (see chapter 5).

Epistemology is concerned with the methods and theories of "how we know what we know," in other words, the nature and origin of knowledge. **Metaphysics** is concerned with the methods and theories of "the way things are" and the systematic investigation of "reality." For the remainder of this chapter, we'll focus on the philosophical areas of epistemology and metaphysics in relation to adventure programming and key educational models.

Philosophical Models Supporting Adventure Programming

Let's look for a moment at five philosophers: Socrates, Plato, Aristotle, William James, and John Dewey. While a detailed discussion of the work done by these individuals is beyond the scope of this book, let's examine some of the areas where their ideas have supported adventure programming.

We can trace the foundation of Western thinking and education to the roots of the work of certain Greek philosophers: Socrates, Plato, and Aristotle. Plato believed that **virtues**, such as wisdom, bravery, temperance, and justice, were key qualities for young people to acquire in order to assume leadership roles in an ideal society. He also believed that the best way for young people to obtain such virtues was through direct and purposeful experience, often by involving them in situations that impelled them into action (Hunt, 1990). For example, the best way to become wise, brave, temperate, and just was thought to be by practicing wise, brave, temperate, and just acts that actually required people to be virtuous.

While differing in approaches (e.g., Plato with rationalism and Aristotle with empiricism), both Plato and Aristotle identified virtues, such as danger, risk, and safety, as important components for human growth. Based on work by Plato and Aristotle, Wurdinger (1995) identified three fundamental ideas that support the basic tenets of adventure programming: direct experience provides one of the best means for learning, building moral character or virtues in people is highly desirable, and the need to take risks is critically important to human growth and development.

Based on this approach to logic, William James evolved a pragmatic approach to philosophy. **Pragmatism** is based on the belief that the value of any learning experience is determined by the degree of learning that occurs from the actions and consequences of such learning experiences. As stated by Kraft (1985): "... Pragmatists do not ignore theorizing or rational inquiry, but rather subject all theory to the crucible of experience to test its 'cash value.' James shared the general American distrust of purely theoretical or intellectual activity and kept asking the question 'What difference does it make?'" (p. 8). The **pragmatic maxim** summarizes the pragmatic approach to philosophy. This maxim states that theories, experiences, and any learning only possess value if they are practical, that is, if they help an individual learn and apply new learning to everyday life.

James's book *Talks to Teachers and Students* (1900) discusses 11 aspects of the maxim that examine the utility of experiential education. A summary of James's aspects includes

- clients learn best by her/his own activity,
- client interest is of significant importance to learning,
- sensory experience is basic,
- effort and vigor make for good education,
- education modifies behavior,
- good education is holistic,
- imitating exemplary behavior is sound learning,
- love and understanding are important to learning,
- effective learning is interdisciplinary,
- respect for individual differences is essential, and
- sound education is specific (Donaldson and Vinson, 1979, pp. 7-8).

In the early 20th century, several educational philosophers began to reshape education. Among these innovative educators was John Dewey, the parent of modern experiential education. Dewey (1938) wrote widely on the value of experience in formal education. His ideas were pragmatic and easy to read. He called for education to be real: about life itself, not mere preparation for life. He saw the teacher's role as enabling students to learn about things they were interested in—not directing them to learn from a sterile curriculum. He thought that students should be taught to solve problems in a cooperative manner, rather than to memorize facts in a competitive race for the best grades. He believed that a democratic process encouraged free and critical thinking, while the acceptance of authority quenched all the fire of questioning. Kraft (1985) paraphrased several aspects of Dewey's work that apply to adventure programming:

(1) Individuals need to be involved in what is being learned, (2) learning through experiences inside and outside of the classroom, and not just through teachers is vital, (3) learning must be immediately relevant for learners, (4) learners must act and live for the present as well as the future, (5) learning must assist learners in preparing for a changing and evolving world (p. 8).

When applied to adventure programs, one of Dewey's most critical concepts is the idea of what determines whether an experience possesses educational value or not. Specifically, Dewey based the educational value of any experience on the principles of interaction and continuity. **Interaction** refers to the ability of an experience to balance the present applications of client learning, such as objective and subjective conditions or external and internal conditions, in such a manner that clients are able to extract the true potential from the current experience. **Continuity** refers to the ability of the experience to positively contribute to future learning of the client, that is, how well the client will be able to generalize the experience in the long-term. Dewey viewed experiences that do not meet the principles of interaction and continuity as miseducative. We'll discuss how these two measurements apply to the concepts of facilitation and transfer later in this book (see chapters 14-17).

COGNITIVE, BEHAVIORAL, AND EXPERIENTIAL THEORIES OF LEARNING

Remember, epistemology is the study of the nature of knowledge and the limitations of human understanding. We can group such theories of learning into several categories. For the purposes of this book, we'll examine three categories here: behavioral, cognitive, and experiential.

Behavioral theories of learning are founded on an empirical epistemology, which ignores the usefulness of conscious thought and personal experience in favor of external conditioning and control. Behavioral theories are criticized by Torbert (1972, p. 39), who likens this approach to stimulus and response conditioning in which the "learner is treated as a manipulable black box whose external behavior is to be changed. Phenomena such as 'attitudes,' 'values,' and 'insight,' referring to events within the black box are irrelevant. This total control conforms closely enough to social learning situations in schools (except that schools tend to use their control in inconsistent, ineffective ways)." The obvious drawback to behaviorist approaches occurs when learners become dependent on the conditioning environment: the application of external control in the form of an authority figure such as the teacher, the reward, or punishment system.

Cognitive theories of learning are based on a rational and ideal epistemology where teaching emphasizes acquiring, analyzing, retaining, and recalling abstract symbols or "tidbits" of information. Cognitive theories consider the procedures used to absorb and remember information. For example, rote memorization of unrelated facts employs the short-term memory, while meaningful learning of concepts that fit into an existing schema (or bank of related knowledge) makes use of the long-term memory. Hence, if memorized information can be connected in context to existing information, then learning will likely be retained for longer periods. For example, you might study for a test by associating new facts with old memories.

In contrast, **experiential** theories of learning tend to be holistic in nature, incorporating cognition and behavior with conscious perceptions and reflections on experience. Coleman (1979) describes two ways to learn a symbolic language. The first way is experiential in nature and is the "way all children learn a first language: the 'natu-

ral' way, by being in the linguistic environment, by trying and failing and finally succeeding, in making oneself understood and understanding others. It is a painful, time-consuming, and emotion-producing experience, but an effective one" (p. 7). The second way is cognitive and is the "typical method of school learning of a second language: [memorizing] the rules of grammar, the meanings of words, not in terms of experience, but in terms of the words of the first language one knows. This process is less painful, less emotion producing, and less effective" (p. 7). According to Coleman (1979), the difference is that the experiential way "grounds each word, each phrase in a rich bed of experience. One remembers a word, a phrase, because of the very emotions it provoked when it was not understood by another or when it was understood and evoked a response from the other. One cannot forget it, because its usage is an intrinsic part of the fabric of experience that constitutes one's life" (p. 8).

Experiential learning can differ from traditional cognitive learning in many ways. Coleman (1979) summarized the major differences between information assimilation, the main avenue by which most traditional cognition is conveyed, and experiential learning by outlining the sequence of each approach (see figure 2.1).

Comparing Information Assimilation and Experiential Learning

Information assimilation, the main avenue of cognitive learning, begins when the learner receives data in the form of symbols, such as numbers in a book or words in a lecture, about a general principle or particular illustrations of the principle. In the second step, the learner assimilates and organizes the information as knowledge, indicating that she has truly learned the information, rather than merely memorized it. In the third step, the learner infers a specific application from the general principle, implying cognitive intelligence, which is the ability to apply learning. The fourth and final step involves actually applying the learning, proving it useful. This sequence progresses from structure to substance.

Experiential learning, however, reverses the four-step sequence of information assimilation, moving from substance to structure. It begins when the learner acts, then observes the causes and effects of the action. Next, the learner derives understanding of the cause and effect from the

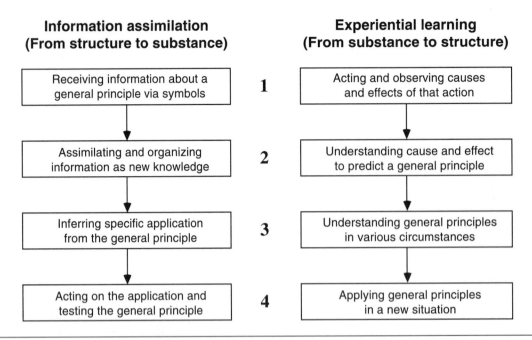

Figure 2.1   A comparison of information assimilation and experiential learning.

observations, so that he may predict events based on similar circumstances. Then, the learner understands the general principle from which such observations and understandings might arise, for example, by forming a working hypothesis. Ultimately, the learner applies the action in a new situation, staying within the limits of the generalized principle, for example, by testing the hypothesis. With additional and more varied actions, the learner broadens and deepens this generalization of principles to determine the limitations of the hypothesis.

In comparing the two approaches, Coleman (1979) found information assimilation more time efficient but often less effective in achieving client gains than experiential learning. In other words, the learner can assimilate information quickly and with little effort, yet may retain little. Furthermore, information assimilation depends on a symbolic medium, which can exclude those learners not fluent in the language used. "For children, adolescents or adults who have not mastered the complex systems of symbols used in reading, mathematics and other disciplines, [this] model leads to almost guaranteed failure, as they are unable to translate the learnings into concrete sequences of action" (Kraft, 1990, p. 180). This criticism is echoed by teachers and employers, who frequently state that students know a lot, but have difficulty doing anything with it. Part of this concern is due to institutionalized

education's failure to address the last two steps of information assimilation, generalization and application.

In contrast, experiential learning "emphasizes a student's ability to justify or explain a subject rather than to recite an expert's testimony" (Joplin, 1981, p. 20). The emotions associated with experiential learning often aid in learning retention. This approach, however, may be time-consuming and the quality or quantity of learning may vary more widely because each individual may experience somewhat different learning as a result of experiential activities. Experiential learning also tends to be more intrinsically motivating, since the "action" of learning can be found in the first step, as opposed to with information assimilation, in which the action is located in the last step. Initiating learning through action in an attempt to influence or control your environment can provide the impetus to complete all steps of the learning process. Schools often try to bypass this motivational shortcoming of information assimilation through extrinsic motivation, for example, by mandating attendance, requiring certain courses, and assigning grades in order to encourage learning. Lastly, experiential learning sometimes falls short (as does information assimilation) when addressing the last two steps—generalizing and applying the learning. If learners reflect on the experience, however, they often overcome this difficulty.

Certainly, we do not intend to set up an adversarial relationship between experiential learning and information assimilation; instead, we wish to outline their differences and complementary nature. Kraft (1990) stated that experiential educators who "use 'real life' experiences as their major teaching/learning tool, often ignore or denigrate what laboratory learning theorists have discovered, not recognizing that our carefully [planned experiential] programs make use of the same principles only in a different setting" (p. 176). As an outdoor leader, you stand to benefit from employing both approaches since the strengths of one compensate for the weaknesses of the other. Information assimilation bypasses the need for learners to repeat the centuries of experiential learning that has preceded them. For example, consider whether or not clients need to actually experience frostbite or hypothermia in order to understand them!

For more detailed presentations of how many of these and other philosophical tenets and concepts have been developed, refer to Crosby (1981), Dewey (1916, 1938), Hunt (1990), Kraft (1985), and Wurdinger (1995).

DEFINING STRUCTURES IN ADVENTURE PROGRAMMING

The following list defines many of the key terms used in this book, including the discipline of experiential education, the profession of adventure education, and the field of effective outdoor leadership. As an overview, this glossary helps frame the context of the information that follows in this and subsequent chapters.

We can loosely define **experiential education** as "learning by doing with reflection." This philosophy is based on the belief that people learn best by direct and purposeful contact with their learning experiences. Simply put, the best way to learn about problem solving is not to read about it in a book, but to actively practice solving problems in a "hands-on" setting. Such learning experiences are realistic: physically active, cognitively meaningful, and affectively engaging. These experiences require learners to accept responsibility for their own actions and to learn from guided reflection on their experiences (Kraft, 1985). Indeed, reflection on experience is a necessary precursor to learning, for without reflection, learning loses much of its potential value.

Outdoor education follows the experiential philosophy of learning by doing. It takes place primarily, but not exclusively, through involvement with the natural environment. In outdoor education, the emphasis for a subject of learning is placed on relationships concerning people and natural resources.

Four relationships in outdoor education have been identified: interpersonal, intrapersonal, ecosystemic, and ekistic (Priest, 1986). **Interpersonal relationships** refer to how people get along in a group of two or more people. These aspects include communication, cooperation, trust, conflict resolution, problem solving, and the like. **Intrapersonal relationships** refer to how an individual gets along with her/himself. These aspects include self-concept, confidence, self-efficacy, and so on. **Ecosystemic relationships** refer to the interdependence of living organisms in an ecological system, in other words, basic biological concepts such as the web of life, the food chain, and the energy pyramid. **Ekistic relationships** refer to the key interactions between human society and the natural resources of an environment. In other words, how people influence the quality of the environment (water pollution or strip mining) and how, in turn, the environment influences the quality of their lives (clean drinking water or the value of beauty).

Historically, two branches of outdoor education have been identified: **adventure education** and **environmental education**. Truly functional outdoor education incorporates all four relationships across both branches.

Adventure education is the branch of outdoor education concerned primarily with interpersonal and intrapersonal relationships. The process of adventure education involves the use of adventurous activities that provide a group or an individual with compelling tasks to accomplish. These tasks often involve group problem solving (e.g., often requiring decision making, judgment, cooperation, communication, and trust) and personal challenge (e.g., testing competence against mental, social, or physical risks). To maximize safety, adventure professionals structure risk in a manner that causes participants to perceive it as being enormously high, while in actuality it is much lower than perceived and more acceptable as a medium for producing functional change and growth. By responding to seemingly insurmountable tasks, participants often learn to overcome self-imposed perceptions of their capabilities to succeed. They are able to turn limitations into abilities; as a result, they learn a great deal about themselves and how they relate to others.

Environmental education is the branch of outdoor education concerned primarily with ecosystemic and ekistic relationships. While commonly thought of as a separate area, you can clearly see that neglect of the environmental side of outdoor education threatens the very naturalness and solitude you and your clients seek in the outdoors.

Recreation refers to the activities that take place during an experience known as leisure, which we'll define shortly. **Outdoor recreation** is simply any activity done outdoors at leisure. Gardening is an outdoor recreational activity, as is racing cars or walking a dog in a park.

Outdoor pursuits are a human-powered form of outdoor recreation. They represent the self-propelled activities performed in outdoor settings. Some common examples include walking, backpacking, rock climbing, mountaineering, skiing, snowshoeing, orienteering, bicycling, spelunking, sailing, kayaking, rafting, and canoeing. They do not include other outdoor recreational activities that are motorized, such as snowmobiling, motorcycling, car racing, and power boating, nor animal-powered, such as horseback riding and dog sledding. While these are defi-nitely outdoor recreation, they often lack the human-powered, low-impact environmental philosophy that frequently accompanies outdoor pursuits.

For an experience to qualify as **leisure**, it must meet three criteria: the experience is a state of mind; it must be entered into voluntarily; and it must be intrinsically motivating of its own merit (Neulinger, 1981). Moreover, the process is more important than the product. For example, writing for a magazine in order to make money is work; while writing for sheer pleasure in which the process is enjoyable is leisure.

Adventure experiences can be leisure experiences. For a leisure experience to qualify as an adventure experience it must meet the three criteria of leisure, as well as a fourth criterion: the outcome must be uncertain (Mitchell, 1983).

Uncertainty of outcome can stem from any number of factors. The outcome of an adventure is uncertain when information that is critical to the completion of a task or the solution of a problem is missing, vague, or unknown. For example, on an outdoor journey, the outcome is uncertain when the necessary skill or confidence may be lacking; when the leadership influence, task definition, or group morale may appear unclear; and when the weather might be somewhat unpredictable. These conditions all lead to uncertainty and therefore risk.

Risk is the potential of losing something of value. The loss may lead to harm that is physical (e.g., broken bones), mental (e.g., psychological fear), social (e.g., peer embarrassment), or financial (e.g., lost equipment). From moment to moment, no one can be fully sure that a loss will actually occur, hence the uncertainty, which creates adventure in a leisure experience. Risk is created by the presence of danger.

Danger gives rise to risk, but they are not the same. We may classify dangers as either perils or hazards that may result from both people and their surroundings. **Perils** are the sources or causes of a potential loss. A lightning bolt is one example of a peril that leads to the risk of electrocution. **Hazards** are the conditions or circumstances that influence the probability or likelihood of a loss occurring. An intense thunderstorm is a hazard that includes the peril of lightning bolts.

Human dangers, whether perils or hazards, originate in the leader or participants in a group. Peer pressure, lack of attention, horseplay, and incompetence are all examples of human dangers. These tend to be subjective or are usually under the control of the group and its leader. **Environmental dangers**, whether perils or hazards, come from the natural surroundings. Avalanches, whitewater rapids, poisonous plants or animals, and temperature extremes are all examples of environmental dangers. These tend to be much more objective than human dangers and are rarely under the control of the group or its leader.

Accidents are unexpected occurrences that result in a loss, such as illness, injury, or fatality. Accidents generally become emergencies when the group or the leader is not prepared to respond correctly. The potential for an accident is greatly enhanced when human and environmental dangers occur simultaneously. For example, when kept separate, whitewater rapids and horseplay may be fine, but allowing them to occur at the same instance greatly enhances the possibility of an accident. This does not mean an accident will always occur, just that one is possible.

Incidents, or **close calls**, are the unforeseen happenings that do not develop into emergencies. Through effective leadership, some accidents may be prevented or the consequences reduced. We can think of incidents as minor accidents in which the losses tend to be more acceptable, such as minor cuts, scrapes, bruises, and the like. But losses that are acceptable to one person may not

be acceptable to another. For example, the possibility of death may be acceptable to some Himalayan climbers, while a bump on a child's head may not be to the child's mother.

Safety refers to procedures put in place to reduce the likelihood of an accident or incident. Safety procedures may be proactive or primary (completed before an experience); active or secondary (in effect during the experience to avoid dangers or respond to an accident); or reactive or tertiary (carried out after the fact). Examples include equipment inspection prior to embarking on the adventure as a proactive safety procedure, first aid for and evacuation of an injured victim as an active safety procedure, and paperwork done to report close calls or actual injuries as a reactive safety procedure.

Challenge is the act of engaging personal competence in risky situations. Risks are present in every adventure experience, creating the uncertainty that makes an experience adventurous. To engage in a challenging adventure experience, adventurers choose to use their competence to risk and resolve the uncertainty of the outcome. If they choose not to make use of their competence, then the outcome is generally dictated by the random element of chance. Without utilizing some element of competence, adventure experiences are not considered challenging.

Competence is usually a combination of skill, attitude, knowledge, behavior, confidence, and experience. As with perception of risk, each adventurer has a perception of personal competence that may or may not be accurate.

We can never know actual values of risk and competence with absolute certainty. At best, we may only estimate them. Professionals develop greater abilities to perceive risk and competence more accurately through valid experiences. Effective outdoor leaders with sound judgment and adequate experience generally possess greater abilities to facilitate safer experiences—but not always.

We can use facilitated adventure experiences to enhance learning. By manipulating perceived values of risk and competence while keeping real values at acceptable levels, facilitated adventure experiences are possible. Depending on the objectives and precise control of such a facilitated experience, misperceiving novices will slowly come to recognize relative levels of risk and competence through reflection on the experiences. Since the levels of risk and competence are structured by the outdoor adventure leader, the importance of effective leadership becomes both obvious and paramount.

PRODUCT OF ADVENTURE: AFFECTIVE ASPECTS

The product of adventure programs can be cognitive (e.g., the acquisition of facts), physical (e.g., technical skill development), or affective (i.e., emotional or social development). We can generally classify affective learning as two inter-active products: development of individuals through improved intrapersonal relationships (i.e., emotional development), and development of groups through enhanced interpersonal relationships (i.e., social development). Secondary aims may also relate to the environmental relationships, but the product of most adventure programs are people who understand themselves more fully and relate to others more effectively. The following are some of the many affective outcomes expected from adventure programming:

Intrapersonal: Emotional and Individual

New confidence in oneself

Increased willingness to take risks

Improved self-concept

Enhanced leadership skills

Increased logical reasoning skills

Greater reflective thinking skills

Interpersonal: Social and Group

Enhanced cooperation

More effective communication skills

Greater trust in others

Increased sharing of decision making

New ways to resolve conflicts

Improved problem-solving skills

Enhanced leadership skills

Since the major focus of many adventure programs is on individual and group development, we'll look more closely at the dynamics of individual social psychology and stages of group development in chapters 4 and 5. These theories are important foundations for any outdoor leader. For now, however, we'll examine the process of adventure.

PROCESS OF ADVENTURE

While there are many theories as to how the process of adventure learning achieves the products we have outlined, probably one of the earliest efforts was the Outward Bound process first described by Walsh and Golins (1976). In their efforts, the authors described adventure education as a process in which the "learner is placed into [a] unique physical environment and into [a] unique social environment, then given a characteristic set of problem solving tasks [creating a] state of adaptive dissonance to which [the learner] adapts by mastery, which reorganizes the meaning and direction of the learner's experience" (p. 16). In other words, the process of adventure education involves the use of adventurous activities (e.g., outdoor pursuits, ropes courses, initiative games) to provide groups or individuals with challenging problem-solving tasks to accomplish.

Walsh and Golins (1976) listed seven key elements of an adventure experience: the learner, the prescribed physical environment, the prescribed social environment, the tasks, a state of adaptive dissonance, and the transfer of new learning. Their model incorporates these elements. See chapter 11 for a diagram and more detailed information.

Learner

The learner needs to be motivated and able. In other words, the learner cannot be closed to learning and has to be capable of physically performing the tasks, of cognitively thinking about and reflecting on the experience, and of affectively dealing with any extreme stress that may arise.

Physically and Socially Unfamiliar Learning Environments

Placing participants into an unfamiliar learning environment can foster the development of a variety of beneficial dynamics. Such environments are often valuable because they present such a stark contrast to learners' familiar environments, often allowing participants to see old behaviors patterns in a new light with a richer perspective as well as permitting participants to notice behavior patterns that they may have overlooked in familiar settings. Unfamiliar physical environments may also allow participants to "try on" new behaviors in an environment that does not encompass some of the limitations or fears of familiar settings. Successful new behaviors may serve as first steps toward integrating behavior changes into more familiar settings.

An unfamiliar yet prescribed social environment can also have a great deal of bearing on the success of adventure programs. Walsh and Golins point to the need for creating an "interdependent peer group with anywhere from 7-15 individuals who have a common objective" (p. 5). Four group dynamics that support adventure programming in a group of this size include the following:

a. The group needs to be large enough to produce a wealth of differing behaviors, yet small enough so that separate subgroups diversify and form around these behaviors.

b. The group needs to be large enough that conflict will result from differing client opinions, yet small enough that the group possesses the ability and resources to resolve any conflicts.

c. The group needs to be large enough to create a collective force through which individuals can and cannot reach certain goals working separately, yet small enough that the group can also support each client's individual goal.

d. The group needs to be large enough that a supportive state of reciprocity occurs [i.e., "an exchange system where by strengths and weaknesses can be traded off within a group" (p. 6)], yet small enough that the group members can contribute their individual strengths, and through such exchange, utilize the strengths of others.

The unfamiliarity of the learning environment that is full of social and physical risks can also be highly stimulating, enhancing the likelihood that clients will learn. Furthermore, the uniqueness can act as an equalizer, placing learners on par with one another; no one has the outdoor experience to be seen as the "expert," so preexisting hierarchies may dissolve or be put aside, allowing people to begin to think for themselves.

Characteristic Problem-Solving Tasks

Tasks in adventure programs should be

- organized—structured by you to suit the group's skill, needs, and maturity,

- incremental—sequenced with increasing complexity, consequences, and uncertainty,

- concrete—limited by time or space and solved for a real purpose: learners know what they are doing and why they are doing it,

- manageable—solvable with the resources of the group and with use of new learning achieved from previous task completion,

- consequential—learners get real and naturally derived feedback from the situation, not from you as reward or punishment, and

- holistic—learners need to apply everything at their disposal in a combined, synergistic manner.

Adventure "problems" generally present themselves as a challenge and, in some cases, initially seem impossible but actually are quite reasonable. Provocative problems can dramatically elicit new learning, and clients are more likely to remember lessons learned in this manner for a long time.

Lessons Learned Through Adaptive Dissonance

The lessons learned in adventure experiences generally arise from a learner's adaptation to a state of dissonance, or the difference between the way things are perceived by a learner and the way that learner would like them to be (see also chapters 4 and 11). Humans like harmony and generally will seek to change a currently less desirable situation into a more desirable one. By taking action to create change and by reflecting on the effectiveness of associated actions, the participant can learn valuable lessons. In the case of adventure experiences, the lessons are often about individual behavior, group behavior, or the environment.

Leader

As a leader, you direct the learning process by performing a number of roles, which may include the following:

- Translator—helping the learner to interpret and reflect on the experience

- Initiator—engineering the experiences

- Trainer—teaching skills and conditioning learners for the difficulties ahead

- Maintainer—keeping energy and motivation levels high

- Authority—holding influence within the group
- Guardian—being responsible for group safety
- Exemplar—modeling behavior patterns expected of the group

According to Walsh and Golins (1976), the leader "requires the ability to be empathetic, genuine, concrete, and confrontive when necessary. [This means utilizing] reflection, openness, esteem and acceptance of others, not to be the know-it-all, but the exemplar of spirited, insightful, compassionate" (pp. 11-12).

Transference of New Learning

The transference of learning from the adventure experience to real life often begins with the mastery of new learning, or the sustained successful completion of tasks. When the learner solves a problem in a manner following the six characteristic problem-solving tasks, she is rewarded with positive feelings of self-worth and being part of the team. The purpose behind achieving this mastery is to generalize the successful strategies and associated feelings to other situations. Because transfer is one of the most critical features of adventure programming, we'll examine this concept more closely in chapter 14.

ADVENTURE PROGRAMMING APPLICATIONS

When adventure is deliberately used to achieve the purposes and benefits we have listed, it is

Sidebar 2.1

HALLMARKS OF GOOD ADVENTURE PROGRAMMING

The following attributes are shared by successful outdoor adventure programs.

Experiential: Good adventure programming is active, rather than passive. It emphasizes hands-on conditions because people learn best by doing and reflecting on their experiences. Activities use perceived risk, yet are relatively safe. These activities are rarely the message or product to be learned, but are more often the medium or process through which learning takes place.

Dramatic: The excitement and emotional nature of good adventure programming activities focuses attention and sharpens minds. Engaging activities demand an increased level of involvement and consciousness. When appropriately engaged, the ability to learn also increases.

Novel: Good adventure programming activities offer a unique context and uncertainty of outcome. People are placed in situations in which no group member is considered to be an expert; therefore, adventures tend to equalize people, breaking down the hierarchical barriers and apprehensions that often exist in organized groups.

Consequential: Errors have potential ramifications in outdoor adventures, such as getting wet in a canoe or falling on a rope, unlike in a classroom simulation for which points are lost. Furthermore, success and failure is supported by those who really matter: peers and self.

Metaphoric: Adventures are a microcosm of the requirements needed for and changes taking place in the real world. The behaviors demonstrated by individuals and groups during these activities parallel the way they act and what happens to them in daily life. As such, new learning, including skills, coping strategies, and bonding among people, can be analogously applied to future efforts at school, home, work, or play or on the streets.

Transferable: Testimonials by past participants support the utility of experiential education, and limited research studies substantiate that new learning does indeed show up in daily life.

People utilize adventure experiences to approach their lives from a fresh perspective and with an improved level of effectiveness (Gass, 1985, 1991).

Structured: Tasks are custom-tailored to meet the needs of the client group in good adventure programming activities. Challenges sequentially increase with complexity and difficulty as people become more competent and need more risk in order to retain a certain level of challenge.

Voluntary: People are not forced to participate in good adventure programming activities. This dynamic gives learners the freedom to learn information and skills that are intrinsically motivating. This independence in the way people learn is often more important than what they learn. It begins with the individual's state of mind and moves toward a leader's confirmation and testimony verifying personal perceptions.

Concrete: In a good adventure program, problems are task-oriented with constraints as in the real world. The activities are intriguing, fun, and invigorating, motivating everyone to get involved. The experiences provide opportunities to experiment with new behaviors and skills in a safe environment that supports risk taking.

Holistic: Good adventure programming may incorporate cognitive, affective (social or emotional), and physical and psychomotor learning; may use all the senses; or may accommodate a variety of learning styles.

called **adventure programming**. As you saw in the four vignettes in the preface, we can categorize adventure programming as one or more of four types: recreational, educational, developmental, or therapeutic. The purpose of a program should be based on the client's needs, rather than on the "type" of client. Consider that corporate clients can engage in more than just developmental adventure programs, for example, sometimes they want a recreational program at a company picnic or conference. And educational programs are not just for school children, for example, therapeutic programs for school children at risk of dropping out are quite common in the profession.

Recreation

Recreational adventure programming is aimed at having fun, learning new activities, or becoming reenergized through adventure. Examples include enjoying a canoe club outing or learning how to rock climb. We can characterize participants in these programs as people focused on enjoying the adventure. Recreational adventure programming can change the way people feel, by reenergizing or revitalizing them. In addition, they may learn a new outdoor skill, then transfer that skill to their own lifelong leisure pursuits.

Education

Educational adventure programming is aimed at understanding concepts, enriching the knowledge of old concepts, or generating an awareness of previously unknown needs through adventure. Examples include teaching the importance of working together as a team or demonstrating the impact of a new way to solve problems. We can characterize participants in these programs as people focused on learning through the adventure. Educational adventure programming can change the way people think by allowing them to see life's issues from a fresh perspective. They gain new attitudes, then transfer these attitudes to the way they conceptualize daily life.

Development

Developmental adventure programming is aimed at improving functional behaviors and training people to behave in new and different ways through adventure. Examples might include finding positive means to communicate with or trust one another. We can characterize participants in these programs as wanting to enhance their interactions in a specific setting, such as school or work. Developmental adventure programming can change the way people behave by showing them successful ways to interact with others. They learn new behaviors, then transfer these behaviors to specific real-life settings, such as the office or classroom. The efficacy of this type of program depends on the degree of transfer from the adventure to the participant's reality. In order to accomplish this, adventure experience coordinators often employ strategies such as thorough diagnosis of a participant's needs, preplanning, action planning, and follow-up service.

Therapy

Therapeutic adventure programming is aimed at changing dysfunctional behavior patterns, using adventure experiences as forms of habilitation and rehabilitation. Examples include dealing with alcohol abuse or overcoming low self-esteem resulting from physical abuse. Participants in these programs generally possess patterns of dysfunction or destructive behavior that may limit or incapacitate their abilities to function in their communities. Therapeutic adventure programming can change the way people behave, sometimes by showing them the impact of negative behaviors, offering them beneficial alternative behaviors, and augmenting what they may already do well. Clients in therapeutic adventure programs often learn new strategies for coping with personal issues, then transfer these strategies to critical aspects of their daily lives.

EFFECTIVE OUTDOOR LEADERS SHOULD

Given these defining terms, products, and processes of adventure experiences, and types of adventure programs, are there philosophical tenets that guide adventure programs? While discussed in several other sources identified earlier, one set of philosophical guidelines that should be present (when possible) in the practices of effective outdoor leaders include the following:

☞ *Unless safety is an issue, allow clients to take as much responsibility to solve problems for themselves as possible.* The uncertainty of an adventure experience (created by challenging activities in unfamiliar environments with unknown outcomes) is generally aided by not "rescuing" participants from problems and by not helping them.

☞ *Encourage "challenge by choice."* Forcing people to perform or get involved in an adventure can reduce and even eliminate their perceived freedom of choice. Coercion limits clients from "owning" their success or failure. Instead they often attribute the outcome to the outdoor leader. Furthermore, injured people may be able to claim negligence against the leader, citing they were made to comply against their will.

☞ *Adapt adventure experiences to suit the varying levels and needs of all members in a group.* Leaders should recognize adventures are a state of mind that often fluctuate according to participants' perceptions of situational risks and personal competence. A range of challenges should be made available in the same activity (different water craft for paddling) or at the same site (various climbs on a cliff) so that participants can select (in consultation with the leader) a level of risk that suits their level of competence.

☞ *Deal in perceived risk with acceptable or recoverable outcomes.* Creating conditions that appear risky, but keeping real dangers as low as possible by using correct safety procedures, heightens the perception of challenge. Dealing in real dangers (where a backup system is not possible due to the nature of the activity or site) are best reserved for participants who have overcome their misperceptions about risk and are astute in perceiving their own level of competence.

☞ *Empower clients by encouraging them to take active roles in safety, and creating challenges that require client competence to counter the risks of the adventure.* This approach avoids "adventure amusement," where clients have absolutely no responsibility for their own care or actions. Instead, they should be put in the primary positions of responsibility and safety whenever possible, with leaders only present to supervise or "back up" the safety systems.

☞ *Create situations where the consequences (positive or negative) are natural outcomes from the clients' actions (e.g., delivered by the environment), rather than artificial ones (e.g., from the leader).* Learning from mistakes can provide invaluable information. Leaders should generally avoid positions where they give reward or punishment for successes or failures. The negative consequences should be real and natural (e.g., getting wet, walking extra distance when lost, putting tents up in the dark, and going without hot drinks when the stove won't light) as should the positive ones (a beautiful view and sense of accomplishment from reaching the journey's end).

SUMMARY

In the manner we are referring to it in this book, philosophy addresses the concepts of epistemology, which is the cornerstone of how and what we know, and metaphysics, which is the way the world is, or how a person's reality is created and viewed. Possessing a knowledge of how and what we know about adventure programming allows us as professionals to develop a stronger practice, that is, the set of rules that define and provide a professional activity with its structure of what it should be attempting to accomplish as well as how it should be doing this. Without a solid philosophical underpinning, you can lack proper direction as a leader, the ability to match experiences to meet particular client needs, the ability to know how to select one technique over another as more appropriate, the ability to communicate why one procedure is better than others (or even important to use at all!), and so on.

Outdoor education is a discipline within the profession of experiential education. Outdoor education has two branches: the fields of environmental education and adventure education. Environmental education deals with ecosystemic and ekistic relationships, while the affective aspects of adventure education address intrapersonal and interpersonal relationships.

Outdoor recreation is considered to be any activity done outdoors, while outdoor pursuits are those activities that are human-powered, not motorized or animal-powered. Leisure is an experience for which the process of the experience is far more important than the product, which is the opposite of work. Adventure experiences are related to educational leisure experiences when participation is voluntary, motivation is intrinsic, adventure is perceived as a state of mind, and the experience outcome is uncertain.

The uncertainty of outcome is possible because of the presence of risks inherent to the activity. Risk, or the potential of losing something valuable, arises from dangers that can be classified as either perils, which are sources of the loss, or hazards, which are conditions that influence the likelihood of loss. Sources of dangers occur from the environment or the humans who participate in adventures within that environment. Accidents and incidents occur more often when both the environmental and human dangers combine to interact at the same instant. Safety is the collective procedures used to reduce dangers and associated injuries.

Challenge results from the interplay of risk and competence. Participants in adventures use competence in a manner that hopes to resolve the uncertainty of an adventure by creating a positive outcome. An adventure without the active engagement of participants' competence is merely subject to chance or random event outcomes. Because the participants are not involved, they cannot attribute success or failure to themselves and thus may not gain any empowerment from the adventure.

Facilitated adventure experiences are purposefully structured adventures in which empowerment of an individual or the group is the goal. As an outdoor leader, you are responsible for coordinating these facilitated experiences and maximizing the learning, safety, and environmental protection. You can do this through effective leadership: a process of purposeful action which creates meaningful conditions and may influence the outcome.

One model used to describe the process associated with adventure programming is the Outward Bound process model. In this process, a learner is put in unique environments to solve problems and adapt to the accompanying dissonance by mastering new learning. The seven key elements of this process are the learner, the physical environment, the social environment, the tasks, a state of adaptive dissonance, and the transfer of new learning. Adventure programming, deliberately used for enhancing relationships, can be recreational, educational, developmental, or therapeutic, depending on the program's purpose. Active experience, drama, novelty, consequences, metaphors, transference, structure, voluntary participation, concrete tasks, and holistic content are all hallmarks of adventure programming.

QUESTIONS TO THINK ABOUT

1. Make a list of the philosophical tenets you believe support the premise of adventure programming, guiding how it should be

conducted. Add elements you believe to be missing.

2. Draw and label a diagram that shows the relationships between the terms defined in this chapter.

3. Given examples of current adventure programs representing each of the four programming types (see also preface), compare and contrast what might occur with adventure programming in each of these situations.

4. Examine the components of the section "Effective Outdoor Leaders Should" and the "Hallmarks of Good Adventure Programming." Do you agree with all these statements? Would you add any conditions or exceptions to make them stronger or more applicable to certain populations? Would you add any statements?

REFERENCES

Carroll, L. (1916). *Alice's adventures in wonderland*. Chicago: Rand McNally.

Coleman, J. S. (1979). Experiential learning and information assimilation: Toward an appropriate mix. *Journal of Experiential Education*. 2(1)), 6-9.

Crosby, A. (1981). A critical look: The philosophical foundations of experiential education. *Journal of Experiential Education* 4(1), 9-16.

Dewey, J. (1916). *Democracy and education*. New York: The Free Press.

Dewey, J. (1938). *Experience and education*. New York: Macmillan.

Donaldson, G.W., & Vinson, R. (1979). William James: Philosophical father of experienced-based education. *Journal of Experiential Education* 2(2), 6-8.

Gass, M.A. (1985). Programming the transfer of learning in adventure education. *Journal of Experiential Education* 8(3), 18-24.

Gass, M.A. (1991). Enhancing metaphoric transfer in adventure therapy programs. *Journal of Experiential Education,* 14(2), 6-13.

Gass, M.A. (1992). Theory and practice. *Journal of Experiential Education,* 15(2), 6-7.

Hunt, J.S. (1990). Philosophy of adventure education. In J. Miles & S. Priest (Eds.), *Adventure education*. State College, PA: Venture, 119-128.

James, W. (1900). *Talks to teachers and students*. New York: Henry Holt.

Joplin, L. (1981). On defining experiential education. *Journal of Experiential Education*, 4(1) 17-20.

King, K. (1988). The role of adventure in the experiential learning process. *Journal of Experiential Education* 11(2), 4-8.

Kraft, R. (1985). Toward a theory of experiential learning. In R.J. Kraft & M. Sakofs (Eds.), *The theory of experiential education*. Boulder, CO: Association for Experiential Education, 4-35.

Kraft, R.J. (1990). Experiential learning. In J.C. Miles & S. Priest (Eds.), *Adventure education*. State College, PA: Venture, 175-183.

Mitchell, R.G. (1983). *Mountain experience: The psychology and sociology of adventure*. Chicago: University of Chicago Press.

Neulinger, J. (1981). *The psychology of leisure*. Springfield, Illinois: Charles C Thomas.

Priest, S. (1986). Redefining outdoor education: A matter of many relationships. *Journal of Environmental Education* 17(3), 13-15.

Torbert, W.R. (1972). Learning from experience toward consciousness. New York: Columbia University Press.

Walsh, V., & Golins, G. (1976). *The exploration of the Outward Bound process*. Denver: Colorado Outward Bound School.

Wurdinger, S. (1995). *Philosophical issues in adventure education*. Dubuque, IA: Kendall/Hunt.

chapter 3

History of Adventure Programming

World War II was in full skirmish. German U-boats were successfully torpedoing merchant marine and naval vessels crossing the North Atlantic between Britain and North America. Sailors, thrown overboard by the explosive strikes into cold water, were dying in record numbers. A curious occurrence was noted by observers: the younger sailors were the ones dying, while the older sailors were able to survive. An owner of one shipping company remarked: "I would rather entrust the lowering of a lifeboat in mid-Atlantic to a sail-trained octogenarian than to a young sea technician who is completely trained in the modern way, but has never been sprayed by saltwater" (Miner, 1990, p. 59). Why the difference? What could be changed in the faulty training of strong young sailors to increase their self-reliance and compassionate support of their colleagues?

The formal beginnings of adventure experiences as a programming tool began in the 1940s with attempts to answer the very questions this vignette poses. While some authors identify the Egyptians, who explored their world in 2500 B.C. as the first adventurers (Ewert, 1989), many trace the start of adventure programming to the question of the "decline" of youth evidenced by the deaths of young sailors.

In this chapter, we'll look at the history of outdoor adventure programming; if you are interested in the earlier history of recreation, leisure, or sport as precursors to adventure programming, we encourage you to seek out texts in these fields.

BEGINNINGS OF ADVENTURE PROGRAMMING

Kurt Hahn can be viewed as the "grandparent" of adventure programming. Hahn was born in 1886 in Germany to Jewish parents, a wealthy industrialist father and an artistic mother. He was influenced early in life by Plato's *Republic* and by an English education (at Oxford from 1910 to 1914). After World War I, Prince Max of Baden, Germany's last Imperial Chancellor, and Karl Reinhard, a German educator, helped Hahn to found a coeducational boarding school in 1920, called Salem Schule (translated as shalom, or peace, school) on Lake Constance. At Salem, the curriculum emphasized personal responsibility, equality, social justice, respect, and service to the community.

Unfortunately, these principles stood in opposition to the Nazi movement and so did Hahn. In

1932, he spoke out publicly against Hitler, particularly in response to Hitler's "Beuthen telegram," in which Hitler demanded that five storm troopers be released and honored despite their convictions and death sentences for trampling a young communist to death in front of his mother. With the rise of the Third Reich, Hahn was persecuted by the Nazis and imprisoned for his statements, beliefs, and religion. He was later released at the request of the British government and exiled from Germany. He went to the United Kingdom and in 1934 opened Gordonstoun School in an abandoned Scottish castle (Richards, 1990).

Gordonstoun operated on the Hahnian principles developed at Salem, but with the start of World War II, this school was expropriated by the British armed forces. Hahn moved to Wales where, after joining forces with Lawrence Holt, Director of the Blue Funnel shipping line, and Jim Hogan, a British educator, he turned his attention to solving the problem of the dying sailors as well as the needs of other youth. They believed that younger sailors and other youth needed to be provided with an experience that would turn the youths' attitudes around. The result of their work came to be known as **Outward Bound**, named after the term given to sailing ships as they left the safety of a harbor and headed for the open seas.

Outward Bound Program

Outward Bound began in 1941 at Aberdovey in Wales, not as a military basic survival training center, but as a program for youth, many of whom were destined for armed service at that time.

Many of the youngsters were sponsored by Holt's shipping company; many more were supported by other organizations, such as police and fire departments, local governments, schools, and industry. Outward Bound courses were originally one month long, because on the last day of the month, these company apprentices would have to go home in order to receive their paychecks from work! A typical course consisted of orienteering, search and rescue training, athletics, small boat sailing, ocean and mountain expeditions, an obstacle course, and service to the local communities (Miner, 1990).

How did Outward Bound accomplish its goals in the early days? Let's look at how the program used an obstacle course, a predecessor of the modern ropes or challenge courses of today. Young sailors would swing on old hawser ropes, cross rope bridges between tree tops, and climb up and down roped cargo nets or smooth wooden walls. The obstacle course was meant to mimic the settings of ships at sea. But not only was this training meant to prepare youth for the task of abandoning ship, it was also devised to increase self-confidence as well as the ability to work well with others in society. Holt probably summed up the Hahnian principle of the school best with the comment, "The training at Aberdovey must be less a training *for* the sea than *through* the sea, and so benefit all walks of life" (Miner, 1990, p. 59).

After the war, the principles of Outward Bound were expanded to address continuing issues of social decline, particularly in youth. The six ways in which youth attitudes and abilities were in decline that concerned Hahn the most included the following (Richards, 1990, p. 69):

1. **Fitness**, due to modern methods of locomotion
2. **Initiative** and **enterprise**, due to the widespread disease of "spectatoritis"
3. **Memory** and **imagination**, due to the confused restlessness of modern life
4. **Skill** and **care**, due to the weakened tradition of craftsmanship
5. **Self-discipline**, due to the ever-present availability of stimulants and tranquilizers
6. **Compassion**, due to the unseemly haste with which modern life is conducted

One way early outdoor programs and their leaders thought they should address the declines was through the provision of a "moral equivalent to war." In describing this concept, James (1967) saw that war, while producing a host of immoral actions and destructive consequences, often produced behaviors that brought out the best in people faced with adversity. James believed the aims of society would be advanced if some mechanism could be produced that continued to develop these moral and beneficial qualities in people without the destructive and immoral aspects of war.

In response to these declines and the widespread needs of British youth, a second school opened on Eskdale Green in the mountains of England's Lake District in 1950. For the next decade, several new schools sprang up around Britain. In 1958, the first school was built outside of Britain in Lumut, Malaysia. In 1962, the first American school opened in Marble, Colorado and several more followed, scattered around the United States. Today, Outward Bound operates 41 centers in 24 countries (Outward Bound International, 1994, p. 2) and works with all types of clients: at-risk urban youth, recovering substance abusers, business executives, and so on.

Kurt Hahn died in 1974, having remained active throughout his retirement. Credited with the legendary and innovative Salem Schule and Gordonstoun, Hahn's visionary thinking also led to the creation of several other programs: the United World Colleges, one on each continent, attended primarily by international students; the Round Square Schools Conference, supporting community-based service learning; and the Duke of Edinburgh Award, a high school achievement scheme. Outward Bound, by far the most famous of his achievements, also helped shape the United States Peace Corps and numerous other outdoor adventure programs (Miner, 1990).

GROWTH OF ADVENTURE LEARNING PROGRAMS

As the Outward Bound movement in America began to expand, the need for several other types of adventure programs also grew. Paul Petzoldt, chief instructor with the Colorado Outward Bound School in 1964, identified the need to better prepare Outward Bound instructors through leadership courses. To meet the need, he proposed the creation of the Wyoming Outward Bound School to teach instructors to be better outdoor leaders. But Josh Miner, founder of Outward Bound in the United States, had his hands full running the Colorado school and trying to start new programs in Minnesota and Maine. In 1965, Petzoldt got together with another Outward Bound instructor, Ernest "Tap" Tapley, and created the **National Outdoor Leadership School** (NOLS) in Lander, Wyoming (Bachert, 1990).

One of the more notable adapted Outward Bound programs is **Project Adventure**. In 1970 America, Outward Bound was beginning to influence certain elements of educational reform. Educators were searching for a way to tap into the benefits of adventure learning from Outward Bound for the mainstream high school curriculum. Project Adventure began as an attempt to modify the month-long Outward Bound experience into several high school subjects: physical education, science, biology, social studies, history, drama, English, and counseling.

Jerry Pieh (son of Bob Pieh, who started the Minnesota Outward Bound) was a principal at Hamilton-Wenham High School in Hamilton, Massachusetts. In 1971, he received a three-year grant from the U.S. Office of Education to start Project Adventure as a collaborative venture between teachers and former Outward Bound staff. The key to its success was the fact that everything was connected: lessons learned in team cooperation and problem solving during physical education class were applied in group projects in other courses (Prouty, 1990).

In 1974, at the end of the three-year test period, an evaluation of the Project Adventure grant showed it to have been successful with some very significant changes in student self-concept and locus of control. That year, the Office of Education awarded Project Adventure the status of National Demonstration School. They touted the program as a model to be disseminated to other schools. Through annual dissemination grants from the National Diffusion Network, Project Adventure staff shared their work with over 400 schools across the United States during the next six years. Karl Rohnke, author of the early group initiative and ropes course books, and Dick Prouty assumed its leadership in 1981. Since the program had grown well beyond the expectations of the high school administrators, Project Adventure separated from the educational system and incorporated as a nonprofit organization. In the decade that followed, Project Adventure branched out to work with youth agencies, psychiatric hospitals, government offices, treatment centers, colleges, universities, corporations, and job training sites (Prouty, 1990). Today, it has four offices in the United States and representatives in Australia, New Zealand, and Singapore.

In 1976, Paul Petzoldt looked for a new medium through which he and others could establish outdoor leadership training programs. He then began leading intact groups of students from midwestern universities into the Wyoming wilderness. Through discussions with several university professors, the concept for the Wilderness Use Education Association came into being in 1977 (they later dropped the "Use" in the title to become the WEA). While NOLS was a facility-based school, WEA became a membership organization composed of departments from a few American universities such as Western Illinois University (Lupton, 1990). At the time of publication of this text, WEA was headquartered at Colorado State University in Fort Collins, Colorado. Thus, Petzoldt is credited with beginning both the National Outdoor Leadership School (NOLS) and the **Wilderness Education Association** (WEA).

Another membership organization with roots in Outward Bound is the **Association for Experiential Education** (AEE). Outward Bound, Project Adventure, NOLS, and WEA have all been long-time members of AEE. In 1974, Outward Bound sponsored a conference on the use of outdoor pursuits in higher education at Appalachia State University. In 1976, after several more conferences at other universities collaborating with Outward Bound (including one in Canada), organizers formed the AEE and incorporated the organization the next year in Boulder, Colorado (Garvey, 1990).

At the time of publication of this text, AEE had over 500 organizational members and 2000 individual members. AEE had an international scope by the 1990s, and indirectly influenced the creation of several AEE-like organizations in other countries around the world. The organization holds international conferences yearly as well as seven regional conferences every spring around North America. AEE also publishes the *Journal of Experiential Education*. We highly recommend this publication as well as the *Journal of Adventure Education and Outdoor Leadership* from England as the foremost sources for leading-edge thinking and writing in the profession of adventure programming.

HISTORY OF OUTDOOR LEADERSHIP PREPARATION

We can trace the formal beginnings of outdoor leadership preparation to Great Britain. From this country, parallel programs have developed throughout the United Kingdom, Australia, Canada, Europe, New Zealand, and the United States. Let's examine the development of these programs.

Great Britain

Great Britain was the first nation to institute a formal training program for outdoor leaders, and its evolution has had three distinct stages: certification, qualification, and occupation standards. The influence of Outward Bound had brought about explosive growth in the use of the outdoors by British youth and school groups. Coupled with this growth was an increase in accidents by poorly led groups of young people, which represented 65 percent of all mountain res-

cues in the decade following the war (Jackson, 1972). Early in 1958, an initial meeting chaired by Lord John Hunt, leader of the first successful Mount Everest expedition and director of the Duke of Edinburgh Award Scheme, led to the formation of the Mountain Leadership Training Board in 1961 with the mandate to certify mountain leaders to care for groups in the outdoors (Parker & Meldrum, 1973). Thus began the first stage of certification (for more on certification, see page 35).

The Mountain Leadership Certificate program trained and assessed leaders in the basic skills "required to take a party on walking and camping expeditions in mountainous areas of the United Kingdom under normal summer conditions. It [was] intended as an essential requirement for teachers, youth leaders, and other adults wishing to take young people on to the mountains and to show them how to enjoy their mountain walking with safety" (Langmuir, 1969, p. 63).

The curriculum of the early Mountain Leadership Certificate program was decidedly

hard-skill oriented. The components of the summer certificate included navigation, hill walking, camping and expeditions, security on steep ground, river crossing, exposure (hypothermia), effects of heat, weather, lightning, and mountain rescue. A winter certificate was added in 1972 in response to the "Cairngorms disaster" in which several school children died of hypothermia in the mountainous Cairngorms region of Scotland in 1971. It was intended for leaders of groups in winter conditions as found in the Scottish Highlands. The components of the winter certificate included snow and ice climbing, belaying on snow and ice, snow shelters, frostbite, snow cover and avalanches, and avalanche search and rescue (Langmuir, 1973). As a direct result of the Cairngorms disaster, the Hunt Committee on Mountain Training, again chaired by Lord Hunt, was formed to take a close look at the certification scheme. Thus began the second stage of qualification.

Published in 1975, the Hunt Report raised some critical points. First, the committee stated they had "serious reservations about the value of confering [sic] certificates on large numbers of adults who are not professionally engaged in mountain training. Furthermore, certification in any sphere carries its own limitations, in that it tends to prescribe in a rigid manner the content of a course of training, making it more difficult to provide imaginatively for varying needs" (BMC, 1975). Second, the certificate was seen by the committee as having an inflated value, given that it merely met a minimum standard in a field in which the maximum might be more appropriate. Third, the granting of a certificate appeared to attract people who otherwise might not have been interested in mountain activities. Fourth, requirement of the certificate by many agencies prevented the involvement of leaders who lacked the certificate, but who had greater experience than required by such a certificate. Fifth, local educational authorities and other groups had used possession of a certificate as an inappropriate guarantee of the leader's ability (BMC, 1975).

The Hunt Committee made three major recommendations. First, training programs should continue, but the approach should be more varied in content, more flexible in nature, and more responsive to individual needs. Second, they recommended the abolition of certificates and the institution of a reporting method giving the conditions under which assessment took place. Es-

sentially this meant assessors would suggest further training for candidates, based on candidates' strengths and weaknesses. Third, they suggested renaming the Mountain Leadership Certificate Program (BMC, 1975).

A year later, the Hunt reforms were adopted, and the British Mountain Leadership Training Board (BMLTB, the newly adopted name) now offered a qualification, rather than a certification, in outdoor leadership. This was a move overlooked by many North American proponents of certification who recommended following the British success story. Yet, ironically, the British scheme no longer certified leaders! Instead, it provided the "opportunity to gain minimum technical competence for leading parties in the hills. It [did] not provide a professional mountaineering or instructing qualification, nor a professional qualification. The completion of a training course alone [was] in no way a qualification in itself" (Langmuir, 1984, p. 360).

Rather than certify the individual to be a leader, the program placed the responsibility on the candidates as well as on the agency that had hired them. The BMLTB clearly stated that it was the "responsibility of the employer or organiser [sic] to decide whether a leader possessed the personal attributes needed for leadership" (Langmuir, 1984, p. 361). They also stated that in nonmountainous terrain, the qualification should not be a requirement, and that plenty of competent outdoor leaders may be known to possess the informal qualities of leadership, but may not have obtained the formal qualification. In no way should the possession of a leader qualification absolve employers from the responsibility of evaluating any potential job applicant.

Nonetheless, the curriculum remained relatively unchanged with the exception of new classes on access, conservation, and "party leadership." This latter component was an effort by Ken Ogilvie to inject some "soft" skills into the profoundly hard-core curriculum of the BMLTB. In response to a report on leadership in outdoor activities (The Sports Council, 1991) calling for greater development of interpersonal skills in leaders, Ogilvie (1993) wrote a text entitled *Leading and Managing Groups in the Outdoors*. With chapters on aims and values, personal experience, thinking about leadership, leadership models and leadership styles, leader awareness, leader attitudes and approaches, and leadership skills, this book was the first attempt to consider that leaders were more than mere competent technicians.

To date, these ideas have yet to be incorporated into the BMLTB scheme, which still remains hard-skill–oriented.

In 1986, the British Department of Employment began a reform of vocational qualifications for all professions in the UK. Three years later, the profession of sport and recreation came under consideration and the third and present stage of occupational standards began. A committee of experts was established to define professional standards (called National Vocational Qualifications, or NVQs) in five occupational areas: coaching, teaching, and instruction; facility management and operations; sport development; playwork; and outdoor education, training, and recreation. The framework of NVQs and standards was completed in 1992 for the outdoor profession and may be applied to everyone who works in the outdoors, from school teachers to social workers and outdoor center staff.

Although the NVQs specific to outdoor education, training, and recreation were still under development at the time of this text's publication, they appeared to consider more than just hard skills. One particular outdoor occupation—development training, which is the use of experiential methods with youth and corporations—has encompassed meta- and process competencies as well as the technical ones (Doughty & Loynes, 1993). Despite this refreshing approach, many of the other outdoor occupations appear stale and rigid from a North American perspective. Only time will tell if this stage will bring about true improvements over past efforts.

Other European Nations

Mountain leader training boards also exist in Ireland, Northern Ireland, Scotland, and Wales. These boards have close ties to the BMLTB, and their curricula have much in common. With the recent trade coalition among European nations, the BMLTB has begun to influence the preparation of leaders in France, Spain, Germany, Italy, and many other countries. Prior to this influence, however, trends in the United Kingdom already had had far-reaching impacts, directly and indirectly, on other British Commonwealth nations.

Australia

Until recently, outdoor leadership development in Australia has been conducted at the state level. Several Australian programs exist in the states of Victoria, Tasmania, South Australia, and Western Australia. The Australian outdoor leadership movement began in 1969 when the Victorian Bushwalking and Mountaincraft Advisory Board offered the first course based closely on the British Mountain Leadership Certificate program. Over the years, the Australians adapted British training materials to suit local conditions (Lingard, personal communication, April, 1984).

Subsequently, other interested organizations in Tasmania, South Australia, and Western Australia copied the Victorian scheme. The majority of these schemes still offered a certificate, but it was a certificate of course completion and not a certificate of leadership. The trend was away from certification of the leader and toward the qualification of having completed the initial training as in the qualification stage in Britain (Tomalin, personal communication, May, 1984).

Programming in Western Australia, which is geographically separated from the other states, has taken a slightly different track. Its "Expedition Leader Course" was formulated on the belief that the "values and qualities for good judgment in a leader emerge from a continuing learning dynamic rather than from a training scheme using knowledge already created and stored" (Manfield & Pearse, 1991, p. ii). In addition to the technical (hard) and people (soft) skills, its curriculum focused on the integrated skills of problem solving, organization, group management, and instruction.

In the Western Australian program, leadership development took place over several years through the primary, secondary, and tertiary education system. Children learned basic outdoor skills throughout their schooling, and then, as university students, they "studied" to become leaders. We found a similar pattern, independent of government schemes, in exemplary college programs, such as the outdoor education degree program created at the Bendigo Campus of Latrobe University-College of Northern Victoria.

Recent developments have seen meetings by representatives of the different Australian states for the purposes of developing a national leadership preparation scheme. For example, the Australians have begun a National Outdoor Recreation Leadership Development (NORLD) project to develop a nationwide approach to provide a common leadership preparation curriculum (NORLD, 1994).

New Zealand

In 1977, organizers in New Zealand established the provisional Outdoor Training Advisory Board (OTAB). Funded for six years, the OTAB sought to develop an outdoor leadership preparation scheme. A close look at the Hunt Report, published in Britain, and the adaptations of Australia gave the board a unique direction for development (Abbott, personal communication, March, 1984).

The board decided to include several key points in their preparation program. First, the scheme would be open-ended, not presenting a certificate, which would imply the end of training. Second, the scheme would be flexible enough to respond to varying training needs of participants. Third, training would be offered at several levels. Fourth, a modular approach would enable people from a wide variety of outdoor activities to benefit from the training. Fifth, the scheme would be open to input from the many agencies involved in outdoor recreation in New Zealand and thus allow for exchanging of ideas. And sixth, the responsibility for assessment would lie with the participant and not with a panel of experts (Abbott, 1981).

The aims of the board were simple: develop a framework for coordinated leader training, advise existing programs, and act as an information clearinghouse (Toynbee, 1982). The unique aspect of this board was its role as an advisory agency. It did not offer an outdoor leadership program of its own; rather, it assisted other agencies and outdoor associations with their own training programs. As an advisory board, they oriented the mandate for action toward securing resource personnel for courses, avoiding duplication of training courses, and making recommendations on standards and course offerings (Trist, personal communication, February, 1984).

When government funding cutbacks failed to support OTAB, a collection of active outdoor leaders formed the New Zealand Outdoor Instructors Association (NZOIA). NZOIA supports the "concept of continual training, updating techniques and experience on an ongoing basis while working within high professional standards both in terms of instruction and safety parameters" (NZOIA, 1989, p. 3). NZOIA is careful to state that any assessment of a leader's competence is not a guarantee, but is instead simply an indicator of demonstrated expertise at a specific time, in a particular place, and under a certain set of circumstances. The New Zealand Mountain Safety Council and the New Zealand Department of Education run similar leadership schemes for club members (recreational programs) and school teachers (educational programs), respectively.

Canada

Outdoor leadership in Canada has been examined by three provinces: Nova Scotia in the east, British Columbia in the west, and Ontario in the center of the country. Since 1979, Nova Scotia has operated a scheme based partly on the British Scheme and partly on some of the New Zealand adaptations. Patterned after the advisory board in New Zealand, the Nova Scotia Outdoor Leadership Development Program (NSOLDP) consists of an information clearinghouse, a service program providing instructional resources, and an open-ended course in outdoor leadership training. Upon completion of the course, graduates are not granted a certificate, but rather are encouraged to continue developing as outdoor leaders (NSOLDP, 1988).

The province of British Columbia investigated outdoor leadership as early as 1978. In 1981, the Federation of Mountain Clubs of British Columbia (FMCBC), a representative body of 31 outdoor clubs and organizations, issued a press release stating their opposition to mandatory leadership certification (FMCBC, 1981). A survey of outdoor leadership development in British Columbia, undertaken by the Outdoor Recreation Council, confirmed this belief, with only 16 percent of the 138 respondents preferring an outdoor leadership certification scheme (Todd, 1983).

The Council of Outdoor Educators of Ontario (COEO) has wrestled with the issue of certification since 1970. A task force on certification of outdoor leaders recommended not developing their own certification program (COEO, 1977). In a COEO-commissioned work, Rogers (1979) proposed an outdoor leadership development model with certification of technical skills only as a parallel requirement for leadership preparation. The proposal itself was noncertifying and consists of three stages very similar to the British and Australian schemes.

United States

While a number of programs in the United States, such as the National Outdoor Leadership School and Project Adventure, provide certificates of completion of outdoor leadership and adventure education courses, the only organization that purports to certify outdoor leaders is the Wilderness Education Association (WEA).

WEA administers the National Standard Program for Outdoor Leadership Certification within the existing context of university programs. WEA states that certified outdoor leaders "are able to teach others to use and enjoy the wilderness with minimum impact; safely lead others in the wild outdoors; exercise good judgment in a variety of outdoor environments and conditions; and demonstrate a basic standard of outdoor knowledge and experience" (Cockrell & LaFollette, 1985). WEA states that their certification "allows potential employers, parents of youth taking trips into the wilds, insurance companies, wild lands administrators, or others interested in the protection of wilderness users and areas, to know that these certified outdoor leaders have been trained in decision making, safety, and conservation" (WEA, 1984). While WEA has taken this stand in regard to certification, the organization has many opponents, and its certification is not recognized by any government agencies at this time.

The Association for Experiential Education has chosen program accreditation as an alternative to leadership certification. AEE recognized that leadership was only one part of the strategy to increase safety and decrease environmental impact in adventure programs. Even if leaders are certified or qualified to perform their roles effectively, many other aspects of the program can prevent them from being safe or environmentally appropriate. For example, competent leaders without the correct equipment, sent to the wrong location, with an unprepared group could cause enormous damage, despite their best efforts to the contrary.

Program accreditation grew out of an in-house safety review process begun by Outward Bound (Wade, 1983) and was perfected by adding a voluntary peer review process (Gray, 1990; Rubendall, 1992). Today, AEE offers program accreditation services for its membership, one aspect of which is staff qualification. Because they are central to what this book is about, let's discuss the trends and issues of leadership certification and program accreditation further.

ISSUE OF CERTIFICATION VERSUS ACCREDITATION

As we have seen, the world has passed the point of deciding whether or not to *prepare* outdoor leaders. The problems of increasing outdoor accidents and environmental damage, coupled with the associated rise in search and rescue costs, insurance premiums, and resource user regulations, have all combined to make a solution to the problem of competent outdoor leadership both appropriate and necessary. A question facing the field in the past has been whether or not to *certify* those leaders after preparation and, if certified, to what extent? Hunt (1985, p. 24) has summed up this concern well, by stating that the key issue in the certification conflict was the "attempt to conflate [confuse] being safe with being certified!"

As we saw with the British programs, the concern appears to revolve around beliefs that certificates guarantee competence and that certificates encompass all the critical components of outdoor leadership (see "The Certification Workshop" on page 36). This true scenario demonstrates some of the shortcomings of certification. Supply and demand economics can influence, if not determine, the training and assessment standards or curriculum content for certification. In other words, fewer available leaders with a need for more can make getting certified very easy for novices, while an overflow of leaders can make getting certified very difficult for experts.

Rogers (1979) was careful to point out that outdoor leadership is not a case of certification, but is rather an ongoing process of preparation that takes place over a great deal of time and is never fully completed for the leader who aspires to be safe. Safety rests on a leader's judgment; this has been a focal point of an intense debate on the topic of certification for outdoor leaders in years gone by. "Regardless of how extensive and thorough a certification system may be, it cannot [ensure] nor certify that leader's judgmental capabilities in a short time" (Swiderski, 1985, p. 20).

Certification of outdoor leaders will always be an issue, but it is no longer a trend (Priest, 1987). As we have seen, the history of outdoor leadership preparation schemes in Australia, Canada, New Zealand, and the United Kingdom shows a tendency to prefer alternatives to certification. Probably the most visible American alternative is the accreditation of adventure programs as practiced by the Association for Experiential Education (AEE). Clarifying the certification versus accreditation issue will help you understand the dynamics involved as well as future trends facing the field in these areas.

"THE CERTIFICATION WORKSHOP"

When I was a young camp director, I took some of my staff to a certification workshop: we needed to be certified as canoeing leaders. Although we were all keen to get a leader certificate (level 1—capable of teaching canoeing), if we were really competent, we could get a certificate as a leader trainer (level 2—capable of instructing other leaders) or even a master trainer (level 3—capable of independently running certification workshops like the one we were attending).

At the certification workshop, we were required to take one day of core lectures and then a day of examinations, choosing three out of five activity sessions from canoeing, kayaking, power boating, rowing, and sailing. I signed up for canoeing, power boating, and rowing. My first choices of kayaking and sailing were full, and I was denied access because of the popularity of these. I elected to take the leftovers that had ample space available due to an enormous demand for certified leaders in these activities. Besides we had a power boat at camp, and I had been in a rowboat once before!

As you might expect, we all worked very hard in the canoe handling tests, which were extremely demanding because high winds blew across the lake. With many years of experience, I almost missed passing, but luckily I was awarded a level 1 leadership certificate in canoeing!

I had even more difficulty in the rowing test. We had to row directly toward the dock and pivot at the last minute to approach side-on. The maneuver required a complex stroke of oars in opposite directions. I had practiced this move unsuccessfully for about an hour when my turn came to be tested. I nervously approached as slowly as I could with observers shouting for me to row faster! Expecting to crash head-on into the dock, I clumsily made my move and without realizing it parked my boat neatly beside the dock. The only one in the group to succeed on the first try, I was awarded a level 2 leader trainer certificate in rowing, despite never having rowed before!

Things were the worst in the power boating test. I had trouble reversing engines and backing up the boat. I bumped the dock repeatedly during practice. When the motor stalled and wouldn't restart, I pulled the cowl off and removed, cleaned, gapped, and replaced the spark plugs. After considerable effort, I finally managed to get the motor running, but time had expired, and I had missed my testing opportunity. Imagine my surprise when I received by mail my level 3 master trainer certificate in power boating and a note explaining how the tester had been impressed by my ability to troubleshoot engines!

Certification

Senosk (1977) defined certification as a process guaranteeing that certain minimum standards of competency had been met or exceeded by an outdoor leadership candidate and as evaluated by a certifying agency. According to Ewert (1985, p. 17), certification was a "means to [ensure] that only qualified people may systematically engage

in the formal teaching and/or leading of individuals in the outdoor adventure situation." Many experts have questioned certification as a valid means of determining the competency of an outdoor leader (Green, 1982). Yerkes (1985, p. 12) summarized the argument: ". . . Some outdoor professionals thought that we should implement certification before the government did it for us. Other outdoor leaders proclaimed that it was an infringement on their professional domain and that no one had the right to regulate this change."

At least two sides of this controversy exist. Advocates of certification believe that certification can protect the consumer and the environment, maintain public safety, establish a caliber of excellence, motivate outdoor leaders to higher standards, lower insurance premiums, and provide some support in case of litigation (March, 1980; Rollins, 1983). Skeptics argue that certification is costly and time-consuming, establishes a "closed shop monopoly" by excluding experienced but uncertified people, tests only specific skills, does not evaluate a leader's capacity for judgment, and may attract the wrong people for the wrong reasons (Cockrell & LaFollette, 1985; Green, 1982). Priest (1988) felt that a compromise was possible. Since research had shown that proponents and opponents seemed to agree that hard skills of leadership were certifiable, yet that certification was not desirable for soft skills, "Could the two groups have wanted the same end product, but referred to it in different terms? A solution to this long standing problem seems possible. . . . Let the certificate be one of skills and not one of leadership" (pp. 42-43).

While some organizations have established in-house certification processes for their staff and potential outdoor leadership candidates, no certification process has been recognized or accepted by the adventure programming field in North America. Research (e.g., Bassin, et al., 1992) has established that program accreditation has been favored by the profession as an alternative to certification.

Accreditation

We can define **accreditation** as the recognition that a program or institution has met certain predetermined standards of operation. Wade (1983) first suggested accreditation as a viable alternative to certification, stating that "such a system of peer reviews has been in operation within the Outward Bound schools" (p. 6) in the United States for almost two decades. In a related step, Gray (1990) designed a voluntary peer review process on a regional basis for AEE, modeled after an Outward Bound safety review process detailed by Wade and Fischesser (1988). Gray cited reduced insurance premiums, marketing advantages, and reduced program costs for accredited programs as some immediate benefits beyond the expected improvements in educational quality,

accident prevention, environmental impact, and ethical behaviors.

In the state of Virginia, Cockrell and Detzel (1985) found 70 percent of adventure programming professionals supported the idea of accrediting outdoor adventure organizations, rather than certifying individuals. A study of AEE member organizations showed 62 percent supported adventure program accreditation as opposed to 38 percent who supported certification (Bassin et al., 1992). Respondents felt that "accreditation was the only viable alternative to certification because more professional credibility would be gained and there would be less dependence on the unpredictable human part of the equation" (p. 25), being responsible for safety. On the basis of this research, AEE chose voluntary accreditation conducted under external peer review.

In the accreditation process, the AEE reviews team the program or institution as a "whole" in terms of meeting specific standards of operation. Accreditation is the final and critical step in verifying program quality. Early steps include self-evaluation and self-training, internal evaluation and internal training, conferences and external training, external consultation, and external peer review (Williamson & Gass, 1993).

The first step of **self-evaluation** and **self-training** occurs when outdoor leaders consider what took place during a particular aspect of the program and consciously make adjustments in their own actions. For the second step of **internal evaluation** and **internal training**, which follows a program, the staff and administrators meet to discuss how to do things differently next time. The third step, which consists of **conferences** and **external training**, is an opportunity for outdoor leaders to gain new experience and learn from others by interacting with peers, informally sharing ideas, attending outside courses, and going out on their own personal expeditions. The fourth step, **external consultation**, involves bringing in authorities for their advice to formally train staff or to create new program components, such as advertising and marketing, risk management planning, or communicating. The fifth step, **external peer review**, involves inviting outside experts to take a look at the program and give feedback on what could be changed before the sixth and final step of accreditation is undertaken.

The standards for accreditation address several topic areas, such as philosophical, educational, and ethical concerns; risk management; staffing; transportation, including land-, water-, and air-based travel techniques; and environmental, emergency, and cultural skills. The *Manual of Accreditation Standards for Adventure Programs* (Williamson & Gass, 1993) devotes a chapter to each of these areas. Within each chapter, standards cover general issues, environmental understanding, human understanding, conduct for the activity, emergency procedures, clothing and equipment, and nourishment for each topic area.

Program accreditation retains the strengths of leadership certification without being bound by some of its weaknesses. For example, accreditation provides adventure programs with the ability to achieve standards without losing the flexibility to determine how these standards are met. It allows you as a leader to deviate from those standards when doing so is clearly in the best interest of a participant's safety, growth, or psychological well-being. Accreditation takes a systemic view of the process of adventure programming rather than dividing it into individualized categories such as leadership. In adventures, during which uncertainty is prevalent, your best judgment for safely conducting an activity could differ from the standard. In those particular instances, remember that standards are basic guidelines that you must apply to the spirit of the situation, not the mandated letter of practice under all circumstances (Gass & Williamson, 1995).

EFFECTIVE OUTDOOR LEADERS SHOULD

☞ Understand the history of the adventure programming profession and the outdoor leadership field. Rather than just know programs, people, places, and dates, they should comprehend the relationships among these.

☞ Understand how and why these programs, people, places and dates have evolved over time and how various programs and aspects have impacted one another. By knowing the influences of the past, they should be able to better predict the trends of the future.

☞ Understand the pros and cons of leadership certification and program accreditation.

☞ Understand that a certificate is not a guarantee of maximum competence, but is limited evidence of minimum competence, and bear this in mind when applying for work.

☞ Understand the five-step sequence of accreditation.

SUMMARY

Kurt Hahn is responsible for Salem Schule, Gordonstoun School, United World Colleges, the Round Square Schools Conference, the Duke of Edinburgh Award Scheme, and most important, the creation of Outward Bound. Many of Hahn's principles were based on his perceptions of social declines he observed in youth. Outward Bound went on to operate 41 centers in 24 countries and to influence the United States Peace Corps and numerous spin-off programs: Project Adventure (Outward Bound in schools) the National Outdoor Leadership School (Wyoming Outward Bound dedicated to developing leaders), the Wilderness Education Association (leadership certification through universities), and the Association for Experiential Education (a collection of adventure organizations and individual members). As the international body for adventure programming, AEE holds conferences, distributes books, and publishes journals: all are excellent resources for professional development.

Since 1961, the influence of the "original" British Mountain Leadership Certificate Scheme has spread throughout Australia, New Zealand, Canada, and the United States. Begun originally as a certification scheme, the program operated by the Mountain Leadership Training Board is now a qualification scheme for aspiring outdoor leaders. Reforms resulting from the Hunt Report have altered the format of the program. Today, the program no longer certifies outdoor leaders, and new developments in National Vocational Qualifications may bring new changes to leadership training.

Australia was the first to adapt the British programs, adding the concept of initial appraisal sessions and advisory panels for training and assessment. Several state-wide leadership schemes are presently contributing to the development of a national strategy for outdoor leadership preparation. Looking to Australia as well as to the changes in Britain, New Zealand developed an advisory, rather than a certifying, role.

Today several groups offer independent leadership training programs. Based on observations of the successful New Zealand scheme, Canadian programs in British Columbia, Ontario, and Nova Scotia appear to be moving away from certification. Two programs in the United States still certify outdoor leaders; however, a nationally recognized program without certification has yet to arise in this country.

Yet, outdoor leadership preparation is necessary. While certification of leaders will always remain a contentious issue, it is no longer a trend. Why? Certification has several serious shortcomings that have moved the profession toward program accreditation instead of leadership certification. The Association for Experiential Education (AEE) has responded with a program accreditation process composed of five steps leading to accredited status: self-evaluation and self-training, internal evaluation and internal training, conferences and external training, external consultation, and external peer review.

QUESTIONS TO THINK ABOUT

1. What were the factors that contributed to the development of Outward Bound?

2. Trace the path of Outward Bound's influence on adventure programming.

3. From these past influences, what future directions do you expect the profession of adventure programming in North America to take?

4. Identify examples from your own culture of Hahn's six areas of decline.

5. What were the factors that contributed to the development of the British MLTB?

6. Trace the path of the British MLTB's influence on outdoor leadership.

7. From these past influences, what future directions do you expect the field of outdoor leadership in North America to take?

8. Differentiate between certification and accreditation. Discuss situations in which one might be preferable over the other, and vice versa.

REFERENCES

Abbott, C. (1981, October). Flexible leader training: The history and philosophy of the New Zealand Outdoor Training Advisory Board. In *Proceedings of the National Outdoor Education Conference* (pp. 52-55). Maroon, Queensland, Australia.

Bachert, D. (1990). Historical evolution of NOLS: The National Outdoor Leadership School. In J.C. Miles & S. Priest (Eds.), *Adventure education* (pp. 83-88). State College, PA: Venture.

Bassin, Z., Breault, M., Fleming, J., Foell, S., Neufeld, J., & Priest, S. (1992). An AEE organizational member preference for leadership certification or program accreditation. *Journal of Experiential Education* 15(1), 21-26.

British Mountaineering Council. (1975). *The Hunt committee report on mountain training.* Manchester, UK: Author.

Cockrell, D., & Detzel, D. (1985). Effects of outdoor leadership certification on safety, impacts and program. *Trends* 22(3), 15-21.

Cockrell, D., & LaFollette, J. (1985). A national standard for outdoor leadership certification. *Parks & Recreation* 20(6), 40-43.

Council of Outdoor Educators of Ontario (COEO). (1977). *COEO task force report on certification.* Toronto: Author.

Doughty, S., & Loynes, C. (1993). *The training of development trainers: Proposed standards.* Ambleside, Cumbria: Lancaster University.

Ewert, A. (1985). Emerging trends in outdoor adventure recreation. In G. McLellan (Ed.), *Proceedings - 1985 National Outdoor Recreation Trends Symposium II.* Atlanta, GA: USDI National Park Service.

Ewert, A. (1989). The history of outdoor adventure programming. *The Journal of Adventure Education and Outdoor Leadership* 6(4), 10-15.

Federation of Mountain Clubs of British Columbia (FMCBC). (1981, May). *Mountain leadership certification press release.* Vancouver, BC, Canada: Author.

Garvey, D. (1990). A history of the AEE. In J.C. Miles & S. Priest (Eds.), *Adventure education* (pp. 75-82). State College, PA: Venture.

Gass, M.A., & Williamson, J. (1995). Accreditation of adventure programs. *Journal of Health, Physical Education, Recreation and Dance* 66(1), 22-27.

Gray, D. (1990). *A pilot model for a New England peer review program.* Unpublished manuscript, Association for Experiential Education.

Green, P. (1982). *The outdoor leadership handbook.* Tacoma, WA: The Emergency Response Institute.

Hunt, J.S. (1985). Certification controversy. *Camping Magazine* 57(6), 23-24.

Jackson, J. (1972). *Notes on party leadership.* Manchester, UK: Mountain Leadership Training Board.

James, W. (1967). The moral equivalent of war. In J.J. McDermott (Ed.), *The writings of William James* (pp. 668-669). New York: Random House.

Langmuir, E. (1969). *Mountain leadership.* Edinburgh, Scotland, UK: Scottish Sports Council.

Langmuir, E. (1973). *Mountain leadership* (Rev. ed.). Edinburgh, Scotland, UK: Scottish Sports Council.

Langmuir, E. (1984). *Mountaincraft and leadership.* Edinburgh, Scotland, UK: Scottish Sports Council.

Lupton, F. (1990). WEA History. In J.C. Miles & S. Priest (Eds.), *Adventure education* (pp. 89-95). State College, PA: Venture.

Manfield, L.M., & Pearse, J.K. (1991). *A-WAY: For the expedition leader*. Albany, WA: Denmark Printing.

March, W. (1980). Assessing outdoor leaders: The catch-22 of wilderness leadership certification. *Foothills Wilderness Journal* 7(2), 16-17.

Miner, J. (1990). The creation of Outward Bound. In J.C. Miles & S. Priest (Eds.), *Adventure education* (pp. 55-66). State College, PA: Venture.

National Outdoor Recreation Leadership Development (NORLD). (1994). News on the National Outdoor Recreation Leadership Development strategy. *Outdoor Update* 2 (p. 1). Hobart, Tasmania: Author.

New Zealand Outdoor Instructors Association (NZOIA). (1989). *Instructor's logbook*. Wellington, NZ: Hillary Commission for Recreation and Sport.

Nova Scotia Outdoor Leadership Program (NSOLDP). (1988). *Leadership development*. Halifax, NS, Canada: Author.

Ogilvie, K.C. (1993). *Leading and managing groups in the outdoors*. Sheffield, UK: NAOE Publications.

Outward Bound International. (1994). *Outward Bound International: To serve, to strive and not to yield*. Rugby, England: The Outward Bound Trust.

Parker, T.M., & Meldrum, K.I. (1973). *Outdoor education*. London, UK: Dent.

Priest, S. (1987). Outdoor leadership certification: Always an issue, but no longer a trend. *Bradford Papers Annual* 2, 37-44.

Priest, S. (1988). Agreement reached on the issue of outdoor leadership certification? *Bradford Papers Annual* 3, 38-43.

Prouty, D. (1990). Project Adventure: A brief history. In J.C. Miles & S. Priest (Eds.), *Adventure education* (pp. 97-109). State College, PA: Venture.

Richards, A. (1990). Kurt Hahn. In J.C. Miles and S. Priest (Eds.), *Adventure education* (pp. 67-74). State College, PA: Venture.

Rogers, R.J. (1979). *Leading to share, sharing to lead*. Sudbury, Ontario: Council of Outdoor Educators of Ontario (COEO).

Rollins, R. (1983). Leadership certification revisited. *California Association for Health, Physical Education, and Recreation (CAHPER) Journal* 50(1), 8-9.

Rubendall, R. (1992). *Heartland peer review practices*. Boulder, CO: Association for Experiential Education.

Senosk, E.M. (1977). *An examination of outdoor pursuit leader certification and licensing within the United States in 1976*. Unpublished Master's Thesis, University of Oregon.

The Sports Council. (1991). *Leadership in outdoor activities: Report of the interim working group*. London, England: Author.

Swiderski, M.J. (1985). Stop going around in circles. *Camping Magazine* 57(6), 20-22.

Todd, A. (1983). *Leadership development program: Summary of survey results*. Vancouver, BC, Canada: Outdoor Recreation Council.

Toynbee, P. (1982). Improving leadership training. In *Proceedings of the National Outdoor Education Conference* (pp. 132-136). Wellington, New Zealand.

Wade, I.R. (1983). *Alternative to certification programs*. Unpublished manuscript.

Wade, I.R., & Fischesser, M. (1988). *The safety review manual: A guide to conducting safety reviews for assessing and upgrading safety in outdoor adventure programs*. Greenwich, CT: Outward Bound USA.

Williamson, J., & Gass, M.A. (1993). *Manual of accreditation standards for adventure programs*. Boulder, CO: Association for Experiential Education.

Wilderness Education Association (WEA). (1984). Pamphlet. Driggs, ID: Author.

Yerkes, R. (1985). Certification: An introduction behind the growing controversy. *Camping Magazine*, 57(6), 12-13.

chapter

4

Individual Behavior
and Motivation

The cover of *Time* magazine for August 29, 1983 displayed a picture of "Daredevil Ben Colli" with the caption "Wheeeeeeee! Chasing Thrills and Adventure." The subject of the photograph was infamous for his high-speed rappelling descents from atop skyscrapers. The cover story, entitled "Risking It All" contained stories of bungee jumpers, mountain climbers, swimmers, runners, paddlers, parachutists, pilots, and sailors. The author of the piece (Skow, 1983) wrote: "There have always been adventurers, footloose and sometimes screwloose, and their 'Why not' has always stirred alarming and delicious fears in settled souls whose timid question is 'Why?'" (p. 52)

To help you deliver your adventure program more effectively, it helps to better understand individual behavior during adventure experiences. In this chapter, we'll explain some of the social psychology theories that have contributed to the present body of knowledge regarding human motivation in times of risk and adventure. To show you real-life applications of these theories, we'll include pertinent examples of common outdoor activities.

PHYSIOLOGICAL AND PSYCHOPHYSIOLOGICAL FACTORS

The uninitiated public often ask "Why? Why would anyone in their right mind climb a mountain, paddle a river, descend a ski slope, or jump out of an airplane?" Mallory's historic answer "Because it's there," made in reference to his plan to ascend Everest in 1924, sheds little light on what motivates people to take risks in the first place. The idea that some people are "adrenaline junkies" and that they are addicted to thrill seeking may seem somewhat humorous. On closer inspection, however, physiological studies suggest that this may be closer to the truth than experts or laymen originally suspected.

Endorphin High

Endorphins are hormone-like chemicals released into the bloodstream during times of stress. Their chemical structure resembles narcotic compounds such as opium, and they have similar effects on the nervous system without the negative side effects that often accompany illicit drugs. The well-known "runner's high" that dulls sensations of pain and gives feelings of limitless strength or endurance to marathoners is just one positive example of endorphins in action.

We humans have a need for a certain amount of stress in our lives to maintain the level of endorphin secretion we have come to expect. Some people have enough stress in their daily lives. Others have greater needs and often fulfill their desires by consciously seeking stimulation through risk-taking adventures (e.g., Bunting, 1987; Schreyer, White, & McCool, 1978; Selye, 1974; Zuckerman, 1979). While this explanation of motivation is based in human physiology, other theories examine the social psychology of adventure.

Optimal Arousal

In the book *Why People Play*, Ellis (1973) discusses his **optimal arousal theory of play**, asserting that the human brain is a continually active organ in need of ongoing stimulation. Deprived of external stimulation, for example during sleep, the brain manufactures its own arousal in the form of dreams. This optimal behavior is easily observed in children (most of Ellis's work was conducted in the children's play laboratories), during which without external stimulation from a parent or friend, they will seek their own arousal in the form of imagined or other independent play. Since adventure is seen by some as a form of adult play (Carpenter & Priest, 1989), the optimal arousal theory of play behavior may apply to adults as well.

The level of arousal of the brain is related to the amount of information it is receiving. The more information received in a set period of time, the higher the arousal; the less information coming in, the lower the arousal. People may be over- or underaroused by the conditions around them, and levels of arousal in the same situation differ for various people. Based on these principles, a unique level of "optimal arousal" exists for each individual. Ellis believed this was the point at which performance is at its maximum. Figure 4.1 diagrams the relationship between performance and arousal.

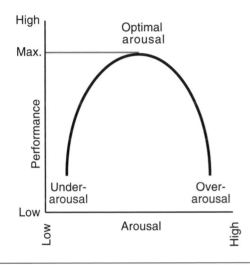

Figure 4.1   A graphic representation of optimal arousal theory.

For example, a mountaineer who is climbing an easy route may be underaroused to the extent that performance drops off. It may also be the case that the mountaineer climbs a difficult route, becomes overaroused, and experiences a similar decrease in performance. Most mountaineers usually seek that particular level of difficulty that is optimally arousing, leading to the best climbing performance. The unique point to Ellis's theory is that people like to perform their best and will purposefully seek out conditions that produce a state of optimal arousal. Since adventure is considered adult play, theories such as Zuckerman's (1979) identification of **sensation seeking** have been adopted as possible reasons to explain why people test and push their limits by taking risks.

Flow State

Csikszentmihalyi (1975) wrote a book entitled *Beyond Boredom and Anxiety* in which he observed and interviewed a wide cross section of

the public, including chess players, poets, dancers, surgeons, and rock climbers. All subjects of his study identified a similar state of being they experienced when fully involved in their chosen activity, which he later termed **states of flow.** "Flow describes a state of experience that is engrossing, intrinsically rewarding and outside the parameters of worry and boredom" (M. Csikszentmihalyi & I.S. Csikszentmihalyi, 1991, p. 150). Studies on flow suggest that people are motivated to participate in adventure experiences because of the intrinsic feelings of enjoyment, well-being, and personal competence they achieve. These positive effects are the reasons people return to adventure programming in an effort to recapture the feelings.

Csikszentmihalyi and Csikszentmihalyi (1991) outlined six characteristics that make the flow-producing experience worthy of repetition to the participant:

1. People experiencing flow clearly know the goals they are trying to achieve and receive **immediate feedback** about how they are doing.

2. **Action and awareness merge** as they see themselves fully engrossed in the activity with pure, uninterrupted concentration.

3. This merging is made possible by their centering on a **limited stimulus field** in which they consciously screen out potential interruptions and unimportant information.

4. They experience "self-forgetfulness" by losing touch with physical reality or by gaining a **heightened awareness** of their inner workings.

5. They enjoy a **feeling of control** over personal actions and the environment during which an awareness of control may be present or a worry over lack of control may be absent.

6. The flow experience is **autotelic**: so enjoyable and meaningful that they desire to repeat the activities in hopes of reproducing such a state, regardless of their reasons for first trying the activity.

Participants can only experience flow when the opportunity to take action is balanced with the individual's capacity to act appropriately. Figure 4.2 illustrates this point.

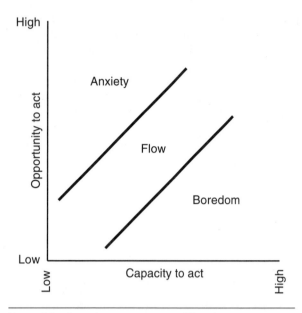

Figure 4.2   A graphic representation of flow theory.

For example, an expert paddler has a high capacity to act, while a novice paddler has a low capacity. Flatwater offers little opportunity to act, while difficult whitewater gives plenty of opportunity. If you place the expert paddler on flatwater, then she experiences feelings of boredom, or underarousal, since her capacity for action exceeds the opportunity. If you place the novice on whitewater, then she experiences a feeling of anxiety, or overarousal, since the opportunity for action far outweighs the capacity. Csikszentmihalyi (1975) asserted that the flow states exist between boredom and anxiety where opportunity and capacity can achieve a synergistic balance. In this example, the novice paddler on flatwater and the expert in whitewater could each be able to experience flow if their capacities matched their opportunities.

Antecedents of Adventure

Mitchell (1983) noted the lack of important conditions or antecedents in Csikszentmihalyi's theory on the experience of flow. He proposed including the identification of several important conditions that "constitute and potentiate [augment] the flow experience" (p. 154) to enhance Csikszentmihalyi's theory. These antecedents included freedom of choice, state of mind, intrinsic motivation, outcome uncertainty, and competence engagement.

First, Mitchell suggested that in order for an adventure to create the experience of flow, it must be completely voluntary, meaning individuals are free to choose their level of involvement. One way leaders meet this condition in adventure programs is by implementing Rohnke's (1988) axiom of "challenge by choice," under which no one is coerced into taking risks.

Second, adventures are individually specific because each person brings his own level of competence to the experience. Moreover, adventures are specific to the situation because each setting has a different level of inherent risk. As a result, adventures are experienced differently by different people: an adventure is a state of mind.

Third, people initially engage in adventure for a variety of reasons. But those motivated by intrinsic reasons (e.g., joy, happiness, independence, and self-development) generally continue to participate year after year. Most people do not seek extrinsic rewards, such as status or money, in adventure experiences.

Fourth, Mitchell defined adventures as undertakings with uncertainty of outcome. Too much uncertainty of outcome, however, is overarousing; too little is underarousing. Thus, unattainable goals could produce panic due to anxiety in a participant and too easily achieved goals could lead to complacency due to boredom. Neither of these situations will result in flow or a positive learning experience, and also could create dangerous conditions. To make the best of an adventure, participants should feel challenged, yet in control of the situation. If a facilitator or friend were to give away answers or rescue a participant by providing solutions to a problem, the amount of uncertainty would change and the experience would be altered (Goffman, 1981). Except in situations of safety, ethical adventure leaders avoid helping participants too much.

Last, the client must be actively engaged in her adventure with the opportunity to influence the outcome and resolve the uncertainty by applying personal competence to the risky situation. The approach used by some adventure programs in which the client is removed from the experience and cared for by the leaders—as if in an amusement park—can negate the empowering effect of an adventure. The individual cannot learn unless she has an active role in the experience, including the benefits and consequences of her actions. Of course, as a leader, you must intercede in truly dangerous situations.

STAGES OF ADVENTURE

After 20 years experience in observing and interviewing participants in outdoor adventures, Mortlock (1984) proposed four stages people experience in any outdoor journey: play, adventure, frontier adventure, and misadventure. According to Mortlock, participants can be in any one of the four stages at any time, whether novice or expert, depending on the amount of fear present in the activity.

- Play is characterized by the absence of fear. We can describe play as pleasant or fun and as boring or a waste of time.

- Adventure is characterized by some fear being present. Participants in the adventure stage are in total control of the situation, but are being challenged to some extent.

- Frontier adventure involves a high degree of fear. In frontier adventure, participants experience the risk of physical harm and no longer feel in complete control.

- Misadventure encompasses too much fear and often results in failure. The outcome of misadventure may be as simple as personal dissatisfaction or as serious as physical or psychological damage. Participants may experience a bruised ego, scrapes, and splinters, which we consider acceptable and recoverable outcomes, or may suffer fractures, emotional breakdown, or even death, which we consider unacceptable and nonrecoverable outcomes.

Mortlock reserved play as the stage to learn new skills in. He felt that adventure and especially frontier adventure must be strived for in an outdoor experience, as these make life worth living. Last, the condition of misadventure was where people learned best from their mistakes, provided they were not permanently injured.

We cannot overstate the role of fear. Fear is the human response to risk and, as such, you should consider it a healthy and much-needed reaction. Nonetheless, there are times when you must help participants deal with their fears of risky situations. Several coping strategies have been suggested by Ewert (1989) to decrease fear: desensitization, which is gradual exposure by building up to the big risk through progressively risky activities; flooding, which is careful and prolonged exposure to the risk once encountered; modeling, which is the observation of the techniques used by others to manage their fear; and rehearsal, which is the application of those techniques with repeated practice.

Adventure Experience Paradigm

Martin and Priest (1986) combined the ideas from previous works, developing their own model: the **adventure experience paradigm**. The adventure experience paradigm explains participants' behaviors, based on the variables of risk and competence. We can define risk as the potential to lose something of value and competence as the capability of individuals to deal effectively with the demands placed on them by their surrounding environment.

In this model, the interaction of risk and competence creates the challenge. Challenge cannot exist without the presence of both situational risk and personal competence engaged in an effort to resolve uncertainty. Depending on the amount of risk and degree of competence interacting together in an adventure experience, five conditions of challenge are possible: exploration and experimentation, adventure, peak adventure, misadventure, devastation, and disaster (Priest & Baillie, 1987). Figure 4.3 presents a diagram of this relationship between risk and competence.

This diagram illustrates that when a person with a high degree of competence performs a low-risk activity, the result is a condition of exploration and experimentation, similar to Mortlock's (1984) play stage during which new skills are learned,

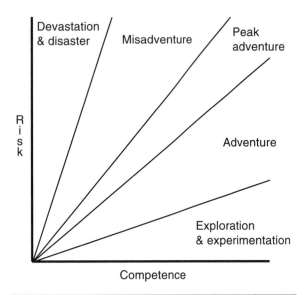

Figure 4.3 A graphic representation of the adventure experience paradigm.

tested, and honed. As competence decreases or risk increases or both, the participant moves into the adventure. When the two components are balanced and matched, a condition of peak adventure results, similar to Csikszentmihalyi's (1975) state of flow. As risk exceeds competence, the potential for misadventure arises; when risk becomes very high and competence is very low, devastation and disaster may occur.

Consider "average" skiers at the start of the ski season. They begin on the gentle "bunny hills" where the risk of falling is minimal and their competence to ski is maximal. This is exploration and experimentation: the skiers can practice their turns and stops to gain confidence. When ready, they move out onto green (i.e., easy and beginner) runs where the risk of falling increases and their skiing competence may decrease. This is adventure, in which participants work harder at skiing and feel more challenged. On the blue square (i.e., moderate and intermediate) runs, they find peak adventure, at which their competence to ski is perfectly balanced with the risk of falling, and they feel "on the razor's edge" as they descend the slope, uncertain whether they will be successful in the product, but confident they will do their best in the process. The black diamond (i.e., difficult and expert) runs provide a little misadventure for these average skiers, because the risk of falling outweighs their competence to ski at this advanced level. When they fall, they consider it to be a minor mishap from which they can recover. They

may be bruised, embarrassed, and covered by snow, but they will not suffer permanent damage. Devastation and disaster would come in the out-of-bounds areas: the back gullies and avalanche slopes where a fall means a broken limb—or worse yet—death! Obviously ethical adventure programs deal with the conditions up to and including misadventure, because people learn well from their mistakes. But devastation and disaster are not a purposeful part of ethical adventure programs.

Martin and Priest (1986) proposed that the goal of an outdoor adventure experience for an individual is to reach peak adventure [similar to Ellis's (1973) concepts of seeking optimal arousal] since this is the realm in which you can experience flow and the most positive benefits of adventure experiences. However, the "key to application of the adventure experience paradigm lies in the perceptions of the individual" (p. 19). Individuals can misperceive both the real risk and their actual competence and, as a result, overshoot or fall short of the goal of peak adventure.

By integrating the concept of misperception in their model, Martin and Priest identified nine types of individuals (see figure 4.4). Let's look closely at three of these: the astute individual, the timid and fearful individual, and the arrogant and fearless individual.

The **astute** individual correctly perceives the level of risk as well as correctly perceives her competence to perform the activity and so possesses a high probability of experiencing a condition of peak adventure. The **timid and fearful** individual misperceives adventure in two ways: she overestimates the risk of the activity and underestimates her competence to perform it. The timid and fearful individual will fall short of peak adventure and perhaps drop into exploration and experimentation, because real risk is actually lower and real competence is actually higher than her perceptions. In contrast, the **arrogant and fearless** individual misperceives adventure in ways opposite to the timid and fearful individual: she underestimates the risk of the activity and overestimates her competence to perform it. The arrogant and fearless individual will overshoot peak adventure and perhaps experience devastation and disaster, because real risk is actually higher and real competence is actually lower than her perceptions. Figures 4.5 and 4.6 portray these latter two profiles.

Adaptive Dissonance

When a person has two different and conflicting thoughts, a cognitive, affective, or psychomotor

COMPETENCE

	Over-perceived	Correctly perceived	Under-perceived
Under-perceived	Fearless and arrogant	Bold	Naive and innocent
Correctly perceived	Assured	Astute	Insecure
Over-perceived	Carefree and exaggerated	Overawed	Timid and fearful

(Left axis label: R I S K)

Figure 4.4 The nine types of individuals, based on perceptions of risk and competence.

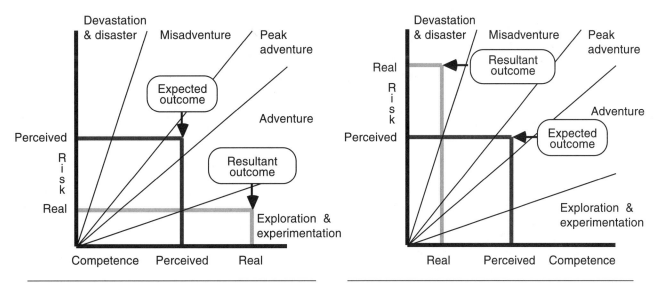

Figure 4.5 An adventure experience paradigm profile for the timid and fearful individual.

Figure 4.6 An adventure experience paradigm profile for the arrogant and fearless individual.

(Festinger, 1957; Walsh & Golins, 1976). A common example in outdoor activities occurs when participants look at completing a ropes course and choose to focus on the danger and difficulty, while you as the outdoor leader explain the safety of the belay ropes and the ease of balancing when not looking down. In this instance, the participants are struck by the paradox of opposing views. Both seem sensible and correct, but the participants are unwilling to accept both as true and so are motivated to resolve the dissonance, perhaps by testing either view through an

attempt to complete one element of the ropes course. The strength of their motivation to attempt the ropes course is partially a function of how big a gap exists between their expectations and your comments. But we'll discuss other motivational influences later in this chapter. For now, let's focus on the role of creating adaptive dissonance.

Priest and Baillie (1987) have discussed the application of the adventure experience paradigm to facilitated outdoor learning situations. The purpose of this model is to help you lead timid and fearful or arrogant and fearless participants toward becoming astute. According to this paradigm, the way to elicit more astute behavior is to create situations with strong adaptive dissonance. In practice, this means presenting tasks that have the appearance of being "difficult" for the timid and fearful, knowing that success is highly probable, and "easy" for the arrogant and fearless, while carefully setting them up for failure. In essence, dissonance between client perceptions and the reality of the adventure can increase the likelihood of a peak experience.

Ethical adventure programs debrief both individuals' experiences, perhaps privately and then within a group. The debriefing helps guide participants to reflect on past experiences, encouraging them to reassess their perceptions of the risk and competence from their previous attempts. As they come to identify, accept, and change their shortcomings, their perceptions move closer to reality, and they eventually become astute (Carpenter & Priest, 1989). With astuteness often comes improvements in self-concept and socialization. Indeed, interpersonal and intrapersonal relationships benefit from such facilitated experiences.

One caution regarding the facilitated adventure experience is that you must structure, control, and supervise the activity. The activity is structured, since you custom fit the level of challenge to the individual; and is controlled, because the risks you manipulate are strictly perceived values while maintaining real values at acceptable or low levels. As the leader, you are the key to the operation and must be sufficiently experienced and astute enough to accurately perceive the risks and the participants' competencies.

THEORIES AND MODELS OF MOTIVATION

The concept of motivation comes from the Latin word *movere*, meaning to move. In this sense, motivation is about why and how individuals move or don't move from one state of being to another. Factors influencing motivation include

- direction of effort, such as confronting a situation or avoiding a situation;
- intensity of effort, or how much effort a person expends in a situation;

- choice of behaviors, such as strategies people use to deal with a situation;
- ability to sustain motivation, for example, how long an individual persists in a situation; and
- resulting behavior change, for example, whether behaviors that result from the situation will be sustained (Sage, 1977; Weinberg & Gould, 1995).

In this section we'll present several theories and models addressing how motivation principles affect adventure programming participants and enhance your ability to appropriately motivate clients toward their goals. Specifically, we'll discuss (1) goal theory, or how a person's commitment to a goal influences his actions, (2) expectancy theory, or how a person's expectations about achieving a goal influences his actions, (3) self-efficacy, or how the belief of whether or not you can accomplish a task affects motivation, and how you can implement various strategies to enhance clients' abilities to be successful, (4) attribution theory and locus of control, or how individuals explain their successes and failures and the influence these attributions have on future actions and emotions, and (5) effectiveness and competence motivation, or how effectiveness of attempts to complete tasks influences feelings of competence as well as how social and interpersonal factors influenced—and were influenced by—these feelings. A final model combines all of these frameworks into one model that outlines risk-taking behavior and competence effectiveness, or how you can use the accuracy of participants' beliefs to influence the probability of success or failure in adventure experiences.

Goal and Expectancy Theories

As the facilitator, your ability to manipulate the risk and competence variables of an adventure experience depends heavily on clients' personal commitments to attaining goals as well as their expectations about being successful. **Goal theory** states that performance is determined by a participant's commitment to goals. These goals may be established by the individual or dictated by others. Participants who are committed to specific and well-defined goals perform at higher levels of competence than those who set general or vague goals (Katzell & Thompson, 1990). Therefore, helping participants to set their own

Sidebar 4.2

ADAPTIVE DISSONANCE AND PERSONALITY TYPES

For timid and fearful individuals in an activity, the adaptive dissonance lies between their anticipated failure and your encouragement that success is imminent. The timid and fearful individuals will expect conditions of misadventure, while you as the leader must have structured and controlled their experiences so that conditions of adventure result (see figure 4.7).

During the debriefing, you can ask questions regarding the participants' initial perceptions of risk and competence. They might typically respond with comments like "It wasn't as dangerous as I had first thought" and "Maybe I can perform better than I give myself credit for!" Following these guided discussions, participants often shift their perceptions closer to reality for the next experience. Overall, the adaptive dissonance is reduced (see figure 4.8).

In time with repeated and varied experiences, coupled with subsequent debriefings, the perceptions of the timid and fearful participants will merge with reality, and they will have become astute. Once astute, you should encourage them to review the overall process of changing in light of how this new learning about themselves might apply to their real lives.

To illustrate, consider a timid and fearful man on a high ropes traverse. The facilitator has structured an experience for which she asks this person to walk across a tightrope 50 feet above the ground with only a rope strung from the far tree for balance and support. Based on perceived values, he is expecting a misadventure or, even worse, devastation and disaster! In actuality, the real values are quite different, since he is belayed. After considerable coaxing and assistance from the facilitator, he completes the traverse and feels elated. The facilitator helps him reflect on his adventure, and after some thought and discussion, he recognizes that the task was not so dangerous and that he really

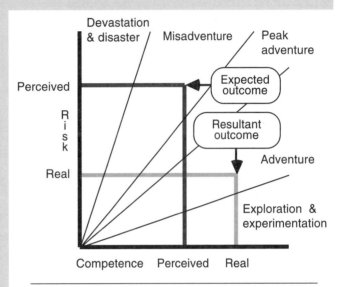

Figure 4.7 Adaptive dissonance between expected and resultant (leader-predicted) outcomes for the timid and fearful individual.

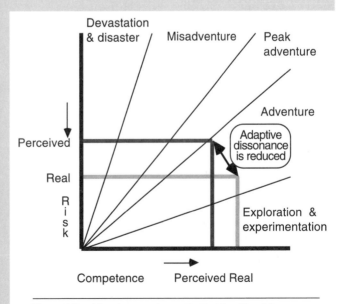

Figure 4.8 After the experience, the timid and fearful individual's perceptions shift closer to reality.

was capable enough to complete it. This learning may later transfer to daily living concerns in which perhaps the man expresses timid and fearful behaviors when meeting new people. In the future, he may be able to take on new friendships with newly learned confidence.

For arrogant and fearless individuals, the adaptive dissonance lies between their apparent sureness and the leader's expression that success is doubtful for this activity. The arrogant and fearless will expect conditions of adventure, but since the leader will have structured or controlled the experiences for gentle failure, the conditions of misadventure will result (see figure 4.9).

Occasionally, arrogant and fearless individuals' behavior is the result of repeated failures in life, and their demeanors are a coping mechanism for dealing with failure. Hence, you must be very careful not to further embarrass these individuals in front of others, reinforcing this personality trait. If such a concern exists, the best approach may be to conduct the activity away from the group, debriefing the individuals separate from and in advance of the shared group discussions. In this way, the arrogant and fearless may respond to questions about risk and competence with answers such as "It may be that that was more difficult than I first thought" and "Maybe I'm not as good as I think!" From these reflections, the arrogant and fearless participants can shift their perceptions closer to reality for the next experience. Once again, adaptive dissonance is reduced (see figure 4.10).

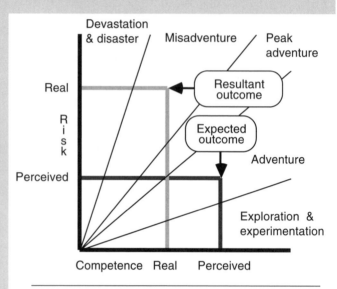

Figure 4.9   Adaptive dissonance between resultant (leader-predicted) and expected outcomes for arrogant and fearless individuals.

With further experience and debriefing, the arrogant and fearless participants will have become astute as their perceptions merge with reality. In the unlikely instance in which they might convert to being timid and fearful from experiencing an overwhelming failure, you can simply structure an easier task for the next activity. Once again, after repeated activities, you can debrief the learning in relation to real life.

Let's consider, for example, an arrogant and fearless woman on a rock climb. The facilitator has structured an experience asking her to climb a

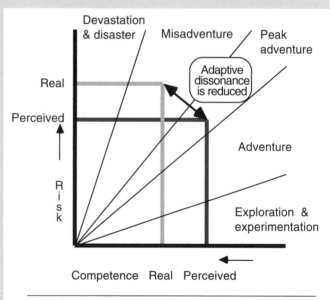

Figure 4.10   After the experience, the arrogant and fearless individual's perceptions move closer to reality.

particularly difficult route, which has previously been the topic of some bragging on her part. Based on perceived values, she is expecting exploration and experimentation or, at best, mere adventure! In actuality, the real values are quite different, since she is belayed, but the facilitator has chosen a very difficult route, expecting her to fail. After considerable effort, she has fallen off the crux of the climb repeatedly and is exhausted. The facilitator now helps her reflect on her misadventure. After some thought and discussion, she recognizes that the task was indeed more difficult than she expected and that she really was not as good as she was saying. This reversal may later transfer to daily living concerns in which perhaps the woman expresses arrogant and fearless behaviors when working on projects as part of a small group. Perhaps next time, she will be more agreeable.

goals, particularly those which require concentrated effort to attain, can be an excellent motivational technique. Certainly, by setting their own goals, participants will have a greater level of commitment to achieving the task.

Expectancy theory takes into account three determinants that motivate people: first, whether their efforts will lead to performance, "Can I do it?"; second, what outcomes are involved, "What's in it for me?"; and third, the value of those outcomes, "Is it worth it?" People are motivated when they expect that effort will result in good performance, which will in turn be useful in attaining desired outcomes (Katzell & Thompson, 1990). Expectancy theory has useful application to outdoor programs as it can help to define exactly how you can motivate individuals to experience peak adventures. Participants provided with sufficient training, emotional support, proper resources, and understanding of benefits will feel more confident about accomplishing a task. This confidence reduces their anxieties and enhances perceived competence, empowering them to tackle greater risks.

Self-Efficacy

Bandura's (1977) social learning theory defines **self-efficacy** as the certainty of an individual's belief that he or she can successfully accomplish a task that tests ability while experiencing risk. It is more than mere self-confidence in your abilities; it is believing that you can successfully execute the behaviors necessary to accomplish the "anticipated and desired" task(s) (p. 192).

Self-efficacy expectations vary in at least three ways: magnitude, strength, and generality.

1. **Magnitude** refers to the degree of certainty associated with success and is heavily influenced by perceptions of risk and difficulty. For example, when working with clients who were afraid of snakes, Bandura offered three ways to confront this issue: looking at pictures of snakes, being in the same room with snakes, and actually touching snakes. Clients varied widely in magnitude as some were 100 percent certain of being able to deal with the less risky task of looking at pictures, and others were only 10 percent certain of accomplishing the more risky task of actually touching snakes. Thus, although any two people may expect success for a given task, they may differ in the magnitude of their certainty of success.

2. **Strength** refers to how long a person will hold on to expectations of success despite contradictory information. For example, a person with a low degree of strength may lose her belief that she can accomplish a task after a single failure. A person with a high degree of strength will be more likely to continue to attempt a task in the face of many failures. Also, a history of succeeding after multiple unsuccessful attempts also plays an important role in building up the strength dimension of an individual.

3. **Generality** refers to the degree of transfer for self-efficacy beliefs from one situation to another. One person may limit efficacy expectations to the performance of identical or closely related tasks, while another may generalize these expectations for success to a wide range of situations. This transfer is more easily accomplished if the individual can see the connections among tasks (see Gass, 1985, 1991, and 1993).

Self-efficacy is based on information interpreted and derived from four internal and external sources: past performance accomplishments, vicarious experiences, verbal persuasion, and physiological arousal. Researchers believe that information gained through success is the most influential and stable source of information because it is based on actual experience. Failures early in learning tend to be more influential than failures in later stages. Moreover, failures that are later overcome by increased effort levels can strengthen self-efficacy levels to a greater degree than failures overcome by chance. Hence, the importance of second tries at certain tasks.

Seeing or hearing about someone else's vicarious pursuit of similar attempts to master a skill or overcome a problem, without negative repercussions, can also enhance an observer's efficacy expectations. The opportunity to observe others of similar competence and being able to hear stories of others' experiences are two positive means for directly enhancing clients' feelings of self-efficacy.

Although gathering efficacy expectations from verbal information is not as strong as those expectations acquired from actual experience, it can serve as a powerful mobilizing factor in combination with the manipulation of adaptive dissonance. Indeed, encouragement—without coercion—from you can enhance self-efficacy.

Since over- or underarousal usually interferes with performance, people experiencing high anxiety or boredom levels might have certain expectations. In addition, expectations of success or failure can further alter arousal levels, since anticipation can confirm positive or negative beliefs about performance. You need to defuse anxiety or boredom associated with setbacks, especially if either emotion becomes debilitating.

Bandura (1977) also suggested that the relationship between self-efficacy and performance is reciprocal: efficacy expectations influence performance and performance outcomes influence self-efficacy. The direction of reciprocity, causing increases or decreases in self-efficacy, also depends on the degree of stress present in the situation. Selye (1974) described stress as coming in one of two forms: **eustress**, which is pleasant and desirable stress, or **distress**, which is unpleasant and undesirable stress, depending on the effect—in the form of emotions and feelings—exhibited by the person under stress.

Attribution, or Locus of Control

According to Weiner (1972), individuals attribute the reasons for their performance outcomes to a variety of causes. These can include ability, effort, luck, task characteristics, attention, and others. Weiner classified these attributions according to a two-dimensional scale. The first dimension, **causality**, ranged from internally to externally attributed causes. The second dimension, **stability,** ranged from stable to unstable causes. As an example, Weiner classified ability as an internal and stable attribute and defined luck as external and unstable.

Later on, Weiner (1979) added a third dimension to his model: **controllability**, or the degree to which the attribution is perceived as under the individual's **locus of control**. This new dimension differentiated attributions such as effort as internally controllable and fatigue as externally uncontrollable. The way an individual perceives a specific attribution, however, is far more important than how it is usually classified (Russell, 1982).

Weiner, Russell, and Lerman (1978 and 1979) found that causality seemed to play an important role in differentiating various effects. Under success conditions, an **internal locus of control** was found to be associated with pride, confidence, competence, and satisfaction. Feelings of gratefulness and thankfulness were linked to **external locus of control** under similar conditions. Under failure conditions, guilt was associated with internal control, while anger and surprise were linked to external control.

Based on this research, Weiner (1985) developed his theory of achievement motivation and emotion. According to him, a person experienced an emotional reaction immediately after an achievement. This general reaction could be either positive (for example, happy), or negative (for example, sad), and was based on the individual's perception of success or failure of the performance. Weiner described these initial reactions as "outcome-dependent," since the reactions were a function of outcome success or failure, rather than a function of attributed cause and control. He found that following the general reaction, an individual carefully thought through the reasons that might explain the outcome cause and control. Once the individual established causality and control, she experienced a secondary specific set of emotions, which were "attribute-dependent." This unique combination of general effects, based on outcomes, and specific effects, based on attributions, influenced future motivation levels and risk-taking behaviors.

By way of illustration, the downhill skier who performs poorly in the moguls feels nonspecific, or general, negative emotions such as sadness—outcome-dependent effects. In trying to figure out the reason why performance was so poor (or causality) the skier attributes failure to a lack of skiing ability, which is internal attribution, and decides that this will not improve due to a strong belief that she cannot change equipment, conditions, and body type, which is external attribution: internal, stable, and uncontrollable. Thus the skier experiences a more specific effect, such as frustration or defeat, which are attribute-dependent effects, and may decide to give up on the sport, which is a behavioral consequence. This example demonstrates the power of attribution to have a destructive, instead of a constructive, impact on motivation.

Effectance Motivation

In his theory of **effectance motivation**, White (1959) felt that individuals were intrinsically motivated to create a positive influence on their environment. If people can successfully meet the demands of the environment through mastery attempts or performance tries, then they will experience feelings of "effectance," or positive effects and emotions. These positive effects, in turn, encourage future mastery attempts under similar environmental conditions. Figure 4.11 presents this model.

As seen in this model, behavior is the result of an urge to gain competence and to have an effect on the environment. Specifically, individuals try a task and, if successful, they equate this with improved competence at that task. This makes them feel good (joy, pleasure, efficacy) and in control of their environment. In turn, these positive effects motivate them to try again. A very simple model, White's theory did not account for a number of extraneous influences, such as the opinions of significant others or the attribution of success, and did not consider the negative side of failure.

About 20 years later, Harter (1978) built White's framework into a theory of **competence motivation**. She expanded his model to include the effects of social and interpersonal factors as

well as the effects of positive and negative experiences. She further hypothesized that the motivational process revolved around perceived competence. Subsequently, Harter (1986) suggested that perceived competence levels were influenced by many factors: success or failure after mastery attempts, perceptions of control, motivational orientation, positive or negative reinforcement from significant others, and characteristics of the task. Figure 4.12 presents a diagram of her model.

But how does this model apply to real life? Suppose a kayaker decides to attempt to run a new set of rapids for the first time. If the level of route difficulty matches the skill level of the kayaker, then we can describe the task as optimally challenging. Achievement of optimally challenging tasks have a greater impact on an individual's perception of himself. If the kayaker is successful in the attempt, then he will experience positive effects, such as enjoyment or intrinsic pleasure. Moreover, success in these situations can increase levels of perceived paddling competence as well as enhance the likelihood that this kayaker will develop internal perceptions of greater control (see also locus of control discussion in previous section). In other words, the kayaker attributes success to internal sources, such as effort and ability. This successful attempt can also receive positive reinforcement and approval from significant others, such as paddling friends. In this case, this information also results in internalized reinforcement, further enhancing internal attribution of feelings. Specifically, the kayaker develops an intrinsic motivational orientation, meaning that activities are chosen for their potential to provide personal satisfaction and meet personally-set standards of performance. In turn, an intrinsic motivational orientation further enhances perceived competence and internal locus of control. These positive perceptions of self augment affective reactions such as pleasure, and the combination of positive effects and perceptions of self, in turn, increase

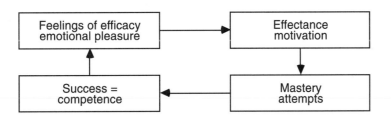

Figure 4.11   The effectance motivation model (White, 1959).

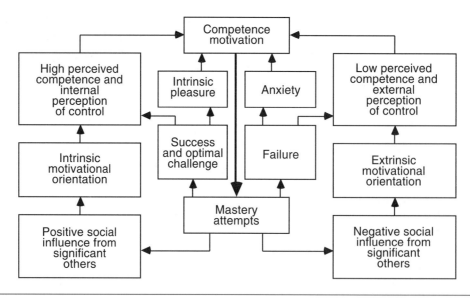

Figure 4.12   The competence motivation mode (Harter, 1978).

motivational levels. Thus, the kayaker is likely to attempt the task again.

In contrast, failure to run the rapids can diminish motivational levels as the kayaker experiences negative effects and perceptions of self. Repeated failure eventually reduces perceived paddling competence levels, possibly leading to external perceptions of control. In other words, the kayaker may attribute the failure to external reasons, such as difficulty of the route or faulty equipment. In addition, the lack of reinforcement and approval from significant others may result in the development of an extrinsic motivational orientation. The kayaker may begin to choose routes that meet other peoples' expectations, striving to meet their external standards of performance. In turn, an extrinsic orientation tends to decrease perceived competence levels, thereby enhancing an external locus of control orientation. Decreasing perceptions of self or negative effects, such as anxiety, further decrease effectance motivation. Thus, the kayaker may not attempt that route or similar ones ever again.

Risk Taking and Competence Effectance

Priest and Klint (Priest, 1993) have combined all the frameworks we've discussed so far into one theoretical model, partially founded on the research and partially rooted in experience. The model revolves around the idea of using competence effectance (i.e., the belief of one's personal competence if correctly perceived) to increase a

client's chance of success in an adventure experience as well as to enhance the possible ramifications.

The model is a series of closed-loop paths, connecting key constructs such as perceived risk, perceived competence, competence motivation, competence performance, arousal, intrinsic feelings, extrinsic influence, self-efficacy, attribution, and locus of control. The model is comprised of three parts, designated as neutral, positive, and negative feedback loops. Figure 4.13 shows the neutral loop.

The left side of the loop describes the three levels of risk that participants can select on the basis of their efficacy expectations. If people are feeling less competent, they are likely to select a lower level of risk; if they are feeling more competent, they are likely to select a higher level of risk; and on rare occasions, they may select a level of situational risk that perfectly matches their personal competence. This latter condition results in a challenge of peak adventure, optimal arousal, state of flow, or what is commonly termed "living on the razor's edge!"

Regardless of the level of risk they choose, people can either perform sufficiently or insufficiently. This evaluation is usually a subjective assessment of personal performance. If participants believe they have performed sufficiently for the level of risk chosen, then challenging conditions of adventure result (e.g., exploration and experimentation). If participants think their performances were insufficient to meet the risks involved, then the challenging conditions of mis-

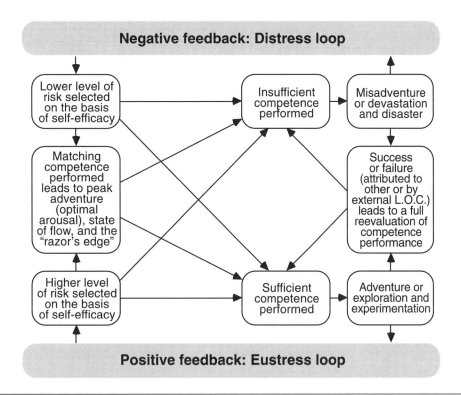

Figure 4.13 The neutral feedback loop of the risk taking and competence effectance model.

adventure are possible, perhaps leading to devastation and disaster.

Following this decision, participants begin to attribute, or justify, the way things turned out. Obviously, your role in helping people to correctly attribute their adventure outcomes is extremely important. If people attribute their successes or failures to external sources, that is, to something other than themselves, then they may reevaluate their performances and possibly change their minds about whether they performed sufficiently or not. If they "own" their successes or failures by attributing them to internal sources, then they may enter into either of the other two loops. Note that if people experience a condition of misadventure or devastation and disaster, they enter into the negative feedback loop, or distress. And if the challenge is one of adventure or exploration and experimentation, they enter into the positive feedback loop, or eustress. Figures 4.14 and 4.15 offer a closer examination of these two loops to help you better understand the model.

The negative loop of distress (see figure 4.14) begins with a perception of failure resulting from misadventure and attributed to internal sources, such as personal performance. The failure can cause direct, negative intrinsic feelings, such as

feeling "bad" about yourself, or cause indirect, negative extrinsic responses, such as comments of disappointment from significant others. Through a decrease in perceived competence, these negative feelings can lead to lower feelings of competence motivation. For example, people who believe they cannot accomplish a task will experience anxiety when facing the same level of risk. Because of this, when emerging from the negative feedback loop, such participants will tend to select a lower level of risk in the neutral loop.

The positive loop of eustress (see figure 4.15) follows a similar pattern, but, naturally, the effect is the reverse of the negative loop. It begins with an internally attributed perception of success resulting from adventure. This success leads to direct, positive intrinsic feelings, such as feeling "good" about yourself, and to positive extrinsic responses, such as comments of approval from significant others, indirectly building on the "good" feelings. Through an increased perception of competence, these positive feelings generally lead to a greater level of competence motivation. For example, people who believe they can accomplish the task will experience boredom with the same level of risk. Because of this, when emerging from the positive feedback loop, such

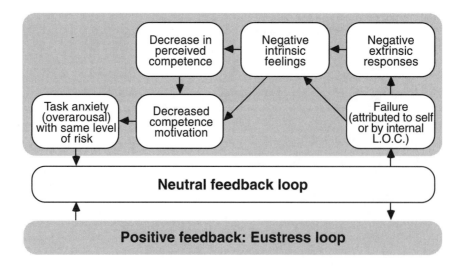

Figure 4.14   The negative feedback loop of the risk taking and competence effectance model.

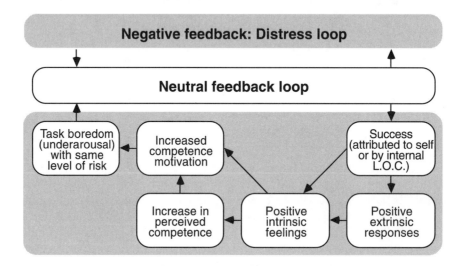

Figure 4.15   The positive feedback loop of the risk taking and competence effectance model.

participants tend to select a higher level of risk in the neutral loop.

For example, consider a participant engaged in an adventure learning opportunity who is timid and fearful about what lies ahead. The first task set for this individual created by you as the facilitator is an easy rock climb, initially viewed by the individual as unattainable. The discrepancy between the task and the client's perception of competence creates adaptive dissonance, or mental argument, within the participant's mind. Resolving this dissonance and attempting the task requires some encouragement, rather than coercion, from you.

Assume for a moment that the individual overcomes the difficulty of a climb, performing with sufficient competence, experiences an adventure in the exploration and experimentation realm, and considers the experience "successful." If the individual attributes the success internally to personal effort, then the individual enters into a positive feedback loop, or eustress. The individual feels good, or positive, intrinsic feelings, and receives praise and congratulations from others, or a positive extrinsic response. This, in turn, leads to the belief that an improvement in personal capability has taken place as perceived competence increases; thus, the desire to do better next time is likely because competence motivation has increased. Since repeating the same climb would be underarousing for similar levels of risk, the individual will likely select a higher level of risk, based on the self-efficacy belief that success is achievable where failure initially seemed evident.

For this new level of higher risks, three performance scenarios are now possible. First, the individual may perform at a sufficiently competent level and return to eustress—if an internal locus of control is in effect and if success is attributed to self. Second, a perfect match of competence with the new choice of risk may occur, leading to the condition of peak adventure. In this case, the individual will attempt to maintain the condition for as long as possible, eventually falling off to one side or the other. The third possible scenario is that the individual may perform at an insufficient level of competence and cross over to the side of distress, or misadventure—even to devastation and disaster.

Consider for a moment what happens if the latter scenario occurs. Insufficient competence performance for the new risk leads to a condition of misadventure—or worse, devastation and disaster—and the feeling of having failed. If the individual attributes failure to himself, then he enters the negative feedback loop of distress. The individual feels bad, or has negative intrinsic feelings, and may even receive some sarcasm and blame from others, or negative extrinsic responses. This, in turn, leads to the belief that personal capability has dropped off, that is, perceived competence decreases, and the desire to stop trying arises, that is, competence motivation decreases. Since repeating the same climb would create anxiety in this case, in other words, would be overarousing for similar levels of risk, the individual is likely to select a lower level of risk next time, based on the self-efficacy belief that he may again fail at an activity for which he had originally expected to experience success.

Say that this individual chooses a new level of lower risk. Once again, three performance scenarios are now possible. First, the individual may perform at an insufficient level of competence and remain in distress, especially if he continues to attribute his failure to internal causes. Second, a perfect match of competence with the new level of risk may lead to the condition of peak adventure. As before, the individual may attempt to maintain this condition for as long as possible. Third, and more likely with the help of a competent facilitator, the individual may perform at a sufficient level of competence and cross back to the positive side of eustress.

If the individual attributes success or failure to other external sources, such as the facilitator,

which can happen if the participant is coerced or given too much encouragement, or to equipment, luck, or weather, which are frequent complaints from novices, then a full reevaluation of personal contribution to the task must be undertaken, and the individual may recognize that he experienced a different challenging condition instead. This change of mind may make the difference between entering one loop or the other. With or without a facilitator, human beings are likely to follow this sequence as they vacillate back and forth between the looped pathways until they become fully astute: both accurate and correct in their perceptions of situational risks and personal competence.

EFFECTIVE OUTDOOR LEADERS SHOULD

☞ Be vigilant about monitoring group members' arousal levels, be aware of the effects over- or underarousal can have on performances, and do what is necessary to see that clients are optimally aroused whenever appropriate and desirable.

☞ Help participants to balance opportunities to act with personal capacity for action, so that they may possibly experience states of flow and the related benefits.

☞ Be sure that the antecedents of an adventure are present within each experience: freedom of choice, state of mind, intrinsic motivation, outcome uncertainty, and competence engagement.

☞ Understand the role that fear plays in an adventure and be prepared to help participants cope with their concerns accordingly through desensitization, flooding, modeling, or rehearsal mechanisms.

☞ Understand the varying conditions of challenge that can arise from the interaction of risk and competence and be able to help participants recognize these in relation to the level of risk and competence present in an adventure.

☞ Understand the role of adaptive dissonance and know how to structure and control adventure experiences to create healthy adaptive dissonance in clients.

☞ Help participants set their own goals to enable greater commitment as well as provide sufficient training, emotional support, proper resources, and benefit comprehension to increase motivation.

☞ Be aware of the impact that past performance or physiological arousal can have on self-efficacy and be capable of sharing vicarious experiences or using verbal persuasion, but not coercion, as methods of participant encouragement.

☞ Monitor how participants attribute success or failure and assist them with proper attribution to either internal or external locuses of control.

☞ Guide the reflection of participants in examining their levels of competence and performance of tasks in relation to their emotions and motivation to complete tasks.

☞ Note the impact that successful or failed attempts at mastery will have on participants' perceived competence and how this, in turn, will affect their levels of motivation.

☞ Be aware of the impact that perceived competence and levels of motivation will have on participants' feelings of self-efficacy and selections of risks in an adventure experience.

SUMMARY

Ellis's play theory of optimal arousal suggests a reason for human engagement in adventure: people will purposefully seek out conditions of optimal arousal that permit maximal performance. Csikszentmihalyi's flow state model details what they can experience in an adventure: goal clarity, immediate feedback, merging of action and awareness, concentration on a limited stimulus field, self-forgetfulness, heightened self-awareness, personal control, and autotelic enjoyment. Mitchell lists the necessary antecedents of adventure as freedom of choice, state of mind, intrinsic motivation, outcome uncertainty, and competence engagement. Mortlock traces the stages in an outdoor journey, based on the level of fear present: play (no fear), adventure (some), frontier adventure (lots), and misadventure (too much).

Martin and Priest's adventure experience paradigm combines the work of these four into a graphic representation of the relationship between risk and competence. Through this paradigm, the creators explore how the combination of risk in the adventure experience and participant competence interact to create one of five conditions of challenge: exploration and experimentation, adventure, peak adventure, misadventure, and devastation and disaster. Priest and

Baillie describe how adaptive dissonance can be used to create astute individuals within the adventure experience paradigm. Adaptive dissonance is the state between what clients know they can do and what they are not able to do, that is, tasks they are unsure of whether they can accomplish or not. Accomplishing such tasks generates a strong sense of mastery, leading to astute learners.

In addition, it's important to understand the concepts concerning motivation in adventure programming. Motivation refers to why and how individuals move or don't move from one state of being to another. Factors influencing motivation include the direction of effort, intensity of effort, choice of behaviors, ability to sustain motivation, and the resulting behavior change. Theories important to note include the following: goal theory, or how a person's commitment to a goal influences actions; expectancy theory, or how a person's expectations about achieving a goal influences actions; self-efficacy, or how the belief of whether or not a person can accomplish a task affects motivation and how you as an outdoor leader can implement various strategies to enhance a client's ability to be successful; attribution theory and locus of control, or how individuals explain their successes and failures and the influence these attributions have on future actions and emotions; and effectance and competence motivation, or how effectiveness of attempts in completing tasks influences feelings of competence as well as how social and interpersonal factors influenced—and were influenced by—these feelings. A final model from Klint and Priest combines all of these frameworks into one model outlining risk-taking behavior and competence effectance, or how the accuracy of participants' beliefs are used to influence the probability of success or failure in adventure experiences. The model makes use of Seyle's concepts of distress and eustress to theorize how people change perceptions on the basis of experience and how astuteness is developed through adventure experiences.

QUESTIONS TO THINK ABOUT

1. Considering Csikszentmihalyi's flow state, can you recall a time when this occurred with you on an adventure experience? If so, try to describe what was happening and why it was occurring. How might you

replicate such an experience for others as an outdoor leader?

2. Discuss the similarities between Csikszentmihalyi's six characteristics of flow and Mitchell's five antecedents of adventure. Create a list of conditions you would like to help foster in adventure experiences to enhance the likelihood that clients will reach their goals.

3. Differentiate among the four sources of self-efficacy and explain the relevancy of the three domains of self-efficacy. Select an adventure activity (e.g., rock climbing, challenge course) and provide examples from this activity that represent sources for increasing self-efficacy levels in clients.

4. What does motivation mean to you? Choose one of the theories of motivation and explain how you would create conditions to help motivate a client.

5. Recall a time when you led a group on an adventure, then explain their individual behaviors by applying the adventure experience paradigm and the competence effectance theory.

REFERENCES

Bandura, A. (1977). Self-efficacy: Toward a unifying theory for behavioral change. *Psychological Review* 84, 191-215.

Bunting, C. (1987). Challenge activities and stress management. In J.F. Meier, T.M. Morash, & G.E. Welton (Eds.), *High-adventure outdoor pursuits: Organization and leadership* (pp. 28-35). Columbus, OH: Publishing Horizons.

Carpenter, G., & Priest, S. (1989). The adventure experience paradigm and non-outdoor leisure pursuits. *Leisure Studies* 8(1), 65-75.

Csikszentmihalyi, M. (1975). *Beyond boredom and anxiety.* San Francisco: Jossey-Bass.

Csikszentmihalyi, M., & Csikszentmihalyi, I.S. (1991). *Adventure and the flow experience.* In J.C. Miles & S. Priest (Eds.), *Adventure education* (pp. 149-155). State College, PA: Venture.

Ellis, M.J. (1973). *Why people play.* Englewood Cliffs, NJ: Prentice-Hall.

Ewert, A. (1983). *Outdoor adventure and self-concept: A research analysis.* Eugene, OR: Center of Leisure Studies, University of Oregon.

Ewert, A. (1989). Managing fear in the outdoor experiential education setting. *Journal of Experiential Education* 12(1), 19-25.

Festinger, L. (1957). *The theory of cognitive dissonance.* Evanston, IL: Row & Peterson.

Gass, M. (1985). Programming the transfer of learning in adventure education. *Journal of Experiential Education* 10(3), 18-24.

Gass, M. (1991). Enhancing metaphor development in adventure therapy programs. *Journal of Experiential Education* 14(2), 6-13.

Gass, M. (1993). *Adventure therapy: Therapeutic applications of adventure programming in mental health settings.* Dubuque, IA: Kendall-Hunt Publishing, Inc.

Goffman, E. (1981). Fun in games. In M. Marie-Hart & S. Birrell (Eds.), *Sport in the socio-cultural process* (pp. 40-91). Dubuque, IA: Brown.

Harter, S. (1978). Effectance motivation reconsidered. *Human Development* 21, 34-64.

Harter, S. (1986). Cognitive-developmental processes in the integration of concepts about emotions and self. *Social Cognition* 4, 119-151.

Katzell, R., & Thompson, D.E. (1990). Work motivation: Theory and practice. *American Psychologist* 45(2), 144-153.

Martin, P., & Priest, S. (1986). Understanding the adventure experience. *Journal of Adventure Education* 3(1), 18-21.

Mitchell, R.G. (1983). *Mountain experience: The psychology and sociology of adventure.* Chicago: University of Chicago Press.

Mortlock, C. (1984). *The adventure alternative.* Cumbria: England Cicerone Press.

Priest, S., & Baillie, R. (1987) Justifying the risk to others: The real razor's edge. *Journal of Experiential Education* 10(1), 16-22.

Priest, S. (1993). A new model for risk taking. *Journal of Experiential Education*, 16(1), 50-53.

Russell, D. (1982). The causal dimension scale: A measure of how individuals perceive causes. *Journal of Personality and Social Psychology* 42, 1137-1145.

Sage, G. H. (1977). *Introduction to motor behavior: A neuropsychological approach.* Reading, MA: Addison-Wesley.

Schreyer, R.M., White, R., & McCool, S.F. (1978). Common attributes uncommonly exercised. *Journal of Health, Physical Education, and Recreation (JOHPER)* 49(4). Also in J.F. Meier, T.M. Morash, & G.E. Welton (Eds.), *High-adventure outdoor pursuits: Organization and leadership* (pp. 36-42). Columbus, OH: Publishing Horizons.

Selye, H. (1974). *Stress without distress.* New York: Lippincott.

Skow, J. (1983, August 29). Risking it all: The spirit of adventure is alive and well. *Time.* 52-59.

Walsh, V., & Golins, G. (1976). *The exploration of the Outward Bound process.* Denver: Colorado Outward Bound School.

Weinberg, R. S. & Gould, D. (1995). *Foundations of sport and exercise psychology.* Champaign, IL: Human Kinetics.

Weiner, B. (1972). *Theories of motivation: From mechanism to cognition.* Chicago: Rand McNally.

Weiner, B. (1979). A theory of motivation for some classroom experiences. *Journal of Educational Psychology* 71, 3-25.

Weiner, B. (1985). An attribution theory of achievement motivation and emotion. *Psychological Review* 92, 548-573.

Weiner, B., Russell, D., & Lerman, D. (1978). Affective consequences of causal ascriptions. In J.H. Harvey, W.J. Ickes, & R.F. Kidd (Eds.), *New directions in attribution research*, vol. 2 (pp. 59-90). Hillsdale, NJ: Erlbaum.

Weiner, B., Russell, D., & Lerman, D. (1979). The cognitive-emotion process in achievement-related contexts. *Journal of Personality and Social Psychology* 37, 1211-1220.

White, R. (1959). Motivation reconsidered: The concept of competence. *Psychological Review* 66, 297-333.

Zuckerman, M. (1979). *Sensation seeking: Beyond the optimal level of arousal*. Hillsdale, NJ: Erlbaum.

chapter

5

Group Development
and Dynamics

Thirteen people signed up for the month-long adventure experience. They arrived with many questions, fears, and uncertainties. Being unfamiliar with one another, they tended to feel uncomfortable in this unfamiliar environment and kept to themselves. Conversations were characterized by "small talk" about conventional topics. As essential equipment and food was distributed, they started to interact with one another and make simple decisions about packing gear and sharing loads. In starting their journey, the group began to confront and solve realistic problems, group interaction was stimulated, and members were challenged physically, socially, and emotionally.

As the journey became more demanding, including difficult decisions made during lengthy travel in extended periods of darkness, group members became "stressed-out" and exhibited anger, rebellion, confusion, and disillusionment, and the situation deteriorated into chaos. Members with common interests sought each other out for comfort. At times, the group divided into subgroups. In some instances, members became upset at the leader for refusing to solve problems for them. Power struggles leading to conflicts were common during established routines such as camp chores or navigation responsibilities.

As the expedition reached its midpoint, members were still trying to establish their group identity. They tried to deal openly with problems as these arose and restore harmony by coming up with a behavioral contract. In time, as members spoke freely about themselves and others, the group became more open. They began to seek help by directly asking for it or by indirectly expressing self-doubts. Leadership was shared among group members, and more supportive behaviors became common.

Due to a newfound sense of independence, the group relied less on their appointed outdoor leader, chose to navigate in a remote setting with the leader acting as a "shadow," accepted sole responsibility for their decisions or behaviors, and resolved their own crises and conflicts. The whole group worked together as a cohesive team, experiencing the success of high performance. Communication, trust, cooperation, and support became prevalent. Positive feelings were present, and all group members expressed a sense of satisfaction.

The final days of the expedition were hectic and filled with emotion, nostalgia, and a feeling of success. Some members experienced a loss of confidence, a fear of leaving, and feelings of anger or anxiety. Others reverted back to earlier behaviors, such as denying that the group was important to them, in attempts to salvage their egos. On completion, the group participated in closing activities designed to reinforce their senses of accomplishment. Following this closure, most members realized that their journey was nearly over. They returned equipment, debriefed, and celebrated the trip. The next morning they departed for home.

Groups tend to evolve through a series of progressive stages. While occasionally groups may skip, repeat, reverse, or even exhibit some stages simultaneously under certain conditions, these stages of growth are generally quite predictable and sequential. Each stage exhibits specific and reoccurring characteristics with transitions between stages tending to be gradual rather than sharp.

STAGES OF GROUP DEVELOPMENT

Numerous researchers have tried to order, number, and name these stages; most theories contain five distinct stages (e.g., Kerr & Gass, 1987; Jensen, 1979; Tuckman & Jensen, 1977). As you can see in the opening vignette, in the first stage, the group comes together and begins to sort out tasks and relationships. In the second stage, concerns arise in the way members relate to one another as they work on tasks together. In the third stage, the group begins to overcome its concerns, establishing its ground rules for tasks and relationships. In the fourth stage, the group is working efficiently as a team, enabling them to accomplish a high level of output in both tasks and relationships. In the fifth and final stage, the group closes down, or breaks up, and members move on to other tasks and relationships, perhaps within a new group.

Of the many labels used, the five-stage model of forming, storming, norming, performing, and adjourning has become widely accepted (Tuckman & Jensen, 1977).

1. **Forming** is characterized by the discomforts, concerns, feelings, and doubts members experience in a new group.

2. **Storming** participants begin to meet the needs of the group, to question authority, and to feel more comfortable about themselves and their relationships.

3. **Norming** involves members addressing appropriate and necessary standards of behavior through which a greater sense of order prevails.

4. **Performing** finds the group concentrating on the tasks at hand with mutual support and interaction among group members evident as well.

5. **Adjourning** provides closure of the task, including the imminent end of relationships.

The main strengths of this model is that it is easy to use, it is widely applicable to different types of adventure programs, and it provides useful information for you concerning the progress of a group (Jensen, 1979).

Task and Relationship Dimensions for Each Stage

We can further divide the functions within a group into the **task dimension**, or work undertaken by the group, called "products," and the **relationship dimension**, or group members' interactions with one another, called "processes." Examining how your orientation to these two dimensions interacts within the five stages of group development will help you apply appropriate leadership styles and strategies to suit client needs.

In the forming stage, the group comes together for the first time, and its members typically strive to become better acquainted with one another. The task dimension in this stage is characterized by acceptance of the task, yet a lack of investment in common purposes. Members are not yet committed to the bigger picture or the group's direction and may prefer to work alone. At the same time, they are relatively dependent on you for support and guidance for completing tasks. They attempt to discover the nature of a task and determine what their roles may be in accomplishing that task. In terms of relationships, they tend to feel uncomfortable when they meet for the first time or anxious as they wonder how they will fit into the group. Individuals' past experiences with other groups, for example, in schools, churches, or clubs, or on sports teams, influence how they view this new, small-group environment. Members are often reluctant to discuss personal views and opinions, so conversation tends to be superficial and stereotypical. Some quickly form impressions, deciding which strangers they will befriend or which they will try to avoid.

In the storming stage, the group works through tough times as interpersonal issues come to the forefront. Their behaviors begin to push the limits of acceptability as they try to figure out the "pecking order." Issues can include, but are not limited to, problems of status, communication, and defining group values. Attempts at influencing one another begin, and power struggles often follow. The task dimension contains possible resistance to roles and confrontation with overlapping responsibilities. The underlying dysfunctional behavior, however, generally remains more of a relationship concern than a problem of the task dimension. Relationships are fraught with rebellion against influence (perhaps against you as the leader) and conflict among member personalities—often because past frames of reference may not apply to the present situation. The group membership may become polarized around decisions to the point of becoming very opinionated. This polarization, if allowed to run its course, may erode the group's efforts and lead to competition. At this point, members often reveal their personal agendas as they begin to assert and defend their individuality. Behaviors may be marked by jealousy, hostility, distrust, and defensiveness. Interactions may become disruptive, unhealthy, incompatible, and ineffective. Friction grows, anxiety is high, disagreements abound, and angry arguments may be common. A pecking order often develops on the basis of power and influence.

In the norming stage, the group creates new ground rules characterized by renewed hope. Satisfied members comply to their roles, becoming more involved with the group task. They adopt and accept their workloads. An atmosphere of cooperation emerges as the group starts to openly collaborate on projects. Members genuinely offer help to others and willingly accept assistance in return. The group's purpose is clear, and a strong sense of team identity exists. Relationship aspects in this stage include conflicts that resemble "sibling-like" rivalries and deeper emotions characteristic of close friendships. Members seem more tolerant of differences and ease into relationships that tend to be much more cohesive and intimate. They have dealt with most previous resistance and have created a set of mutually accepted operating principles. Personality clashes typically have dissipated, and past arguments have been replaced with harmonious dialogue. An attitude of "we" instead of "me" often prevails as members become much less dependent on you for leadership.

In the performing stage, the group tends to work very well together. Tasks are competently accomplished by members, resulting in productive outcomes. As a high achieving team, members are preoccupied with getting the job done and doing it well. They are proud of the group and are committed to making relationships work. They may experience minor setbacks, but these rarely amount to lasting or real conflicts in this stage. They have fully established the pecking order; however, they have based it on members' skills and resources, rather than on their power and influence. Group members admire and respect the strengths and weaknesses of others, and their roles tend to be less rigid. They conduct their roles in a way that allows them to balance tasks

and relationships—as a leader might attempt to accomplish in this stage.

Last, in the adjourning stage, the group wraps up loose ends, bringing work to a close usually with feelings of adjourning anxiety. Members may begin to miss the deep level of focus they have achieved in performing their work and have trouble coping with closure. Members may also reflect on their effectiveness in accomplishing their tasks. They may encounter difficulty facing up to unmet goals or making plans for the future. The adjourning stage places members in a situation in which they must find new resources for meeting these needs. Members can accomplish this in a positive manner, for example, by reviewing experiences to summarize benefits, incorporating growth into future interactions; or in a negative way, for example, by denying that the experience is over or regressing to previous negative behaviors often seen in the storming stage. The relationship aspect of this stage follows a similar pattern. Members may begin to miss the deep level of connections they have made to others. Although members are disbanding, they frequently feel that they can stay in touch if a need exists, and modern communications makes this departure easier. Nevertheless, some members may deny the end, especially if the group held emotional significance for them, and reunions may be necessary to ease the transition.

Appropriate Leadership Style for Each Stage

As a leader, you play a critical role in the development of a group through these stages. In considering the various roles, or "styles," you can employ to assist group development, we can arrange the styles on a continuum from laissez-faire, in which you do nothing to control the group, to dictatorial, in which you exert total control over the group. Since neither of these styles have ever been considered appropriate for outdoor leadership, three styles between these two extremes have become more acceptable: autocratic, democratic, and abdicratic (see chapter 18 for further details on flexible outdoor leadership styles).

Since leadership is a process of influence, these three outdoor leadership styles are defined by the amount of influence, or decision-making power, held by the group or by the leader. The **autocratic** style involves your making decisions and then convincing the group to follow. In a **democratic** style, you and the group share various responsibilities in making decisions. For an **abdicratic** style, you abdicate decision-making responsibility to the group, but remain closely involved in case the need arises to intervene in the process.

The conditional outdoor leadership theory (COLT) is a model that predicts the appropriate leadership style on the basis of the leader's concern for task, relationship, and conditional favorability (Priest & Chase, 1989; see figure 18.4, page 242, for a detailed discussion of this model). As concern for task, or getting the job done, takes precedence, an effective leader utilizes an autocratic style. As concern increases for relationship aspects, an effective leader employs an abdicratic style. Intermediary values or an equal balance of both concerns favors the democratic style. Changes in the favorability of conditions (e.g., environmental dangers, leader proficiency, group unity, member competence, and characteristics of the decision) can also shift the style in one direction or the other. Note that these conditions may sometimes be a greater determinant of appropri-

ate leadership style than task and relationship dimensions.

Figure 5.1 details typical levels of leader concern for the task and relationship dimensions of each stage in group development (Attarian & Priest, 1994). Attarian and Priest suggested the appropriate leadership style to use with a group during each stage ranges from autocratic through democratic to abdicratic and back again.

During the forming stage, you should invest a great deal of time and effort into the group's task: setting goals, orienting members to new roles, and developing a sense of group identity. Your concern for relationship development should take on an important, yet less direct, role. Examples include facilitating healthy interactions among members, encouraging members to clarify their reasons or expectations for being in the group, and creating a comfortable atmosphere of sharing. Devoting a great deal of energy informing the group as to how they should relate to one another can be quite patronizing and inappropriate for leaders. Instead, you should support members through "being" types of messages,

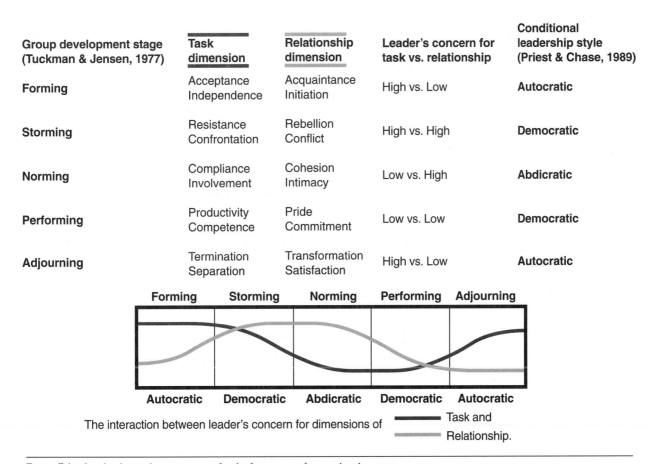

Group development stage (Tuckman & Jensen, 1977)	Task dimension	Relationship dimension	Leader's concern for task vs. relationship	Conditional leadership style (Priest & Chase, 1989)
Forming	Acceptance Independence	Acquaintance Initiation	High vs. Low	**Autocratic**
Storming	Resistance Confrontation	Rebellion Conflict	High vs. High	**Democratic**
Norming	Compliance Involvement	Cohesion Intimacy	Low vs. High	**Abdicratic**
Performing	Productivity Competence	Pride Commitment	Low vs. Low	**Democratic**
Adjourning	Termination Separation	Transformation Satisfaction	High vs. Low	**Autocratic**

Forming   Storming   Norming   Performing   Adjourning

Autocratic   Democratic   Abdicratic   Democratic   Autocratic

The interaction between leader's concern for dimensions of ▬▬▬ Task and ▬▬▬ Relationship.

Figure 5.1   Leadership styles appropriate for the five stages of group development.

such as "Glad you're here" and "Welcome to a program that can be a great experience for you" (Mitten, 1995). Concurrently, you must empower the group to determine its own path toward developing positive relationships. Given a direct concern for task and an indirect role for relationships, it is often appropriate to select an autocratic leadership style.

As the group enters the storming stage, conflicts tend to erupt and your concern for relationships should rise to balance your concern for task. At this stage, it is typically appropriate to employ a democratic style, remembering that the conflict and confrontation that often occurs is typical for groups progressing through an adventure experience. As a leader, you should not try to avoid or prevent the storming stage, rather, you should welcome it, using it to the advantage of the group. The storming stage permits members to express grievances, change issues that are inappropriate, and test to see that the group is truly sincere in its support of one another. You should create an environment that permits members to speak their minds without fear of retribution or retaliation. You can create this atmosphere by explaining how conflict is a natural and important step in the evolution of a high-performing team. At the same time, you should not ignore the task dimension. At this stage, your concern for both should be about equal: you need to adapt goals, restate priorities, adjust roles, and refocus efforts on getting the job done as well as address the troublesome interpersonal issues.

A comfortable calm often follows the "storm" as the group begins the norming stage. At this time, you should be primarily concerned with relationships, since the task of creating operating principles is already well in-hand. In this situation, it is helpful to apply an abdicratic style, simply supporting group members in their efforts to work out their own ground rules for future behaviors. Since established norms are a key to success in this stage and to moving on to the next stage, we encourage you to facilitate group discussion, acting more like a peer or colleague whenever possible and appropriate. Subsequently, if new members join the group, you must introduce newcomers to the existing guidelines and encourage the group to reexamine their norms, including the new members in the picture.

As a high performing team, the group "kicks into high gear" and begins to produce top-quality work. Now the concern for task returns as productivity becomes important; however, your concerns should be low because the group is in control of the situation. Once again, with concern for task and relationship being relatively equivalent, a democratic leadership style is probably most appropriate. At this point, you should act as a resource and often remind members that the group could not have reached this pinnacle of performance without passing through the earlier stages of development. Most of your attention should be focused on maintaining the group in a high performance mode while remaining aware that reoccurrence of past problems or the appearance of new crises may occur. If this happens, the group could slip back one or two stages, and you will need to flex your leadership style accordingly.

As with the forming stage, during the adjourning stage you should invest a great deal of time and effort into the group's task of creating a sense of closure for the experience: helping clients integrate what they've learned into the future, helping them to organize future reunions, helping them overcome any difficulty accepting changes, and facilitating ongoing communication. Your concern for relationship development should again take on an important, yet indirect, role. Remember, group members may regress to earlier dysfunctional behaviors under the stress of closure. Once again, we recommend that you become more autocratic, focusing more concern on task and relatively less concern on relationship.

Leadership Strategies for Each Stage

Both understanding the five group development stages and knowing the appropriate leadership style for each stage gives you a guiding framework to determine the best strategy to assist groups in meeting the goals of recreational, educational, developmental, or therapeutic groups as outlined in chapter 2. Recall that these goals are having fun, learning skills, and being entertained for recreation; understanding new concepts, enriching old ones, and becoming aware of needs for education; improving functional behaviors and training positive actions for development; and changing specific behaviors in order to remedy a social dysfunction for therapy. Consider these strategies for each of the five stages.

Forming. For recreational groups, you must clearly specify program goals, objectives, and your expectations of group members. When possible, encourage member participation and group interaction. For example, at the beginning of a backcountry skiing course, you should take the time to describe the course goals and activities. Following this explanation and review and with clients' input, you should determine if these goals and associated activities meet their needs, then make necessary changes to help individualize learning.

For educational and developmental groups, encourage exploration and involvement in relation to the process of *how* the group wishes to approach client needs and goals. Clarifying goals and group expectations is often a major portion of this process. While you may typically use highly structured activities, you must encourage group members to participate in the process of making sure that individual differences are permitted. For example, say some members of the group have stated that they have a very strong fear of heights. During an initial trust fall activity, you should adapt the exercise to respect these individuals' needs.

For therapeutic groups, you and the group should begin by examining the goals and expectations of group members, as well as their congruency with the goals assigned by the sponsoring or overseeing agency. During this process, you should help the group explore individual differences in conjunction with the options available to the group. Through this process of clarification, you should help group members understand individual needs and the expectations of the sponsoring or overseeing agency. For example, a judicial system conducting wilderness programming for juvenile offenders expects leaders and participants to follow certain standards during a course to increase the therapeutic value for each individual.

Storming. In storming, you should recognize that conflict can be beneficial and so relate it to the goals of most programs. With recreational experiences, you should structure activities so that individuals are able to express themselves. It is important, however, to remain clear about which decisions can be made by the group and which will be made by you.

With educational and developmental groups, it is important that you allow for potential struggles in the group to occur, yet ensure that the group atmosphere remains open and safe. In permitting group decisions, it is essential that

you not intercede in the process unless necessary. If you overrule group decisions, members may lower or invalidate their opinions of their decision-making abilities. This discounting can create an atmosphere in which members are less willing to express themselves. For example, if three members of the group are continually late to activities, you might initiate a group discussion about how this affects the group, but you must allow the participants to generate their own possible solutions to the problem.

With therapeutic groups, you should strive to clarify the "storming" (or "power and control") issues in regard to the purpose of the group. For example, ask "Why do you think the three of you are having such a hard time with this? Are there ways this is related to the issue that brought you here? Are there exceptions to when you are able to deal appropriately with what is occurring?" With therapeutic groups, you have the added responsibility to help clarify appropriate and inappropriate behaviors as the group works through issues. You must enforce limits, but these limits should have some relevant purpose for their existence. In other words, create rules that have purpose rather than rules for rules' sake.

Norming. In norming, you should support the group as they establish their own set of operating principles. For recreational experiences, as participants gather more skill and competencies, members either become a group or remain a collection of individuals. For the group to attain a sense of mutual reciprocity, a sense of cohesiveness must occur among individual members. If this process occurs, individuals will generally experience the benefits of each other's talents as they work together to achieve established goals. You should strive to help the group see that common goals are well-defined and can help develop the skills of each individual in the group. For example, if a group involved in learning whitewater canoeing skills has decided to paddle a class III rapid, you should support the group in their team planning efforts while also working on specific techniques with each person to develop individual skills, ensuring that each person remains safe throughout the experience.

In educational and developmental programs, you should encourage greater levels of responsibility. When appropriate, you should also be flexible in allowing participants to further adapt goals and activities to their own needs. You should help facilitate increased interdependency among group members as well as personal independence, encouraging participants to become less dependent on you. In other words, you should encourage group members to see you more and more as a resource, rather than as a leader. When appropriate, for example, if the group has agreed that their goal is to climb a particular mountain, you should help participants take ownership of their behavior by providing feedback and clarifying issues as needed.

In therapeutic programs, you should continue diagnosing problem areas, offer new perspectives, and support positive achievements. Through appropriate techniques of clarification and confrontation, you and the group should jointly explore possible ways that individuals can meet their needs without compromising the rights of others. For example, if "Jesse" hits "Sam," a series of questions you ask might include "Jesse, what did you want when you hit him? What is another way of getting Sam's attention? Which method gets Sam's attention and

keeps your friendship? What are ways you have used in the past where you have been noticed and the group made you feel like you belonged?"

Performing.　In the performing stage with recreational groups, you should help the group achieve its own goals by encouraging individuals to increase initiative and responsibility for their skill development. Effective leaders often monitor the group, supporting its inclination to work independently. For example, as our whitewater canoeing group continues to develop, you should encourage members to take on increasing numbers and levels of responsibilities involved in conducting experiences; for example, allow them to check out safety systems or take responsibility for scouting whitewater sections before entering them with a canoe.

With educational and developmental groups, you should also encourage group members to take on increasing responsibility for their actions, eventually reaching the point at which the group could achieve complete independence from you. Acting as a resource, you should help the group clarify its goals instead of directing the group toward its goals, helping them make minor adjustments to increase the likelihood that they will meet their goals. For example, suppose two members fall far behind while ascending a mountain. Rather than reminding the group of what its goals were, you should ask the group to clarify the purpose of the activity, then encourage members to use a group process to resolve the issue.

In therapeutic programs, you should clarify what progress has been made in the group, then help individuals transfer this knowledge to other situations outside of the group. You should remain supportive but may begin to take a devil's advocate position, perhaps representing the point of view of others outside of the group. An example in an at-risk youth program might be saying "As a group you've all agreed that it's alright to swear while we are in this group; but if I were a potential employer and heard you using that kind of language, what do you imagine I would think?" (Kerr & Gass, 1987, p. 45).

Adjourning.　By the adjourning stage of recreational programs, group members should have achieved high or adequate levels of independent skill competency. At this stage, you should encourage participants to consolidate what they have gained as individuals working in the group and to apply what they have learned to other technical situations.

In educational and developmental programs, you should help group members by encouraging them to review and evaluate what the group has learned. Effective leaders often help the group summarize areas of progress, helping individual members to transfer newly acquired knowledge to other situations outside of the group. When appropriate, you may also choose to provide alternatives for people to reconnect in the group. For example, follow-up strategies such as mentoring meetings, reunion socials, coaching schemes, and refresher programs may all be useful ways to maintain the momentum of change.

In therapeutic programs, you should focus on clarifying gains, encourage the transfer of learning, and help clients address the tendency to regress to previous dysfunctional behaviors. Regression during closure is particularly common with therapeutic populations. In addition, you should help members access helpful resources outside of the adventure experience. Consider a group of young offenders who have made excellent progress in their wilderness therapy program. When returned to their original, dysfunctional environment, they are likely to experience pressures to repeat old behaviors. Your challenge is to find a substitute for the offenders' therapy group that will work in their everyday environments, thereby countering any factors that may tend to reverse the changes they have experienced. Often helping them find suitable support networks of other functional rehabilitated offenders can go a long way toward preventing further recidivism.

OTHER FACTORS AFFECTING GROUP DYNAMICS

The use of small group dynamics to attain recreational, educational, developmental, or therapeutic goals is central to the process of adventure programming. Effective leaders often utilize the strength of the group to help bring about individual behavior changes. In using small group development as a tool for creating change, you must keep in mind several other considerations:

1. Individual needs. While the model focuses on group development, you must also be aware of the unique needs of each participant. Participants may have goals separate from the group that demand consideration. You should strive to blend individual and group needs together so that the two forces interact in a manner that achieves the highest degree of success.

2. Variation in development. Remember that groups will progress through the stages of development at different rates and directions. Moreover, individual members within the same group will grow at different speeds. This variation in development often makes allowing for different individual outcomes especially important. For example, some participants may progress to a point in a group at which they feel comfortable, whereas others may still be questioning whether they are willing to make a commitment to the group. You should recognize that group members can regress as well as advance through these stages. For example, varying degrees of regression to earlier stages is often evident in therapeutic programs as participants approach the end of the experience and are not yet ready to separate.

3. Group restructuring. Inserting or removing members from a group will affect its development and the dynamics of every interaction within the group. Since everyone plays a role within the group, when a person is added or removed, the group will go through some form of restructuring. This restructuring process can often result in regression to earlier stages of development.

4. Members' unique characteristics. Other characteristics of the membership, such as age and gender, will influence group development. Intelligence, cognitive processing ability, and the capacity to integrate new learning will also accelerate or delay the evolution of groups. You need to make adjustments in the program to accommodate these needs. One example of this might be to include facilitation methods that are appropriate for the group or particular population (e.g., school children verses corporate executives—see chapters 14-17).

EFFECTIVE OUTDOOR LEADERS SHOULD

☞ Know the five stages of group development and the various characteristics associated with each stage.

☞ Be able to identify which stage of development their group is in and, as a result of this identification, be able to employ a correct leadership style as well as apply appropriate leadership strategies to bring about change and growth.

☞ Be able to differentiate between how recreational, educational, developmental, and therapeutic groups vary in their stages of group development and identify strategies as to how to foster the development of members in these groups through the various stages.

☞ Be able to identify factors that affect group dynamics as well as how to adjust for these factors within a particular group's process of development.

SUMMARY

In the past, leaders have often relied on repeating past occurrences and the "magic" of groups to reach their intended goals. By understanding group development, however, you can choose activities, leadership styles, and effective strategies that are appropriate for the needs of a group in a particular stage. When you accomplish this, your program will "flow," or have a sense of natural timing that allows participants to get the most out of their experiences. While it's true that groups will develop regardless of your level of involvement, knowledge of how you can affect this growth will often be the difference between your providing a valuable experience and your simply helping people to survive an adventure program.

Many theorists have postulated their own multistage models of group development. Tuckman and Jensen's (1977) model is generally the most commonly used framework, listing five stages: forming, storming, norming, performing, and adjourning. These stages describe the coming together of individuals to make a group and the conflict that leads to developing acceptable ground rules, which, in turn, permits a period of high achievement before the experience and the group relationships end.

Apply one of the three common leadership styles (autocratic, democratic, and abdicratic) to each of the five stages, depending on the situation. The style you choose should be a function of your concern for task or for relationship as well as for conditional favorability. By correctly identifying the group's stage at any particular time, you can employ the best style, thereby helping the group move to the next stage of development. Indeed, if you are familiar with the five stages

and the three styles *and* their possible interactions, you can effectively guide a group through the process of evolution to ultimately reach and sustain top performance as a team.

Use your knowledge of the stages and leadership styles as a framework to guide you as you determine the best strategy to help groups meet recreational, educational, developmental, or therapeutic goals. In forming, examine program goals and group expectations, then alter the program as necessary to accommodate these. Help individuals clarify their similarities and differences and to share their fears and concerns. In storming, recognize the benefits of conflict while not permitting it to occur at the expense of others. Draw attention to acts of danger while maintaining an open and supportive group atmosphere by encouraging the group to solve its own problems. In norming, help the group establish their own norms and see issues from new perspectives. Clarify and confront issues, encouraging members to consider ways they may meet their needs without compromising the rights of others. In performing, get the group to share its talents and to offset its strengths and weaknesses. Shift responsibility and accountability to the group but remain supportive by occasionally taking opposing sides or acting as a resource for advice and assistance. In adjourning, summarize the group's learning and progress and help members transfer what they have learned to their everyday lives. Provide alternatives to the support the group offered and use follow-up strategies to maintain changes.

You should note, however, that this group development model does not account for individual development, evolution of group dynamics at different rates and in different directions, adding or subtracting members, and the specific characteristics and competence of the group. Yet, by understanding group development, you will be well equipped to select the best activity, to express the correct leadership style, and to apply appropriate strategies to help a group grow toward its next stage.

QUESTIONS TO THINK ABOUT

1. Describe a group (preferably one you were a member of) and its behaviors in the five stages of the group development model.

2. Discuss the style and strategies used by the leader of that group. Were the leadership

style and strategies effective? How could the style and strategies have been improved?

3. What will you do differently in each of the five stages with the groups you will work with?

REFERENCES

Attarian, A., & Priest, S. (1994). The relationship between stages of group development and styles of outdoor leadership. *Journal of Adventure Education and Outdoor Leadership* 11(3), 13-19.

Jensen, M. (1979). Application of small group theory to adventure programs. *Journal of Experiential Education* 2(2), 39-42.

Kerr, P.J., & Gass, M.A. (1987). A group development model for adventure education. *Journal of Experiential Education* 10(3), 39-46.

Mitten, D. (1995). Building the group: Using personal affirming to create healthy group process. *Journal of Experiential Education* 18(2), 82-94.

Priest, S., & Chase, R. (1989). The conditional theory of outdoor leadership style. *Journal of Adventure Education and Outdoor Leadership* 6(3), 10-17.

Tuckman, B.W., & Jensen, M.A. (1977). Stages of small group development revisited. *Group & Organization Studies* 2(4), 419-427.

PART
II

Practical and Organizational Skills for Outdoor Leaders

chapter

6

Technical Skills

The day was perfect. A warm breeze blew across Maria's face as she stood on top of the cliff, having just set up four independent sets of anchor systems for rock climbing. The progressions for climbing, based on the students' objectives, were in place for the day's lessons. She could see James, her coinstructor, briefing the group on the day's activities and laying out the safety procedures. The day progressed wonderfully and in the final discussion no one felt it could have gone much better.

The day was terrible. An unexpected ice storm had settled over the mountain range, covering everything with three inches of ice. Several tents in the group had collapsed during the night, and the group had retreated into cramped, yet convenient, snow caves they had built earlier. Following the planned route to the summit was out of the question due to unstable snowpack conditions, so the group took a secondary route that required a less technical—but much longer and more arduous—experience of "post-holing" for several hours. Such a change required a number of adaptations in the program that the staff implemented with input from students. At the end of the day, while students and staff members alike agreed that the experience was a total drag, in the final discussion no one felt it could have gone much better.

As seen in both vignettes, technical skills serve as one of the foundations for conducting any adventure experience. Although technical skills are not always the "product" of adventure programs, they always serve as the "process" through which people grow. Without appropriate knowledge of such skills, you may find the task of conducting adventure experiences to be dangerous—if not impossible. As a leader, you may be blessed with tremendous facilitation techniques or great organizational capabilities, but without technical skills to serve as the underlying medium for conducting such activities, knowing these techniques and having certain other capabilities are useless.

In writing this chapter, as well as the other "hard skill" chapters (7 and 8), we do not intend to describe in detail how to conduct all of the technical aspects of each skill area in adventure programming. Unfortunately, space does not allow for this, but you can find numerous books written on each skill alone. The list of books at the end of this chapter is a good place to start.

What we will provide in these chapters, however, are some of the key, specific competencies you should possess to enable you to effectively teach and lead certain adventure activities. Please note, however, that these competencies change according to geographic areas, client populations, client goals, and environmental conditions. These competencies only become valuable when they are guided by the accommodating judgment required of outdoor leaders.

GENERIC, METASKILL, AND SPECIFIC COMPETENCY AREAS

In conducting adventure programs, no matter what the activity, you need to be capable in a variety of **generic competency** areas. These areas are comprised of those skills applicable to *all* adventure experiences. Examples of these areas include weather interpretation, first aid, trip planning, appropriate level of performance, skill, physical fitness, and mental awareness above and beyond the call of the activity, location, participants, and anticipated adversity.

Furthermore, you need to be capable in areas of **metaskills,** or those areas that combine hard and soft skills into a workable design. Examples of these areas include leadership style, problem-solving and decision-making skills, experience-based judgment, effective communication, and ethical behavior (see also chapters 18 through 23).

In addition, you need to be capable in several **specific competencies**—those skills unique to the particular activities chosen for the adventure program. For example, paddling and rope handling are two skills that you need only if you are actually going to be kayaking or canoeing and climbing or doing challenge courses. In this chapter, we'll outline the specific competencies you need to master for eight of the most popular adventure activities. We have based our guidelines on two main works: *Safety Practices in Adventure Programming* (Priest & Dixon, 1990) and the *Manual of Program Accreditation Standards for Adventure Programs* (Williamson & Gass, 1993).

SPECIFIC TECHNICAL-SKILL COMPETENCIES

The eight adventure activities in this chapter include backcountry travel, top-rope rock climbing and rappelling, mountaineering, challenge (ropes) courses, caving or spelunking, flatwater and whitewater paddling, on-road and off-road bicycling, and cross-country skiing. The vast majority of these specific skills are technical in origin, that is, they are related to activity performance. Although we'll mention some of the specific safety, environmental, and ubiquitous "other" competency skills here, we will not consider any of the generic safety or environmental competency skills until the next two chapters, or the metaskills until chapters 18 through 23.

One final reminder: Competence in technical, safety, and environmental skills alone does not constitute effective outdoor leadership. Such competence is merely a start; you must build on your capabilities by adding the skills we'll discuss in later chapters in this text. For example, the organizational skills of trip planning (chapter 9) or risk management (chapter 10) are the same for most programs, regardless of the activity. Being properly skilled in all areas will give you a greater "cushion of competence" to fall back on in times of need!

Backcountry Travel

Activity: As a backpacking leader, you should possess knowledge of appropriate travel techniques, such as the locking-knee rest step on uphill grade, switch-backing in steep, open country, and choosing an appropriate stride length and cadence on various slopes. You should know about specific equipment selection for the conditions encountered, for example, which packs, footwear, tents, and sleeping bags are appropri-

ate for which conditions; correct equipment use, such as equally loading backpacks, adjusting suspension straps, erecting tents, and refueling and lighting stoves; equipment care, such as waterproofing boots; and equipment repair, such as fixing broken tents or packs and unclogging stoves or water filters. You may also need to know how to improvise emergency rescue equipment, for example, how to fashion a stretcher from pack frames or by weaving one with rope.

Safety: Common injuries in backpacking tend to be joint strains and sprains. You should be aware of participants with weak leg joints or back or neck problems. In addition, you should know how to perform specific warm-up stretches for various body parts (e.g., legs, hips, neck, shoulders). Furthermore, you should understand the unique concerns that come from all possible weather and terrain interactions, such as combining steep hills in freezing rain. Finally, you should have adequate plans for finding lost hikers and for supervising a group in wilderness conditions.

Environmental: For backcountry travel in wilderness areas, unique considerations may be necessary, such as the need to obtain land use permits. You should be aware of local trail etiquette, for example, whether or not downhill hikers have the right of way. You should be especially aware of the resource impact potential for highly used camping areas.

Other: When traveling off-trail, technical terrain can be a challenge for leaders. This may include steep scree slopes or slippery snow slopes. More injuries generally happen during the descent than the ascent, usually because people are tired and relaxed after having reached a summit. When appropriate, you need to be well prepared for rock falls or avalanches, ensuring that everyone wears a helmet. You should anticipate the possibility of people slipping, perhaps causing an ankle sprain. Encourage people to use appropriate hiking techniques for the area, such as treading carefully, facing the hill, avoiding leaning too far into the slope (like climbing a ladder), digging the feet into the hillside without loosening debris, keeping one eye uphill for falling debris, and not lingering downhill from others moving above them. Fixing a hand line may be necessary with appropriate procedures, including only allowing one person on it at a time, since a sideways stumble can dislodge several others who might be holding on.

River crossings are occasionally part of backpacking experiences. Crossing a slippery log high above the water or jumping along stepping stones may be more dangerous than simply wading across a river. So you should know how to use a combination of various methods to ford a river, such as human tripods, chains of people, upstream hand lines, third-leg poles for added stability, extra flotation, and Tyrolean traverses. For rocky fords, you may need to consider wearing shoes, sandals, or boots as well as helmets if the risk of head injury exists. In addition, you may need to prevent people from wearing baggy clothing that may fill with water, causing them to submerge. It is generally appropriate in such situations to have everyone unbuckle waist belts and sternum straps, and loosen shoulder straps, so that a pack may be quickly removed in the water, and not pin or drag someone under.

You must understand and be able to "read" river-crossing characteristics on-site, including downstream dangers, air and water temperatures, water murkiness, footing stability, water depth, flow rates, current speed, length of crossing, and obstacles. Moreover, you may need to pay particular attention to preplanning rescue attempts in case someone is swept downstream, including remembering that ample visibility and danger-free river space are needed for floating, drifting, swimming, and reaching the nearest bank. Certainly, you should know group members skill levels, especially swimming abilities and strength and balancing capacities, making sure skill levels match the type of crossing you choose. In addition, you need to give careful consideration to the time of day because, for example, snow melt and runoff can be greatest in the afternoon; avoid fording rivers that might be beyond group capabilities. Remember: it may be better to wait for levels to subside or find another location.

Addressing many other factors can make fording a river safer. When conditions warrant extra assistance on either bank, you should consider placing a person with a throw bag downstream from the crossing point. You may need to consider belaying people from either or both banks. You might want to keep knives handy to cut any ropes that may get tangled up with people in the water. You may need to test all crossings before you permit any participants to cross, possibly leaving a qualified staff member to cross last. When river temperatures are cold, be prepared to deal with immersion hypothermia. Finally, you may need to think ahead about how to communicate over the noise of the river.

Top-Rope Rock Climbing and Rappelling

Activity: As a rock climbing leader, you should know appropriate movement techniques, such as laying back, jamming, chimneying, and using counterforce; belaying techniques, such as using the body or devices for friction and using backup belay systems; anchor systems, such as natural, artificial, solid, independent, equalized, and redundant; spotting for bouldering; knot tying; forming harness tie-ins and anchor clip-ins; and communication signals. You should know about specific equipment selection for the conditions you may encounter, such as when to use dynamic or static ropes, webbing, carabiners, harnesses, and helmets; correct equipment uses, such as how to fit and dress in harnesses and helmets; equipment care, such as not stepping on nylon software or dropping aluminum hardware; and equipment replacement, such as regularly logging usage and making visual inspections for wear and tear. You may also need to know how to improvise emergency lowering and raising techniques, including litter lowering, Z-pulley raising, and knot jumping.

Safety: Common injuries in rock climbing include joint dislocations. You should be aware of participants with a history of separated shoulders, elbows, or fingers. In addition, you should assess clients' overall physical fitness and psychological readiness to climb. Encouraging the removal of all jewelry (e.g., knives, rings, bracelets, necklaces, earrings) and any sharp objects from pockets (especially pens and pencils) to prevent shear injuries or impalements is an appropriate safety measure. You should know how to perform specific warm-up stretches of body parts (e.g., arms, neck, shoulders, hips, knees). Furthermore, you should understand the unique concerns that come from possible weather and terrain interactions, such as the danger of combining exposed people on cliff faces with lightning. Moreover, you should have clear plans for specific supervision of individual climbers and belayers as well as general group management. Finally, you may need to inspect climbing sites for environmental dangers, such as potential rock falls, loose holds, uneven ground, and sharp objects.

Environmental: For rock climbing, unique considerations may be necessary for site preservation, such as avoiding bird nests and rock paintings, and conservation, including keeping wire from brushing lichen and avoiding pulling out plants in cracks, dragging ropes around trees, using too much chalk, excessive bolting, bashing pitons, glue fixing holds, and chipping rock to make new holds. You should be aware of local rules for the climbing site, including bolting practices and whether you must boulder only in dedicated areas.

Other: If you work with clients on climbing walls, you should know if the wall construction follows acceptable standards. You may also need to know about the principles and technology of the facility you are using, noting safe working load, minimum breaking strength, anchor systems, base padding, wall materials, artificial holds, and regular safety inspection reviews.

Rappelling (or abseiling) can often be conducted as a stand-alone adventure activity that is separate from top-rope rock climbing. In this instance, the competencies we have listed for climbing may also apply to rappelling. Competencies that usually differ from rock climbing competencies include appropriate movement techniques, such as proper body shape, hand positions, foot placement, and "free rappelling" past overhangs; equipment use and care of rappelling devices; and additional communication signals for rappelling. As a rappelling leader, you should use separate and independent rappel and belay systems when appropriate. One common example of this is a rappel device connected to the harness at a point different from the belay tie-in knot and rappel ropes and belay ropes each having their own anchor systems. In addition, you should know that common rappelling accidents can include clothing or hair getting caught in ropes or devices, coming off the rappel rope (rappelling off the end of the rope), anchor failure, and equipment damage, for example, high-speed descents can overheat friction devices and melt ropes.

Mountaineering

Activity: In addition to some of the rock climbing techniques, as a mountaineering leader you may need to know snow climbing techniques, including post-holing, ice ax self-arrest, roped group travel, and glissading; ice climbing techniques, including French and American cramponing techniques and placing ice tools; and glacier travel techniques, such as step cutting, walking in echelon formation, and crossing snow bridges and crevasses. You may also need to know these special techniques: belaying, including boot ax belays; anchors, including correct use of bollards, buried "dead" objects, flukes, picket, and ice screws; knots, such as pre-positioned Prussik and butterfly; and harness tie-ins to a chest harness in order to prevent inversion with a heavy pack on.

You should know about specific equipment selection for the conditions you may encounter, including when to pack shovels, ice tools, crampons, crevasse rescue kit, altimeters, and eye protection from snow blindness or flying ice chips; correct equipment uses, including how to walk in crampons and how to carry an ice ax and swing ice tools without injury; equipment care, including not stepping on nylon software with crampon spikes and checking anchors for melting under pressure; and equipment repair, such as how to fix crampons and snowshoes. You should know how to improvise emergency lowering and raising techniques, such as how to do crevasse rescues, Bilgeri lift, Prussiking, and Z-pulley raising. You should know how to build emergency snow shelters, mark the return route with wands, and melt large quantities of snow for adequate fluid intake.

Safety: Naturally, you should possess a thorough understanding of mountain safety. You should know information pertaining to snowpack or ice history (age, depth, layers, crystals), seasonal precipitation trends, spring runoff, freeze and thaw cycles, weather forecast, temperature, and time of day. This information can be critical to determining and predicting the stability and characteristics of the routes you choose. You should also know how crevasses and snow bridges are formed, the likelihood of avalanches, and the impact of sun and temperature on snow bridge, crevasse, and serac stability. In addition, you may need to know how to perform on-site inspections to examine snow crystals and layers or ice strength, color, water content, and underlying foundation.

Injuries in mountaineering are most often associated with high altitude. Thus, you should be aware of the possibilities of high altitude mountain sickness, hypothermia, frostbite, and cerebral or pulmonary edema. Furthermore, you should understand the unique concerns that come from possible weather and terrain interactions, such as combining altitude with high winds (e.g., winds can increase rapidly at higher elevations) and avalanches (see cross-country skiing). Moreover, you may need to inspect mountaineering sites for environmental dangers, including looking for potential avalanches, lightning, ice fall, and snow bridge collapse. Certainly, you should assess clients' physical fitness and psychological readiness for the routes you choose. As with rock climbing, accidents are more likely during the descent when people are tired and careless after reaching the summit.

Environmental: You need to understand the consequences of improper waste disposal, for example, dumping it into crevasses. This practice is becoming less tolerated due to the large increase in wilderness use (see chapter 24).

Challenge (Ropes) Courses

Activity: As a challenge course leader, you should know the difference between high elements, requiring belaying protection, and low elements, requiring spotting—not catching—protection, as well as the differences in safety protocols for skills, such as dynamic belaying and static belaying with "transfers" between elements. You may need to know appropriate movement techniques, such as ascending, crossing, and descending high elements; belaying techniques similar to rock climbing but also including backup belay systems, dynamic and static belays and transfer methods; anchor systems, which includes regular inspection of permanent anchors in addition to the rock climbing anchoring techniques; spotting for low elements and group initiatives; knots; harness tie-ins; anchor clip-ins; and communication signals, which include static transfers in addition to the rock climbing communication techniques. You need to know about specific equipment selection for the conditions you may encounter, such as when to use dynamic or static ropes and how to use spin static devices and shear reduction blocks; correct equipment uses, including how to fit and dress in harnesses and helmets; equipment care, including not dropping aluminum hardware or stepping on nylon software; and equipment replacement, including regularly logging usage and making visual inspections for wear and tear. In addition, you need to know how to improvise appropriate emergency lowering techniques, for example, performing "cut-away" rescues, evacuating physically injured people without an ambulance present, and mobilizing people who are psychologically frozen by their fear.

Safety: Injuries on challenge courses can include heart attacks (rates rise rapidly, often reaching maximum rates), shear injuries, joint dislocations or hyperextensions while lifting or from dropping people, and minor cuts, scrapes,

bruises, and splinters. You should be aware of participants with a history of cardiac risk factors, back concerns, and separated shoulders, elbows, or fingers. It is wise to encourage the removal of jewelry, especially rings, bracelets, necklaces, and earrings, and any sharp objects from pockets. Encourage participants to wear long-sleeve shirts and long pants even on hot days and to tuck in loose clothing. You should know how to perform specific warm-up stretches (e.g., arms, neck, shoulders, hips, knees). You should understand the unique concerns that come from all possible weather and terrain interactions, such as not combining people on wires with lightning and high winds. Moreover, you may need to have clear plans for specific supervision of individuals, such as first time belayers, as well as for general group management, including dealing with congestion on elements and horseplay. You should inspect the area for environmental dangers, such as sharp sticks, hanging tree limbs, exposed rocks, uneven ground, and equipment dropped from above. And, of course, you should assess clients' physical fitness and psychological readiness for participation.

Environmental: For challenge courses, unique considerations may be necessary for site preservation, including not disturbing bird nests or tree growth, and conservation, such as avoiding through-bolting small diameter trees, girdling trees with ropes or cables, and compacting soil around roots.

Other: You generally need to ensure that the course is properly constructed, making sure it meets appropriate standards, and is regularly inspected for dangers such as detached cables or ropes, loose clamps or strand vises, missing bolts or nuts, frayed cable or rope ends, split poles or planks, overexposure to ultraviolet light, weather damage, tree diseases, and root system damage. You should know about the principles and technology of the facility you are using, for example, its safe working load, minimum breaking strength, ground anchor integrity, guy line or belay cable fastenings, and regular safety inspection reviews. You should also be experienced at recognizing and repairing—or not using—damaged elements. Finally, you may need to know how to secure the challenge course to avoid creating an "attractive nuisance."

Caving or Spelunking

Activity: As a caving leader, you should know horizontal and vertical movement techniques, such as walking, crawling, slithering, squeezing, getting unstuck, negotiating water hazards, rappelling, ascending with ladders and with aid gear; belaying techniques; anchor systems; knots; harness tie-ins; anchor clip-ins; and communication signals. You may need to know about specific equipment selection for the conditions you may encounter, which are similar to rock climbing but may possibly include a minimum of three different light sources per person and a rescue kit containing full-length static rope, wire ladders, ascenders, anchors, carabiners, and pulleys; correct equipment uses, such as fitting and wearing special clothing and gear; equipment care, including not stepping on nylon software and not dropping aluminum hardware; and equipment replacement, including regularly logging usage and making visual inspections for wear and tear. You may need to know how to improvise emergency lowering and raising techniques, such as litter lowering, Z-pulley raising, and knot jumping.

Safety: Common accidents in caving include head injuries, getting stuck in a tight place, and reacting to fear. Certainly, you must be aware of participants with a history of claustrophobia or fear of the dark. You need to consider using helmets as well as taking sufficient food and water for an extra 24-hour stay. You should understand the unique concerns that potential weather and terrain interactions may cause, such as knowing that combining heavy rains with deep passages in which cave flooding occurs can drastically alter the appearance and availability of routes. You should have plans for specific supervision of individual cavers, such as for those who may need extra help in tight squeezes, as well as general group management, such as how you'll keep everyone together in the dark. You may need to inspect caving sites for environmental dangers, such as potential rock fall, loose holds, and uneven ground. In addition, you should assess clients' physical fitness and psychological readiness to cave in the dark.

Environmental: Caving is often conducted in an especially sensitive setting. Unique considerations may be necessary for site protection, for example, properly removing and disposing of all litter and human waste and leaving survey markers or prehistoric artifacts intact. You need to be aware of local rules for the caving site, such as no smoking, marking walls, contacting bats or other animals, touching or damaging cave formations, dumping spent carbide, or tampering with cave gates. You may need to secure special permission to enter caves, understanding that caves and cave-dwelling animals are protected by law in most areas.

Flatwater and Whitewater Paddling

Activity: As a paddling leader, you need to know appropriate flatwater and whitewater techniques, such as power strokes, turning strokes, corrective strokes, braces; capsize techniques, including group, individual, boat-assisted self-rescues, and paddling a swamped boat; swimming techniques, such as drownproofing, treading water, and floating through rapids; boat dynamics and maneuverability, including spins, forward, reverse, and straight tracking, side slips, eddy turns or peelouts, bracing, U-turns, landings, rolling, and ferrying; boat transportation, such as rooftop or trailer tie-downs, turn signals, safe loading and unloading, and carrying; knots, such as the trucker's hitch; and river communication, including using whistles and signals. You need to know about specific equipment selection for the conditions you may encounter, such as helmets in whitewater, using type III or V personal flotation devices (PFDs), dry bags, flotation devices, spray decks, bailers, sponges, foot pumps for inflatables, repair kit, a rescue kit containing haul ropes, pulleys, carabiners, anchors, knife for fouled lines, and a saw for cutting through wood in strainers; correct equipment uses, such as how to fit helmets, use throw bags, and wear PFDs while in a boat; equipment care, including appropriate waterproofing and proper securing of gear; and equipment replacement, such as regularly logging usage and making visual inspections for wear and tear. Clothing can be a special concern since people may remain wet for the entire day. You may need to think about recommending functional clothing such as wet suits or dry suits (e.g., when the sum of air temperature and water temperature are less than 50° C or 122° F) and footwear that protects feet, allowing for walking, but not interfering with swimming. You also may need to know how to improvise emergency rescue techniques, including securing people, securing equipment, dealing with pinned boats, Z-pulley dragging, and knot jumping.

Safety: Common injuries in paddling can be joint dislocations and reacting to fear. You should be aware of participants with a history of separated shoulders, elbows, or fingers as well as how proficient each participant is in water. You should know how to perform specific warm-up stretches (e.g., arms, neck, torso, shoulders). In addition, you should understand the unique concerns that come from all possible weather and terrain interactions, such how to deal with wind and lightning on open water. You should have plans for supervision of individual paddlers, such as proper positioning for rapid running, as well as general group management, including maintaining visual contact on open water. You may need to inspect paddling areas, portages, and access or egress points for environmental dangers, such as moving water, submerged stumps, prevailing winds, water temperature, or uneven ground. As always, you should assess clients' physical fitness and psychological readiness to paddle.

Environmental: For paddling, unique considerations may be necessary for site preservation, such as avoiding beaver constructions, and conservation, such as using existing portage trails, avoiding expanding damage around put-in and take-out areas, and preventing water contamination from poorly packed stove fuel. You should be aware of local rules for the paddling area, including river courtesy and whether or not fires must be only below high-water line. You must avoid exceeding weight and personnel limits for boats as well as consider the effect that the equal or unequal distribution of supplies will have on those limits.

Other: When appropriate, you need to conduct appropriate swim tests and capsize drills prior to paddling flatwater, and rapid drills prior to paddling whitewater. For river trips, you should obtain recent information on river volumes and flow rates. As you probably well know, whitewater generally demands extra attention from leaders. You may need to scout rapids in advance, pair paddlers so that weak teams are not created, and stagger teams through the rapids, sending one craft at a time through, so that stronger teams may assist weaker ones and congestion doesn't lead to collisions. In addition, you may need to make room in eddies for other crafts that may want to enter.

High water combined with low-water bridges or narrow chutes can be very dangerous. As flow rate increases, so does the power of the river, generally making rescues more difficult and errors more serious. Strainers or sieves permit water to flow through without opposition, but can trap crafts and people. The enormous water pressure, coupled with such a pinning, can destroy the craft and drown a trapped person. Hydraulic reversals (or souse holes) can happen when water drops over an object (usually linear like a weir, low water dam, or rock ledge) and may create a

depression in the river surface. Top water can flow back upstream into the hole in order to fill it in, thus forming a kind of vertical washing machine or whirlpool effect that is extremely difficult to get free from.

You must brief participants on what to do if they are thrown into whitewater: float with head up, look ahead for dangers, place feet downstream and in front to push off from obstacles, hold onto craft for extra flotation and visibility, remain upstream of the craft so as not to be pinned against obstacles, and do not stand up against the current; instead, wait for an eddy opportunity, kick toward shore, and abandon the craft if necessary. You should explain how to handle whitewater and moving water dangers on the river, such as fallen trees, strainers, hydraulics, undercut rocks, pinning, standing waves, eddies, chutes, waterfalls, weirs, dams, and shallows.

On-Road and Off-Road Bicycling

Activity: As a bicycling leader, you need to know appropriate on-road and off-road travel techniques, such as how to deal with movement in traffic, high-speed turning, single-file spacing, gear selection and cadence for inclines, weight distribution, front and back brake use, when to walk, jumping, hopping, ascending, descending, and falling safely; and communication techniques, for example, to warn of traffic or obstacles. You need to know about specific equipment selection for the conditions you may encounter, for example, ensuring that bikes are tough enough for the terrain and have adequate gear ratios, effective brakes, rear view mirrors, antennae flags, and ample water bottles, and that participants are wearing protective eyewear, footwear, brightly colored clothing, gloves, and helmets; correct equipment uses, such as how to fit the bike to the body size and how to pack, equally load, and suspend panniers; equipment care, including daily inspections of tire pressures, brake or gear cable tension, power train lubrication, bottom brackets, pedals, headsets, wheel trueness, and bolts; equipment repair, such as how to fix flats, adjust cables, true wheels, repack bearings, and pack a repair kit containing spare inner tubes and tires, pump, patch kit, screw drivers, pliers, and adjustable wrench; and equipment maintenance, ensuring, for example, regularly scheduled replacement of tires, chains, and cables.

Safety: Common injuries in bicycling are generally associated with collisions and repeated use or stress injuries. You should be aware of participants with a history of weak knees or hips and back or neck problems. You should know how to perform specific warm-up stretches (e.g., arms, legs, neck, shoulders, hips, knees). You should understand the unique concerns that come with all possible weather and terrain interactions, for example, the dangers of combining rain with oil on the road or loose gravel on curves. You need to have clear plans for specific supervision of individual cyclists, including how to maintain direct visual contact and how to make verbal contact to warn of dangers, as well as general group management, such as placing a motorized support vehicle behind the group to warn approaching motorists on long road trips, in heavy traffic, or with beginners. You may need to inspect bicycle paths for environmental dangers, such as uneven surfaces, sharp objects, traffic volume, shoulder width, and safe places to rest, which may include places other than the shoulder. As always, you should assess clients' physical fitness and psychological readiness to bike.

Environmental: For bicycling, unique considerations may be necessary for site protection, such as avoiding startling animals or destroying vegetation by locking up and skidding the back wheel or detouring, and conflict resolution, such as warning others of approaching cyclists, sharing trails with other users, dismounting if necessary, and pedaling under control and at a reasonable speed. You need to be aware of local rules of the road, including traffic laws and regulations, or for the area, such as "no bikes in legally designated wilderness." You need to properly dispose of used rubber tires and conservatively apply chain lubricants, taking care not to spill any oil into the environment.

Other: If you bicycle in reduced visibility conditions, such as at night, dawn, or dusk, or in fog, wear appropriate reflective clothing and use bike lights and reflectors; be sure to carry spare batteries and bulbs. If you bicycle deep in wild backcountry areas, where breakdowns could mean a long walk out for help, carry sufficient survival gear.

Cross-Country Skiing

Activity: As a skiing leader, you should know appropriate uphill and downhill techniques, such as diagonal striding, single and double poling, skating, telemarking, snowplowing, step turns, parallel turns, sidestepping, angular traverses,

and herringbone; falling down and getting up with a heavy pack on; and waxing techniques for expected conditions as well as mohair or nonwax alternatives. You need to know about specific equipment selection for the cold weather and steep terrain you may encounter, such as how to select durability of skis, poles, boots, snow shovels, and saws; correct equipment uses, including how to fit skis and poles to body height and weight; equipment care, including how to fix loose bindings, broken ski tips, broken poles, and scraped bases; and equipment repair, ensuring that you carry a kit containing wire, pliers, screwdrivers, and duck tape, as well as spare ski tips, pole shafts, pole baskets, and bindings. You typically need to understand the importance of layered clothing for when people frequently shift between standing still and heavily exercising, and correctly fitting hand and footwear to prevent frostbite resulting from cutoff circulation. You also should know how to build emergency shelters, such as snow caves, igloos, or quinzees; how to improvise evacuation sleds from skis and packs; and how to obtain adequate fluids by having enough fuel to melt plenty of snow.

Safety: Common skiing injuries include joint dislocations or major bone fractures. You should be aware of participants with a history of separated shoulders, elbows, or fingers and previous fractures. You should know how to perform specific warm-up stretches (e.g., arms, neck, shoulders, hips, knees). You should understand the unique concerns that come with all possible weather and terrain interactions; for example, combining high winds with leeward slopes that create deep snow deposition zones can be dangerous. You should have clear plans for specific supervision of individual skiers, such as careful observation of descent areas where falls can result in greater injury, as well as general group management, especially, for example, in avalanche country. You may need to inspect skiing sites for environmental dangers, such as potential for avalanches and uneven surfaces. You should also assess clients' physical fitness and psychological readiness to ski.

Environmental: For skiing, unique considerations may exist for waste disposal when the soil is covered by snow. You need to be aware of local rules, such as not disturbing the trap lines or caches of others.

Other: When crossing frozen lakes or rivers, you must be certain that the ice is thick enough to support the group's weight, for example, by spreading out, keeping ropes and long poles handy, not resting in large groups, and avoiding stream areas near the water's edge. You also need to watch out for "bottomless" snow in the springtime, in which water percolating beneath the snow has melted away the lower layers, creating a deep cavity beneath a thin surface.

Avalanches can be a major concern while cross-country skiing. In these areas, you need to know how to identify avalanche potential, such as leeward hillsides, overhanging cornices, slope inclines and orientations, lack of ground cover, recent storms, sustained winds, new snowfall, temperature fluctuations, snow layering, and crystal types. When appropriate, you need to know how to avoid exposing people to avalanche dangers, for example, by avoiding old slide paths, sticking to ridge tops and valley bottoms, crossing suspect slopes one person at a time, loosening equipment, zipping up clothing layers, not kicking deep steps, traveling quickly, and resting only in protected locations. In anticipated avalanche locations, you need to carry and know how to use transceivers or beacon locators; these must be turned on and worn on the body of each person. You also need to carry an appropriate number of snow shovels and a selection of avalanche probes—or ski poles and tent poles that can be converted to probes. Finally, you need to be competent at responding to avalanches; for example, you should designate an observer to watch for further danger, mark last-known location of victim, hastily search downhill from there, probe suspect areas, locate beacons, and dig up all hits.

EFFECTIVE OUTDOOR LEADERS SHOULD

☞ Understand the difference between as well as the interaction of generic, meta-, and specific skill competencies for the activities they will lead, placing these in the context of the geographic areas, client populations, client goals, and environmental conditions where they will lead.

☞ Be specifically competent for the activities they will lead.

SUMMARY

Technical skills are a foundation for conducting adventure experiences. Although these skills are not always the "product" in adventure programming, they are always the "process" through which people learn. Without technical skills, you will be ineffective. To be an effective outdoor leader, you must possess a wide variety of generic competencies that apply to all adventure experiences, no matter what the activity. You also must have expertise in the specific competencies that are unique to the activity.

The activity-specific competencies tend to be mostly technical skills but include unique safety and environmental skills. Competence in these specific areas alone is not sufficient for outdoor leadership, but is definitely an important start. Refer often to the descriptions of appropriate practices for each of the eight activities we have described in this chapter as you strive to become an effective leader.

QUESTIONS TO THINK ABOUT

1. Select four of the activities that you are willing to lead, then compare your competencies to the specific competencies listed for each activity.

2. Are you ready to lead these four adventure activities? Why or why not?

3. What will you do to make up for any shortcomings you have in these four areas?

4. Say that you are going to lead a challenge (ropes) course experience on one day for a group of 13- to 14-year-old students and the next day for a group of 50-year-old corporate clients. How will your specific technical-skill–competency concerns differ between the two days?

5. Select one of the eight activity areas in which you feel knowledgeable. Give examples of how each of the following four factors—geographic areas, client populations, client goals, and environmental conditions—would change the specific technical-skill competencies listed in this section.

REFERENCES

Priest, S., & Dixon, T. (1990). *Safety practices in adventure programming*. Boulder, CO: Association for Experiential Education.

Williamson, J., & Gass, M.A. (1993). *Manual of program accreditation standards for adventure programs*. Boulder, CO: Association for Experiential Education.

FURTHER READING

Backcountry Travel

Cockrell, D. (1991). *The wilderness educator: The Wilderness Education Association curriculum guide.* Merrillville, IN: ICS Books.

Gilchrist, J., & Lee, J. (1984). *Orienteering instructor's manual.* Willowdale, Ontario: Orienteering Ontario.

Hart, J. (1984). *Walking softly in the wilderness.* San Francisco: Sierra Club Books.

Kjellstrom, B. (1976). *Be expert with map and compass: The complete orienteering handbook.* New York: Charles Scribner's Sons.

Lowry, R., & Sidney, K. (1985). *Orienteering: Skills and strategies.* Willowdale, Ontario: Orienteering Ontario.

Lowry, R., & Sidney, K. (1987). *Orienteering: Techniques and training.* Willowdale, Ontario: Orienteering Ontario.

Seaborg, E., & Dudley, E. (1994). *Hiking and backpacking: Outdoor pursuits series.* Champaign, IL: Human Kinetics.

Simer, P., & Sullivan, J. (1983). *The National Outdoor Leadership School's wilderness guide.* New York: Simon and Schuster.

Rock Climbing

British Mountaineering Council. (1988). *Development, design, and management of climbing walls.* Manchester, England: British Sports Council.

Cinnamon, J. (1994). *Climbing rock and ice: Learning the vertical dance.* Camden, ME: Ragged Mountain Press.

Fyffe, A., & Peter, I. (1990). *The handbook of climbing.* London, England: Pelham Books.

Graydon, D. (Ed.). (1992). *Mountaineering: Freedom of the hills* (5th ed.). Seattle: The Mountaineers.

Long, J. (1994). *How to rock climb* (2nd ed.). Evergreen, CO: Chockstone Press.

Loughman, M. (1981). *Learning to rock climb.* San Francisco: Sierra Club Books.

Rohnke, K. (1981). *High profile: A manual for building wooden block climbing walls.* Hamilton, MA: Wilkscraft Creative Printing.

Watts, P. (1996). *Rock climbing: Outdoor pursuits series.* Champaign, IL: Human Kinetics.

Mountaineering

Chouinard, Y. (1978). *Climbing ice.* San Francisco: Sierra Club Books.

Cinnamon, J. (1994). *Climbing rock and ice: Learning the vertical dance.* Camden, ME: Ragged Mountain Press.

Fyffe, A., & Peter, I. (1990). *The handbook of climbing.* London, England: Pelham Books.

Graydon, D. (Ed.). (1992). *Mountaineering: Freedom of the hills* (5th ed.). Seattle: The Mountaineers.

Lowe, J. (1979). *The ice experience.* Chicago: Contemporary Books.

March, B. (1988). *Modern snow and ice techniques.* Milnthorpe, England: Cicerone Press.

Roscoe, D.T. (1976). *Mountaineering: A manual for teachers and instructors.* London, England: Faber and Faber Limited.

Challenge (Ropes) Courses and Group Initiatives

Rohnke, K. (1989). *Cowstails and cobras: A guide to games, initiatives, ropes courses, and adventure curriculum.* Hamilton, MA: Project Adventure.

Rohnke, K. (1989). *Silver bullets.* Dubuque, IA: Kendall/Hunt.

Rohnke, K. (1995). *Quicksilver.* Dubuque, IA: Kendall/Hunt.

Webster, S.E. (1989). *Ropes course safety manual: An instructor's guide to initiatives, and low and high elements.* Hamilton, MA: Project Adventure.

Caving or Spelunking

Halliday, W.R. (1973). *American caves and caving.* Scranton, PA: Harper and Row.

National Speleological Society, Inc., Cave Avenue, Huntsville, AL 35810.

Flat- and Whitewater Paddling

Gullion, L. (1987). *Canoeing and kayaking: Instruction manual.* Newington, VA: American Canoeing Association.

On- and Off-Road Bicycling

Bikecentennial, PO Box 8308, Missoula, MT 59807.

Bridge, R. (1979). *Bike touring: The Sierra Club guide.* San Francisco: Sierra Club Books.

Canadian Cycling Association, 1600 James Naismith Drive, Gloucester, Ontario K1B 5N4.

Coello, D. (1985). *The mountain bike manual.* Salt Lake City: Dream Garden Press.

Cuthbertson, T. (1979). *Anybody's bike book.* Berkeley, CA: Ten Speed Press.

International Mountain Bike Association, PO Box 2007, Saratoga, CA 95080.

National Off-Road Bike Association, PO Box 1901, Chandler, AZ 85244.

van der Plas, R. (1988). *The mountain bike book.* New York: Velo Press.

Cross-Country Skiing

Gillette, N. (1979). *Cross country skiing.* Seattle: The Mountaineers.

Tejada-Flores, L., & Steck, A. (1981). *Backcountry skiing.* San Francisco: Sierra Club Books.

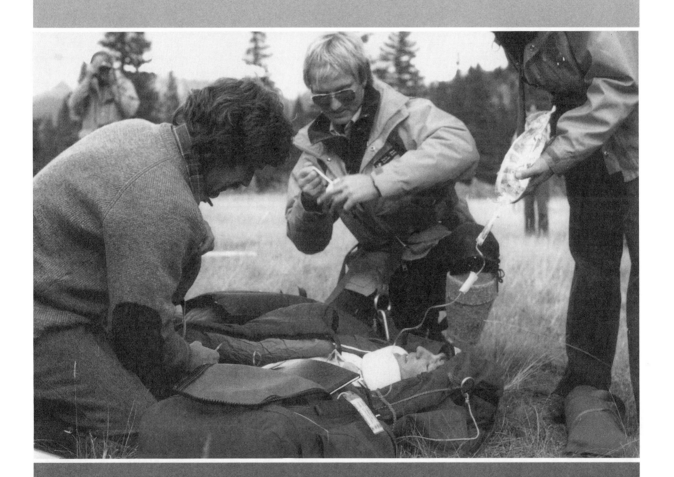

Safety Skills

The weather had deteriorated badly. The wind was blowing horizontal sleet, and the group members were drenched and shivering in their cotton t-shirts as the leader pressed on. Base camp was only a few miles away now, and although they were tired, the group believed they could make it home. Besides, the camp would have a hot meal waiting and dry sleeping bags to finally rest in. As the skies became dark, the group fumbled around in the only daypack they had brought with them (on what was to have been a short hike) and found a single flashlight. As the dimming beam barely projected their way down the narrow trail, the group stumbled their way back into camp, often falling. Not until after several members had been treated for hypothermia did the leader notice that one member was missing: still lost on the trail!

Raffan (1984) described the role of an outdoor leader in safety management as being similar to a slot machine. Every time you take a group outdoors, the slot machine spins and brings up a "lemon" or two in the form of dangers. When a sufficient number of dangers have accumulated—and if you have not attended to these lemons—the "jackpot" pays off with an accident. How many potential "lemons" can you count in the opening scenario?

As with chapter 6, "Technical Skills," our purpose in writing this chapter is not to provide detailed "how to" safety procedures for every skill area in adventure programming. What we will provide, however, are some of the general guidelines you, as an outdoor leader, should possess in regard to safety procedures and protocols of adventure experiences. Please note, however, that these competencies change according to geographic areas, client populations, client goals, and environmental conditions.

ACCIDENT THEORY

As we stated in chapter 2, **safety management** refers to all those procedures put into effect for the purpose of reducing the possibility of accidents. We can then define **accidents** as unexpected occurrences that result in an injury or loss. Such losses can be **physical**, such as fractures or death, **social**, such as being embarrassed in front of peers, **emotional**, such as being afraid of a situation, or **financial**, such as not getting your money's worth or losing or damaging equipment.

Generally, most accidents occur when two types of dangers, human and environmental, combine and interact at the same time to create an **accident potential** (see figure 7.1), which may lead ultimately to an accident. The accident potential itself is the risk probability or the likelihood that an accident will occur. A high level of accident potential does not mean that an accident will definitely occur, only that the likelihood of one is increased. This probability is greatly influenced by the relative strengths and numbers of dangers present, as well as the proactive, active, and reactive countermeasures you take. While it is not possible for you to "predict" these percentages with certainty, knowledge of these factors and judgment based on this knowledge can help you determine more accurately, yet still subjectively, potential risk.

One key concept of this diagram (figure 7.1) is that a large majority of accidents occur when both forms of dangers are present. For example, when the human danger of inappropriate horseplay combines with the environmental danger of wet ground, the risk of someone slipping during an activity is enhanced. If only one danger is present without the other, for example, horseplay without wet ground or wet ground without horseplay, the likelihood of an accident is decreased. But the moment both interact at the same instant, the accident potential greatly increases.

Let's examine, now, another important concept: the likelihood of an accident depends on the number and strength of dangers. For example, hypothermia can occur because of a variety of dangers such as rain, wind, or cold on the envi-

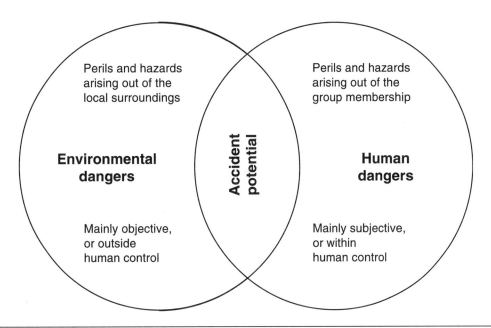

Perils and hazards arising out of the local surroundings

Environmental dangers

Mainly objective, or outside human control

Accident potential

Perils and hazards arising out of the group membership

Human dangers

Mainly subjective, or within human control

Figure 7.1 The accident equation (modified from Alan Hale's 1983 work).

ronmental side, and poor equipment, inexperience, fatigue, or hunger on the human side. The number of dangers are cumulative: in this case, three environmental dangers and four human dangers. Remember, the interaction of these dangers greatly enhances accident potential, which becomes a product of the relative strengths of the dangers. In other words, the greater the interaction between dangers, the more likely the accident. To illustrate this interaction, if the relative intensity of dangers remained the same, we can view the interaction in this case as being 12 times greater (3×4) than if each side had a single equivalent environmental and human dangers alone (1×1). As dangers accumulate, the risk probability also rises.

Danger Classification

Since the interaction of human and environmental dangers generally increases the chance of an accident, let's take a closer look at the specifics of these two aspects of danger. As we mentioned in chapter 2, we can classify **dangers** as either perils or hazards. **Perils** are the sources of injury or the cause of the loss, such as a lightning bolt. **Hazards** are conditions that accentuate or influence the chance of an injury or loss occurring, such as a storm. The presence of danger, whether a peril or a hazard, gives rise to risk. For example, the risk of being electrocuted (accident) is created by two dangers: the presence of a storm (hazard)

that increases the probability of lightning bolts (peril) striking a person.

By knowing the difference between perils and hazards and by being able to identify and label them in the field, you may reduce the chance of your group encountering undesirable risks. By way of illustration, consider mountaineering involving glacier travel to a summit. Crevasses (cracks in the moving ice) and seracs (towers of ice moving along with a glacier) are obvious perils to the mountaineer. You may avoid them by skirting the section of the glacier where they are most prevalent. However, when the route goes through such an area, sometimes you simply cannot avoid these perils. Instead, you should deal with them in a safe manner by also considering the hazards associated with these perils.

Temperature, which of course varies according to the time of day, sunlight, and other climatic conditions, is a hazard that increases the likelihood that the ice will move as it warms up. Experienced mountaineers attempt to avoid the risk of being injured from the peril of moving ice by choosing the correct time to encounter those perils—when hazards are minimal. One common practice suggests beginning a summit bid in the dark around midnight, using headlamps, getting on summit for dawn, and being back to camp by noon—all before temperatures rise. In the heat of the afternoon, the mountaineers may then relax, eat lunch, and watch the glacier come apart far above them, knowing that they have reduced the likelihood of dangers by appropriately addressing perils and hazards. In summary, perils will always be present in adventures. Knowing how and when these perils are impacted by hazards can help you reduce the cumulative dangers on either side of the accident equation.

Danger Analysis

You've seen how to deal with the specific perils and hazards of ice melting, but how do you generalize danger analysis from this one situation to other situations? Use the following 10-step procedure of **danger analysis** as one way you may be able to reduce the chance that accidents will happen, or if one does, that you minimize its consequences to acceptable and recoverable levels (Priest & Baillie, 1987).

The 10 steps, summarized in figure 7.2, include the following:

1. **Plan ahead.** Admit it can happen to you! If you have the attitude that it can't happen to you, you are fooling no one but yourself. Sometime in your career as an outdoor leader, there is a high likelihood that an accident will occur despite your best efforts. The matter is not *if*, but *when*! The key is being ready to deal with almost anything that can happen and keeping a humble attitude as a leader. Preplanning is essential! Know what you will do for each potential accident *before* it happens.

2. **Search for dangerous situations and conditions.** Maintain a continuous search to identify dangers. You must remain vigilant for dangers in any situation. Imagine what might happen at any time. This is often accomplished by keeping a watchful eye open for all suspect circumstances and by always being prepared to ask "What if?" When many dangers are present, take this as a warning to be extra alert and cautious. Always take the appropriate actions for dealing with dangers.

3. **Point out potential dangers.** Once you identify dangers, draw clients' and coleaders' attention to them. For example, making clients aware of wet and slippery ground, an environmental danger, and the level of horseplay, a human danger, can reduce the likelihood of an accident because recognition of the potential for an accident is often enough to change behavior.

4. **When appropriate, remove elements that contribute to dangerous situations.** If drawing attention to danger doesn't deal with it, then remove the danger as long as removal does not increase the risk of this or another danger occurring. For example, removing a loose rock, an environmental danger, that could fall on a person or be tripped over on the trail makes good sense, provided you don't throw the rock carelessly and hit someone else or start an avalanche of many loose rocks. Furthermore, you may, at times, view

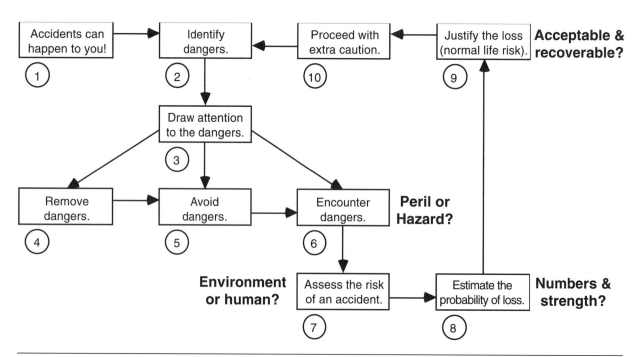

Figure 7.2 A 10-step procedure for analyzing dangers in adventure programs.
Adapted from Priest and Baillie, 1987.

the actions of one client as creating a potential accident risk, a human danger, to the other members in the group and choose to remove that individual, provided such removal does not place the group or person in any further danger.

5. **Avoid dangerous situations.** If you cannot remove the danger, then attempt to avoid it. This may mean rerouting an expedition, adapting the old route; changing an activity altogether to a new design, adopting a new plan; or calling a halt and canceling the program, aborting the activity. Note that the purposeful encountering of dangers is occasionally necessary and sometimes desirable. Beyond the obvious dangers sought by adventurers as a means to challenge themselves, some potential dangers have benefits. For example, the human danger of horseplay is sometimes good: consider water fights helping cool people on a hot day during a river trip. In other cases, the environmental danger of hot sun helps to warm people on a cold winter's day. These potential dangers can be positive, provided you encounter them while avoiding combining them with other dangers. For the examples noted, you should have PFDs and sunscreen lotion available to prevent dangers from combining.

6. **Identify and classify dangerous situations.** If you cannot remove or avoid the danger, then it is likely that you will have to encounter it and therefore must classify the dangers as either perils (source of the loss) or hazards (conditions that influence probability of loss). This classification should enable you to encounter the peril when hazards are at a minimum, thereby reducing the risk of an accident (e.g., traveling in areas of ice fall when the sun does not increase the likelihood of falling ice). This information can often be obatined by addressing the question: "What hazards (the sun in this case) will accentuate the perils (ice fall) that may be encountered?"

7. **Assess risk and reclassify danger.** If you cannot avoid the danger, then assess the risk of a potential accident. Next, you should reclassify the dangers as either environmental, based in the surroundings, or human, based in the group. This reclassification can enable you to recognize if the potential for overlap of the two forces and the risk of an accident exist. Ask yourself the question: "What is the likelihood that the human and environmental dangers will overlap and combine to create an accident potential?"

8. **Estimate potential losses.** If a combination of human and environmental dangers appears imminent, then estimate the probability of loss. Answer these two questions: "How much overlap can be expected? How probable is it that this combination will lead to an accident?" Recall that more numerous and stronger dangers lead to a greater likelihood of an accident. Therefore, you should identify and assess the number and strength of dangers in the human and environmental categories. Absolute numbers do not necessarily mean that accidents are proportionately likely—simply that the more dangers present, the more combinations among these dangers possible, and the more likely an accident will occur. In some cases, the dangers will not combine at all. For example, lost tent poles and excellent summer weather indicate minutely small probabilities. In other cases, the dangers cannot but combine. For example, a novice skier and a rocky hillside may well be an almost certain accident waiting to happen.

9. **Minimize losses.** If the risk of an accident appears probable but still not an absolute certainty, then choose a course of action for which the outcome of an accident is more likely to be both acceptable and recoverable. If leaving behind rock climbing protection and ropes will enable a group to back off of a life-threatening mountain storm, lose the gear or go back and recover it at another time and accept the fact that the losses are merely financial and not more "costly."

10. **Make appropriate adjustments.** If the loss from an accident occurs (e.g., an injury), make preplanned, appropriate adjustments (e.g., evacuation). But before you can accomplish this, you have to do that preplanning! Decide what your injury countermeasures will be before an accident occurs. Once these are employed, proceed with appropriate caution, continuing to search for new dangers that may arise and combine with the already existing dangers.

Please note that outdoor leaders need not use all steps to increase safety—the safest trip may be one that discovers in planning ahead that the adventure experience isn't appropriate given the environmental conditions and the client populations. Even if you follow these steps, no guarantees exist that a more severe accident will not still happen. But knowing how to quickly and accurately use the preceding steps (without having to lug this book along on the trip!) is one method of creating safer experiences.

Inhibiting Factors

Figure 7.3 shows six factors that can inhibit your ability to use the danger-analysis process appropriately. These inhibiting factors include new or unexpected situations, inappropriate attribution, relaxed concentration, smelling the barn, risky shift phenomenon, and poor or unsound judgment.

1. **New or unexpected situations** mean that you are less likely to competently address situations because you have limited or no experience in dealing with them. Examples include using routes for the first time; changes in group dynamics through regrouping, new leadership structures, or new forms of supervision; leading activities for the first time; and conducting experiences in new course sites or new areas (Meyer, 1979). One reason for the high value of "pre-site investigations," which is scouting new areas prior to bringing participants there in similar conditions, is that it decreases the chance of surprises, as well as informs you of potential "teachable moments."

2. **Inappropriate attribution** refers to the tendency of some outdoor leaders to take credit for good happenings, internally attributing them to personal skills, and to place blame on something else, such as bad weather or faulty equipment, when things go wrong, externally attributing problems. This is often because of exaggerated pride, or the need to please others, "look good," or the desire to live up to real or perceived expectations. But beware! Such behavior can prevent you from taking the first step in the danger analysis procedure: you may simply refuse to consider that an accident could happen to you!

3. **Relaxed concentration** involves outdoor leaders who drop their guard due to fatigue, distraction, or carelessness. With your guard down, you are less likely to be constantly looking for dangers and will not be sufficiently alert to proceed with caution. We have often seen this behavior in parties descending from mountain peaks; in groups egressing from a river run when, for example, once the paddling part is over, sprained ankles on the carry-out may be more common than at the access or carry-in when people are more attentive to dangers; and on ropes courses or during group initiatives when, for example, some spotters have the tendency to

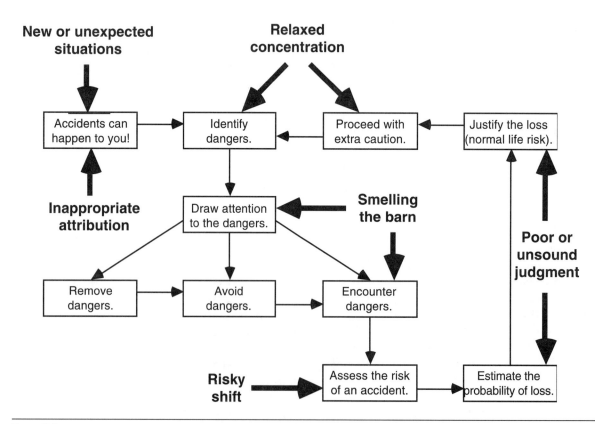

Figure 7.3 Five inhibiting factors at work in the danger analysis procedure.

relax their concentration once someone reaches the top of a wall or when a person is climbing down a ladder. Familiarity with dangers can also breed contempt as you become desensitized to ongoing dangers. For example, spending all day skiing in potential avalanche conditions without evidence of any slides may incorrectly and positively reinforce the belief that these slopes are not really that dangerous.

4. **Smelling the barn** and rushing to get back is a behavior shared by some horses and outdoor leaders. When you attempt to maintain a time schedule—despite falling behind—or see that the end is in sight, you may forget to point out dangers to others or may tend to encounter dangers that you might normally put more energy into removing or avoiding. Given the peer pressure to get home to a warm shower or a hot meal, you must resist the temptation to allow these goals to become more important than safety.

5. The **risky shift phenomenon** addresses the idea that when people are in groups, particularly when they are inexperienced, they tend to make riskier decisions than when they are by themselves (Meier, 1981). This can sometimes be seen in novice group members when they are reluctant to express their fears, especially when courage is socially desirable, and "go along," participating in higher risks than they would on their own. This shift can also be seen when some members abandon personal responsibility, choosing to transfer the responsibility for taking risks to other group members, thinking this will make them safe, or to you—generally without informing you. When this occurs, you might find the group making decisions it really does not want to pursue; no one wishes to appear cowardly and many are reluctant to admit being in too far over their heads! For reasons such as these, you may underestimate the group's level of risk. You must be aware of this possibility, especially when peer pressure between group members is present.

6. **Poor or unsound judgment** always inhibits many aspects of outdoor leadership, and safety is no exception. One common source of poor or unsound judgment is when you misperceive what is occurring. Such misperception inhibits your ability to estimate the probability of loss and to justify that loss in terms of everyday living. Since good judgment is so vital to adventure programming safety, you should evaluate your judgment on a continual basis (see "Questions to Think About" in chapter 10). As you evaluate yourself, you should also consider the open and honest critiques of colleagues. Although the method may be threatening to you, your judgment can be greatly improved by small groups of leaders gathering to truthfully discuss their close calls, near misses, epic journeys, and embarrassing mistakes, without fear of retribution from adventure program administrators.

SAFETY COUNTERMEASURES

Despite a thorough danger analysis and attention to factors that inhibit your judgment, accidents can and do happen! In the event of such an accident, a sequence of countermeasures may prove useful to you as you attempt to minimize the impact of the accident. We can divide safe countermeasures to accidents into three categories, based on the timeliness of their application: proactive or primary, active or secondary, and reactive or tertiary.

Proactive or primary safety procedures refer to carrying out all practices before a program to avoid an accident or at least to prepare a suitable response to one. Examples of preventative or proactive measures include equipment inspection, safety briefing, skills training of staff, completion of legal paperwork, review of potential environmental and human dangers, and close inspection of client health forms.

Active or secondary procedures refer to all actions taken during the program, usually as a result of an accident. Examples of responsive or active measures include first aid, search and rescue, evacuation, on-site recording of injury data, and response procedures.

Reactive or tertiary refers to all actions that occur after an accident. Examples of follow-up or reactive measures include informing next of kin and the sponsoring organization, final accident documentation, making contact with legal counsel or insurance representatives, and scheduled visits to the injured client at home or in the hospital.

Program Safety

Safety policies should be developed by adventure programs with specific guidelines to suit their particular situations. Such policies may contain a philosophy statement, program goals, learning objectives, the methods to evaluate behavioral outcomes, and an explanation of how these all relate to safety (Priest & Dixon, 1990).

Safety policies and guidelines should be written in a staff manual. The guidelines should apply to both staff and clients alike, or if reason exists for different safety policies, these should be noted.

In turn, as an outdoor leader, you need to be familiar with the safety guidelines in the staff manual. Then you should help clients to understand that they are responsible for contributing to their safety as well as the safety of others taking part in the activities. Make sure clients understand that due to the nature of adventure activities, everyone has a role to play in maintaining safety through awareness and a responsible attitude. Such an attitude includes being cautious about safety concerns and working to develop the ability to ask questions when in doubt. Awareness includes looking out for one another's best interests and the presence of human or environmental dangers. Sharing the concepts of accident theory (see figure 7.1 on page 89) can go a long way toward empowering clients in their own responsibility for safety.

For adventure programs involving field trips or expeditions (any travel away from the usual residential site), the additional elements of a **risk management plan** often need to be completed. This plan can contain, but may not necessarily be limited to, educational rationale for the activity, specific details on the activity times and places, emergency contact phone numbers, a proposed itinerary with anticipated dangers and expected countermeasures, a route map with escape plans, a summary of health information for all group members, a budget of expenses, and a list of supplies or equipment (Priest & Dixon, 1990). Staff members should take copies of the plan along on the trip as well as leave copies with responsible people who will inform the authorities, and take the necessary action, in case the group is overdue. See also chapter 9, "Trip Planning," and chapter 10, "Risk Management" for further information.

The addition of a **safety committee** to develop and monitor program safety practices can be tremendously beneficial. Part of their responsibility can be to collect, analyze, interpret, and act on incident and accident data collected by staff. Such a committee is often comprised of program staff representatives, technical experts, and outside advisors. The committee's purpose is usually to regularly review and endorse the program's safety practices and to take responsibility for collecting, analyzing, interpreting, and acting on their findings.

Documentation

Paperwork is a necessary part of safety management, and you should complete appropriate forms for all accidents, incidents, field trips, and expeditions. If a client is injured on an adventure program, an **accident report form** should be completed by outdoor leaders connected with the accident. Since programs can learn from mistakes, subsequent analysis of the information collected on such forms can go a long way to prevent and reduce future accidents. The same dangers that led to incidents could also have caused accidents had some small thing been done slightly differently. Therefore, completing an **incident report form,** and analyzing the information on it, can also do much to help avoid accidents in the future.

Accident Response Procedures

In response to an accident in your group, you may wish to consider following the sequence of procedures outlined in figure 7.4. The sequence is based on eight steps of response: A = Airway, B = Breathing, C = Circulation, D = Diagnostic exam, E = Evacuation plan, F = Find resources, G = Get assistance, and H = Helicopter usage (Priest & Dixon, 1990).

The most qualified person is usually recognized as the individual in charge of the accident response situation. This person is usually the senior outdoor leader unless her expertise is required elsewhere. Response measures are generally organized and issued by this person. Given enough extra people present to respond, you should organize the group into three subgroups: a trauma team, which gives first aid and comfort and stabilizes the victim; a travel team, which is in charge of alerting and directing outside resources to assist with the injured person; and a transport team, which plans rescue and evacuation procedures as well as helps the individual in charge to monitor the well-being of rescuers.

The trauma team is generally comprised of the most competent first aid members of the group. They are responsible for (1) assessing the situation, asking "Who is injured? What are the dangers present?" (2) approaching the victim, asking "Will the person giving first aid be placed in any danger by doing so?" and (3) neutralizing any dangers present, drawing attention to, avoiding, or removing them if possible. Of course, this team is also responsible for providing first aid, such as checking and readjusting or removing

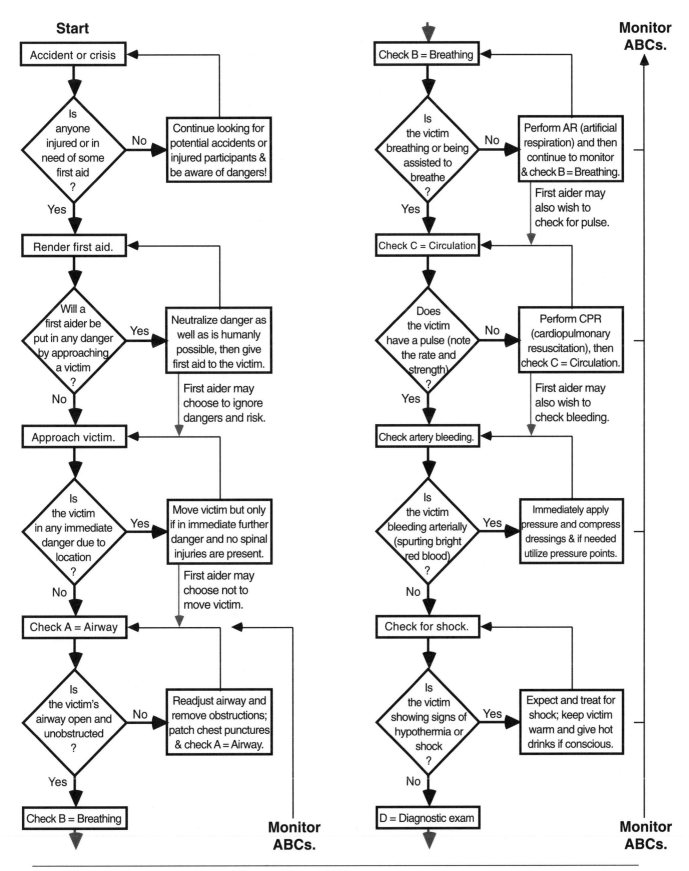

Figure 7.4 An accident-response sequence (Priest and Dixon, 1990).

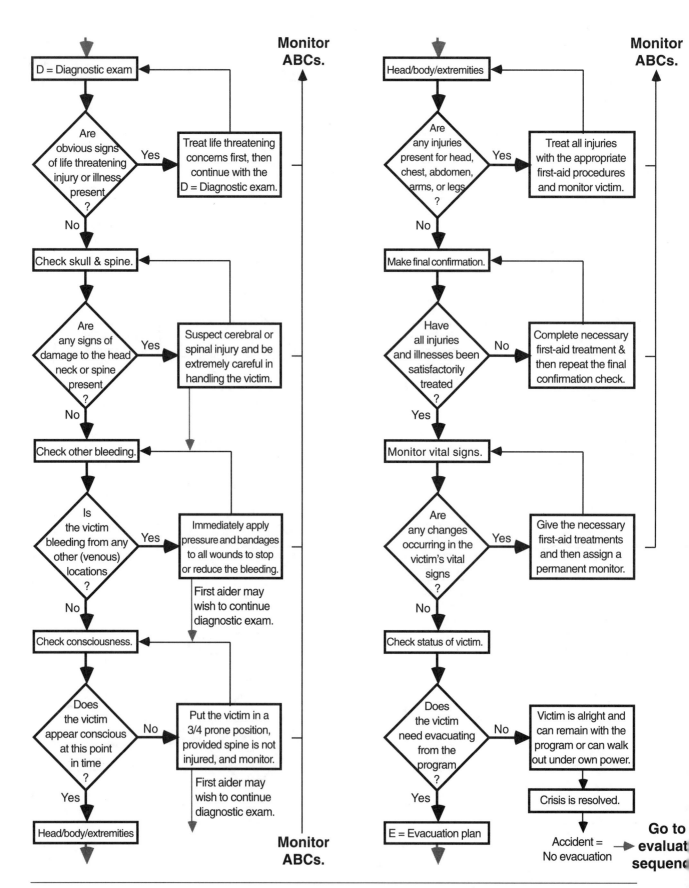

Figure 7.4 *(continued)*

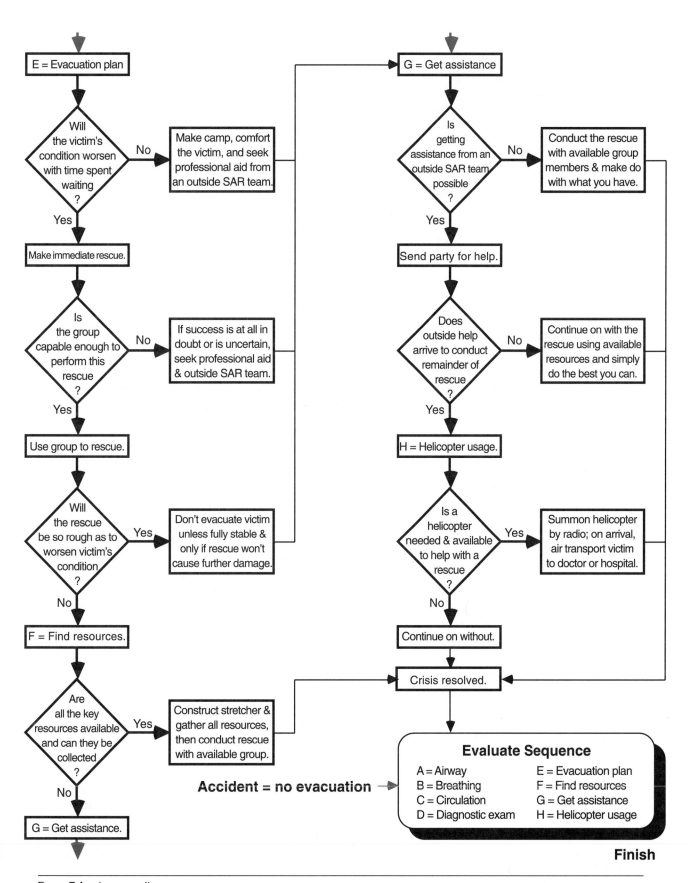

Figure 7.4 *(continued)*

obstructions and rechecking for further obstruction (A = Airway); performing artificial respiration if necessary and continuing to monitor (B = Breathing); and taking pulse and performing cardiopulmonary resuscitation (CPR) if necessary (C = Circulation). They also conduct a thorough exam (D = Diagnostic), looking for signs of consciousness, arterial bleeding, spinal damage, shock, fractures, and minor bleeding. In short, they triage and treat the victim as necessary, double-check the examinations, and continue to monitor and record vital signs until a person with a higher level of medical training arrives. Even when this occurs, trauma team members may continue working with the injured parties to ensure medical continuity.

The transport team is responsible for evacuating and transporting the victim (E = Evacuation plan). One part of the team locates and marks the evacuation route in coordination with the travel team, while the other part collects needed materials for evacuation and transport (F = Find resources). When appropriate, they are responsible for the arduous task of littering the victim to the pick up zone or out of the wilderness. This requires a great deal of effort and constant vigilance for the safety of the victim. Some members of the trauma team may double as transport team members when possible. The transport team also possesses the critical function of overseeing the safety of the entire group, ensuring that no more participants become victims. In this way, they are also the "temperature" team, responsible for continual monitoring of rescue team members' body temperatures, getting a stove lit to boil water for hypothermia, or locating a source of cool water for hyperthermia.

If outside assistance is needed, a separate travel team may be sent ahead of the transport and trauma teams. The travel team is in charge of alerting and directing outside resources to assist with the injured person, such as additional medical help, evacuation assistance, external program personnel, or police. This may include activating a cell phone, radio, location devices, signal flares or fires, or the like. If necessary, this team must summon an ambulance for evacuation from accident site (G = Get assistance) or air support for emergency medical evacuation (H = Helicopter usage). If such messages need to be sent out on foot to such resources, written directions and a copy or a summary of the accident report should accompany the party going for help. The party should consist of at least three, and preferably

four, people in case one of them gets injured along the way. The party going for help should be self-sufficient and should stay together and carry their own accident response kit. They may also be responsible for flagging the return route for the search and rescue (SAR) team and marking it on a grid-referenced map, maintaining an evacuation report, and attaching a copy of the victim's health form to the victim. This form will greatly assist the SAR team and the medical staff on arrival at a hospital. In addition, the SAR team providing the assistance will need to know the extent of the victim's injuries and the intended evacuation route. If possible, returning with the SAR team can be extremely helpful.

In the event of an obvious fatality, do not disturb the victim's body—only a coroner or appointed police officer may give permission to remove it. Accurately flag and document the accident scene, disturbing it as little as possible. If a camera is available, take photographs and measure any relevant distances, depths, or heights. Triple-check all measurements. Contact the program's director and the local authorities (in that order), sticking to facts and avoiding all speculation or admission of guilt.

Do not discuss the matter with any media, referring all inquiries to an appointed program representative. This person will deal with all public relations matters, including notification of relations and follow-up telephone calls. This representative will also deal with the hospital or the morgue, prepare a press statement (victim's name is not released until next of kin have been contacted) for the media, and screen subsequent inquiries and requests for interviews.

Safety Reviews

A **safety review** is an accepted method of checking the safety procedures of your program. Your safety committee can perform this review as a proactive measure prior to an accident or incident or as a reactive measure after an accident or incident or both. In general, its purpose is to provide a fresh perspective on safety through involving external peers who can provide truthful and critical advice in a supportive manner. In best-case scenarios, programs utilize two forms of safety review: internal review from ongoing efforts of the in-house safety committee and external review by periodic involvement of outside experts or peers. The purpose of these two forms of review are to compare the program safety performance with known state-of-the-art procedures and common practices (Wade & Fischesser, 1988).

With safety reviews, a small team of people generally observe the program in action as well as behind the scenes. During observation, they collect data concerning the safety practices and procedures of the program. From these data they infer whether the program under review is operating within safety guidelines and what changes might improve the overall level of safety, based on their experiences working with a variety of other programs. They discuss their findings with the appropriate program representative or the safety committee, providing a chance for feedback. At the end of the visit, the committee generally presents a written report, summarizing the review methods, results, and recommendations for changes.

Some of the areas a safety review committee may examine include the following: philosophy statement, program goals, learning objectives, the methods to evaluate behavioral outcomes of clients, educational rationale for the activities, communication, transportation, specific details related to the activity times and places, emergency contact phone numbers, a proposed itinerary with anticipated risks and expected countermeasures, a route map with escape plans, a summary of health information, a budget of expenses, a list of participants and their supplies and equipment, a schedule for monitoring and maintaining equipment, litigation protection, liability or accident insurance, health care procedures, accommodations, food service, procedures for screening participants, activity and site selection, staff recruitment, staff supervision, staff training, staff assessment, staff to participant ratios, and the involvement and influence of the safety committee—with particular emphasis on the collection, analysis, interpretation, and action taken regarding incident and accident data (see also figure 7.5; Priest & Dixon, 1990).

Note that programs with a long-standing history of established safety procedures and reviews may wish to pursue external recognition through such vehicles as program accreditation by a governing body or association, such as the Association for Experiential Education.

SKILL AREAS

Last, but not least, you should be skilled in appropriate safety areas for the particular adventure experiences you are providing. Examples of safety skills that may be appropriate include weather interpretation, body temperature regulation, navigation, survival, water safety skills, first aid, and search, rescue, and evacuation.

Weather Interpretation

You should be able to predict weather, based on current weather reports, perhaps obtained by radio; on your observations of present conditions, including clouds, precipitation, wind speed, wind direction, and temperature; and on your familiarity with local prevailing patterns. You should be capable of dealing with weather extremes, especially thunderstorms and the threat of lightning.

Body Temperature Regulation

You should be able to prevent and treat hypothermia and hyperthermia, including knowing the five pathways of body heat loss and their regulation, understanding human thermophysiology (areas of high heat loss and metabolic effects of food, water, drugs, alcohol, and tobacco), and recognizing the signs and symptoms of hypothermia (stumbling, incoherence, disorientation, shivering, or no shivering at all) and hyperthermia (headaches, nausea, cramps, excessive sweating, or no sweating at all). Moreover, you must be capable of providing the correct treatment for the different phases of hypothermia and hyperthermia by learning proper techniques of decreasing or increasing heat losses and of warming or cooling victims as necessary.

Navigation

You should be able to navigate in the worst possible terrain that you expect to encounter during an adventure activity. This means being able to read a map, including being able to measure distances by scale ratios and from bar scales, cite grid references, convert among map north, true north, magnetic north, or grid north directions, and interpret colors, symbols, contour lines, and other features. You should be able to use a compass, including taking map and field bearings, converting between these by accounting for local magnetic declination, traveling on that specific bearing, and triangulating locations with two or more bearings. You should be able to orienteer, including aiming-off, using attack points and steering marks, avoiding obstacles, using back bearing, and using catching features and hand-

General questions . . .

Does the program clearly state philosophy, mission, goals, and objectives in a safety policy?
Does that safety policy explain the educational rationale behind putting people at risk?
Do program guidelines apply to staff and participants alike or is there a double standard?
Are safety (risk) management plans completed for each adventure activity or field trip?
Do these plans contain the necessary safety preparations and emergency information?
Are accident response kits (including first-aid materials) present for all activities?
Are emergency communication links available between field staff and outside medical help?
Are drivers appropriately licensed to drive vehicles and transport numbers of passengers?
Are safety practices, such as seat belts and equipment checks, in place for transportation?
Is equipment tested and used properly in the program? Is a repair and maintenance log kept?
Are participants warned and informed of the risks and responsibilities prior to acceptance?
Are the preenrollment orientation materials sent to participants accurate and adequate?
Do participants complete an appropriate health and medical disclosure form and waiver or release?
Are staff competent in dealing with participants' typical and emergency health care issues?
Is there a policy statement concerning the use and abuse of alcohol and other drugs?
Are participants screened for health concerns or do they take a preenrollment medical exam?
Are activities or sites chosen for potential to meet program goals and educational objectives?
Are participants properly briefed and progressively prepared for each activity or site?
Are participants coerced or forced into a particular activity or are they challenged by choice?
Does the program conform to local resource regulations and correctly apply for use permits?
Do on-site and local facilities adhere to the public laws governing their proper operation?
Does the program have a safety committee? Does it monitor and sanction safety practices?
Are accident and incident data reported, compiled, analyzed, and acted on accordingly?
Do job contracts include procedures for training and assessing staff? Are these followed?
Do acceptable staff-participant ratios exist for all adventure activities and sites?
Do staff have the necessary combination of hard, soft, and metaskills required for their jobs?
Are staff competent at the adventure activities they run and familiar with the sites they use?
Do staff anticipate dangers and are they capable of responding to accidents while in the field?
Are staff appropriately qualified or certified in first aid and CPR? Is such evidence on file?
Are written procedures in place to handle the most commonly expected emergency accidents?

Before the review . . .

Establish guidelines for conduct of the review: who, what, where, when, why, and how much?
Appoint a representative liaison between program or safety committee and safety review team.
Select mutually acceptable team members, avoiding controversial or political appointments.
Examine existing paperwork, including brochures, reports, reviews, forms, manuals, lists, and logs.
Inform staff of pending interviews and encourage open and honest sharing of concerns.

During the review . . .

At the introduction, discuss particular areas of safety concern and attempt to ease anxieties.
Maintain professional, diplomatic, and tactful behavior throughout the safety review.
Explain the review to participants who ask; avoid public criticisms that may be overheard.
The review content may be patterned after items on this list or other items may be included.
The team may wish to divide responsibilities for observing, interviewing, reading, and so on.

After the review . . .

Orally present findings in private to key program personnel, including safety committee.
Make sure statements about safety practices or observed behaviors are factual, not opinionated.
Exchange new ideas for improving safety through two-way communication with feedback.
Balance negatives with positives; permit personnel the chance to explain any disagreements.
Submit a written report giving requirements, recommendations, suggestions, and observations.

Figure 7.5   Questions to ask for a safety review.

rails. You should be able to route-find, including noting checkpoints along the path of travel, contouring between points of similar elevation without losing altitude, and choosing routes of travel, based on expected terrain, vegetation, party strength, or other variables.

Survival

You should be able to cope under the worst possible conditions in the event that you are lost, injured, or caught out in the elements during an adventure activity—with or without your group. You need to have a positive survival attitude, including being able to admit you're lost, to keep from panicking, to comfort others, and to prioritize needs: protection from the elements, finding sustenance, and being found. You should be able to light fires with wet wood or insufficient fuel supply; to build shelters that are easily constructed, insulated, and ventilated; to signal for help, including using international distress and ground to air signals; and to secure nonpoisonous food and water in various settings. Remember the food rule: if unsure, don't consume!

Lifesaving and First Aid

You should be able to swim and provide CPR and first aid. This is one area that certification is welcomed and accepted by most adventure programs. You may wish to obtain your certifications in lifeguarding and as a wilderness first aider or emergency medical technician (EMT). For whitewater activities, we recommend that you seek appropriate training in moving water safety and rescue techniques. Knowledge of how to properly use a full-accident response kit, including a first-aid kit is critical for every outdoor leader.

Search, Rescue, and Evacuation

You should be able to locate missing people and remove them from danger. You should be capable of designating a safe base camp; interviewing people to obtain pertinent information, and recording their comments; performing quick or hasty searches of high-probability areas such as nearby trails, rivers, or meadows; performing coarse or fine-line searches, side-by-side walking through a square grid; constructing stretchers appropriate for the method of carrying, lowering, or raising; and lastly, you must be able to recognize when the search is beyond your resources and decide to seek a professional SAR team.

EFFECTIVE OUTDOOR LEADERS SHOULD

☞ Understand the principle concepts of accident theory and danger classification.

☞ Be able to execute the 10-step danger analysis procedure and to avoid the six inhibiting factors that may interfere with the procedure.

☞ Be able to execute an accident-response procedure, including completion of the appropriate documentation.

☞ Be able to establish preventative measures, such as trip planning, safety policies, review committee, and program accreditation.

☞ Be skilled in the safety areas of weather interpretation, temperature regulation, navigation, survival, swimming and lifesaving, first aid, search, rescue, and evacuation, and, if insufficiently skilled in any of these areas, seek out appropriate training.

SUMMARY

Safety management is aimed at client protection and is a collection of procedures designed to reduce accidents that might cause injury or other loss. Most accidents occur when human and environmental dangers combine and interact at the same moment to create an accident potential, or the probability of risk. This is the likelihood that an accident will happen, not the certainty that one will occur. The more dangers present, however, generally the greater the risk of an accident. We can classify dangers as perils or hazards. Perils are the sources of loss, and hazards are the conditions that accentuate the chance of a loss. When you must encounter perils, you should seek to do so when hazards are low and therefore the least influential.

A 10-step danger analysis procedure may help you reduce the risk of an accident or to minimize the accident's impact. First, admit it can happen to you! Second, continually seek to identify dangers. Third, draw attention to identified dangers. Fourth, remove the dangers. Fifth, avoid the dangers. Sixth, encounter dangers in a controlled manner if you cannot remove or avoid them. Seventh, assess the risk of an accident from combining dangers. Eighth, estimate the probability of loss resulting from an accident. Ninth, justify that the outcome of the potential accident will be acceptable and recoverable. Tenth, proceed with caution! Six factors that can inhibit these ten steps include new or unexpected situations, inappropriate attribution, relaxed concentration, smelling the barn, risky shift phenomenon, and poor or unsound judgment.

If an accident occurs within a group, follow a sequence of eight response steps: A = Airway, B = Breathing, C = Circulation, D = Diagnostic exam, E = Evacuation plan, F = Find resources, G = Get assistance, and H = Helicopter usage. The group, with the most senior level outdoor leader in charge when appropriate, breaks into three teams: trauma, travel, and transport and temperature teams.

If and when things do go wrong, you should have proactive, active, and reactive safety countermeasures in place, ready to use. Filling out paperwork can be part of these countermeasures, possibly including accident report forms, incident report forms, and safety management plans. A safety policy helps guide adventure programs in their management of safety and dangers. A safety committee monitors and sanctions the safety practices according to the organization's policy, and collects, analyzes, interprets and acts on incident and accident data collected on the forms. The committee also plays a role in conducting internal and external safety reviews for the purpose of comparing program safety procedures with state-of-the-art or common practices.

QUESTIONS TO THINK ABOUT

1. List all the "lemons" (i.e., dangers) in the introductory vignette.

2. Explain the overlapping circles diagram of accident potential (figure 7.1) and the difference between the two types of dangers, hazards and perils.

3. Apply the danger analysis procedure to a real outdoor activity, describing its strengths and weaknesses in regard to your performance in that activity.

4. Relate a time when an inhibiting factor has interfered with your analysis of danger.

5. Differentiate among the three forms of countermeasures: primary, secondary, and tertiary.

6. Use the accident response procedures (A through H) to respond in a simulated accident exercise and discuss their effectiveness in bringing about a successful resolution. Identify the roles of the three subgroups in the accident response procedure, noting how their roles may vary, depending on various conditions and geographical area.

7. Plan your next trip, completing the necessary safety management plan documentation.

8. Review an adventure program using the questions listed in figure 7.5.

9. As an outdoor leader, assess yourself in all of the safety skills, detailing how you intend to improve on any shortcomings in each skill.

REFERENCES

Hale, A. (1983). *Safety management for outdoor program leaders*. Unpublished manuscript.

Meyer, D. (1979). The management of risk. *The Journal of Experiential Education* 2(2), 9-14.

Priest, S., & Baillie, R. (1987). Justifying the risk to others: The real razor's edge. *Journal of Experiential Education* 10(1), 16-22.

Priest, S., & Dixon, T. (1990). *Safety practices in adventure programming*. Boulder, CO: Association for Experiential Education.

Raffan, J. (1984). Images for crisis management. *The Journal of Experiential Education* 7(3), 6-10.

chapter

8

Environmental Skills

The group marched single file across the meadow to reach the moss-covered high ground. On arrival, they pitched their tents close together in the small area beside the lake and began digging ground trenches to drain expected rainwater away from the tent sides and into the nearby marsh. Once camp was established, the leader designated tasks to the group: collecting rocks for the campfire ring, cutting trees with a hatchet for firewood, and digging a meter-deep hole with a shovel to serve as a group latrine. That night, the group burned their garbage in a large bonfire and what they couldn't burn, they buried in the latrine along with their leftover evening meal. The dishes were cleaned in the lake!

While such misuses and abuses of the natural environment have occurred since the beginning of humankind, the consequences of such actions have only recently reached catastrophic proportions, particularly in areas that are the most sensitive to human intrusion, such as wilderness areas. One of the main reasons for this calamity is the large increase in the world's population combined with the exponential growth of human use of wilderness areas. In summarizing the growth trend in outdoor adventure pursuits, Ewert (1989) pointed to some of the following factors in the United States alone:

- The number of cross-country skiers rose from 2,000 in 1964 to 500,000 in 1974.
- Nearly 30 million participants enjoyed the activities of backpacking, canoeing, Nordic skiing, mountain and rock climbing, and board sailing in 1986.
- Of the top 10 fastest growing forms of outdoor recreation in 1985, half were outdoor adventure pursuits, including board sailing, board surfing, mountain and rock climbing, horseback riding, and sailing.

Probably one of the best indicators of the growth in adventure activities is the measure of retail sales of outdoor gear. In 1996, the sales of outdoor adventure specialty gear was projected to total nearly $10 billion, reflecting a strong record of stable growth over the past 10 years. Experts predict continued growth in the future (Outdoor Retailer 1997 Media Kit, 1996).

Given the enormous number of people who seek adventure in the outdoors, you and your groups can no longer afford to travel and camp in ways that cause such a high level of damage to the environment. With anticipated future increases in these already enormous numbers, such damage to the environment will inevitably destroy the very beauty that produces enjoyment of the outdoors. Since every action in the outdoors has some small impact, it is becoming even more imperative for all of us to find ways to "leave not a trace" or at least to minimize these impacts when traveling through, camping in, or adventuring in the outdoors. Besides guiding participants in adventure settings, the teaching of minimum-impact techniques to groups is even more essential so clients will be indoctrinated into similar belief systems and behaviors when they return to outdoor settings independently.

Probably one of the strongest evolutions toward protecting outdoor areas has been the establishment of the Leave No Trace (LNT) organization in North America. The mission of this organization is to "educate wildland user groups, federal agencies, and the public about minimum-impact camping" (Leave No Trace, 1996). The LNT organization publishes the following pamphlets addressing specific environmental areas and conditions: *North America, Rocky Mountains, Southeastern States, Backcountry Horse Use, Western River Corridors, Temperate Coastal Zones, Desert & Canyon Country, Pacific Northwest, Rock Climbing, Alaska Tundra*, and *Northeast Mountains*. The LNT's guidelines encompass six principles adapted for use in varying environmental areas and conditions: (1) plan ahead and prepare, (2) camp and travel on durable surfaces, (3) pack it in, pack it out, (4) properly dispose of what you can't pack out, (5) leave what you find, and (6) minimize use and impact of fires (Leave No Trace, 1996). We encourage you to contact this organization for guidelines addressing specific environmental areas and conditions.

As with chapter 6, "Technical Skills," and chapter 7, "Safety Skills," our purpose for writing this chapter is not to provide detailed "how to" procedures for every environmental skill area in adventure programming; you should get these specifics from other sources, such as the LNT. What we will provide in this chapter, however, are some of the general guidelines you should follow to implement minimum-impact procedures and protocols during outdoor travel. We have divided these general guidelines into several categories: planning, hiking and travel, and camping and campsite behavior. Please note, however, that these competencies will change according to geographic areas and environmental conditions. What will be appropriate in one type of area may not be called for in another environmental setting.

But before we get into specifics, let's consider a philosophy that should override all other guidelines: "A thing (an act in the outdoor environment) is right when it tends to preserve the integrity, stability, and beauty of the biotic community. It is wrong when it tends to do otherwise" (Leopold, 1966, p. 222). The principles of Leopold's "land ethic" should serve as the foundation for your program's environmental policies and procedures, complete with written lists of acceptable and unacceptable behaviors in the environments you commonly use for adventures. These policies should extend beyond the treatment of environments by also addressing the various cultures, whether native, urban, rural, or wilderness, that your groups may interact with during your adventures. Specifically, these policies might dictate the way participants interact with and respect others, dress, and act, for example, honoring native traditions, wearing local clothes, leaving farm gates as found, and remaining quiet in the wild.

PLANNING FOR AN ENVIRONMENTALLY APPROPRIATE EXPERIENCE

Outdoor leaders have always known that proper planning before they enter an outdoor environment with a group serves as one of the key elements in leading a safe and successful trip. The same holds true in setting up an environmentally sound trip. For example, forgetting a stove may necessitate lighting a wood fire; leaving the tent poles at home may require the cutting of vegetation for a replacement.

The Leave No Trace organization lists several aspects to consider when preparing an environmentally sound outdoor experience (Leave No Trace, 1996):

1. Know the area and what to expect, including knowledge of the area for safety and educational purposes and how "populated" your wilderness experience will be to try to prevent overuse problems. Other ideas include (a) working with local experts, such as park service employees, land owners, and regional outdoor enthusiasts, to learn about the sensitivity and popularity of the area you intend to travel through; (b) obtaining appropriate permits or permissions prior to the trip; (c) planning to camp in appropriate places; (d) considering whether you need to travel off-trail or not, and, if you do travel off-trail, following practices that minimize your impact on the land; and (e) planning to travel in areas that handle hiking and camping abuse better than others, such as using dry trails instead of wet and muddy ones, and remembering that low altitude zones are quite often less sensitive than alpine zones; forested or sandy areas handle groups better than certain meadows or other areas of fragile vegetation.

2. Stick to an appropriate group size because large groups—those greater than 10—can have a greater impact than smaller ones.

3. Select appropriate equipment. Certain equipment, such as lightweight stoves, freestanding tents, and collapsible water carriers, can be extremely helpful in creating less of an impact on the environment than the alternatives of building fires, making shelters from natural materials, and needing to camp right next to a water source. Buying program equipment of earth tone colors can reduce visual impact on the environment.

4. Repackage food before leaving for the outdoors to greatly reduce the likelihood of litter, broken glass, and "surprise openings and spillage" in clients' packs. Several examples include removing food from cardboard boxes and placing in reusable ziplock bags, emptying contents from glass containers and placing into reusable plastic containers, etc.

HIKING AND TRAVELING WITH MINIMAL IMPACT

The axiom "Leave nothing but footprints; take nothing but photographs; kill nothing but time" is an excellent guide for traveling in outdoor environments. But it may not be enough. Even footprints can be damaging. Hard-soled footwear, whether boots, shoes, or sandals, can tear the fragile surface of a meadow and accelerate erosion on hillsides. Reduce the effects of human intrusion on specific areas, for example, by avoiding trampling vegetation when moving off-trail, by traveling as a dispersed group rather than a mass, and by hiking on surfaces that are durable or highly resistant to human impact.

Other principles advanced by the LNT organization (1996) include the following: (1) Stay on the trails, for example, don't short-cut switchbacks or walk on planks or rocks in muddy places, (2) in alpine and subalpine areas, walk on trail or exposed rock, (3) when taking rest breaks, do so on durable surfaces, such as exposed rock or bare ground, and (4) if going off trail is necessary, keep your group small (less than six), walk only on durable surfaces, spreading out if appropriate for the site to diminish trampling and to prevent creating new trails, and avoid fragile areas, such as alpine areas and marshes.

CAMPING AND CAMPSITE BEHAVIOR

Nowhere is the potential for environmental impact greater than at a campsite. When a group is situated in the same area for a prolonged period of time, their inadvertent or careless misuse of resources can bring about irreparable damage. You and your group should be able to camp in outdoor environments, leaving only minimal traces of your visit. Furthermore, you should all be prepared to teach no-trace camping to others.

Many factors enter into the process of campsite selection: flat and dry ground, shelter from the elements, lack of insects, proximity to drinking water, ground cover, and the absence of danger. In environmental terms, the most important decision is whether to use an existing campsite or establish a new one. Ultimately this choice forces you to use some judgment about the an-

ticipated impact of the group and its size. Large groups may do better to use existing campsites, while a small one may be able to make less overall impact at a new site.

Although your decisions will vary depending on conditions, as a general guideline use established sites to reduce impact. If such sites do not exist, some helpful guidelines are to stay at least 50 meters from creeks and rivers and trails and at least 100 meters from ponds or lakes. Note that in some regions, guidelines may be as great as one-third kilometer or one-quarter mile away from water sources, trails, or private property. Also consider how the layout of a campsite might influence the creation of new trails between tents and toilet areas and how the cooking area may be repeatedly downtrodden by people hanging around and shuffling their feet to keep warm while waiting for meals. Think about "rotating" areas of congestion so wear and tear is dispersed; this may mean moving sites if appropriate.

Pitch tents on sand, duff, or mineral soil, avoiding vegetated areas. When erecting a tent or other shelter, do not dig drain channels around the base of the tent or shelter as this can leave permanent scars. Instead, pitch tents on elevated sites to eliminate the need for trenching. Don't sweep away vegetation or organic materials to get to the ground; set up the tent on top of these natural cushions.

When breaking camp, make sure that you completely remove any string tied to vegetation for supporting the tent. Fill in tent stake holes, replace any rocks or logs that you moved, and scatter a little ground duff or cover over any compacted areas. The LNT organization also recommends brushing out footprints or matted grass with a stick (Leave No Trace, 1996). Perform a final site check to locate any lost equipment or leftover litter, then bag trash and carry it out.

Waste Disposal

The LNT organization suggests four guidelines for disposing of fecal matter: avoid polluting water sources, eliminate contact with insects and animals, maximize decomposition, and minimize the chances of social impacts (Leave No Trace, 1996). The technique most often recommended for the disposal of human wastes (fecal matter, liquid foods, or dish washing water) is to use individual "cat holes." Dig a small pit about six inches into the humus and bacteria-rich layer of topsoil. Then, normally, you should bury fecal matter in the top few inches of the humus layer of soil where bacterial action can speed the degradation processes. Leaving fecal matter on the surface of hot and dry or cold and wet ground in remote areas sometimes aids a faster breakdown than burying it. Locate cat holes at least 100 meters from any water or trail, remembering that this distance may be greater in some circumstances. Consider using natural alternatives for toilet paper, such as snow or appropriate stones and sticks. If toilet paper and feminine hygiene products are used, ensure that they are carried out in doubled plastic bags. For certain activities or places, special practices will supersede those we have outlined. For example, carry out all human wastes when spelunking in caves.

Cat holes are not necessary for urination. While posing little threat to human health, the odor of urine can be unpleasant, and the salts in urine can cause animals to dig up the ground. Leave No Trace generally recommends urinating on rocky or sandy areas away from camp and water sources (Leave No Trace, 1996).

Fire Building

Before building a fire, ask yourself if it is needed. Stoves can provide for all of the needs of people traveling in the outdoors.

If, however, you want a fire for cooking or need one for survival, use an existing fire pit or carry a fire pan, a large tin can with holes in it. You should only use "dead and down" wood as fuel. Don't break off or cut the branches of living green trees. Cover all traces of past fires by dispersing cold, white ashes to the wind, burying black charcoal, scattering leaves, and duffing over any scars. Be safe by not building the fire near any combustible items, such as tree roots, logs, or tents, and by keeping a large supply of water on hand to extinguish any runaway flames. If building the fire in a pristine area without any previous scars, then avoid leaving any trace by making a platform or "mound" fire on bare flat rock with a deep layer of sand and gravel spread over the exposed rock to prevent charcoal staining. Leave No Trace (1996) generally recommends using these fire structures over pit fires. Of course, clean up mound fires as you would any others.

Washing and Cooking

Use of soap to wash hands, bodies, or dishes is rarely necessary. Sand is an effective scouring substitute. If soap is absolutely necessary, use it sparingly since high concentrations of soap left on dishes can cause diarrhea. Pick a so-called "biodegradable" soap with a low phosphate content. Lather first and then rinse well away from water, over deep mineral soil. Soaping, brushing teeth, or washing clothes should take place 100 meters away from water or camp, the same as using the toilet. Dig a dump hole only for the disposal of dish washing water or other liquids but not solid foods—you should carry these out.

Cook and handle food well downwind from camp as bears or other local animals will likely be attracted by the aroma and securely store food in strong animal-proof containers hung high among the trees. If possible, reuse leftover food in the next meals. Don't bury it in the ground as animals may dig the food up and eat it. Pack and carry all that you packed and carried in! Don't burn or bury litter and leftover food. Use stoves, ensuring that you pack an ample fuel supply, instead of open fires, which consume wood. In many areas, this fuel supply is diminishing, and its use can interfere with important biological or degradation processes that are integral parts of the local ecosystem.

Nonintrusive Behaviors

Since people seek solitude almost as often as they seek nature, social impacts are also important while adventuring in the outdoors. Consider the visual impact of brightly colored equipment and clothing in the outdoors. Except in emergencies and hunting seasons, avoid neon colors; instead, attempt to use more subtle earth tones. Unless it is to avoid a potential accident, don't flag trails with brightly colored surveyor's tape. Noise as well as bright colors can "pollute" others' experiences. Select campsites so as not to interfere with the view and privacy of other campers.

EFFECTIVE OUTDOOR LEADERS SHOULD

☞ Understand that every action has the potential to impact the natural environment and so take the necessary precautions to protect that environment when traveling or camping outdoors with a group.

☞ Teach these low-impact techniques to their groups with a purist approach so that if the groups water down the techniques, they will likely apply enough techniques that the impact will be appropriately low.

SUMMARY

Minimum-impact travel involves avoiding or reducing the damage caused by humans moving through an environment. For the most part, this means carrying out litter, solid food waste, and sanitary products as well as burying fecal matter, liquid foods, and dish washing water. You should also keep in mind the social impacts of noise, visibility, and privacy. Your program should be respectful of the environment and its indigenous populations.

No-trace camping involves avoiding or reducing the damage caused by periodically stopping in an environment. Give special consideration to using existing campsites or carefully creating new ones. Remember to set up camp well away from water. Locate toilet, cooking, and washing areas well away from camp and water. Avoid fires but if one is necessary, avoid inappropriate fuel consumption, fire spreading, and charcoal scarring. Finally, erect tents without disturbing vegetation or ground cover.

QUESTIONS TO THINK ABOUT

1. Identify all the environmental impacts present in the introductory vignette.
2. Comment on the minimum-impact travel techniques used on the last trip you took as a participant.
3. Detail the no-trace camping techniques you will use on the next trip you take as a participant.
4. As an outdoor leader, how will you teach group members to use these techniques?

REFERENCES

Ewert, A. (1989). *Outdoor adventure pursuits: Foundations, models, and theories*. Worthington, OH: Publishing Horizons, Inc.

Leave No Trace. (1996). PO Box 997, Boulder, CO 80306. Phone: 303-442-8222, Fax: 303-444-3284.

Leopold, A. (1966). *Sand County almanac, with other essays from Round River*. New York: Oxford University Press.

Outdoor Retailer 1997 Media Kit. (1996). Outdoor Retailer, One Penn Plaza, 10th Floor, New York, NY 10119-1198. Phone: 800-950-1314, Fax: 212-279-4453.

chapter

9

Trip Planning

As an extremely competent outdoor leader, Anthony preferred to rely on his judgment and experience to organize expeditions. He was a master of logistics, but when his group arrived at the first campsite, the tent poles were nowhere to be found. Luckily, the weather was mild and he was able to improvise poles from nearby deadwood. In retrospect, he remembered that the tent bodies and flys were stored separately from the poles in his equipment room, and he resolved to change this procedure on return. He also realized that trying to juggle all those trip logistical tasks in his memory had led to one dropped and forgotten item. He asked himself "What else would go wrong?"

R elying on experience alone was an error in this case. Reserve judgment based on experience (see chapter 20) for times of uncertainty and improvisation, such as when deciding how to replace lost equipment. In situations for which the tasks are common and repetitive, such as trip organization, use checklists to reduce mistakes, reducing the chances that you'll leave anything important behind.

We have written this chapter like such a checklist, and we encourage you to customize the list by adding your own local operating procedures or by changing the order of items. We'll also discuss planning and keeping organized during the trip—while traveling and at camp—as well as after the trip. So let's get packing!

BEFORE THE TRIP

Generally, when planning a trip, you should consider 14 items in the following order: rationale, activities, locations, routing and scheduling, participants, groups, staffing, equipment, food and water, accommodations, transportation, communication, budgeting, and safety and risk management. Then, triple-check each aspect for any errors or omissions.

1. Rationale

The first item to consider for any trip is the reason or rationale for going. A trip should usually be a response to meeting the clients' specific needs for recreation, education, development, or therapy through adventure (see chapter 2). Next, identify and write down the purposes, goals, and objectives for the trip. You should base all trip planning that follows on these.

2. Activities

You should choose activities for their ability to meet client goals and learning objectives as long as they fit the trip rationale, and not because you and the rest of the staff enjoy doing them! Be certain that the activities you choose are consistent with the clients' readiness within an overall program, taking into account several factors, including emotional maturity, physical skill levels, social development, and cognitive abilities. Pick activities that are risky enough to provide an adventurous learning experience and engaging enough to challenge participants, but appropriate for reducing the actual risks encountered. Activities should fit within a progression of learning through which subsequent experiences build on previous ones. Sequence activities so that their difficulty, complexity, required preparation, and prerequisites increase over time. Consider how well these activities foster independence from you, rather than dependence on you. Have extra activities in mind as backups in case drastic changes in the weather prevent the trip from going as planned. Be prepared to change activities if safety is a concern.

✓ *Check*: Does the chosen activity match the needs as established by the trip rationale? If not, modify the activity and then recheck its compatibility before continuing.

3. Locations

You should choose locations for their ability to meet program goals and learning objectives, and not because you enjoy visiting those specific sites for your own fun. Review locations that may be conducive to the selected activities. Obtain information from maps, aerial and satellite photos, guidebooks, club newsletters, and other appropriate sources. Areas should feature scenery, terrain, vegetation, weather, risks, routes, and campsites that compliment the needs of the trip. Compare and contrast the suitability and practicality of each area by considering the (a) time and distance needed to travel there, (b) time and distance to obtain emergency services, (c) ease and cost of obtaining permission to visit the area, (d) user regulations, (e) capacity of the local environment to handle size and type of group, and (f) possible crowding or conflicts with other user groups.

Select the best location and conduct a site reconnaissance, or pre-site investigation. This "recon" visit benefits you during the trip by decreasing the chance of getting lost, increasing the quality of decisions, enhancing the success of accident response, and improving the learning of participants from you and your coleaders' intimate knowledge of the best teaching sites. When using recon information to plan a route or schedule times, remember that leaders generally move faster than participants and that available daylight and weather variations may exist in other seasons. After you have confirmed the choice of location, secure the necessary permits and permissions to park, enter, travel, and stay overnight in the area. Be prepared to change locations if safety becomes a concern, having potential backup plans in place.

✔ *Check:* Does the location you chose match the needs as established by the trip rationale? Is it compatible with the selected activities? If not, modify the activity or location and then recheck compatibilities before continuing.

4. Routing and Scheduling

Map out a route connecting places of interest, such as teaching sites, camps, and viewpoints. In doing so, consider the route length, daily distances, available campsites, access and egress points, escape routes, including for inclement weather, injurious accident, or getting lost, order of site usage, and best direction to travel. Build in contingencies, such as rest days, long breaks, obstacle delays, shortcuts, and side trips. For example, with a canoe circuit, you can drop several extra loops from the route if the group is delayed or add some in if the group is ahead of schedule.

Determine the duration of the trip, then select from available dates. Prepare a flexible itinerary. Often, it is helpful to work backward from the expected time of return. Calculate times for travel on all routes, including driving time to and from the trip area. Consider the influence that the following will have on travel speed: distance, terrain, elevation change, route width and linearity, route conditions, vegetation cover, weather, temperature, season, time of day, available daylight, group size, pack weights, and participant fitness or competence. Although the group may not stick to the route or the schedule, this plan can serve as a guideline for adjusting the plan, since performance during early days often dictates changes in expectations in later days.

✔ *Check:* Do the route you chose and the schedule you set match the needs as established by the trip rationale? Are they compatible with the activities and location? If not, modify the routing, scheduling, activities, or location and then recheck their compatibilities before continuing.

5. Participants

Since the overriding concern in any adventure program should be based on the needs of the participant, you should check that they are sufficiently prepared for the activities, locations, routing, and scheduling. Do not accept participants unless they meet the appropriate criteria, carefully considering, for example, those who may be forced into the trip by a program eager to fill vacancies.

Consider whether these prerequisites may provide appropriate criteria for participant acceptance: the completion of prior courses or tests, such as a swim test before canoeing; emotional and social maturity, such as compatibility with others or attitude toward the environment; health and fitness, including strength, flexibility, balance, agility, coordination, and cardiovascular endurance; and competence, including aspects such as ability, skill, experience, and confidence. If appropriate, arrange for pretrip training and informational sessions, possibly in similar settings to eliminate any weaknesses in technical, safety, or environmental skills. Consider several other concerns in planning: number of people, for example, plan for a range and expect a few to add or drop; gender and ages, recognizing that legal restrictions may apply; interests, striving to correlate with levels of motivation and energy; and special needs, disabilities, or medications.

Ensure that participants are well informed prior to the trip. Provide written information well in advance and offer an orientation meeting when appropriate; for example, you may wish to invite the parents or guardians of child participants. On the written information, include program philosophy, trip details, and any prerequisites or preparations that prospective participants should complete. In orientation meetings, introduce leaders and other participants. Explain the trip activities, nature, reason, and purpose. Address potential fears by openly discussing safety procedures and possible risks. As other trip details become available, pass these on to participants by mail, phone, fax, e-mail, or through another meeting.

Distribute, complete, and collect important paperwork, such as legal or medical forms. If appropriate, recommend additional personal accident or medical insurance for those who need it. Screen participants' health histories, having those with questionable health, such as cardiac concerns, undergo an appropriate medical exam or seek physician's permission prior to their involvement. Pay close attention to participants who appear to be at-risk for a heart attack, such as those who have a personal or family history of attacks, have high blood pressure, are over 40, are obese, smoke, or are sedentary, and if in doubt, consider preventing their participation.

Designate and inform participants of a responsible contact person who will act as an intermediate between the group and their friends and family. If the group is overdue, they can let the contact know about their delay, and concerned family and friends can phone the contact to get the latest news.

✔ *Check:* Do the participants match the needs as established by the trip rationale? Are they compatible with the routing, scheduling, activities, and location? If not, modify the appropriate trip components and then recheck their compatibilities before continuing.

6. Groups

Form the participants into groups. Pick group size to maximize learning opportunities, optimize relationships among members, and minimize environmental impact. Typical group sizes may range from 6 to 16, averaging about 10 or 12. Bigger groups are generally more difficult to supervise or manage, allowing some members to hide in the crowd. Smaller groups generally have

fewer group interactions to generate valuable dynamics. Size may also be restricted to as low as four to six people per group in some heavily used areas to protect nature. A minimum size of four makes sense in case of an injury. While a first person stays with the injured second person, the third and fourth can go for help. Sending two people for help is good in case one gets injured on the way out.

Once groups have been formed, outline the ground rules and regulations, overview the routing and scheduling, detail probable dangers and safety procedures, discuss possible environmental impacts, distribute food and equipment lists, and assign roles or duties for the trip. Plan for plenty of time for the formation of the group (see chapter 5) and appropriate facilitation of experiences.

✔ *Check:* Do the groups match the needs as established by the trip rationale? Are they compatible with the participants, routing, scheduling, activities, and location? If not, modify the appropriate trip components and then recheck their compatibilities before continuing.

7. Staffing

Select staff and be certain they work well together under all expected conditions, including adverse ones. Maintain an acceptable leader to participant ratio. This ratio will vary according to the level of risk expected on the trip, the level of competence found in the group, and the purpose of the outing. To start with, a minimum of two leaders per group is a good guideline. This permits you to "bracket" the group with one of you "scouting" at the front and the other "sweeping" up the rear. In an accident, if the victim is a leader, another leader remains to take control and respond as needed.

Designate leaders and assistant leaders for each group, then clarify their roles to prevent conflict that can polarize or split the group. As a leader, you must see the bigger picture and take overall responsibility. Assistants should attend to smaller details and fill in the missing pieces. You generally oversee the tough decisions, while assistants often serve as a valuable sounding board for ideas. For example, you should typically oversee emergency situations, while assistants may act as messengers, monitor the victim, supervise the remaining group, or accompany the victim during evacuation. If leadership is to be shared, agree on roles and responsibilities well in advance of the trip. The staff members must communicate effectively during the adventure as well.

✓ *Check:* Do the staff match the needs as established by the trip rationale? Are they compatible with the groups, participants, routing, scheduling, activities, and location? If not, modify the appropriate trip components and then recheck their compatibilities before continuing.

8. Equipment

Prepare three equipment and clothing lists: individual, group, and safety. On the individual list, include not only items to bring but also those *not* to bring, such as watches, hair dryers, loud radios, drugs, and alcohol. Check to ensure that participants have the right gear, especially clothing and other appropriate "essentials" for each person. Have them bring in their own equipment for inspection and to determine proper fit. Explain the layering concept to participants, then check that they have adequate layers (wicking, insulating, and protecting) for both average and worst conditions.

Obtain and inspect group and safety equipment. Decide what pieces of equipment you and your coleaders will carry. Remember to carry extra food and spare clothing for emergencies. Divide the remaining gear equitably among group members by considering their relative levels of fitness and available pack space as well as the weight and volume of the equipment. People may wish to weigh their packs to ensure that they will be carrying less than a third of their body weight. Obtain specialized equipment, such as that needed for canoeing or mountaineering, then teach participants during the pretrip training sessions how to use such equipment properly. Keep abreast of innovations in outdoor equipment in order to better inform participants of what works and what does not.

✓ *Check:* Do the equipment lists match the needs as established by the trip rationale? Are they compatible with the staff, groups, participants, routing, scheduling, activities, and location? If not, modify the appropriate trip components and then recheck their compatibilities before continuing.

9. Food and Water

Count the total number of meals and categorize them as either breakfasts, lunches, dinners, or snacks. Prepare a menu for each meal in each category. Consider the nutrition, taste, palatability, perishability, cooking ease, and cleanup effort for all meals. Keep in mind the number of stoves and the amount of fuel required to prepare the meals. Recognize that melting snow, cooking at higher altitudes, or boiling without a pot lid will all require more time and fuel to accomplish.

For each meal, calculate the amount of food needed to feed the total number of participants in each group. Combine these menu contents into a single shopping list. Purchase this food and then repackage it for minimum waste of food and packaging (e.g., removing food from cardboard boxes and placing in reusable ziplock bags, emptying contents from glass containers and placing into reusable plastic containers, etc.). Label and distribute food equitably among group members. Try to keep a single meal's contents together with the same person. If the total volume or weight are extreme, consider arranging a food drop or cache at one or more points during the trip.

Decide on water purification preferences. Boiling will require extra fuel and will take extra time to purify. Chemical treatments involve a form of iodine tablets or crystals, and some people do not like the taste. Filtering may demand a system that correctly deals with both bacterial and viral components, and good systems are often expensive and occasionally troublesome. Carry sufficient water at all times—extra for arid areas.

✓ *Check:* Do the food and water provisions match the needs as established by the trip rationale? Are they compatible with the equipment, staff, groups, participants, routing, scheduling, activities, and location? If not, modify the appropriate trip components and then recheck their compatibilities before continuing.

10. Accommodations

Accommodations can range from hotels, such as on the road to and from the trip location, to huts and shelters in more popular and less wild areas, to campsites, which are the norm for most backcountry outings. Some of these facilities may require advance reservations and can often involve a cost for their use. Book and pay for obligatory accommodations in advance.

✓ *Check:* Do the accommodation arrangements match the needs as established by the trip rationale? Are they compatible with the food, equipment, staff, groups, participants, routing, scheduling, activities, and location? If not, modify the appropriate trip components and then recheck their compatibilities before continuing.

11. Transportation

Remember that traveling to and from the trip site is usually the most dangerous aspect of any outing. Therefore, focus on safety for all transportation issues. Arrange for transport vehicles, taking into account insurance requirements, shuttling services, and parking arrangements. Keep a photocopied record of all driver licenses and any rental agreements. Have staff take some form of a defensive driving class.

Ensure that drivers have the correct license for the vehicle driven and the number of occupants. Be certain they are experienced at driving and backing up this type of vehicle and any trailer that may be attached. Give them a map, directions, and a list of meeting places, making sure these places have phones to reach the contact person if a delay occurs. Remind them of the rules of the road (e.g., seat belts, speed limits, frequent rest stops) and what to do in case of a traffic accident. Decide whether several vehicles will travel independently, catching up at meeting places, or together in convoy fashion.

Do not operate vehicles with more people and equipment than their designed capacity, which you can determine by the number of seat belts in the vehicle and manufacturer's carrying capacity information. Have an appropriate safety-belt rule, such as passengers must wear a seat belt while the vehicle is in motion. Mandate conditions in which passengers do not distract the operator of the vehicle while it is in motion. Consider headlight use when vehicles are being used for transportation during the daytime as well as nighttime. Have guidelines for staff to consider during diminished driving conditions; for example, if visibility is limited to less than 100 yards, the driver pulls the vehicle over to the first safe spot, turns on the four-way flashers, and waits until visibility increases. Rotate staff driving time to reduce driver fatigue; for example, do not allow anyone to operate a vehicle for more than five hours at a time or for more than three hours if the operator has been performing vigorous activity for more than eight hours that same day.

Check that all vehicles contain the correct safety equipment, such as first aid kit, repair tools, fire extinguishers, chains, flares, reflectors, and spare tires, and that attachments, such as roof racks, hitches, trailers, lashings, and equipment, are safely secured. Make sure staff know how to appropriately use this gear, such as how to change a tire in an appropriate manner. Stow any gear carried inside the vehicle safely so as to avoid creating projectiles in a crash situation. Conduct a pretrip vehicle check, checking tire pressure, lights, fluids, brakes, belts, cables, hoses, and gauges, and discuss loading, unloading, and onboard rules and safety with participants and staff. Count heads before leaving any meeting place.

Unload and load the vehicle in an orderly fashion. Have appropriate protocols for loading, such as allowing only two people to load or unload the roof rack at any one time. Unload vehicles on the side of the road only in the event of an emergency; instead, try to unload or load the vehicle in parking lots or on appropriate side roads.

When parking vehicles, remove all valuables, leave nothing in view, and place the vehicle out of the way of other vehicles. Decide whether to hide keys nearby or take them along. A spare set of keys permits both options. When shuttling, attempt to leave at least one vehicle at each end of the trip so that a group retreat, for instance, due to weather or accident, places a vehicle at your disposal.

✓ *Check:* Does the transportation match the needs as established by the trip rationale? Is it compatible with the accommodations, food, equipment, staff, groups, participants, routing, scheduling, activities, and location? If not, modify the appropriate trip components and then recheck compatibilities before continuing.

12. Communication

In the event of a serious accident, establishing communication with outside medical expertise is critical. In this case, communication can range from citizen-band walkie talkies or radios with dedicated frequencies, to cellular phones, to sending people out to get help. When other forms of communications fail, the latter is an excellent fallback option. Unless the group is very small, try not to send only one person for help in case that person is injured while alone.

Communications may also be useful for getting up-to-date information about weather or fire dangers, for breaking a large group into several smaller subgroups, and for changing outside arrangements, such as pick-up times and places. In choosing a form of communication, consider cost, including monthly rental and annual licensing fees; maintenance, including replacing parts or recharging batteries; limitations, such as line of sight versus repeating stations; function, including the possibilities of loose connections or freezing up in cold weather; and care, such as battery life or moisture encroachment. Above all ask "Are the batteries charged?"

Note that easy access to the outside world can severely reduce the "wilderness state-of-mind" common to many outdoor adventures. Having ready contact can also encourage groups to overextend themselves, confident that these communications will help them. You may wish to consider not announcing the possession of communications as well as having communications "fail" once in a while!

✓ *Check*: Do communications match the needs as established by the trip rationale? Are they compatible with the transportation, accommodations, food, equipment, staff, groups, participants, routing, scheduling, activities, and location? If not, modify the appropriate trip components and then recheck compatibilities before continuing.

13. Budgeting

Budget for vehicle costs, including rental, gasoline, oil, tolls, extra mileage, shuttle drivers, parking; food per person per day; equipment, including purchase, rental, and repair; permits, including camping and user fees; staff costs, including salaries, benefits, and personal expenses; and miscellaneous, such as advertising, facility rental, maps, telephone, and faxes. Balance these expenses against any income expected from the participants. Since the number of participants can also fluctuate, build in an appropriate buffer of costs to account for that extra person who might necessitate renting a more spacious vehicle or hiring an extra leader. Always plan on having enough spare cash to pay for expenses during the trip and carry a credit card for unexpected emergencies.

✓ *Check:* Do the budget arrangements match the needs as established by the trip rationale? Are they compatible with the communication, transportation, accommodations, food, equipment, staff, groups, participants, routing, scheduling, activities, and location? If not, modify the appropriate trip components and then recheck compatibilities before continuing.

14. Safety and Risk Management

Complete a safety and risk management plan for every trip, possibly including (a) a brief educational rationale; (b) specific details on the activity times and places, proposed itinerary with anticipated dangers and expected countermeasures, a route map with escape plans, and emergency contact phone numbers, including police, hospital, and rescue; (c) summary of participant qualifications, health information, and completed emergency contact and next of kin forms for staff as well as participants; (d) signed legal forms; (e) a budget of expenses; (f) locations of nearest phones, medical facility, and important emergency agencies and their phone numbers, including search and rescue services and the nearest park service office; (g) appropriate information, systems, and forms in place for staff when they need them, such as search and rescue procedures, missing person report forms, crisis and fatality response forms and guidelines, and accident incident response forms and guidelines; (h) blood-borne pathogens handling procedures; (i) alcohol and drug policies; (j) media and information dispersal information; and (k) individual, group, and safety lists of clothing and equipment. Obtain the necessary approval from the supervising organization and double-check insurance coverage for all aspects of the trip.

Leave copies of the plan with the designated contact person who will inform the authorities, respond to inquiries from participants' families and friends, and take the necessary action if the group is overdue or in trouble. Give a copy of the plan to each leader on the trip as well.

✓ *Check:* Do the safety and risk management plans match the needs as established by the trip rationale? Are all 11 pieces (a through k) of information included in the risk management plan? Are they compatible with the budget, communication, transportation, accommodations, food, equipment, staff, groups, participants, routing, scheduling, activities, and location? If not, modify the appropriate trip components and then recheck compatibilities before continuing.

Triple-Check

Immediately before departure, get the latest weather forecast or tidal charts and check the local conditions for icy roads, muddy trails, river flow rates, snow depth, and the like. Encourage participants to telephone one another in case they have overslept their alarms. Let them determine their own car pool arrangements in order to reach the initial meeting place.

✓ *Double- and triple-check*: Check all 14 steps forward and then again backward. Is everything compatible? Make the final decision to *go* or alter, adapt, abandon, or abort the trip! Last, establish and continually refine criteria to determine if the plan needs changing in midstream. Stay flexible!

DURING THE TRIP

While on the trip, you hold responsibility for the safety of your groups and for balancing this safety against the group's inevitable impact on nature and against the learning that comes from encountering risks. Therefore, you should attend to these concerns in order of priority: safety, nature, learning, enjoyment, and completing the trip as planned.

Completing the trip by sticking to a route or a time schedule is one of the major causes of fatal accidents. You must be prepared to alter, adapt, abandon, or abort a trip, according to your judgment. Participants having fun and enjoying themselves is an added bonus on any trip, but not if it is at the expense of learning, nature, or safety!

As a reminder for what was planned before the trip began, when it comes to learning, you must ensure the receptivity, recognition, response, and reflection of participants (Priest, 1988). To create learning opportunities, set behavioral learning objectives that are within the reach of each participant. Preparing ahead of time, including holding pretrip sessions on terminology and basic concepts, may be appropriate. Keep activities exciting and enjoyable to motivate. Keep participants well fed and watered and at stable body temperatures. When clients aren't cold, hungry, hot, or thirsty, they are receptive to learning. Keep an eye on group development issues and how they are influencing group and individual behavior.

Reflection is a key component in a client's ongoing learning progress. Build in plenty of time for reflective debriefing discussions and implement some other forms of reflection, such as writing in a journal, discussing in pairs or trios, drawing, painting, acting out dramatic skits, composing poetry, telling stories, dancing, or soloing (self-introspection).

When it comes to nature, you must protect the environment. This means clearly communicating appropriate behaviors, such as expecting participants to respect private property, to not litter, to stay on trails, to avoid taking shortcuts on switchbacks, and to travel quietly so that others might see wildlife. Consider the area's carrying capacity by using stoves instead of fires, avoiding the creation of new campsites, burying sanitary wastes in the top soil layer, sharing the resource with others, leaving no trace, and cleaning up the mess left by less considerate users.

When it comes to safety, you must ensure the health of participants. This means continual monitoring of weather, terrain, route finding, participants' locations, body temperatures, and morale and energy levels. Make sure everyone knows where the accident response kit (ARK) is kept. Conduct ongoing danger assessment and accident analysis. Brief participants as to impending dangers. Examine dangers by, for example, scouting rapids, digging avalanche pits, or crossing a river first before participants encounter them. Immediately stop any unsafe actions, such as horseplay. Anticipate unsafe actions at the start of most activities when an initial explanation may not have been clear to some people.

Traveling

Frequently count heads while traveling on trails, over open water, down rivers, into caves, or across mountain slopes. Prior to beginning activities, discuss with participants what to do for emergencies, such as if they're injured or lost, and conduct appropriate stretching or warm-up sessions to prevent injuries and reduce the potential for fatigue. As people begin to exercise they can get warmer, so plan an early stop to adjust clothing and to maintain a comfortable body temperature. Before beginning, know and share with clients how the route is marked, for example, tree blazes, paint spots, metal signs, or rock cairns, and what special markings might be used to indicate junctions or changes in direction.

Review the first leg while participants follow along on their own individual maps. Remind them what to do if they become lost or separated from the group. Use a buddy system when appropriate, such as pairing weak participants with strong, and encourage participants to keep tabs on their buddies while traveling along the route. Instruct participants to leave their packs or some other item on the route in plain view if they leave the route for any reason, such as photography or sanitation needs. Discuss sanitation procedures. Model desirable behaviors, such as picking up litter and not taking shortcuts.

Pace the group by traveling at an appropriate speed, which should be equal to that of its slowest member. Develop a group consciousness about how to accommodate varying speeds of group members, for example, by placing slow people near the front, fast people at the back, and redistributing carried loads. Travel single file, unless route conditions permit different group configurations. Keep the group between a designated scout (first group member) and sweep (last member), using appropriate ways to communicate if a stop is needed; for example, have scout and sweep stay close enough to see each other or call one another by whistle or voice.

Take regular rest stops to recover breath, adjust clothing, eat and drink, gather group together, discuss previous leg, plan for next leg, or view scenery. At rest stops, as the last tired people arrive and take off their packs, allow clients time to rest and do not immediately strike out on the next leg of the journey until new arrivals are rested. Perform a site check of the area, counting people, looking for dropped gear, or rechecking for litter before leaving.

Break large groups into smaller ones, maintaining reasonable spacing and contact between subgroups. Assign a scout and sweep to each subgroup and give separate equipment to each subgroup when appropriate, such as first aid kit, spare rope, or radio. Stagger subgroups through obstacles and dangers, such as rapids, avalanche slopes, and river crossings, so that they may assist one another.

Stop at trail intersections or places of possible confusion. Count heads before continuing. When appropriate, such as in a well-known area with a competent group, leave one person at each intersection to wait for the next person. On arrival, that next person takes a turn at waiting while the other person continues. You and your coleaders can then move throughout the line, taking different positions in the group, alternating scout, sweep, and observer roles. Each position has its pros and cons.

Scout from the front when route-finding is difficult, when you expect dangers ahead, or when a "runaway" group needs holding back. A front position, however, can cause the group to become too dependent on you, lose track of where they

are, or be unaware of existing dangers. They may also lose motivation if a scouting leader exerts too much control.

Sweep from the rear when the group is spread out, when tired or straggling members need extra motivation and encouragement, or when others might benefit from navigating at the front. A rear position, however, can cause the group to become too independent of you, allowing them to get far ahead of the group or even get lost or into other trouble. They may be frustrated by too little control from a sweeping leader.

From in the front or at the rear, you may have difficulty seeing what is going on in the group. If this is a concern, observe from the middle when noting group interactions, such as cliques or conflicts, when checking on participant health, such as fatigue or temperature, or when encountering difficult obstacles, such as avalanche slopes or river crossings. This position allows you to move freely and unobtrusively through the group as well as to be relatively close to everyone in the event of an accident. As an observer, you can also stop at any obstacle and assist or advise participants as they pass it. When in the middle, be careful not to let a group spread out too far ahead or too far behind.

At the Camp

Select a campsite on the basis of appropriate criteria, such as

- environmental appropriateness, following the Leave No Trace organization's guidelines (see chapter 8);
- flatness, remembering that a slight incline may be desirable;
- safety, avoiding avalanche zones or nearby hanging dead branches;
- drainage, not digging any trenches;
- surface, not damaging vegetation or moving soil;
- lack of insects, keeping in mind that a breeze can discourage them;
- proximity to water, not coming so close as to pollute it;
- protection, using trees for rain or wind breaks;
- shade or sunshine, noting the direction of sunrise and sunset;
- aesthetics or scenic views; and

- proximity to other groups whose presence may detract from the group's need for solitude and privacy.

Double-check that tents are correctly situated and erected so as to properly shelter participants from exposure to the elements.

Identify dangerous areas to avoid. Designate procedures and places for food storage, cooking, eating, disposal, or sanitary concerns. Encourage people to use a flashlight as night falls. Manage gear by keeping the campsite tidy and well-organized, especially before going to bed. Keep in mind that disorganized equipment can be lost if covered by overnight snow. If possible, hang extra food between two trees well above ground to avoid animal inquiry and avoid taking food into the tent when in bear country. Clean up on departure and pack out all trash.

In Difficult Conditions

Effective leaders normally keep an eye on their "back" routes by frequently looking behind them to where the group has been. This is often done in case the forward passage is blocked and retracing steps becomes necessary. In selecting routes, consider the dangers of traveling in dry canyons prone to flash flooding, river valleys with obligatory crossings, mountain ridges with cliff bands and lightning hazards, snow slopes with avalanches or slips potential, glaciers with serac or crevasse movement, and scree slopes with rock fall or a high chance of twisted ankles.

If traveling at night, carry emergency bright lighting, wear eye protection for unseen sharp branches, wear reflective clothing if helpful, and plan for diminished vision. In reduced visibility, such as under fog or in a snowstorm, familiar terrain can quickly become unfamiliar and supervising or controlling a group can be extremely difficult. For appropriate circumstances, consider roping the group together to prevent anyone from getting separated from the group. On poorly indicated routes as in reduced visibility and when marking is sparse, let a route-finder go out on a rope, looking for the next marker, while the group waits at the last known marker. If the next marker is found, the group can follow the rope and leave the safety of the last marker. You should have the group repeat this slow process until this very difficult situation changes for the better.

BACK HOME AND OTHER PLANNING TASKS

Evaluation is valuable, and you should plan for it in advance, rather than leaving it to the last minute. Provide opportunities for participants and coleaders alike to give you written and verbal feedback. Prepare a written report from the evaluations comprised of a summary of what took place, being especially sure to note deviations from the original safety and risk management plan, and any recommendations for changes next time. Complete any additional paperwork, such as accident and incident reports.

Wash, dry, and return equipment after the trip. Appropriately dispose of leftover food and equipment. Return vehicles. Balance budget and submit receipts or remaining moneys. Last, plan a reunion, perhaps a potluck dinner with video or slide show, or a follow-up meeting.

For this checklist, we have purposefully omitted those aspects of programming that are not necessarily a leader's responsibility. For example, the jobs of advertising or marketing the trip and the financial or fund-raising tasks typically fall to program administrators. Hiring staff, budgeting, and using computers are roles for both administrators, programmers, and leaders. But such program management topics are the subject for another book. Although operating an adventure program is a requirement of managers rather than leaders, you may still wish to learn the responsibilities that lie beyond trip planning.

EFFECTIVE OUTDOOR LEADERS SHOULD

☞ Be familiar with trip planning procedures. These procedures typically include the areas of rationale, activities, locations, routing and scheduling, participants, groups, staffing, equipment, food and water, accommodation, transportation, communication, budgeting, and safety and risk management.

☞ Be able to write risk management plans, covering the following:

1. A brief educational rationale
2. Specific details on the activity times and places, proposed itinerary with anticipated dangers and expected countermeasures, a

route map with escape plans, and emergency contact phone numbers (e.g., police, hospital, rescue)

3. A summary of participant qualifications, health information, and emergency contact or next of kin forms, completed for both staff as well as participants

4. Signed legal forms

5. A budget of expenses

6. Knowledge of the location of nearest phones, medical facility, and important emergency agencies and their phone numbers (e.g., search and rescue services, nearest park service office)

7. Appropriate information, systems, and forms in place for staff when they need them (e.g., search and rescue procedures, missing person report forms, crisis and fatality response forms and guidelines, accident incident response forms and guidelines)

8. Blood-borne pathogens handling procedures

9. Alcohol and drug policies

10. Media and information dispersal information

11. Individual, group, and safety lists of clothing and equipment

☞ Be well practiced in these procedures so that trip planning flows smoothly and the trip proceeds safely.

SUMMARY

At times when tasks are rare and occasional, you should expect to call on your judgment. But for cases in which tasks are common and frequently repeated, such as trip planning, checklists are an invaluable tool. A trip checklist covers the trip rationale, activities, locations, routing and scheduling, participants, groups, staffing, equipment, food and water, accommodation, transportation, communication, budgeting, safety and risk management. Triple-check every aspect of preparation before the trip. But don't stop there! You have further responsibilities during the trip, including safety, nature, learning, enjoyment, and completion in that order; while traveling on the route, including pace, control, rest stops, and leader position in the line; at the camp, including site selection and organization; in difficult conditions; and after the trip is over, including evaluation and clean up.

QUESTIONS TO THINK ABOUT

1. What are the guiding principles of trip planning?

2. What are the key contents of a safety and risk management plan?

3. Under what circumstances would you change the leader's priority list of responsibility for safety, nature, learning, enjoyment, and completion to some other configuration?

4. What is the best position for you to take in the line of a traveling group and why?

5. What will you do differently in your trip planning after having studied this chapter?

6. Plan a trip from start to finish. Present your trip design to the class, then have them critique it, stressing the positive aspects and areas you may want to improve.

REFERENCE

Priest, S. (1988). The Ladder of Environmental Learning. *Journal of Adventure Education and Outdoor Leadership*, 5(2), 23-25.

chapter

10

Risk Management

A client is on the final pitch of a rock climb of a major peak. The outing is recreational and is led by a certified mountain guide. The client has been correctly instructed in the techniques necessary for the type of climb being done and has completed and signed the usual medical and legal paperwork. After several failed attempts at the overhang crux on this pitch with each failure requiring the guide to lower the client for a brief rest, the client fails once more, but somehow the rope becomes undone from the client's harness. Death results from a long, unprotected fall, and the client's widowed spouse sues the guide, the recreational company, and the harness manufacturer. The lawsuit is settled out of court.

As an outdoor leader, what legal responsibility do you have to prevent accidents such as this one? What more can you do to protect yourself and your adventure program from being sued? In this chapter, we'll examine both your role as an outdoor leader in managing the risks and the role of legal liability in conducting adventure programming.

RISK IS ESSENTIAL

The activities run by adventure programs involve risk and danger, but so does everything else in life! The presence of danger gives rise to risk, and risk is one of the critical components that makes adventure programming popular and successful. State-of-the-art safety procedures are used to reduce the real dangers, yet keep desired perceived risks high. Therefore, **balancing risks and safety** is a central paradox for outdoor leaders: too much risk and the danger of the experience becomes unreasonable; too much safety and adventure program fails to remain adventurous.

The general public considers adventure activities to be dangerous even when appropriate procedures are used, typically because they have difficulty differentiating between real and perceived risk. Yet, research has repeatedly shown that adventure activities are significantly safer than most other traditional physical activities. For example, a 20-year safety study conducted by Project Adventure (Furlong, Jillings, LaRhette, &

Ryan, 1995, p. 5) reported an injury rate of 4.33 per million hours of exposure to Project Adventure activities, which consisted primarily of initiatives and challenge course experiences. This report also showed that participating in a Project Adventure program had injury rates comparable to the fields of real estate, insurance, and finance (which experience a rate of 4.5 accidents per million hours of activity) and lower rates than educational services (8 accidents per million hours) or amusement and recreational services (19 accidents per million hours). The U.S. National Safety Council currently reports that traditional physical education classes experience an accident rate of nearly twice that of Project Adventure activities (9.6 accidents per million hours; Project Adventure, 1987). Higgins (1981) found that Outward Bound courses had a lower ratio of disabling injuries (37.5 accidents per million hours) than either automobile driving or college football (more than 60 accidents per million hours). Meyer (1979) also reported fewer deaths due to outdoor adventures than automobile accidents. Based on these comparisons, adventure experiences are actually less risky than traditional life activities as well as the average person's perceptions.

Even with these statistics and claims, however, as outdoor leaders, we still have difficulty convincing the public and defending the job of deliberately placing people at risk. Thus, you need a clear understanding of the benefits of risk tak-

---

Disclaimer: In this chapter, we'll look at legal systems and insurance schemes in relation to outdoor leadership and adventure programming. But please do *not* take the concepts we discuss as legal advice. Laws vary for different countries, states, and provinces. Program staff should consult a lawyer and other appropriate personnel for advice.

ing in order to determine whether these benefits outweigh the risks. In the unlikely event of an accident, a court of law may come to the same conclusion with the aid of expert witnesses with professional experience or knowledge. A jury, however, without such understanding may make its decision based on misguided, yet common beliefs, which are often developed by the publicity that infrequent, but spectacular, outdoor accidents generate. Such incorrect perceptions in other industries are also common; for example, the general public becomes fearful of flying after a few air crashes—despite the fact that many more people regularly die in home or traffic accidents!

Given that risk taking is an essential element of adventure programming, you must find ways to sensibly manage these risks, instead of trying to prevent them. Of course, one way to protect participants in adventure programs is to follow the safety management practices we discussed in chapter 7. In this chapter, however, we'll go beyond basic safety measures to discuss the concept of risk management. **Risk management** includes those policies, practices, and procedures used by your program to appropriately address potential personal injury and financial losses, protecting your adventure organization from the economic cost of being sued and reducing your organization's financial obligation if a suit is successful. As identified by van der Smissen (1990), the specific objectives of a **risk management plan** are "(a) preventing damage or destruction to property, (b) reducing or preventing possible injury or suffering to individuals, (c) instituting loss-reduction and prevention programs, and (d) shifting through transfer mechanisms those losses which cannot be controlled by other means" (23, p. 3).

After identifying and estimating the extent of risks in adventure programs, van der Smissen (1990, 23.231-23.234, pp. 9-12) states that there are generally four approaches you and your colleagues can take to control risks:

1. **Elimination**—either through **avoidance**, which is identifying the elements of the risk prior to a situation and determining the organization is unable for financial or other reasons to meet the standard of care to conduct the activity appropriately, or **discontinuance**, which is no longer offering a program element because it is too great a risk. If you cannot conduct an activity with the best professional practices,

it should be eliminated from your activity offerings

2. **Transfer**—moving financial risks to another individual or organization, for example, by shifting the costs of major liability claims to a third-party insurance carrier or by contracting for services with a program that can meet the standard of care to conduct the activity appropriately

3. **Retention**—assuming and handling financial losses internally, usually by paying losses from a reserve fund designed for this purpose or "small losses," particularly property losses, can be built into the budget

4. **Reduction**—operating as safely as possible, attempting to decrease accidents as the core of risk management, generally done in conjunction with one or more of the other three approaches to controlling risk

Note that for all risks identified for an activity, the risk management plan should set forth strategies for **both** a financial approach (transfer and retention) and a programmatic or operations approach (reduction).

LEGAL LIABILITY

Liability refers to the degree of legal responsibility or obligation that people or programs have for repairing damages (often by paying money) for injuries to participants. Typically, adventure programs deal primarily with four kinds of liability: contractual, criminal, human rights, and tort. Of these four, **tort liability** is the most common concern of outdoor leaders and falls within the domain of civil wrong, or injury. The field of tort liability is composed of three categories: intentional acts to harm, unintentional acts that harm, and strict liability or liability without proof of fault (van der Smissen, 1990, 1.41, p. 47). Most often the area of unintentional acts that harm (i.e., negligence) will be of concern to you and your outdoor program.

FOUR CONDITIONS OF NEGLIGENCE

Negligence is an "unintentional breach of legal duty causing damage reasonably foreseeable without which breach the damage would not have occurred" (van der Smissen, 1990, 1.42, p. 65). Four main elements comprise negligence, all of which must be established or proven in order for a person to be guilty of negligence and for the injured to receive restitution. These four elements are: (1) a duty to provide a safe environment, not exposing the client to an unreasonable risk of injury, (2) an act which breaches the duty, a failure to perform to the appropriate standard of care, (3) the substandard act was the cause of the injury, and (4) damage or injury did in fact occur (van der Smissen, 1990).

While all four conditions must be established for negligence to be present, the element of primary contention is generally the act (#2 above), which usually revolves around the question "Did the outdoor leader provide the appropriate standard of care?"

STANDARD OF CARE: BEING REASONABLE AND PRUDENT

In outdoor leadership, courts measure the **standard of care** as that of a reasonable and prudent professional. Two points are important to stress. First, whether or not you are a "professional," the court will hold you to the standard of care of what a professional would do in the adventure experience. This is because you are holding yourself out to your clients to know how to conduct adventure experiences. "The standard of care would be measured by the moral qualities, judgment, knowledge, experience, perception of risk, and skill that a person in the capacity of a professional would have" (van der Smissen, 1990, 2.22, p. 43). Second, the court will hold you to and judge you by the quality of being "reasonable." As explained by van der Smissen, "What is reasonable is situational. Reasonableness is usually determined by three situational elements— the activity, the environment conditions, and the participants" (2.22, p. 44).

That is, the standard will vary with the type and kind of activity. For example, a greater degree of expertise is required for whitewater boating, since it is generally viewed as more risky or dangerous than flatwater boating. Understanding the environmental conditions is essential to providing the appropriate standard of care; for example, was the weather properly considered so participants weren't exposed to cold winds

that might result in hypothermia? The standard will also vary depending upon the client population; for example, was the instructor knowledgeable about, and take into account, the particular needs of adjudicated youth, persons with disabilities, individuals on medication, etc.? This is especially true with children, since minors are viewed as requiring a greater degree of supervision, since they are typically viewed as being less cautious and less mature than adults.

The standard of care for these situational elements will be determined from the opinions of one or more practicing outdoor leaders (expert witnesses) as to desirable professional practices, from standards set forth by professional organizations or specialized organizations, and possibly from publications that describe established safety practices in adventure programming.

PROCEDURES TO PREVENT LAWSUITS

As a defendant, aside from the bad publicity of injuring clients and the cost of time and money to defend yourself (even if innocent!), you're sure to suffer a great deal of anguish at the thought of being found negligent. While one cannot prevent all lawsuits in this litigious society, outdoor leaders and adventure programs can reduce the likelihood of being sued, ameliorate the impact when sued, and proactively decrease the chances of successfully being sued. Two such methods are **safety procedures** and **legal procedures**. With safety procedures, those programs with up-to-date and appropriate safety procedures will incur fewer and less severe accidents to start with. This, in turn, will decrease the chance of being sued. This is one reason we have highlighted many such procedures throughout this book (see chapters 6, 7, and 9).

When it comes to legal procedures, you can also reduce the likelihood of your program being sued and also enhance your success in court if sued. Probably the initial "line of defense" is to combine warning and informing with appropriate forms. Specifically, verbally **warn and inform** clients of the risks and responsibilities associated with participating in the adventure program. Be certain they are clear as to what they will be getting into. Make sure you discuss that there may be an accident in the program, that accidents do occur, that you cannot totally guarantee safety, and that they (the clients) also must assume elements of responsibility for their own safety and for the safety of others. Mention examples of the kinds of activities and settings they will be engaged in, paying particular attention to the probable distance from medical aid. Verbally list some of the potential dangers associated with adventure programs and some of the key safety procedures they will be expected to perform. Emphasize that accidents are always possible. Describe a wide spectrum of possible accidents from minor bruises through moderate hypothermia to fatalities.

Completing Written Forms

As important as it is to verbally inform clients of risks, having the participants read and sign a form that alerts them to dangers is equally as important. Written forms range from ones that provide some assistance in case of a legal action, such as an agreement to participate form, to others that may be a contractual agreement that may bar recovery of damages or shift responsibility, such as waiver and release forms with indemnification clauses. Some of these forms state that if clients are injured by an act of ordinary negligence by outdoor leaders they will not hold the leader/program liable, which is known as an **exculpatory agreement**. Van der Smissen (1990) described eight types of written documents that can be used in regard to liability. The first four types of forms are based in tort law and the last four forms are contract law.

1. No document—by participating, if a client understands the nature of the activity, assuming inherent risks found in the activity is implied

2. Agreement to participate, which formalizes the fact that clients are agreeing to participate and assuming inherent risks of the activity

3. Informed consent, used only with adults, which states that they were informed about the nature of the activity or experience and expected outcomes

4. Parental permission, which is a signed statement saying they agree that their child can participate; note that there is no assumption of risk by a participant

5. Covenant not to sue, used only with adults, which is a contract stating that if an injury occurs no legal actions will be brought forward

6. Waiver, used only with adults, which is an agreement that a client will not hold the provider liable for any damages if ordinary negligence is the reason for client losses

7. Release, used only with adults, is similar to a waiver, but releases you from already existing liabilities

8. Indemnification clauses, or "save harmless" clauses, used only with adults, which shifts financial responsibility of any award from damages to someone else other than the outdoor leader/program (often back to the client or parent)

Note that waivers and releases are forms of an exculpatory agreement. Some courts are upholding such contracts; however, your program should not rely solely on exculpatory clauses to protect against liability. Also note that some professionals have questioned the ethical use of such statements.

In a meeting in 1994 in Washington, DC, professionals from the recreation industry met at the Outdoor Recreation Coalition of America (ORCA) "Summit on Outdoor Recreation" to discuss issues confronting the outdoor recreation industry. One landmark working group comprised of the leading experts in legal issues created an invaluable reference called *Developing an Allocation of Risk Document* (ORCA, 1994). This document recognizes that risk is a critical and inherent part of many outdoor recreation activities; and rather than reduce such risks and destroy the very element that makes an activity adventurous, programs should inform clients of these inherent risks so they can make a choice about participating in the activity. The working group emphasized the idea that "participants may not recover from providers for injuries that result from any of the inherent risks of the particular recreational activity. In other words, the provider has no duty to protect the participant from those risks, and has no liability for injuries resulting from those inherent risks" (pp. 3-4). The working group encouraged programs to formulate an allocation of risk document with their own legal counsel, tailoring such a document to their specific needs.

When creating an allocation of risk document (note that all eight forms are considered types of allocation of risk documents), the ORCA group recommended several elements and guidelines. Obviously, such measures need to be selected by the legal counsel supporting your outdoor program, but based on the work of Priest and Dixon (1990) and van der Smissen and Cotten (1995) (note this second form is complementary to the ORCA document), we offer the following as a helpful checklist of potential—but not required—considerations. Look to see that the form includes or does each of the following:

___ Has a title that accurately describes what the form is

___ Identifies who is entering into agreement, for example, outdoor leader or program, client, parent

___ Is clear and explicit, that is, expressed in "clear and unequivocal terms"

___ Has the word "negligence" conspicuously displayed, such as in bold print or underlined, if a waiver

___ Has an easy-to-read print size

___ Adequately describes activity, clearly answering the question "What will the participants be doing?"

___ Describes location of activity, for example, wilderness, ocean, gymnasium

___ States that risk is inherent in activity

___ Warns of some risks involved, for example, "Among the risks are . . ."

___ States that risks listed are not all-inclusive, for example, "But not limited to . . ."

___ Includes "In consideration of participation . . ." in document language

___ Affirms voluntary nature of participation

___ Uses language that is broad enough to cover all programming aspects (i.e., contemplated). Examples may include phrases like: "(1) in all phases of the activity, (2) while using the equipment, (3) while on the premises, and (4) any and all claims arising from" (van der Smissen and Cotten, 1995).

___ Does not contain any fraudulent statements

___ Has exculpatory language conspicuously displayed, such as bold print in a prominent place

___ Covers unique situations, such as lack of quick access to a hospital setting

___ Outlines participant representations:

Staff has been available to explain risks more fully.

Client has no interfering medical condition.

Client can fulfill necessary physical requirements or equipment.

Presence of program staff is no guarantee of safety or lessening of risks.

Client possesses necessary medical, disability, dental, and life insurance coverage.

Client possesses prerequisite competence for difficulty of activity.

___ Appropriate disclaimers

___ Covenant not to sue, waiver, release, and indemnification language

___ Acknowledgment, acceptance, and assumption of risk statements

___ Severability clause, that is, the rest of document remains enforceable if one part does not

___ Final acknowledgment by participant, acknowledging he understands the form and voluntarily agrees to it

___ Document is signed, and possibly even initialed, in appropriate places.

___ Signature is located on form close to exculpatory language.

___ If client is minor, both child and parent or guardian signatures.

Follow this procedure when completing form:

___ Provide participants with plenty of time to read the form, ensuring that it is in the client's language (e.g., Spanish, English, appropriate vocabulary).

___ Use no coercion.

___ Ensure that your verbal language is consistent with that which is written.

___ Read document aloud to clients.

___ Verbally describe document.

___ Reinforce importance of document; for example, do not tell clients to not bother reading it.

___ Ensure forms are completed before programming begins, that is, done prior to van ride to canoeing site.

Agreement to Participate for Minors. If participants are minors, that is, younger than the age of legal consent (under the age 18 or 21 depending on the state) and legally considered children, then you should properly inform both children and parents or guardians about the activity, its risks, and expectations of the participant. You can ask parents to waive their own rights, but they cannot sign away the rights of their children, nor can minors sign (contract) away their rights, since contracts are not binding on minors. Children may sue once they reach the age of legal consent until the statute of limitations expires, which may be several years later.

Minors can, however, sign an agreement to participate, which describes the nature of the activity, the risks of participating, and the responsibilities or expectations in participating in the adventure program or a specific activity. Following such description the child should sign. Then there should be a section for the parent, which first acknowledges they have read the previous description with its risks and responsibilities, and gives permission for the child to participate. The parents or guardian also need to give permission to medically treat children if they become injured. If you want to have the parents waive their own rights or indemnify regarding injury to their child, then an exculpatory clause stating this would come last before their signature.

Health Disclosure. As long as participants are filling out legal forms, you may wish to include some medical paperwork at the same time. Use a **health disclosure form** to collect basic information, such as the participant's name, address, home and work phone numbers, gender, birth date, height, weight, age, blood type if known, first-aid certification with expiration date, social security or social insurance number, medical policy type and number, an emergency contact's name, address, home and work phone numbers, and relationship to the participant, and their doctor's (dentist's or therapist's) name, address, and phone number.

The form may include health history questions with names, descriptions, and dates, regarding disabilities, conditions, prior injuries, fears, illnesses, cardiac concerns, past surgery (local or general anesthetic), current medications with dosages, allergies to foods, drugs, insects, plants, or animals, the wearing of glasses or contact lenses and dentures, smoking behavior, swimming ability, and any other areas that might limit participation. This procedure demonstrates a reasonable and prudent attempt to find out about any problems that participants might have. While

your program cannot be held liable for critical information not disclosed, you should encourage participants to provide truthful and complete answers, guaranteeing them confidentiality, that only staff and medical personnel will have access to the information.

AFTER AN ACCIDENT

Obviously, first aid and evacuation to medical treatment are important concerns after any injury or accident. When providing these, qualified leaders have a duty of care not to worsen the injury by an incorrect response, for example, by resetting a shoulder dislocation in the field when a hospital is only one hour away. Avoid talking with the media, referring them to a program spokesperson or administrator, who should know what to say. Be careful not to admit guilt or a negligent act: it is better to say too little, rather than too much, since more will probably be known later about what truly happened. Keep accurate records, including filling out accident and evacuation report forms, and complete them as soon as possible so you can more accurately recall details. Van der Smissen (1980) highlights five aspects that you should include when completing accident report forms: (1) sequence of the activity, for example, when it occurred and what had preceded the accident in terms of activities, (2) location, such as where the accident occurred, including a diagram, and where other people were (leaders and participants), (3) what happened, including what injured client and other participants were doing, who was involved, and so on, (4) injured participant's role, including what could, should, or might have been done by the injured client to prevent or reduce the accident and cautions and instructions given to client that she may not have followed, and (5) aid procedures, including proactive, active, and reactive measures conducted to assist clients in preventing injury and reducing severity of injury (p. 30). Van der Smissen also suggests not placing opinions on the form about what was believed to be the cause of the accident or stating that your negligence was the cause. You can include oral statements or separate written statements, making recommendations for changes (p. 30).

It is important to note that some lawyers recommend submitting all such records to them as privileged attorney-client information. Thus, control over the information lies in the hands of the outdoor program and its attorney and not the newspapers.

After you have dealt with the accident, it is essential that you contact legal counsel and insurance providers. Note that making quick changes to program procedures as a result of the accident may not be in the program's best interest, as this can suggest the program was operating inappropriately during the accident (van der Smissen, 1980). Make appropriate changes—but only after an accident investigation and program safety committee meeting that takes into account all procedures. Avoid doing anything to anger the injured that may trigger a lawsuit, such as billing them for the activity. Counsel and support anyone involved in the accident. Consider visiting the injured in the hospital or at home if appropriate.

Going to Court

An injury (e.g., death, dismemberment, disability) may result in litigation partly because of the injured person's or their relative's need for fair and just compensation. It may also be due to the overwhelming number of lawyers looking for cases! If a participant decides to sue the adventure program, do not take personal offense: lawsuits are becoming a function of the litigious times we live in. If your program does have the misfortune to be sued, the leaders involved often experience a great deal of personal pain and guilt. Since the lawyer of the injured will attempt to demonstrate that the leaders were negligent, the conduct of the program and leaders will be closely examined and scrutinized in a very detailed manner. In addition to the assistance of your program's attorney, leaders could benefit from counseling support as well.

The insurance company or adventure program (if self-insured) may prefer to settle out of court. This action may save time or money and avoid the negative publicity. In fact, the matter can be settled out of court at any time during the trial proceedings.

If you do find yourself going to court, the incidents and events that will occur are going to vary, depending on the laws of the state, province, region, or country. Here, we'll offer one possible series of events to give you an informal and brief overview of what could occur. Remember, however, that the actual procedure will vary and you can do very little at this point to change the course

of actions; for better or worse, it is in the control of the legal system.

The trial proceedings begin with **pleadings**, during which the plaintiff's lawyer files a complaint outlining a claim and its foundation with the appropriate civil court. Filing the complaint results in a summons being sent to the defendants, notifying them of the claim situation and requesting a formal response. The defendant's lawyer then files an answer to the complaint, normally denying the allegations and listing defenses to the claim of negligence.

A **discovery period** follows during which several steps take place: depositions, which are testimonies of key witnesses under oath; interrogatories, which are written questions and answers exchanged between parties; inspections of health records, legal forms, damaged equipment, or other objects; and examinations, including medical evaluation of the injured. Immediately before the trial, a conference may be held between the two parties for the purpose of encouraging an out-of-court settlement or to shorten the trial by limiting the presentations of witnesses and evidence.

During the **trial,** the purpose is to determine the existence of the four factors (i.e., a duty of care exists, determining breach, causation, and injury compensation). Both parties' lawyers and the judge interview potential jury members to ascertain their capacity for fairness and objectivity.

After opening statements from both sides, **presentation of evidence** begins with the plaintiff, who holds the burden of proof. The plaintiff's lawyer establishes the facts as alleged in the earlier complaint and by calling witnesses and showing documents or other exhibits of evidence. Witnesses answer questions from the plaintiff's lawyer during direct examination and from the defendant's lawyer during cross-examination. The process is then repeated in reverse for the defendant's response to the allegations. The plaintiff's rebuttal and then the defendant's rejoinder follow. After closing statements from both sides, the judge gives instruction to the jury, and they retire to consider their verdict.

Once the jury has rendered its verdict, either party may request a judgment notwithstanding, which is an immediate reversal by the judge to a contrary verdict, a new trial if a mistake was made, or a relief from the judgment by leniency of the judge. If these requests are refused, either party may appeal the decision on the basis of procedural error or abuse of discretion to a higher court. This court will not retry the complaint, but will review the trial record for errors or abuses. This appellate court judgment is binding and may overturn, uphold, or modify the lower court decision. In the end, the plaintiff may still win an award for damages.

For another perspective of what course the legal proceedings may take in the United States, van der Smissen (1980, p. 29) offers a brief but illustrative course of events.

Reducing the Award. The damages award from a successful suit for the injured can be reduced under the concept of **comparative negligence** or fault, which all but six states in the USA have. The **contributory negligence** or contributing fault of the injured (that is, how much of the injury is the fault of the actions of the injured) is compared to the fault of the program, defendant, or provider. The injured receives only that percentage of the fault that is attributed to the program. For example, if there were a $500,000 award and the injured were 20% at fault and the program 80%, the injured would receive $400,000; or if the injured were 80% at fault and the program only 20%, the injured would receive only $100,000. However, in nearly one-half of the states in the U.S., when the injured contributes 50% or more toward one's own injury, then the injured receives nothing at all. Just like leaders, participants are expected to conduct themselves as reasonable and prudent people, and they are held accountable under the comparative fault concept if their misconduct contributes to their own injury.

People who participate in adventure programs know they are engaging in something designed to be risky. Therefore, they are expected to assume some of the responsibility for those risks and the amount of assumption will vary with age, that is, less for children and more for adults, and with information provided them, for example, less for the poorly skilled and more for the highly skilled. Thus the importance of clearly and repeatedly warning and informing participants about inherent and other risks prior to beginning any adventure activity as well as having participants complete appropriate forms.

Remember that although legal experts suggest avoiding any admission of guilt after an accident, they also suggest writing down any dmission of partial responsibility made by participants after someone is injured. While you may feel a sense of responsibility for an accident, this feeling does not always mean that you were legally liable.

Insurance

If all else fails, your program should carry two kinds of insurance: liability coverage to pay awards due to negligence and accident coverage for medical and disability costs. **Liability coverage** may be difficult or expensive to obtain; however, performing a high standard of care and following detailed risk management plans can reduce the difficulty and cost. If insurance is very expensive, programs may pool together to obtain reduced premiums. Check to see that **accident coverage** has a clause covering the extra costs of emergency evacuation, such as the expense of helicopter airtime. Be aware that all types of coverage usually have a predetermined ceiling, or limit, on the amounts of payment. In addition, your program can purchase coverage either for the general program or for one specific event.

Insurance policies are contracts established in writing that precisely describe what is covered and what is not. If an insurance policy contains an **exclusionary phrase** that limits coverage to a list of activities, locations, or clients, then make very sure that the policy list includes all the activities, locations, or clients of your adventure program. Don't assume that any policy provides blanket coverage to all program aspects, as this is rarely the case. If you are planning to work with a particular activity, location, or client that is not listed in the general insurance policy, then consider obtaining further accident and liability coverage specific to the necessary addition. Remember, "An ounce of prevention is worth a pound of cure."

EFFECTIVE OUTDOOR LEADERS SHOULD

☞ Understand the advantages and disadvantages of being seen as working in a profession that deliberately puts people at risk.

☞ Know the history of accident or injury rates as compared with other professions.

☞ Know the concepts of risk management and ways risks are controlled in the adventure profession.

☞ Understand the legal concepts behind liability and negligence.

☞ Understand the legal concepts behind standard of care and inherent risk.

☞ Know the importance of participant forms, including what is written as well as what is verbally stated to clients when they are completing the forms.

☞ Be familiar with the differences among the legal procedures necessary to protect the adventure program, such as warning and informing, signing waiver forms or agreements to participate, completing health disclosure forms, employing comparative negligence defenses, and obtaining accident and liability insurance.

☞ Know the legal differences when working with clients under the age of majority and persons of majority age and how this influences programming.

☞ Know what to do after an accident and how to write up an accident report.

☞ Comprehend their roles in the process of a legal trial.

SUMMARY

Adventure programs deliberately employ risk or challenge to bring about change. Balancing risks and safety is a central paradox for outdoor leaders: too much risk and the danger of the experience becomes unreasonable; too much safety and the adventure program fails to remain adventurous. The general public considers adventure activities to be dangerous even when you use appropriate procedures, typically because they have difficulty differentiating between real and perceived risk in these experiences. Accident statistics show that adventure experiences possess lower rates than traditional physical activities as well as lower risk than the average person's perceptions.

Safety management, or the practices used for protecting participants, is a subset of the broader term of risk management, or the procedures for protecting the adventure organization from liability. Risk management includes the policies, practices, and procedures used by a program to appropriately address potential personal injury and financial losses, protecting the adventure organization from the economic cost of being sued and reducing their financial obligation if a suit is successful. Specific objectives of a risk management plan are preventing damage or destruction to property, reducing or preventing possible injury or suffering to individuals, instituting loss reduction and loss prevention programs, and shifting through transfer mechanisms those losses which cannot be controlled by other means. Four approaches program staff can take to controlling risks are elimination, transfer, retention, and reduction.

Liability refers to the amount of legal responsibility or obligation that people or programs have to compensate for injuries to participants. This often involves financial settlements. Negligence may be found by a court of law if the defendant owed a duty of care to the plaintiff, which is accepted as true in adventure programs if the care was substandard or breached; if the breach caused injury to the plaintiff and if the injury did in fact occur and can be compensated. If this chain can be broken by proving one condition to be false, then a successful defense of liability due to negligence can follow. But reasonable and prudent leaders are expected to operate at or above the standard of care for the particular activity. Courts generally determine standard of care based on expert opinion and publications of common or acceptable practices.

Two obvious preventative measures are to include appropriate safety procedures and to protect by legal procedures. One legal procedure may be signing a form that includes warning and informing people of the risks and responsibilities of participation. Another could include having adults sign an assumption of risks and responsibilities of the activity statement (for example, an exculpatory clause/waiver statement releasing the program from liability due to any negligence). Simultaneous completion of a health disclosure form, which should contain personal details, medical history, and emergency contact information, helps to ascertain in advance any health problems or concerns participants might have.

Five aspects that you should include when completing accident report forms are sequence of the activity, location, what happened, injured participant's role, and aid procedures. Do not place opinions on the form about what was believed to be the cause of the accident or state that negligence was the cause. You may, however, include oral statements or separate written statements to make recommendations for changes.

Do not take offense at litigation, but do protect the feelings of leaders named in a lawsuit. If an out-of-court settlement is not reached, then the claim goes to trial. Pleadings include filing an alleged complaint, which results in a summons, which, in turn, is answered with a defense. During the discovery period, depositions, interrogatories, inspections, and examinations take place. A pretrial conference attempts to encourage settlement or to shorten the trial by limiting evidence presentation. At trial, the judge determines duty of care and a jury determines breach, causation, and injury compensation. The trial proceeds with opening statements, plaintiff's presentation of evidence (direct examination and cross-examination of witnesses), the defendant's response, the plaintiff's rebuttal, the defendant's rejoinder, and closing statements. After the judge instructs the jury, they retire to consider a verdict. The verdict may be followed by requests for changes or appeals for review by either side. Appellate decisions are final and binding.

The amount of a negligence award can be reduced by comparative negligence, which compares the plaintiff's contributions to the accident with the program's accountability, adjusting the amount proportionately. Participants are expected to know and assume the risks of an adventure program, to perform as reasonable and prudent people, and to assume some responsibility for their own injuries.

Your adventure program should consider two kinds of insurance: liability coverage to pay negligence awards and accident coverage to pay for medical and disability costs. Policy coverage may be limited by maximum amounts of payment and by excluding a list of activities, locations, or client types. Your program should check its coverage to be as complete as necessary.

QUESTIONS TO THINK ABOUT

1. What are the benefits of risk taking in an adventure program? What would you say to someone who does not understand your profession of purposefully endangering people? How do you balance risks and safety as an outdoor leader?

2. Define risk management and state its objectives.

3. What are the four approaches to controlling risk? Give examples of each.

4. Define liability and negligence.

5. What are the four elements of negligence? Which one is almost always present?

Which one is usually the center of a defense against negligence?

6. In your own words, explain the concept of reasonable and prudent, then describe what it means to the role of a volunteer outdoor leader with numerous certifications.

7. For outdoor leaders, how do courts determine the standard of care?

8. In order to warn and inform participants, what would you do and say to them in an orientation meeting?

9. What is the difference between a waiver of claims form and an agreement to participate form? When should you use each?

10. What is the difference between signing a release of liability and signing an assumption of risks? When should you use each?

11. What is the reason to include an exculpatory clause about negligence?

12. What does inherent risk mean? Why is this so important to an outdoor leader as opposed to a person leading another type of recreational activity?

13. What elements would you include in a waiver form?

14. What is the most important legal consideration for including minors in adventure programs?

15. Why ask participants for true and full disclosure of their health?

16. Aside from first aid and evacuation procedures, what should you do and not do in response to an accident?

17. What is important to include in an accident report?

18. What is your biggest worry if a claim goes to trial? How will you deal with this concern?

19. What is comparative negligence? Give an example.

20. Differentiate between liability and accident insurance coverage. Give examples of each.

21. What should you be concerned about with exclusionary phrases in an insurance policy?

REFERENCES

Furlong, L., Jillings, A., LaRhette, M., & Ryan, B. (1995). *20-year safety study of Project Adventure, Inc.* Hamilton, MA: Project Adventure.

Higgins, L. (1981). Wilderness Schools: Risk vs. Danger. *The Physician and Sportsmedicine,* 9(3), 133-136.

Meyer, D. (1979). The management of risk. *Journal of Experiential Education* 2(2), 9-14.

Outdoor Recreation Coalition of America (ORCA). (1994). *Developing an allocation of risk document.* Boulder, CO: Outdoor Recreation Coalition of America.

Priest, S., & Dixon, T. (1990). *Safety practices in adventure programming.* Boulder, CO: Association for Experiential Education.

Project Adventure. (1987). *15-year safety study of Project Adventure, Inc.* Hamilton, MA: Project Adventure (also see 20 year study).

van der Smissen, B. (1980). *Legal liability—Adventure activities.* Las Cruces, NM: Educational Resources Information Center (ERIC).

van der Smissen, B. (1990). *Legal liability and risk management for public and private entities.* Cincinnati: Anderson Publishing (also see 1997 supplement).

van der Smissen, B., & Cotten, J.D. (1995). Everything you always wanted to know about waivers—But were afraid to ask. Handout presented at the 1995 AAHPERD Convention in Portland, OR.

PART
III

Instruction in Adventure Programming

chapter

11

Experiential
Education

Well then, if risks must be run, should not one run them where success will improve people?

—Plato, in Grube, 1974, p. 128

I assume that amid all uncertainties there is one permanent frame of reference: namely, the organic connection between education and personal experience; or, that the new philosophy of education is committed to some kind of empirical and experimental philosophy. But experience and experiment are not self-explanatory ideas. Rather, their meaning is part of the problem to be explored. To know the meaning of empiricism we need to understand what experience is.

The belief that all genuine education comes about through experience does not mean that all experiences are genuinely or equally educative. Experience and education cannot be directly equated with each other. For some experiences are mis-educative. Any experience is mis-educative that has the effect of arresting or distorting the growth of further experience.

—Dewey, 1938, p. 25

Most adventure programs are founded on the belief that all forms of learning, behavior change, personal development, and growth occur through actual experiences. At the heart of this belief are the central principles of experiential learning. Experiential learning processes place clients as close as possible to the experiences for learning. Educators create such situations because they believe that the "direct" experience is more valuable for the transmission of knowledge than more "vicarious" forms of learning, such as lectures.

Remember, we can informally define **experiential learning** as learning by doing combined with reflection. It is an active rather than passive process, requiring learners to be self-motivated and responsible for learning, and instructors to be responsible "to," yet not "for," the learner (King, 1988).

Experiential learning is also based on the belief that change occurs when people are placed outside a position of comfort (e.g., homeostasis, acquiescence) and into a **state of dissonance**, or the difference between the current situation and desired future. In such a state, people are challenged by the adaptations necessary to reach a new state of equilibrium, yet are also supported through such processes by leaders and peers. Reaching these self-directed states produces changes that result in growth and learning. One of the major differences between experiential learning and other educational formats is that experiential learning is not a product of learning, but a learning *process* that is implemented under appropriate circumstances.

The Association for Experiential Education (AEE) has defined a series of principles that reflect many of these ideals. This professional organization encourages professionals to follow these principles, most visibly in the AEE's program accreditation process (Williamson & Gass, 1993), ethical guidelines (AEE, 1992), and practices of experiential education (AEE, 1995). These principles include the use of direct and purposeful experiences, which are appropriately challenging to clients and which have natural consequences. The principles we'll outline in this chapter are client based, have present and future relevance, require synthesis and reflection, demand personal responsibility, and are actively and inherently engaging.

1. Adventure programs are based on using **direct and purposeful experiences.** All change and growth has some form of experience as its origin, and experiential methodologies place the client as close as possible to that origin. Why? Because this process can be more valuable for the production and maintenance of positive change than other learning methodologies.

2. Adventure programs focus on **appropriately challenging clients**. Indeed, experiential practices are based upon the belief that change occurs when people are placed outside of positions of comfort and into states of dissonance (i.e., needing to resolve discrepancies), where there are degrees of perceived risk and they must use their competence to regain a state of equilibrium (see chapter 4). Reaching these self-directed states of equilibrium necessitates change, resulting in the type of growth clients are attempting to achieve. In order for this to occur, we strive to place clients in appropriate environments and situations where the level of risk—both real and perceived—also fosters a motivating attitude both to change and to retain the changes.

3. The activities in these programs are also real and meaningful in that they have **natural consequences**. Natural consequences are those that occur from the setting, situation, and circumstances of the adventure experience without human intercession. The ramifications of decisions made or actions performed by clients provide realistic, immediate, and, often, individualized feedback. This means that when appropriate and possible, you should utilize natural consequences to match a client's choices or behaviors, thereby providing the basis for growth. Conversely, artificial consequences occur if a human or human system anticipates or responds to a client's action, causing an artificial consequence to modify the natural consequences.

4. Natural consequences, rather than artificial ones, result in changes that are client based, rather than leader determined. **Client-based changes** begin at a place that is appropriate for each person and progress at each client's pace to an outcome that meets the individual's needs. In this process, clients make personal investments in choosing the type, level, and value of their experiences.

5. Such changes are designed to have **present and future relevance** for the client. Not only are these changes useful in resolving the uncertainty of the adventure experience and attaining a new state of equilibrium, they will also prove useful in helping the client improve daily life.

6. **Synthesis and reflection** are used as elements of the change process. Since change from experience is not always an automatic result, synthesis and reflection enhance the internalization of change for the client. This realization can be achieved in a number of ways, including individual and group discussions, debriefings, solo experiences, journal writing, drawing, or other creative arts. As a professional outdoor leader, you should encourage reflective processes in your clients' work and learning to deepen the experiential process. Adventure programs without a form of reflection in the experiential process are simply not using experiential methodologies.

7. Clients are compelled to become **personally responsible** in their adventure experiences. The activity itself draws clients into action; they are not forced to participate by you or other leaders. Experiential teaching applies methods and activities that encourage personal involvement and personal responsibility, especially challenge by choice, to give clients power and control over their learning.

8. In such a way, clients become **actively engaged** in adventure activities. These experiences inherently require problem solving, curiosity, and inquiry, and they are followed by synthesis and reflection. Clients can deal with new situations by applying what they have learned and identified in previous situations. Remember, the process is active rather than passive, requiring clients to be self motivated and responsible for their own learning and growth. Your job is to facilitate this responsibility, based on each client's particular needs and abilities.

Experience plays a pivotal role in learning. In fact, some authors consider the term "experiential learning" to be a tautology, or a redundancy, (Joplin, 1981) since all learning involves doing, whether you're learning by "doing" a test, a book, or a lecture. But you, as an outdoor leader with knowledge of how people learn from experiences, can provide more effective learning opportunities through your program's adventure activities.

RATIONALE FOR FOSTERING FUNCTIONAL GROWTH

Given these eight principles, you can see the application of experiential learning processes in adventure programming. Like experiential learning, clients of adventure programming achieve learning, behavior change, or growth by being supported through challenging activities in a manner that works best for them.

What is it about adventure programming that produces such positive changes? While more than one method of conducting adventure experiences is generally accepted, several universal components seem to serve as specific rationale for fostering functional growth. Gass (1993) has identified seven principles that summarize this rationale, providing a theoretical framework for conducting such experiences. These principles include action-centered programming, use of an unfamiliar environment, a climate of change, assessment observations, supportive small-group development processes, a focus on successful functioning, and changes in the leader's role.

Action-Centered Programming

As a forum for change, experiential learning helps clients become actively involved in "doing their learning" rather than just "listening to how it is done," which is often the case in didactic, or verbal learning situations. In adventure programs, didactic processes, such as lecturing, are augmented or replaced by concrete actions and experiences. Clients are asked to "walk" rather than merely "talk" their behaviors in adventure programming. The interaction of talk and action becomes observable and multidimensional, involving physical and affective areas for learning as well as cognitive ones. The action-oriented nature of adventure programming also increases the amount of nonverbal interaction between clients (e.g., Gillis & Bonney, 1986), allowing a greater examination of how clients truly interact. Indeed, Mason (1987) pointed out that in many contexts, nonverbal communication is five times more believable than verbal communication. This supports the validity of nonverbal client interaction, which, in turn, creates richer sources of learning, leading to beneficial change.

Unfamiliar Environment

When clients enter into adventure programs that focus on change, they may possess a strong level of resistance, that is, they may be in homeostasis, or a state in which they desire to stay the same. Adventure experiences often reduce such resistance by placing clients in situations that are new and unique, yet supportive. One reason resistance

decreases is that clients have few expectations or preconceived notions about what defines "success" in adventure experiences. They lack the knowledge of what is "correct" or how they are "supposed to act" in unfamiliar adventure experiences. When properly implemented, this dynamic serves to create a "risk-free" atmosphere, freeing clients to explore new learning opportunities, rather than becoming overwhelmed or incapacitated.

Furthermore, such a dynamic can limit self-destructive behaviors, such as dysfunctional behavior when interacting with others, freeing intellectual and emotional energy for adaptation and change. Another benefit is that unfamiliar environments are simplified and straightforward, presenting clear problems for clients to address (Walsh & Golins, 1976). This simplification can limit side issues or external stressors that can complicate or compound many of the everyday concerns confronting them. Not surprisingly, the unfamiliar environment also provides a medium that is clearly in contrast to a client's current reality state. As stated by Walsh and Golins, "Contrast is used to see generality, which tends to be overlooked by human beings in a familiar environment or to gain a new perspective on the old, contrasting environment from which the learner comes. The learner's entry into a contrasting environment is the first step towards reorganizing the meaning and direction of his [sic] experience" (p. 4). Clients are able to see elements of learning they may have overlooked already existing in current situations, because adventure experiences are different or unfamiliar. Clients may also learn new pieces of information that will help them learn when they return to more familiar environments.

Climate of Change

While traditional learning environments are effective in creating positive changes in some cases, at other times these same environments hold little motivation for clients to change. When properly implemented, adventure experiences can introduce conditions that appropriately increase client motivation to change, generally through the use of eustress (Selye, 1974). Eustress, a healthy form of stress, motivates clients to use problem-solving abilities in a functional way, such as trust, cooperation, and communication to accomplish tasks in adventure experiences. One of the features associated with eustress is the concept of "adaptive dissonance" (Walsh & Golins, 1976), in which clients must adapt their behaviors to resolve a difference between present and future states and to achieve states of desired equilibrium. By adapting in this way to create desired change, clients are provided with rich sources for learning. Adventure experiences also provide motivation through clear feedback from consequences arising out of appropriate and inappropriate behaviors. This feedback vividly and accurately represents clients' positive and negative behaviors. A client's interpretation of these behaviors provides both a powerful medium for change and an increased motivation to change.

Assessment Observations

Much of the material used for constructing change is obtained from the actions of clients in adventure experiences. Kimball (1993) relates this construction process to the psychological theory of "projection." Based on this premise, clients project a clear representation of their behavior patterns, personalities, structure, and interpretation on to the adventure activities because of the unfamiliarity and ambiguity of previous experience with the situation. As outlined by Kimball, "Wilderness challenges are high in ambiguity. The client must interpret or structure the task demands as well as his/her own response to it. The challenges of the wilderness expedition offer great latitude in response. The greater the latitude and the higher the stress, the more likely the client will 'project' unique and individual personality aspects into the 'test' situation" (p. 153). Careful observation of responses to a broad and deep selection of different adventure activities allows accurate identification of "lifelong behavior patterns, dysfunctional ways of coping with stress, intellectual processes, conflicts, needs, and emotional responsiveness. When properly observed, recorded, and articulated, these data can be the basis for long term therapeutic goals" (p. 154). These observations become extremely valuable for planning change processes. They are particularly helpful in constructing metaphors, for designing future adventure experiences, and in producing lasting functional change.

Supportive Small-Group Development

Unlike a typical classroom setting, most adventure experiences are conducted in small groups of 8 to 15 people. The small-group setting often serves as a critical factor for behavioral change. Properly orchestrated small-group interactions can exponentially increase a group's ability to accomplish tasks, for example, through reciprocal interactions or sharing in each other's strengths and weaknesses. Small groups can also provide a rich source of emotional safety and support when group members are involved in the product as well as the processes of adventures. For example, as we discussed in chapter 5, conflicts sometimes arise in groups during adventure experiences. By implementing supportive group processes, such as the full-value contract (see page 176) or other group norms that support emotional safety, you can help groups resolve conflict through positive discussions.

Focus on Successful Functioning

Remember, clients often bring problems, or even a history of failure, with them when they start adventure programs. One of the consequences of these problems is that they can heighten defense mechanisms, thereby increasing clients' resistance to change. But in adventure environments, you can give clients opportunities to focus on their abilities—instead of on their disabilities. This orientation can diminish initial defenses, leading to healthy changes, especially if you combine this approach with opportunities to successfully complete progressively more difficult and rewarding tasks. Rather than being resistant to learning, your support helps clients expand their perceived limitations and discover untapped resources or new strengths. You can also encourage clients' efforts by focusing on the potential for becoming personally empowered by establishing and maintaining functional behaviors.

Changes in the Leader's Role

Adventure activities also create several changes in the dynamics between outdoor leaders and clients. One example is changing your role from being a "director" to a "supporter." Here you are able to assume a more approachable position with clients. During shared adventure experiences, you have the opportunity to work with clients during their various challenges, rather than being the source of challenges. These dynamics, combined with the informal setting of the adventure experience, can remove many of the barriers limiting interaction that may exist in other more "formal" educational processes. While still maintaining clear and appropriate boundaries, you can become more approachable, creating richer interactions with clients. All of this can help to bring greater overall change.

EDUCATIONAL MODELS SUPPORTING ADVENTURE PROGRAMMING

Several worthwhile models have been created that explain the experiential process of adventure programming. These include the Outward Bound process model (Walsh & Golins, 1976), the "hurricane-like" spiral of experiential education (Joplin, 1981), a numeric measurement scale for experientiality (Gibbons & Hopkins, 1980), and several experiential learning cycles (Dewey, 1938; Kolb, 1984; Pfeiffer & Jones, 1980; and Priest, 1990).

Outward Bound Process Model

As we outlined in chapter 2, probably one of the most influential models in the brief history of adventure programming is the Outward Bound process model created by Walsh & Golins (1976). It was one of the first efforts to list and organize the elements of this leading adventure program into an interactive and replicable process that could be used by other programs. As shown in figure 11.1, the seven elements of the Outward Bound process model are the learner, prescribed physical environment, prescribed social environment, characteristic set of problem-solving tasks, state of adaptive dissonance, mastery, and re-

organization of the meaning and direction of the learner's experience. Each of these seven elements are important features of adventure programming.

When considering the change process, this model appropriately begins with the learner. Determining the needs, corresponding objectives, and level of motivation of the learner are all key to orchestrating a successful experience—before starting any program. While somewhat dated in their rationale [e.g., the authors point to "ways of minimizing the handicaps of the physically disabled so that he can participate in the mastery peculiar to Outward Bound" (p. 3)], the model presents the idea that learners need to be assessed by instructors prior to the adventure program.

Based on the concept of unfamiliarity, the model states that the adventure environment must stand in contrast to the clients' "home" environments with which they are familiar. The difference between these environments allows clients to receive valuable information from two sources: the elements they overlook in their familiar environments and the elements present in the adventure environment that do not exist in their familiar environments.

The adventure program accomplishes this contrast by using **prescribed physical environments** that are generally multisensory, neutral, and straightforward. Most adventure environments are multisensory: they possess a number of differing features to see, hear, smell, taste, and touch. These environments are also neutral: the "rules" of the adventure experience are not arbitrarily

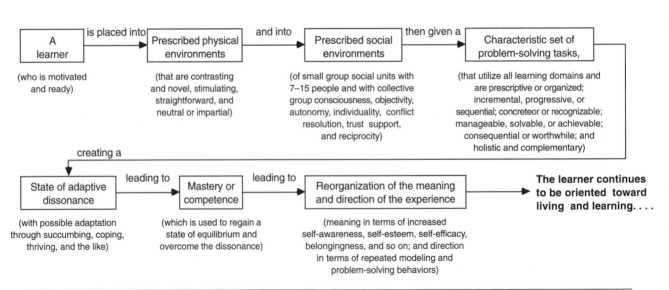

Figure 11.1 The Outward Bound process model (Walsh & Golins, 1976).

made by people. Nor do intervening features, like staff intercession, always buffer clients from the adventure experience: they must deal with what the physical environment presents. The elements in the physical environments used by adventure programs are straightforward and easily identifiable and contain no outside distractions to divert clients' attention.

One of the critical features of Walsh and Golins's work is acknowledging the effect that a **prescribed social environment** has on the success of adventure programs. Their model points to the need for creating a particular group dynamic, that is, "an interdependent peer group with anywhere from 7-15 individuals who have a common objective" (p. 5). Four group dynamics that support adventure programming are all related to size. The group needs to be large enough to produce a wealth of differing behaviors, yet small enough so that separate subgroups do not diversify the group and form around these separate entities. The group needs to be large enough that conflict will result from differing client opinions, yet small enough that the group possesses the ability and resources to resolve any conflicts. The group needs to be large enough to create a collective force with which they may attain certain goals that cannot be attained by individuals working separately, yet small enough that the group can also support each client's individual goals. The group needs to be large enough that a supportive state of reciprocity occurs, which is "an exchange system whereby strengths and weaknesses can be traded off within a group" (p. 6), yet small enough that the group members can contribute their individual strengths, and through such exchange, utilize the strengths of others in areas in which they may be weak.

The Outward Bound process model identifies a **characteristic set of problem-solving tasks** common to the challenges encountered in adventure experiences. These characteristics contribute to the development of competence, functional change, and other positive benefits experienced by clients. These characteristics are organized, incremental, concrete, manageable, consequential, and holistic. Adventure experiences are most successful when they are organized to meet the needs of clients and when they are sequenced progressively, or conducted "incrementally in terms of complexity and consequence" (Walsh & Golins, 1976, p. 7). Thus, clients should begin with easier tasks and gather senses of competency and mastery from accomplishing these tasks, then attempt more difficult tasks with an established base of increased skills and confidence. Adventure experiences are generally concrete and quite easy to define in terms of content, that is, the tasks are easily recognizable (if not visually stimulating), and in terms of time, that is, the tasks generally possess a definite beginning and end. Adventure challenges, while initially appearing insurmountable to many clients, can be managed or accomplished by clients with the resources they possess. In other words, initially these resources and the method in which they need to be coordinated may be unclear to some clients, but their abilities to accomplish the task are based on their abilities to manage resources and personal skills. Adventure experiences are consequential, and the results, positive or negative, generally have an immediate, nonarbitrary, and direct effect on clients. Adventure experiences incorporate learning that addresses a variety of domains, including cognitive, social, emotional, and psychomotor learning. Combinations of these learning domains may provide a more holistic perspective on how to help clients change.

Presenting clients with problem-solving tasks in unfamiliar physical and social environments generally creates anxiety in the form of **dissonance**. This dissonance is generally between where the client currently is, which is facing a problem, and where they would like to be, which is solving the problem successfully. Without changing this dissonance, clients become disempowered, disinterested, or both.

What you must seek to implement are **adaptive dissonance situations**. These are situations in which clients choose to overcome the dissonance the situation presents by adapting their behaviors to meet their intended objectives. Accomplishing this both instills a sense of mastery or competence in clients as well as gives them insights into behaviors they can transfer to their home environments.

While not outlined in Walsh & Golins's model, one feature critical to successfully implementing the concepts of adaptive dissonance and mastery is the concept of challenge by choice. As pointed out by Klint (1990) and Kiewa (1994), possessing the freedom to choose has a direct relationship on a client's ability to experience personal growth and attribute such growth to the client's own efforts, rather than "plain, old luck" or manipulation by a facilitator (see chapter 4). Also critical to the concepts of adaptive dissonance and mastery is the need to "individualize" these focuses, based on client needs. Clients play the major role in determining adaptive dissonance and mastery, based on what they see as enriching and worthy of mastery. Some clients will value externally focused challenges and associated mastery, for example, the experience of conquering the environment, whereas others clients will value more internally-focused challenges and associated mastery, such as the experience of "bonding" with the environment, thereby overcoming self-imposed limits.

The **mastery** or **competence** produced by successfully resolving the adaptive dissonance presented by a situation serves as motivation for behavior change. This is related to Bandura's (1977) theory of self-efficacy, believing that mastering tasks, particularly difficult ones, will increase clients' beliefs that they can successfully accomplish other meaningful tasks (see also chapter 4).

While mastery provides the motivation for change, completing problem-solving tasks in these types of unique physical and social environments also provides clients with information on the **reorganization of the meaning and direction** of change in their lives. The lasting impact of this reorganization is only as strong as a client's ability to transfer change in a manner that is lasting and continuous.

Five-Stage Model of Experiential Education

Joplin (1981) created a five-stage model based on her review of existing experiential programs. The five stages of this model are focus, action, support, feedback, and debriefing. The **focus stage** presents the learning task and helps clients concentrate their attention on this task. The **action stage** involves doing the actual task, which is often a task that is unfamiliar to or stressful for the client. In the **support stage**, the group or you provide security and caring to assist clients in their efforts. In the **feedback stage**, you supply information to clients about their efforts and accomplishments to help advance their learning. In the **debriefing stage**, you help clients learn from their experiences through reflective processes that help them organize and integrate what they've learned. Joplin arranged these steps in a progressive and continuous chain of "hurricane-like" spirals (see figure 11.2).

Based on her model, Joplin further identified eight characteristics associated with experiential processes that apply to adventure programming. These characteristics include student-, not

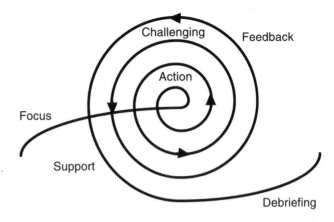

Figure 11.2   One spiral of Joplin's (1981) model of experiential education.

teacher-, based, personal not impersonal, process and product oriented, evaluative for internal and external reasons, holistic understanding and component analysis, organized around experience, perception-based not theory-based, and individual- not group-based learning.

Learning is centered on client needs and interests rather than on your needs and interests. The effective leader individualizes the subject matter to fit the specific client in terms of both the affective and the cognitive. The manner or process by which a learner accomplishes a learning task is valued as much as the product or completion of the task. Evaluation is completed for individuals outside of the learner, such as school personnel, as well as for the learner as an individual. In other words, evaluation is done "by" as well as "to" the client. Learning can be holistic—cognitive, affective, and psychomotor—as well as be expressed or analyzed in a number of differing, yet possibly interconnected components. Experience serves as the central source for learning: the program is built around experiences, and clients acquire personal knowledge primarily through reflecting on their experiences. Thus, you must emphasize clients' abilities to share, explain, and justify what they've learned from their own perspective more than what is the right answer from theoretical "experts." You should encourage clients to judge the level of their accomplishments on what they achieved, rather than just on how they did compared to others in, for example, norm-referenced tests.

Scale of Experientiality

In an attempt to avoid increasing confusion surrounding the definition and applications of experiential education, Gibbons and Hopkins (1980) developed a **scale of experientiality** that outlined various degrees of experiential programming. Their scale refers to the amount of actual experience in the learning situation. Five criteria determine this amount, including the degree to which the

- experience was mediated, that is, the more "direct" the experience, the more experiential,
- client was involved in the planning and execution of the experience,
- client was responsible for what occurred in the experience,
- client was responsible for mastering the experience to the fullest extent possible, and
- experience enabled clients to grow in directions that were helpful to them.

Based on these five criteria, the authors identified five increasing modes of experientiality: re-

ceptive, analytic (examination), productive, developmental, and psychosocial. With two submodes for each mode, a total of ten submodes represented a continuum of experientiality from least to most experiential: simulated, spectator, exploratory, analytical, generative, challenge, competence, mastery, personal growth, and social growth (Gibbons & Hopkins, 1980, pp. 33-34). Each of these mode and submode experiences has a cumulative effect, with the more experiential modes possessing the elements of less experiential modes beneath them (see figure 11.3).

In the **receptive mode**, experiences, or representations of them, are presented to learners who remain a passive audience throughout. In these simulated experiences, learners passively experience slides, pictures, films, or other simulations of reality. In the spectator experience, learners experience the object of the study, but only as an observer.

In the **analytic (examination) mode**, learners conduct field studies in which they apply theoretical knowledge and skill in order to examine an event, analyze an aspect of the environment,

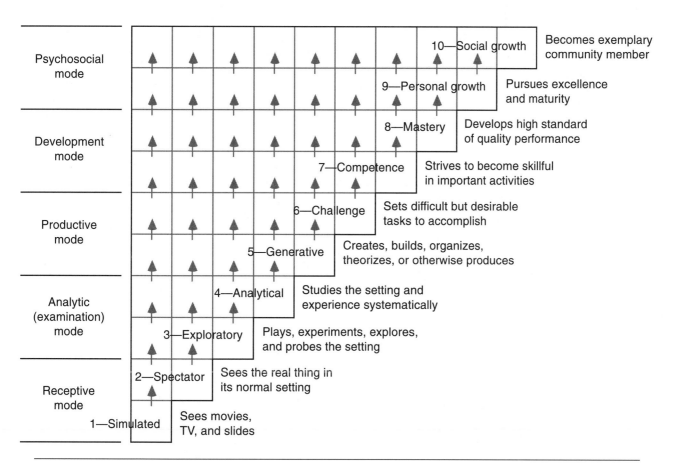

Figure 11.3 Gibbons and Hopkins's (1980) scale of experientiality.

or solve a practical problem. The exploratory experience exposes learners to interesting sites and encourages them to explore the possibilities of the materials at hand. In the analytical experience, learners study systematically, often applying theory to solve problems in practical situations.

In the **productive mode**, learners generate products, activities, and services that have been assigned by you or that they have devised themselves. The generative experience allows people to learn by building, creating, composing, organizing, or otherwise generating products in appropriate settings. Naturally, the challenge experience challenges them or allows them to challenge themselves as they pursue goals of productivity or accomplishment that they must struggle to achieve.

In the **developmental mode**, learners pursue excellence in a particular field by designing and implementing long-term programs of study, activity, and practice. The competence experience encourages learners to focus on a particular field, to practice skills involved, to become absorbed in the activity, and to achieve recognized competence in it. The mastery experience encourages learners to go beyond competence to develop commitment, to set high personal standards in their pursuit of excellence in a field of activity, and to become a master of their chosen area.

In the **psychosocial mode**, learners understand themselves and their relationships with others. They accomplish the tasks presented by their particular stage of development toward maturity and make contributions to the lives of others. The personal growth experience enables learners to gain understanding of themselves as unique individuals and to gain knowledge of effectively and responsibly directing their own activities.

The social growth experience enables learners to become more socially competent with people of all ages and to act in more socially-responsible ways, using their accomplishments in service to the community.

Process of Experiential Learning Models

Several authors have examined the cyclical nature of experiential learning. Dewey (1938) was the first of these. He believed that the "formation of purposes is a rather complex, intellectual operation. It involves: (1) observation of surrounding conditions, (2) knowledge obtained partly by recollection, and (3) judgment, which puts together what is observed and what is recalled to see what they signify" (p. 69). Figure 11.4 represents Dewey's three-step process.

A number of educators, most notably Kolb (1984), constructed models based on Dewey's process. Kolb interpreted a variation of Lewin's experiential learning cycle, creating a four-step recurring model (see figure 11.5). In his model, "immediate concrete experience is the basis for observation and reflection. These observations are assimilated into a 'theory' from which new implications for action can be deduced. These implications or hypotheses then serve as guides in acting to create new experiences" (p. 21).

Pfeiffer and Jones (1980) outlined their model of the experiential learning process for group facilitators (see figure 11.6). Step one involves the action of doing or experiencing in order to generate information for analysis in subsequent steps. Step two incorporates sharing reactions to and observations from the experience in what they termed "publishing," likening this step to computer data input. Step three includes the sys-

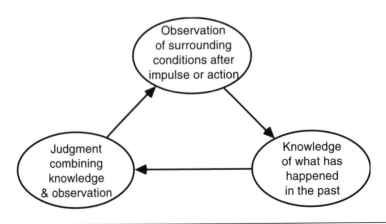

Figure 11.4   Dewey's (1938) process of experiential learning.

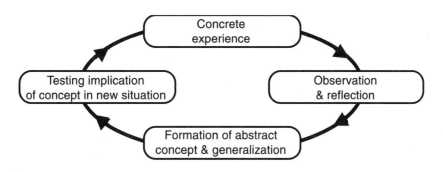

Figure 11.5 Kolb's (1984) interpretation of Lewin's experiential learning cycle.

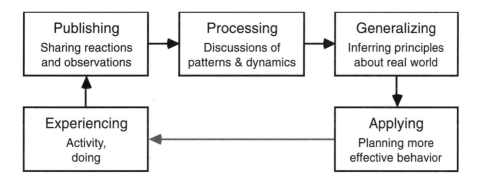

Figure 11.6 Pfeiffer and Jones's (1980) model of experiential learning.

tematic examination of the experience during processing by discussing the patterns and dynamics that arose from the reactions and observations. We can view the combined publishing and processing steps as an "inductive process: proceeding from observation rather than from a priori 'truth' [as in the deductive process]. Inductive learning means learning through discovery" (pp. 3-4). Step four infers principles about the real world by generalizing from the publishing and processing steps. In this step, the learning becomes truly pragmatic by showing its relevance to reality. Step five infers applying new action and planning more effective behavior on the basis of the generalized principles. The cycle repeats, which "is meant to indicate that the actual application of the learning is a new experience for the participant, to be examined inductively also" (p. 7).

Experiential Learning and Judgment Paradigm

According to Dewey (1938), judgment plays the pivotal role in the experiential learning process. He wrote that the "crucial educational problem is that of procuring the postponement of imme-

diate action upon desire until observation and judgment have intervened" (p. 69). In some ways, Dewey might have paraphrased judgment as a sort of ability to "learn how, as well as where, to look before leaping." Priest (1990) explains judgment as a six-step procedure you undertake when information important to the problem-solving or decision-making process is missing, vague, or unknown. In order to allow the problem-solving or decision-making process to continue, you use judgment to substitute reasonable values for the missing, vague, or unknown ones (see also chapter 20).

Specifically, experience-based judgment follows six steps: experience, induce, generalize, deduce, apply, and evaluate (see figure 11.7). First, you collect specific experiences, whether firsthand, observed, or vicarious, and store them in the brain through the senses. Second, you subject these specific experiences to inductive reflection, moving from the specific to the general. Third, you form generalized concepts and store them away in memory (either long- or short-term) as a map of connected concepts. When faced with uncertainty, your brain searches these memory maps for relevant concepts. Fourth, you subject the retrieved concepts to deductive reflection,

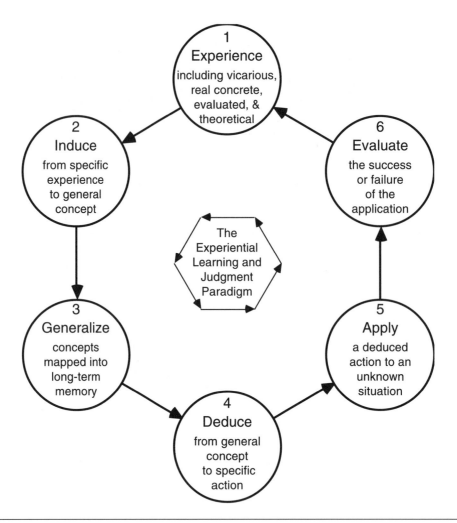

Figure 11.7   Priest's experiential learning and judgment paradigm.
Adapted from Priest, 1990.

moving from the general back to the specific. Fifth, you apply your judgment (prediction, guess, estimation, or even speculation) to the situation as a substitute for the uncertainty. Sixth, you evaluate the effectiveness of this application. The outcome of your assessment acts as new experience for the cycle to repeat. In this way, you refine judgment over time, and learning takes place through repeated reflections on experiences. This process is one that can result in a tremendous amount of client growth.

EFFECTIVE OUTDOOR LEADERS SHOULD

☞ Base adventure programming on sound philosophical principles and educational theories.

☞ Design adventure programs that contain direct and purposeful experiences, that appropriately challenge clients, and that have natural consequences.

☞ Use program activities that are client based, have present and future relevance, require synthesis and reflection, demand personal responsibility, and actively and inherently engage participants.

☞ Conduct adventure programming that is action-centered and that utilizes unfamiliar environments, a climate of change, assessment observations, supportive small-group development processes, a focus on successful functioning, and changes in the leader's role.

☞ Measure the quality of learning experiences by certain criteria such as interaction and continuity, or the scale of experientiality.

☞ Consider the role of service to others in adventure programming.

☞ Understand the combination of behavioral, cognitive, and experiential theories of learning to provide the most effective learning opportunities possible.

☞ Understand the contributions of elements in the Outward Bound process model make to all adventure programming.

☞ Understand how the various multiple-step cyclical models of experiential learning apply to adventure programming.

SUMMARY

Adventure programs use direct and purposeful experiences that appropriately challenge clients and have natural consequences. Adventure experiences are client based, have present and future relevance, require synthesis and reflection, demand personal responsibility, and actively and inherently engage participants. Adventure programming is action centered, and utilizes unfamiliar environments, a climate of change, assessment observations, supportive small-group development processes, a focus on successful functioning, and changes in the leader's role.

The Outward Bound process model describes how change comes from the adventure experience. An adventure places the learner into unique, prescribed physical and social environments, presenting him with a characteristic set of problem-solving tasks. This situation creates a state of adaptive dissonance, leading to increased competence or mastery of these challenges. This success reorganizes the meaning and direction of the learner's experience and has positive implications for the future.

Joplin's (1981) "hurricane-like" spiral model has five stages: focus, action, support, feedback, and debriefing. From the model, she identified eight characteristics associated with experiential processes and adventure programming: student- not teacher-based, personal not impersonal, process- and product-oriented, evaluative for internal and external reasons, holistic understanding and component analytical, organized around experience, perception- not theory-based, and individual- not group-based learning.

We can use a scale of experientiality to measure the amount of actual experience in the learning opportunity. The amount is determined by the degree of mediation, involvement, responsibility, mastery, and potential for growth. Five modes of increasing experientiality are based on these five aspects: receptive, analytic (examination), productive, developmental, and psychosocial. Each mode has two submodes, representing a continuum of experientiality: simulated, spectator, exploratory, analytical, generative, challenge, competence, mastery, personal growth, and social growth.

Dewey's three-step process explains the cyclical nature of experiential learning: observation, knowledge, and judgment. Kolb uses a four-step cycle, an interpretation of Lewin's work: concrete experience, observation and reflection, formation, and testing implications. Pfeiffer and Jones' model has five steps: experiencing, publishing, processing, generalizing, and applying. Priest's experiential learning and judgment paradigm has six steps: experiencing, inducing, generalizing, deducing, applying, and evaluating. In conclusion, all learning is experiential at least to some small degree.

QUESTIONS TO THINK ABOUT

1. In your own words, discuss the concepts expressed by the two quotes at the beginning of this chapter from Plato and John Dewey.

2. Explain the concept of "direct and purposeful experience."

3. Explain the statement: "Instructors are responsible 'to,' and not 'for,' the learner."

4. Take the eight principles advanced by the Association for Experiential Education and show how each should be applied to a specific adventure experience.

5. Provide your rationale for how adventure experiences foster the development of functional growth for clients.

6. Explain the concept of "contrast" and how it adds to client growth.

7. State the strengths and weaknesses of the Outward Bound process model.

8. Clarify when you should use information assimilation and when you should use experiential learning models in adventure programming.

9. Recall your latest adventure program experience and explain the level you were at on the scale of experientiality.

10. Recall your latest leadership experience and explain the level your clients were at on the scale of experientiality.

11. Choose one of the cyclical models that explain experiential learning and describe how this model might apply to an adventure experience you will lead in the near future.

REFERENCES

Association for Experiential Education (AEE). (1992). *Ethical guidelines for the Therapeutic Adventure Professional Group* (TAPG). Boulder, CO: Author.

Association for Experiential Education (AEE). (1995). Principles of experiential education practice. In *Association for Experiential Education Directory and Handbook*. Boulder, CO: Author.

Bandura, A. (1977). Social learning theory. *Psychological Review,* 84(2), 191-215.

Dewey, J. (1938). *Experience and education.* New York: Collier Books.

Gass, M.A. (Ed.). (1993). *Adventure therapy: Therapeutic applications of adventure programming in mental health settings.* Dubuque, IA: Kendall/Hunt.

Gibbons, M., & Hopkins, D. (1980). How experiential is your experience-based program? *Journal of Experiential Education* 4(1), 32-37.

Gillis, H.L. & Bonney, W. C. (1986). Group counseling with couples or families: Adding adventure activities. *Journal for Specialists in Group Work.* 11 (4), 213-220.

Grube, G.M.A. (Ed.). (1974). *Plato's republic.* Indianapolis: Hackett.

Joplin, L. (1981). On defining experiential education. *Journal of Experiential Education* 4(1), 17-20.

Kiewa, J. (1994). Self-control: The key to adventure? In E. Cole, E. Erdman, & E. Rothblum (Eds.), *Wilderness therapy for women: The power of adventure* (pp. 29-42). New York: Harrington Park.

Kimball, R.O. (1993). The wilderness as therapy: The value of using adventure programs in therapeutic assessment. In M.A. Gass (Ed.), *Therapeutic applications of adventure programming in mental health settings* (pp. 153-160). Boulder, CO: Association for Experiential Education.

King, K. (1988). The role of adventure in the experiential learning process. *Journal of Experiential Education* 11(2), 4-8.

Klint, K.A. (1990). New directions for inquiry into self-concept and adventure experiences. In J.C. Miles & S. Priest (Eds.), *Adventure education.* State College, PA: Venture.

Kolb, D.A. (1984). *Experiential learning.* Englewood Cliffs, NJ: Prentice-Hall.

Mason, M. (1987). Wilderness family therapy: Experiential dimensions. *Contemporary Family Therapy,* 9 (1-2), 90-105.

Pfeiffer, J.W., & Jones, J.E. (1980). *The 1980 annual handbook for group facilitators.* San Diego: University Associates.

Priest, S. (1990). Everything you always wanted to know about judgment, but were afraid to ask. *Journal of Adventure Education and Outdoor Leadership* 7(3), 5-12.

Selye, H. (1974). *Stress without distress.* New York: Signet Books.

Walsh, V., & Golins, G. (1976). *The exploration of the Outward Bound process model.* Denver, CO: Colorado Outward Bound School.

Williamson, J., & Gass, M. (1993). *Manual of program accreditation for adventure programs.* Boulder, CO: Association for Experiential Education.

Instructional Methods

The process of education is a lot like learning to swim in a pool that has a shallow end and a deep end. Some people often learn to swim in the shallow end and move to the deep end when they have their basics down. Some people learn by plunging right into the deep end, hoping they learn quickly before drowning. Still others enter the shallow end, wade around slowly with a great deal of trepidation, and never develop the confidence to progress further. In all of these cases, some flounder and a few sink, but the ones who become independent swimmers accomplish this feat because they are able to build on and connect all of the elements of their learning experiences. And although many prefer just to get their feet wet, none are really truly educated unless they venture into deeper waters!

Learning has a "shallow" end and a "deep" end. Shallow learning involves retaining and understanding theory. But knowing theory is rarely enough. To fully learn, you must be able to pragmatically use knowledge by testing whether a theory works in real situations. This deep learning involves utilizing and creating practice from theory. In this chapter, we'll discuss instructional models you can use to help you foster deep learning as well as strategies and skills for successful teaching, including public speaking, teaching tips for effective lessons, and objective and goal setting. You'll be able to directly apply all of the models, skills, and strategies we'll discuss to adventure programming whether your program's focus is on recreation, education, development, or therapy.

FIVE DEPTHS OF LEARNING

We can view learning as having five depths, ranging from a shallow, basic end to a deep, complex end. These five progressively deeper levels are memorization, comprehension, application, generalization, and systemization.

• At the first, or **memorization**, depth of learning, the learner memorizes by repeating factual information and by identifying right and wrong answers. For example, a memorizing learner will be able to list the key rules of belaying (anchor, proper steps to belay, communication signals, and so on). The learner can also identify right or wrong ways to belay, such as not keeping the "breaking" hand on the rope at all times.

• At the second, or **comprehension** depth, the learner is able to explain how processes work and why, when, or where the learning can be used. For the same belaying example, a comprehending learner is able to describe the step-by-step sequence of hand movements for belaying and can detail situations in which belaying may or may not be necessary.

• At the third, or **application** depth, the learner applies her comprehension by practicing or demonstrating the learning in the specific situation for which it was intended or in which she initially learned it. For the belaying example, an applying learner is able to set up and handle a horizontal belay in the classroom and transpose this to setting up and operating a vertical belay in top-rope rock climbing.

• At the fourth, or **generalization**, depth, the learner modifies or adapts the learning to suit new and different environments. For example, a generalizing learner is able to vary the technique from belaying on a river crossing to belaying during a rappel to belaying a lead rock climber. Each situation is different, requiring correct modifications in order to adapt to the new situation.

• At the fifth, or **systemization**, depth, the learner creates new knowledge from her base of existing knowledge. In the belaying example, the systemizing learner is able to find a new and, perhaps better, way to belay. Recent changes to using tubular or camming belay devices, instead of plate or body belays, are examples of systemization at work.

A client's success in reaching a particular depth of learning depends heavily on the instructional methods you choose. In this chapter, we'll look at the inquiry-discovery approach to learning (Hammerman & Priest, 1989), the learning gradient (Priest & Hammerman, 1990), and the Socratic method of questioning.

Inquiry-Discovery Approach to Learning

The **inquiry-discovery approach to learning** is a useful method to teach cognitive concepts. Inquiring and discovering are natural ways to learn, the ways people have always learned on their own without intercession by a leader or instructor. The process begins with a question and the answers follow from rational, logical, and systematic study.

As the name implies, the approach to learning has two segments: inquiry and discovery. **Inquiry** involves three parts: questioning, investigating, and analyzing. **Discovery** also involves three parts: interpreting, understanding, and answering. The relationship between the two segments is cyclical: inquiry leads to discovery, and, in turn, discovery leads to new inquiry (see figure 12.1).

Let's look more closely, now, at the inquiry process. In **questioning**, the process almost always begins with the postulation of a theory, the recognition of a problem, or the formulation of a hypothesis. **Investigating** involves a method or procedure to secure evidence to support the theory, to resolve the problem, or to test the hypothesis. In **analyzing**, you collect information to scrutinize for patterns of relationships, simi-

larities, or differences. Once you identify these patterns, you may move on to discovery, considering and discussing them in relation to the initial theory, problem, or hypothesis you pose during the **interpreting** step. Then, in the **understanding** step, you explain these connections in the context of whether they support the theory, solve the problem, or refute the hypothesis. In this manner, you can explain the original question in the **answering** step, and good answers lead to more good questions.

This sequence is similar to the scientific method with one exception. For the scientific method, the learner formulates a hypothesis or theory, then collects information through a questioning process to see whether the hypothesis is true or not. In the inquiry-discovery approach to learning, however, you assist this process by adding additional questions to the client questioning process. Because of this dialogue, "inquiry and discovery" are time consuming. They involve a high degree of interaction between teacher and learner. As the teacher, you stimulate the learning process by posing questions to learners, causing them to think about what they have observed, what is likely to occur next, and a course of action or steps to pursue in order to bring about a certain action or solve a particular problem (Hammerman & Priest, 1989). In this way, the inquiry-discovery approach moves the learners beyond mere memorization to address the middle depths of learning (e.g., analyzing, interpreting).

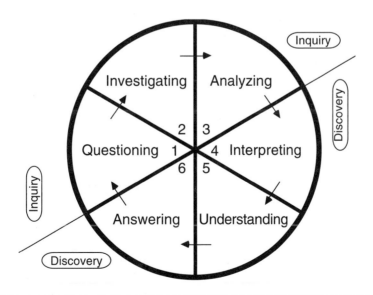

Figure 12.1   The inquiry/discovery approach to learning.
Adapted from Hammerman and Priest, 1989.

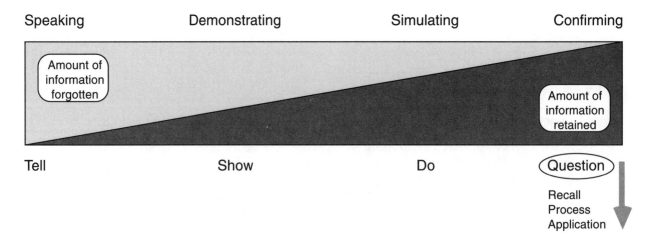

Figure 12.2   The learning gradient.
Adapted from Priest and Hammerman, 1990.

Learning Gradient

The **learning gradient** is a combination of useful methods to teach psychomotor or physical skills, such as how to paddle, climb, or ski. The gradient is a continuum of four methods: **speaking** (telling), **demonstrating** (showing), **simulating** (doing), and **confirming** (questioning) as shown in figure 12.2. In the speaking method, you tell, or lecture, about a particular skill. The client simply assimilates the information. For the demonstrating method, you show the particular skill, and the client watches. In the simulating method, the client does the same skill, and you evaluate the performance. In confirming, the client answers questions posed by you as you test for depth of learning. As the learner progresses along the continuum, the amount of information retained increases.

For example, say you are teaching a lesson in the skill of knot tying. You begin by telling, progress to showing and doing, and then end with questioning. You tell the group information, such as terminology (e.g., standing part, bight) and typology (e.g., knot families, breaking strengths). Once the group has a fundamental understanding of key concepts, you show them how to tie knots one knot at a time, since too much information at once often proves wasteful early in learning. Once the group has seen the various steps to tying one knot, they practice doing the same knot. After they have shown their competence at tying that knot, you ask questions about the application, or "dressed," shape of the knot before moving on to the next tying exercise.

Mere "telling is not teaching" (D. Hammerman, W. Hammerman, & E. Hammerman, 1985). Since people forget most of the information they hear, clients will not learn how to tie knots by being told a large amount of information. Similarly, just seeing several knots being tied is usually insufficient for learning, although demonstration will have greater impact than lecturing. Clients must have practice knot tying before they can even begin to learn. The old adage "I hear and I forget, I see and I remember, I do and I understand" (Confucius) has obvious connections to skills learning. The addition of the statement "You ask me and I know" to this process can further cement what was learned, mirroring the four progressive steps of the learning gradient in a continuum:

- Speaking (telling)—I hear and I forget.
- Demonstrating (showing)—I see and I remember.
- Simulating (doing)—I do and I understand.
- Confirming (questioning)—You ask me and I know.

Socratic Method of Questioning

Both the inquiry-discovery approach and the learning gradient require the correct use of questioning techniques to realize their full teaching-learning potential. Both cases employ the **Socratic method**. As you probably know, this method is named after the Greek philosopher Socrates, who frequently used questions as a way to elicit thinking from his students.

Questions for the Socratic method come in three principle forms: recall, process, and application (D. Hammerman, W. Hammerman, & E. Hammerman, 1985). **Recall questions** ask learners to remember basic principles based on earlier experience. They encompass counting, describing, identifying, matching, naming, observing, remembering, and selecting. **Process questions** ask learners to reason for answers. They involve analyzing, classifying, comparing, contrasting, experimenting, explaining, grouping, implying, inferring, and ordering. **Application questions** ask learners to come up with examples showing they fully understand something by being able to put it in use. They embrace evaluating, extrapolating, generalizing, hypothesizing, interpolating, judging, predicting, speculating, and theorizing (D. Hammerman, W. Hammerman, & E. Hammerman, 1985). These questions help you probe the shallower three of the five depths of learning: memorization, comprehension, and application.

Asking questions of these types in this order (i.e., recall first and application last) is the most effective for confirming learning. For the knot-tying example, recall questions could be "What is this part of the rope called?" or "What kind of knot is this?" Process questions might include "How are these two knots similar and different?" or "What is wrong with this knot?" Application questions might include "How could this knot be used?" or "If I add an extra loop to this knot, what does it become?" For each question, students' thinking processes increase in complexity and sophistication as question types range from recall through process to application.

Questions not only confirm learning as in the learning gradient and guide learning as with inquiry and discovery, they also motivate students to learn. Asking questions, for which learners do not have immediate answers, makes them more likely to remember the answer than when someone else provides it. Therefore, questioning stimulates thinking, for example, through adaptive dissonance, thereby increasing retention.

INSTRUCTION THROUGH PUBLIC SPEAKING

Public speaking proficiency is an essential tool for you to possess as an outdoor leader, but like many people, you may have a great fear of it. Still, called on to teach concepts and skills, debrief emotions and feelings, and introduce adventure activities, you must be a capable speaker. So practice to become an effective public speaker. Try these suggestions for public speaking when making presentations, not speeches:

• Be yourself and act naturally. Don't be false or try to copy someone else's style. Allow spontaneity to occur. Don't read the presentation or make a speech. This can be as boring as reading a textbook aloud! Let your enthusiasm shine through. Don't hold back on appropriate feelings, personality aspects, and convictions.

• Before a presentation, you may find it helpful to conduct voice warm-up exercises, such as resonance, articulation, projection, annunciation, and pronunciation. Casually talking with people or singing alone prior to speaking can substitute for these exercises. Practice relaxation techniques to reduce your apprehension about speaking in public. Deep breathing, listening to soft music, and positive mental imagery (seeing success) can make a big difference in "getting the stomach butterflies to fly in the right formation." Don't dwell on things that could go wrong!

• If possible, arrive early and set up any equipment you need, such as audiovisuals, teaching props, handouts, and the like, and if using notes, be certain they are accessible and in the correct order—but, remember, don't depend on these! If formal introductions are called for, wait to be introduced; otherwise, introduce yourself or have a friend introduce you. Open with a brief story, personal anecdote, dramatic statement, or rhetorical question, but be certain that your opening relates to your presentation's topic. Be careful when telling jokes as openers: they are rarely related to the topic and can distract or alienate an audience. By all means use humor, but only if it is appropriate and natural.

• Know the audience and their levels of competence. Avoid speaking about topics that are "over the heads" of clients, and don't "talk down" to them. Treat an audience with respect. Clients will be reluctant to learn if they perceive you as arrogant or discourteous. Prepare content with the particular audience in mind. Consider their age, education, knowledge, interest, and size when planning. Prior to any presentation, take the time to meet, talk with, and learn about representative members of the audience, especially if they are an unknown group.

• Be enthusiastic and prepared. If you aren't interested in the topic, then clients certainly won't be either! Organize and rehearse the presentation material in a logical order and know the content extremely well; otherwise, expect many mistakes, some disappointed clients, and the occasional mistake of running overtime. So practice speaking to friends who will give you honest feedback. As you refine your presentation, use a tape recorder to double-check the points your friends made.

• During a presentation, move around. When you vary your position, you help focus audience interest and attention. Stand erect, shift eye contact among a variety of people, use effective body language, for example, by using hand gestures instead of nervously playing with coins in your pocket, breathe steadily for voice control, and utilize a variety of speaking methods, including clarity, volume, speed, and pitch.

• Speak with authority. Speak clearly, loudly, and slowly to overcome surrounding noises. Be certain the learners who answer questions also speak clearly, loudly, and slowly so all may hear. Speaking too slowly, however, may permit client's attention to wander, but speaking too fast may prevent clients from assimilating information. Avoid both speaking in a monotone voice and running words together. Distinguish among similar-sounding words by clearly enunciating each syllable. Use voice inflection to vary the pitch of speech and vary volume to highlight important points.

• Give plenty of examples and analogies to connect the presentation to real life. Make these examples clear, emphasizing the key concepts. Summarize the key concepts, highlight them by varying speech volume or tone, and repeat them often for significance. Pause occasionally: silence can be an effective tool. Provide an agenda for the presentation, for example, by displaying the outline on a flip chart, board, or screen; refer to this outline to let clients know how the presentation is proceeding. Use the "signpost" words, that is, the same indicator words as in the agenda, to convey location within the presentation. Avoid slang words and clichés. Use vivid language that is rich in symbolism, imagery, and metaphor. Listing important words on an outline, defining or explaining any new term that clients may not know.

• Notice audience reaction to the presentation. Monitor body language and energy levels. If cli-

ents appear bored, be prepared to shorten the presentation by dropping a few points. If the presentation content is dry and boring, consider using audiovisuals to spice it up. Since "a picture is worth a thousand words," slides, videos, still photographs, and even overhead transparencies can improve the quality of a presentation and therefore the degree of learning that takes place. Address all responses or comments from the audience by paraphrasing or repeating these for all to hear. Don't ignore this input. Instead, praise or reinforce all contributions, then ask clients questions that elicit deeper comprehension.

• While asking questions seems like a relatively simple thing on first examination, you can choose to follow one of several procedures. Ask clear and concise, open-ended questions, that is, ones that cannot be answered with a short response such as "yes" or "no." Pause and allow plenty of time for thinking. If no answers are forthcoming, gently request one from a particular person. Listen carefully to the answer, paraphrase or repeat it for all to hear, and respond to the person who gave the answer. One sure way to reduce the number of answers given by a group is to criticize their ideas. Instead, thank each person for his contribution and probe for greater detail. If an answer given is incorrect, ask further questions that help the learner to discover this fact without letting on you think he's wrong. While trying to understand clients' opinions, you may sometimes find your own logic in error or may see things from a fresh perspective. Always connect answers to the lesson of the presentation, to reality, or to the next question.

• After a presentation, sum up key points and ask clients for their questions (unless clients have been free to interject questions at any time during the presentation). If you don't know the answer to a client's question, say so, pledge to find out, and then follow up with an answer for that client. Seek feedback (verbal and possibly even written) from clients about the effectiveness of the presentation by asking them for their opinions and by observing their use of the presentation content in future learning situations.

DESIGNING EFFECTIVE LESSONS

While the public speaking suggestions fit well with client presentations, this instructional method constitutes only a small amount of teaching in outdoor leadership situations. More common by far are teaching lessons in the outdoors. The fundamentals of public speaking still apply to this instruction, yet a number of tips and tricks can improve your outdoor teaching, including the areas of lesson planning, setting up the teaching environment, getting started, delivering the information, finishing up, and substituting for audiovisual aids.

Lesson Planning

The key to lesson planning is constantly taking the learner's perspective: always ask what the learner might think of the lesson. Although many different ways to plan a lesson exist, they all have some aspects in common with the following procedure:

a. List all the skills and concepts that learners need to get from the lesson.

b. Organize these into a logical flow, or sequence, of learning. Such organization of information is usually, but not always, linear. You can progress from the known to the unknown, from the inductive (which is reasoning from the particular to the general) to the deductive (which is reasoning from the general to the particular) from the general rule to the example, from the observed to abstract principles, from reality to theory, from whole to piece, from simple to complex, from primitive to sophisticated, and possibly the reverse of all these.

c. Once you have organized the skills and concepts into the main body of the lesson, add a conclusion that summarizes what the lesson was about. Be sure to include a review of the main points and some suggestions of ways to apply the lesson to future learning

d. After completing the first three steps, you'll know how to add an introduction that outlines what the lesson will be about and that motivates the learner by explaining the usefulness of the lesson. Be sure to include the purpose of the lesson, its context within the grand scheme of the adventure program or course curriculum, and its possible connection to past learning.

Teaching Environment

In setting up the teaching environment, consider two locations: the indoor classroom and the outdoor setting. In both locations, consider the

clients' comfort in terms of temperature, for example, adjust thermostat or encourage clients to add or remove clothing layers; lighting, for example, adjust light switches or have clients stand facing away from the sun; and air quality, for example, adjust air conditioning or have clients sit away from campfire smoke. Whether in the classroom sitting in chairs or outdoors sitting on the grass under a tree, the format of the lesson should determine the seating formation. For verbal discussion, form a circle, which permits eye contact for all. For two-way exchange of information, that is, lessons with some discussion and some presentation, use a semicircle arrangement. For lecturing, have the group sit in rows.

Getting Started

When getting started, begin with names and introductions. Avoid the usual "introduce yourself" in favor of a name game and partner or group introduction activity. Next, ascertain the clients' expectations. Have them finish sentences like "I expect this program to . . ."; "This experience will help me . . ."; and, "The adventure will be good if. . . ." You can have them write down their conclusions, shuffle them, and then have them read by another for anonymity or put on a wall for all to see. These responses often prove useful for setting goals and objectives (see the last section of this chapter). Once clients have shared their expectations with you, you should share your expectations with clients. Detail leader roles and responsibilities in the lesson or program. This is also the time to demonstrate congeniality. At best, authoritative leaders can make clients feel inadequate. At worst, they can feel foolish and humiliated. But as an approachable leader, you can make clients willing to risk revealing their ignorance about the lesson material and to gamble on asking you for help.

Delivering Information

When delivering information in a lesson, you can choose from different modes, depending on whether you are demonstrating, in which you actually perform the skill, or clients are simulating your demonstrations, copying the movement that you demonstrated. During demonstrations, break skills down into their component parts. For example, the Dufek stroke, used in whitewater paddling, is a combination of four different paddle movements: high brace, standing draw stroke, draw stroke to the bow, and power forward stroke. For students to learn such a complex stroke in one fluid motion demands that you teach it in pieces and then show students how to reassemble the pieces into the greater whole. Pass demonstration equipment around for everyone to see and touch before you use it. Keep an eye open for clients who begin to practice their simulations early, while the demonstration is still occurring. This action may indicate that they have absorbed too much information and are trying to retain it by practicing. If so, break the demonstration down into smaller parts, reminding them to watch first and try later on. Always begin with easy skills or concepts, increasing the degree of difficulty as the learners gain confidence and competence.

When clients are performing simulations, be sure everyone has finished practicing before giving the next demonstration. If clients get left behind at this point, you will expend more energy than usual helping them catch up in the future, especially if they become lost or disinterested. Assign a helper to work closely with those who need extra time to practice. Enlist the aid of talented or quick learners to partner with a peer who needs assistance. Avoid definite statements like "It's simple!" because clients who don't catch on right away will feel even more inadequate. Last, disclose the criteria you're using to evaluate performance in the simulation, then adhere to these benchmarks, so that clients clearly know what you expect of them.

Finishing Up

When finishing up, don't forget to question, confirming learning. Monitor the group for their reactions, and don't let clients sit still for too long. Let them participate for brief times throughout the lesson to ward off boredom in situations in which you are asking clients to assimilate large amounts of information.

Substituting for Audiovisual Aids

Audiovisual aids are useful for breaking the monotony, presenting complex data, stimulating discussion, providing examples, and emphasizing key learning points in a classroom lecture. Unfortunately, slide or overhead projectors, black- or whiteboards, video players, and flip charts are rarely practical or accessible in the outdoors. But drawing in the sand or dirt can be almost as effective as high-tech visual aids. Clients may pay greater attention if you use handouts as substitutes for audiovisual aids since they don't have to continually take notes. Still, the litter and convenience concerns limit the use of handouts in wilderness areas. If you do use handouts, be aware that they may distract clients from presentations, demonstrations, or simulations. Models are another substitute, but their effectiveness can be less than that of high-tech equipment for some clients. For example, you could demonstrate the "ferrying" technique for paddling laterally across river currents by using a stick and string in a gentle stream. This may not be as compelling or convincing as a computer simulation, a movie, or an actual hands-on demonstration. One idea is to use high-tech in preparatory classes before the adventure, then reinforce the application of this information on-site.

OBJECTIVE WRITING AND GOAL SETTING

Goals and objectives form the foundation for all lessons that are taught in adventure programs. The ability to set goals and objectives is critical to outdoor leaders and is almost as important to clients. You, as a leader, should use goals and objectives to define the direction of the adventure program and to prepare and organize adventure experiences. A client should use them to plan for action after the adventure program as they continue dealing with daily life after returning home. In all cases, writing detailed goals and objectives can augment the reasoning processes for both yourself and your clients.

Goals are general intents that stem from the adventure program's purpose. **Objectives** are specific target declarations that clarify and expand on each goal. If, for example, the purpose of a program is to reduce juvenile delinquency in a community, then one goal might be to reduce self-destructive behaviors in at-risk youth who are clients. Furthermore, one of several objectives for this particular goal might be to improve the self-concept of youth clients, as measured by significant rises in their scores on the Tennessee Self-Concept Scale or other assessment tools, through adventure activities conducted over a three-month treatment period. Although you and your clients should write down goals and objectives, consider them to be always in flux, never carved in stone. In addition, a program could use goals and objectives to direct leader or client behavior or performance.

We can divide goals into four different kinds: regular work goals, problem-solving goals, innovative goals, and developmental goals. Let's examine these four types for an adventure program working with female survivors of sexual abuse. Note that we have written these goals with behavior you should target in mind.

- **Regular work goals** are those that make up the major portion of your responsibilities to ensure the safe, effective, and efficient delivery of program services.

  ☞ *Example:* Empower clients by giving them greater control over the experience.

- **Problem-solving goals** give you opportunities to react to major problems that need solving and to prevent program quality from suffering by doing so.

  ☞ *Example:* Intervene in potential flashback situations that may limit client benefits.

- **Innovative goals** are set by you to proactively improve the delivery of program services.

  ☞ *Example:* Anticipate and eliminate barriers to transfer of learning when clients return to society.

- **Developmental goals** are intended to improve your performance so that a program can improve services, adjust to changing market conditions, deliver better quality services, and reinvest in staff.

  ☞ *Example:* Educate staff as to upcoming minor alterations in the boundaries associated with physical contact with clients.

Objectives are extremely detailed and may comprise a more general goal. In other words, one goal may have multiple objectives. With corporate clients, a normal goal is to develop teamwork. Four resulting objectives for this singular goal could be related to trust, support, cooperation, and communication. For example, on completion of the adventure program, clients will have demonstrated

1. trust in group members by completing the Trust Fall into others' arms from a table top,

2. a willingness to accept and offer help as evidenced by sharing at least five ideas during a complex group initiative task without receiving discouraging comments from any group members,

3. an ability to work together without argument under adversity or time deadlines, and

4. effective listening skills by speaking one at a time during all debriefing sessions and not making comments unrelated to the discussion.

Note that we have written these objectives with the participant's targeted behavior in mind. All four of these interdependent objectives identify elements of conduct, conditions, or criteria (Mager, 1984). **Conduct** denotes what you expect a client to do, generally using active verbs to portray either a process or a product of performance. **Conditions** describe the circumstances under which performance takes place. **Criteria** indicates the level of acceptable performance, generally using some measure of evaluation to determine success. Objectives ideally include all three of these elements. For example, after finishing the module on kayak strokes, the novice client will be able to paddle forward and backward, to skull laterally through a meter-wide English gate on flatwater (conduct), with no wind (conditions), and without touching the gate with paddle or craft (criteria).

Another way of writing objectives is to make them SMART: specific, measurable, achievable, realistic, and time-bound.

- **Specific**: You should state the expected outcome with precision. If you want to be richer, then will a dollar donation easily meet your needs?

- **Measurable**: Define the change as an outcome to reach. If you don't know where you are going, how will you know when you get there?

- **Achievable**: Change should be possible to achieve. Setting unachievable objectives merely leads to frustration. Do you have the resources necessary to achieve this objective?

- **Realistic**: You should base the change in actual circumstances. Is change real or valuable if it takes place during an imaginary role-playing exercise?

- **Time-bound:** You should expect the change to be accomplished by a certain deadline. If you have no time limit for completion, will you have the incentive to finish?

Last, adventure programs are typically evaluated based on goals and objectives. For the goal- and objective-setting process to be of any value, the goals and objectives you set must be relevant, concise, and measurable. The more accurate as well as appropriate the goals and objectives, the greater the true reflection of learning achieved.

EFFECTIVE OUTDOOR LEADERS SHOULD

☞ Be aware of models on depth of learning, inquiry-discovery, and the learning gradient.

☞ Be able to apply these models of learning to teach effectively.

☞ Strive to be capable public speakers and teachers.

☞ Be able to set goals and write objectives for learning and performance.

☞ Be capable of delivering effective lessons both indoors and outdoors.

SUMMARY

We can describe the depth of learning on a spectrum from memorization, through comprehension, application, and generalization, to systemization. The ability to reach a depth of learning depends on instructional methods, such as inquiry-discovery, the learning gradient, and the Socratic method, as well as on skills and strategies, such as public speaking, effective teaching, and appropriate objective or goal setting.

The inquiry-discovery approach to learning helps teach cognitive concepts and has six parts arranged in a cycle: questioning, investigating, analyzing, interpreting, understanding, and answering. In short, this is the scientific method with guidance in the form of questions from you, the outdoor leader.

The learning gradient helps teach activity skills and is a continuum of four methods: speaking, demonstrating, simulating, and confirming. In short, you tell the client some fundamental information about the skill to be learned, show the skill, have the client do or practice the skill, and then ask questions to cement learning.

The Socratic method includes three types of questions: the recall of basic principles, the process of reasoning, and the application of learning to new situations. When you ask these types of questions in sequence, as opposed to randomly, they guide, confirm, and motivate learning.

Public speaking is a common fear of leaders, but an important teaching tool. The keys to unlocking the secrets of public speaking are to relax and be yourself, warm up your voice before speaking, know the audience well, prepare well with their needs in mind, rehearse in advance, vary your style of presentation, speak with clarity and authority, use plenty of examples relating them with vivid language, monitor the audience's reaction and adjust accordingly, ask open-ended questions, and seek feedback afterward so you can do better next time. Some crucial tips and tricks for teaching in the outdoors are to plan lessons in a logical progression, to provide a comfortable place for learning, to ascertain client expectations in advance, to share leadership expectations, to break complex skills down into component parts, to question to confirm learning, and to substitute for audiovisual aids.

Prepare, organize, and teach your lessons for your adventure program based on written program goals and objectives. Then, when you're planning for future client change and your program's administrative direction, look at the goals and objectives again. Goals are general intents that stem from the adventure program's purpose. Objectives are specific targets that clarify and expand on each goal. One goal may have several related objectives, and both should remain flexible. Goals come in four types: regular work, problem-solving, innovative, and developmental. Objectives should mention conduct, conditions, or criteria. Make them SMART: specific, measurable, achievable, realistic, and time-bound.

QUESTIONS TO THINK ABOUT

1. Compare the five depths of learning to the six parts of inquiry-discovery learning.
2. Compare the five depths of learning to the four methods of the learning gradient.
3. Compare the five depths of learning to the three types of questions in the Socratic method.
4. Recall the last time you spoke in public. Which of our suggestions did you use and not use?
5. Recall the last time you taught a skill or concept. Which of the teaching tips and tricks did you use and not use?
6. Think of the purpose of any adventure program, then set four goals, one of each of the four types.
7. Write three objectives for each of the four goals you wrote.
8. Contrast conduct, conditions, and criteria with the SMART way to write objectives.
9. Plan an outdoor lesson, using either the six parts of inquiry-discovery learning or the four methods of the learning gradient.

REFERENCES

Hammerman, D.R., Hammerman, W.M., & Hammerman, E.L. (1985). *Teaching in the outdoors* (3rd ed.). Danville, IL: Interstate.

Hammerman, D., & Priest, S. (1989). The inquiry/discovery approach to learning in adventure. *The Journal of Adventure Education and Outdoor Leadership* 6(2), 29-32.

Mager, R.F. (1984). *Preparing instructional objectives.* Belmont, CA: David S. Lake.

Priest, S., & Hammerman, D. (1990). Teaching outdoor adventure skills. *The Journal of Adventure Education and Outdoor Leadership* 6(4), 16-18.

chapter
13

Teaching
Models

Teaching is a lot like whitewater boating: to be successful the work must be divided up into a series of interconnected choices made before, during, and after the whitewater experience. Before each rapid, boaters make important choices about where they intend to go, what they take with them, when they go, and who goes in what order. In the rapids, boaters often choose their speed and route, pause in an eddy, or even move back upstream to retry a segment of a rapid. After the rapids, boaters make choices about evaluating the success of the passage, discussing how to do it better next time, and preparing for the next set of rapids.

Teaching is much the same: when it comes to conducting learning experiences, you have to make choices before, during, and after the experience. In this chapter, we'll describe in detail a range of teaching styles through which you can slowly shift the control over the learning experience from yourself to your clients. The last area of control to be surrendered by you is usually the planning done beforehand, since this has the greatest power and influence over clients' learning. We have based much of the paradigm used to illustrate this teaching process on the ideas of Mosston and Ashworth (1994).

The model in figure 13.1 shows a range of six teaching styles as well as a seventh shared style. The six styles are differentiated by who, you or your clients, predominantly holds the majority of responsibility when making key choices in the preexperience, experience, and postexperience phases of learning.

PHASES OF THE LEARNING EXPERIENCE

Before discussing the teaching styles, let's take a closer look at the phases and their respective options (see figure 13.2).

Preexperience Phase

The **preexperience phase** concerns the set of choices you make before an adventure experience. We can characterize these choices along the lines of the following six questions about teaching.

• **Why?** refers to reasons for teaching; possible uses of information, such as practical or theoretical; depth of information, such as memorization,

comprehension, application, generalization, and systemization (see chapter 12); and whether information will be appropriate or relevant to the needs of the clients.

• **What?** refers to content or subject matter, such as which topics and in what proportions; intended objectives, that is, what the lesson should achieve; expected outcomes, or what should happen; required resources, such as what equipment you should gather and what other logistics you must deal with; and possibly methods of evaluation, that is how clients might be objectively or subjectively evaluated on their performance.

• **How?** refers to methods, for example, how best to use Socratic questioning or modeling techniques; feedback, such as how best to give or receive; evaluation, including how to establish criteria or procedures; and teaching styles, including how best to communicate information.

• **Who?** refers to the clients, who are receptive to learning, and to the group, whom you should teach as individuals or pairs and in small or large units.

• **Where?** refers to the setting, including best location, environment, or weather for teaching, and to positioning, for example, where to place yourself in relation to the clients.

• **When?** refers to scheduling, such as when to start or finish and take breaks, and to sequencing, such as when to teach each piece of information in the "lesson" and when to teach this lesson in the context of all information to be taught.

Experience Phase

The **experience phase** contains all the choices associated with learning during the adventure,

	Preexperience Before: why, what, how, who, where, and when to teach	Experience During: introduction, pace, direction, resting, redoing	Postexperience After: reflection, evaluation, integration, feedback, follow-up
Dictated	Leader	Leader	Leader
Prescribed	Leader	Leader	Client
Directed	Leader	Client	Leader
Consulted	Leader	Client	Client
Interpreted	Client	Client	Leader
Automated	Client	Client	Client
Shared	Leader and client	Leader and client	Leader and client

Figure 13.1 The range of seven teaching styles for adventure programming.

	Preexperience	Experience	Postexperience
WHY:	Teaching reasons Information uses Information depth Client relevance	INTRODUCTION Briefing & framing PACE & rhythm Learning speeds	REFLECTION Gaining meaning Appropriate methods
WHAT:	Subject matter Intended objectives Expected outcomes Required resources Evaluation methods	DIRECTION Adjustments RESTING Teachable moments	EVALUATION Who establishes criteria Procedures used INTEGRATION Linking learning
HOW:	Methods & styles Feedback & evaluation	REDOING Reexperiencing	FEEDBACK Verbal or nonverbal Source, delay, or withhold
WHO:	Clients & groups		FOLLOW-UP Enhancing transfer Alternatives available
WHERE:	Setting & positioning		
WHEN:	Scheduling & sequencing		

Figure 13.2 Decision options for the three phases.

such as introduction, pace, direction, resting, and redoing.

• **Introduction** refers to briefing clients as to the learning experience in a manner that is consistent with the objectives, for example, using isomorphic framing to enhance metaphoric transfer (see chapters 14 and 16).

• **Pace** refers to teaching information with a rhythm that appropriately matches the diversity of client learning speeds.

• **Direction** refers to making minor adjustments on the run as to where the learning is going (sometimes referred to as "thinking on your feet!") since learning rarely progresses according to the preexperience plan.

• **Resting** refers to stopping for a teachable moment or a breather as well as to terminating the teaching session if unsafe, ineffective, or miseducative.

• **Redoing** refers to allowing clients to experience the opportunity to learn once again. For example, repeating a rapid is never the same: it is very different each time, facilitating further learning.

Postexperience Phase

The **postexperience phase** includes the choices you make after clients have experienced learning through adventure. These options focus clients' attention on gaining meaning and relevance from the experience through methods of reflection, evaluation, integration, feedback, and follow-up.

- To encourage **reflection,** you may select from many methods, such as solo contemplation, group discussion, guided debriefing, and individual journal writing, to help clients learn the most from any experience.

- You have several decisions to make for **evaluation,** such as who establishes criteria (you or clients) and which procedures you will use. For example, you might help clients compare or contrast their performances against the learning criteria and the intended objectives or expected outcomes.

- To facilitate **integration**, you must choose the best way to link the learning in the present experience with past and future experiences.

- You can make several selections about **feedback**, including whether to give it, delay it, withhold some part of it, or use verbal or nonverbal channels, and which source to use: yourself, other clients, the individual, or a partner.

- For **follow-up**, you must consider the alternatives available for enhancing transfer, such as holding formal or informal meetings or social reunions, action planning, mentoring or coaching of new behaviors, involving significant others in feedback sessions, and offering professional support groups for alumni.

RANGE OF TEACHING STYLES

The resulting combinations of constraint and restraint of leader-client control create six styles of teaching: dictated, prescribed, directed, consulted, interpreted, and automated. Let's look at these six styles in more detail, examining a specific example of how you could apply each. Then, we'll tie all six together in a single example to show you the similarities and differences among styles. Last, we'll present the seventh style of

shared teaching in which you and your clients share the choices in all three phases of the learning event, giving you some modified examples.

Dictated Style

In the **dictated style**, you hold total responsibility for the choices made in all three phases: preexperience, experience, and postexperience. The clients have little or no control in any of these phases. In the preexperience, you determine the why, what, how, who, where, and when of teaching. During the experience, you "command" the briefing, rhythm, adjustments, breaks, start or finish, and repetition. In the postexperience, you determine the choice of reflection method, evaluation criteria and procedures, learning integration, feedback, and transfer follow-up. In short, you determine every aspect of the learning experience.

The dictated style may seem constricting or overbearing in a profession that aims to empower its learners, but it has its place in a few learning situations. Consider the importance of safety and the need to do things the "right" way to avoid injury. In fact, teaching safety is the best time to employ a dictated style. For example, while you can teach belaying in many different ways, sometimes when consistency is critically important and safety is of paramount concern all clients and staff must belay the same way. For example, if you dictate that everyone must belay the same way, then you can easily survey a group of belayers and immediately spot individual discrepancies.

Prescribed Style

The **prescribed style** is the same as the dictated style with one exception: the clients have control over the postexperience phase. But you still retain responsibility for the preexperience and experience phases. In the preexperience, you still answer the why, what, how, who, where, and when questions and dictate all the critical choices during the experience. But in the postexperience phase, you let the clients determine how they will interpret, evaluate, integrate, and use what they have learned.

The prescribed style is particularly effective in teaching techniques pertaining to skill acquisition and application in specific situations, for example, when learning how to cave, bike, climb, paddle, or ski in certain conditions. Consider the example of tandem paddling techniques necessary to turn a canoe. As you probably know, a combination of opposite strokes performed at the bow and stern can rotate a canoe about its center point. While a number of stroke combinations can be effective in performing this task, such as sweep and reverse sweep, forward and reverse, draw and crossover draw, or push-away and pry, only certain combinations will work in a specific situation because of specific conditions, such as water depth, turning space, stationary water, or moving water. When using this particular teaching style, you prescribe the acceptable technique for the specific condition, then direct the client to execute this technique in this situation. In this way, clients are able to evaluate how certain strokes work in specific conditions and apply this knowledge to future situations. If they fail to execute the proper strokes, they will still learn in the postexperience phase through the natural consequences of their actions. For example, they may get stuck in shallow water by using incorrect strokes. They may even capsize, but since you have set up this type of "controlled" instructional setting, outcomes tend be more recoverable and acceptable.

Directed Style

With the directed style, you hold responsibility for the preexperience and postexperience phases. The clients have control over choices made in the experience phase. Before the experience, you still decide the why, what, how, who, where, and when to teach. After the experience, you determine how the clients will reflect, who will evaluate, where the learning fits in, whether to employ feedback, and how to follow up. But you allow clients to make choices during the actual experience, such as how fast to go, which direction to take, when to rest or stop, and what pieces to repeat.

The directed style is very useful at times when client freedom to choose is important, yet your control over verifying the safety of their choices is equally important. Take tying knots as an example. Most knots can be tied in many variations. Some of these variations can lead to knots that appear correct to the untrained eye, but can fail under certain circumstances. So you should direct clients through tying the many variations and then let them experiment with several knot tying methods. You should even allow the clients the freedom to try their own variations, choosing the one that works best for them. Then, in the

postexperience phase, you perform a final check of each knot's structure so as to confirm its accuracy, giving feedback to the clients on how well they have done. Safety is critical again, as with the dictated and prescribed styles, but you give clients the freedom to tie the knot any way they choose while still double-checking for safety. When you use the directed style, you give clients both direction and the freedom to make their own choices.

Consulted Style

The **consulted style** is the same as the directed style with one exception: the clients have control over the postexperience phase as well as the experience itself. You retain responsibility for the preexperience phase only. So you plan the experience by making critical selections of teaching reasons, contents, objectives, outcomes, methods, styles, locations, positions, and schedules. Once the experience begins, however, you step back and let clients determine how the experience will proceed and how they will interpret their learning.

The consulted style is especially effective for situations in which safety is not critical, and yet consequential learning is very important. One example is setting up camp. You consult with clients as to the basic ground rules and then permit them to explore their own preferences for setting up camp, regarding such aspects as pitching the tent, lighting a stove, and cooking a meal. If the tent is pitched poorly, the stove cannot be lit, or the meal is cooked for too long, then the clients experience feedback in the form of real and natural consequences: the tent collapses in a storm, the meal is cold, or the food gets burned. You do not become involved in providing feedback, because the learning environment does this for you. Instead, your role is to carefully plan the preexperience phase, selecting circumstances that are ripe for consequential learning, but without the risk of injury. As with the directed style, under the consulted style the clients are free to experiment within the experience, but the consulted style goes beyond the directed style, giving additional freedom in the postexperience phase, allowing clients to learn from their mistakes.

Interpreted Style

In the **interpreted style**, you hold responsibility only for the postexperience phase. The clients have control over the preexperience and experience phases. The clients plan and execute the experience, making the best choices about why to learn, what to learn, how to learn, who learns, where to learn, when to learn, which speed to take, whether to stop, and if they should repeat something. Afterward, you guide their interpretation of the experience by making key choices about reflection, integration, evaluation, feedback, and follow-up.

Some people may be reluctant to offer this much control to learners. However, if one aim of adventure programming is to empower free-thinking and self-reliant learners, then you must use this style. Nevertheless, you should only make the decision to use this style (or the automated style) after careful consideration of the ramifications and only after properly preparing clients for this shifting of responsibilities. Major projects, such as expeditions and service learning, are excellent times to use an interpreted style. Clients plan and complete all of the preparations and executions before and during the learning project, while you help them interpret the experience. Like the consulted and directed styles, the interpreted style gives clients control over their experiences. But unlike any of the styles we've discussed so far, the interpreted style also gives clients control over the design of their experiences. Beware, however: this control is not something you should surrender frivolously, particularly when safety is a concern.

Automated Style

The **automated style** goes beyond the interpreted style to give the clients control over making choices in the postexperience phase as well as in the other two phases. Thus, you relinquish responsibility for all three phases and—as hard as it may be—avoid interfering. Clients make all the choices about planning, executing, and interpreting their learning. As the supervising leader, your role is simply to support clients in their efforts to implement their choices.

The automated style is appropriate for clients who have mastered all the fundamentals of a skill and are in the final stages of applying their learning. An excellent example of this is peer leadership. Here, several clients, now leadership candidates, get together and organize a trip for others. They may be taking school children on a nature walk or senior citizens on a bike tour. The leadership candidates take responsibility for ev-

erything associated with the preparation, execution, and evaluation of the trip. Much like planning and implementing their own expeditions under the interpreted style, the automated style both gives them freedom and allows them to interpret the experience for themselves. The key difference here is that feedback comes from the peers—not the experienced, supervising leader. They govern the evaluation of the experience with minimal input from the supervising leader, who observes, often from a distance.

Shared Style

In the foregoing six styles, the responsibility has primarily rested with either you or your clients. In reality, however, the control over choices made in the preexperience, experience, and post-experience phases is not absolute. When you or your clients are in control, one entity has most of the influence to make choices, but the minority still has representation in those decisions. As a result, responsibility, control, and influence generally vacillate between you and your clients so that the six styles do not have precisely defined boundaries. As a result, overlap is possible and styles interact.

A mix of two or more styles at a time is often quite appropriate, hence the need for a seventh style, the shared style. In the **shared style**, you and your clients work together in the preexperience, experience, and postexperience phases. You and they participate jointly in all choices associated with planning, executing, and evaluating the learning event.

The decision to blend two or more of the six styles into a shared style often depends on two factors: safety and consequences. Recall that the dictated and directed styles afford you a great deal of control over setting up and checking experiences in which safety is a major concern. Remember, too, that the prescribed and consulted styles surrendered a great deal of that control to clients when you wanted them to learn from consequences. The key to selecting styles or creating the best blend of styles lies with balancing your concern for safety with your desire for clients to learn from real and natural consequences.

You can easily modify any of the six examples we gave for the first six styles to become shared teaching by the addition of either leader or client influence at any phase and by the inclusion of both at all phases. Consider the two examples of

Sidebar 13.1

THE RANGE AT WORK: LEARNING NAVIGATION

Typically, you may combine all six teaching styles over time in order to move clients from being dependent learners under your direct supervision to becoming independent learners under more indirect supervision. The following six examples for learning navigation show the gradual shift of responsibility, progressing from you to the clients as they become more masterful at learning within each teaching style.

Early in the process, clients identify the position of symbols on a map by grid references. Grid references are six-digit numbers that describe a precise location and so must be done correctly and according to a consistent sequence. Failure to follow the specific sequence can result in an incorrect number that can represent another place up to 100 kilometers away! Such errors could be fatal in certain situations, especially if the grid references were being used to identify emergency pickup points. In these situations, you should teach grid references with a dictated style. Dictate that clients will learn and use only one way to establish grid references. You retain total control over all phases: preexperience, experience, and postexperience.

Later on in the learning sequence, clients begin to take compass bearings on a map and to sight those bearings in the field. Most topographic maps are drawn to true north, but the compass needle points to magnetic north. Due to this phenomenon, clients must learn to account for the angular difference between these two northerly directions, known as declination. Failure to cope with this magnetic declination can cause bearings to be off by a considerable number of degrees. Three methods exist for dealing with declination. First, the true north lines on the map can be redrawn by the clients to line up with magnetic north. In this manner, the difference will be accounted for on the map. Second, once they have taken a map bearing, they can adjust it for declination by adding or subtracting the angular difference to get the field bearing. In this manner, the difference will be accounted for while moving from the map to the field. Addition or subtraction depends on whether the declination is to the east or west of true north, for example, the common phrase "west is best and east is least." Third, when sighting the field bearing, the clients can permit the red tip of the magnetic needle to point to the local declination value instead of true north as indicated on the compass housing. In this manner, the difference will be accounted for in the field. What matters most is not which method is used, but only that some method is correctly used to eliminate the problem of magnetic declination. Given these factors, you can teach magnetic declination with a prescribed style. In this lesson, prescribe several accepted ways to deal with the difference, then allow clients to use what they prefer. You take responsibility for all aspects of the preexperience and experience phases but allow the clients to decide how they will reflect on, interpret, integrate, apply, and follow up on this learning in the postexperience.

Once they have mastered the basics of map reading and compass use, clients often practice these skills through orienteering events. One example is score orienteering for which you provide clients with multiple locations marked on a map, giving them a specified time limit to reach as many locations as possible. More distant locations are worth more points, while closer ones are less valuable. The aim is to earn as many points as possible by visiting the locations selected by the most effective combination of travel routes and times. This is an example of a directed teaching situation. You direct the clients by setting up the experience and controlling their interpretation of it. But you permit the clients to direct the speed and course of their own experiences.

With a reasonable knowledge of navigation, clients are commonly presented with realistic map-reading exercises. In such an exercise, clients may be bicycling from place to place, following a road map. Along the bicycle route you have selected, clients make choices about which way to go and for how far. This route-finding includes you as a member of the group, but you are only present in case of a problem. This is an example of consulted teaching in which you consult with the clients when they have difficulty with the exercise or need other assistance. You take responsibility for the preexperience, but the clients govern the speed and course of the experience and take responsibility for its interpretation and application.

In a last step prior to a solo expedition, clients navigate cross-country for several days by compass. This activity involves their free-form planning of the route at all stages: from picking the area to visit through choosing the campsites to selecting the final bearings between campsites. When they travel, they do so as a group, but without you. You shadow the group from a distance, resisting the temptation to interfere. With an interpreted style of teaching, you help the group interpret what they have learned after the experience but play no deliberate role in planning or running it.

On a solo expedition, clients route-find on their own and plan all aspects of a canoe journey without any help from you. You do not attend the expedition, and each client goes alone on her own route. Obviously, clients must be well prepared for this task, because considerable learning and responsibility have been transferred to them. Such an automated style of teaching is possible because you have done a tremendous amount of work beforehand. You can now afford to allow the individuals to go alone and to let them run on automatic! Therefore, the clients take full responsibility for the preexperience, experience, and postexperience phases. This obviously occurs when clients have moved on to becoming peer outdoor leaders!

belaying (dictated style) and peer leadership trip (automated style) from the extreme ends of the instructional style range.

Belaying involves a high concern for safety and may require that all clients belay the same way under a dictated style. But on the rare occasion that safety is not such a great concern, you can relinquish a little control over the learning experience to the clients. For example, you can give clients some say in learning other acceptable ways to belay, allowing them to select the method that is most comfortable for them. A shared style is appropriate to permit them this freedom, but only if safety is not of paramount concern, perhaps later in the program.

In contrast, the peer leadership example involved a desire for consequential learning, allowing clients the freedom to make mistakes. If in a certain situation safety is a greater concern than it was in our example, then you, as the supervis-ing leader, must exert greater control over planning, implementing, and evaluating the experience. The clients and you should discuss and negotiate much of the trip content, while you might even attend as a group member, rather than shadow and observe from afar. A shared style permits you appropriate control when leaned toward the automated style, but only if safety is a major concern.

SELECTING THE MOST APPROPRIATE STYLE

No single best teaching style exists. The most effective style is the one that suits the situation at-hand and the preference of the leader and clients. Rarely will you find yourself utilizing only one style. Thus, you should be able to select the most appropriate teaching style, based on the maturity, needs, and best interests of the clients, and on your own interest in safety and desire for consequential learning. For example, you could easily teach how to set up camp by pitching a tent, lighting a stove, and cooking a meal (our consulted style example) with another style, depending on the balance of concerns for safety and consequences. In some cases (e.g., with extreme weather conditions), it would be dangerous to use such a style with inexperienced clients when learning shelter construction. As safety concerns increase and consequential learning concerns decrease, you could shift your style from directed through prescribed to dictated, depending on your levels of concern. Similarly, as safety concerns decrease and consequential learning concerns increase, you could shift your style toward interpreted and automated. When in doubt, compromise and utilize a shared style. This "middle ground" gives you the flexibility to meet clients' needs and your desires as well as gives a smooth transition to other styles if called for. For you, the most important point is to shift responsibility to the learners whenever they are ready to accept more obligations and greater accountability.

EFFECTIVE OUTDOOR LEADERS SHOULD

☞ Be able to understand and recognize the elements of the preexperience, experience, and postexperience phases of any lesson.

☞ Be able to identify their level of concern for safety and consequential learning in any experience.

☞ Be able to select an appropriate style of instruction based both on their concerns and the needs of clients.

☞ Be able to use all seven teaching styles and to move between styles as instructional situations change.

☞ Be able to gradually transfer responsibility to the clients by shifting teaching style accordingly.

SUMMARY

The preexperience, experience, and postexperience phases of an adventure can be controlled by either you or your clients while planning, executing, and evaluating the experience. Various combinations of leader or client control create different styles of instruction. These can range from dictated and prescribed through directed and consulted to interpreted and automated. A seventh, shared style blends the elements of these six, depending on your concern for safety or desire for clients to learn from the consequences.

QUESTIONS TO THINK ABOUT

1. Share with colleagues examples of teaching styles discussed in this chapter in which you have been a participant. Did these styles work? Why or why not?

2. Select a lesson you might wish to teach to a group of clients participating in an adventure program. Identify all the elements of the preexperience, experience, and postexperience phases for that lesson.

3. For the same lesson, identify your level of concern for safety and consequential learning. What is the best style for you to use in teaching this lesson and why?

4. For the same lesson, list the elements of preexperience, experience, and postexperience phases that you would control and those that you would allow your clients to take responsibility for. Explain why you and your clients should have the primary power to make each of these choices.

5. Describe how you could modify your preferred teaching style for the lesson to become a shared style.

REFERENCE

Mosston, M., & Ashworth, S. (1994). *Teaching physical education* (4th ed.). New York: Macmillan.

PART
IV

Facilitation in Adventure Programming

chapter

14

The Process
of Facilitation

The day had been long, but extremely successful for the group. While kayaking ended up being the adventure activity taught during the day, much of the group's success seemed to stem from their outdoor leader's ability to orchestrate an enriching experience and to enable them to see valuable connections between kayaking and each of their futures. The group norms established at the beginning of the day (including "Challenge by Choice" and "Full Value Contract," both explained later in this chapter) served as a constant source of mutual support, creating a strong willingness in each group member to try. The leader's assessment of both group and each individual member's needs seemed to grow stronger as the day progressed, and this was evident in the way the leader guided the group in their discussions and solo time, reflecting on the experience. While the gains where achieved by the group, the leader definitely helped to make these gains more attainable in a way that made a difference for everyone.

As the use of adventure experiences for reaching recreational, educational, developmental, or therapeutic goals has grown, so have certain facilitation methods and techniques that increase the likelihood of achieving those goals. In this chapter, we'll give you an overview of these methods; then, in subsequent chapters, we'll delve more deeply into each particular technique.

While experience serves as the source for being able to achieve client objectives in adventure programs, you can employ a variety of facilitation techniques to make attaining these objectives easier. Sometimes referred to by other names, such as processing and debriefing, we can define **facilitation** as "those techniques that are used to augment the qualities of the adventure experience based on an accurate assessment of the client's needs" (Gass, 1993, p. 219). The central purposes of facilitation are to enhance the quality of the learning experience, assist clients in finding directions and sources for functional change, and create changes that are lasting and transferable. Facilitation has been labeled the "cornerstone" of effective adventure-based learning experiences (Nadler & Luckner, 1992).

WHY FACILITATE ADVENTURE EXPERIENCES?

As a young Outward Bound instructor, Rusty Baillie was quoted as saying "let the mountains speak for themselves." He was referring to the innate power and majesty that such environments have to bring about lasting change in people. Clients, however, do not always receive the "message of the mountains," especially if they are first-time adventurers who may be so caught up in the experience that they miss the meaning of the message.

Certainly, without facilitation, people might learn, grow, and change on their own, but perhaps not as effectively as with the aid of facilitation. Years down the road, they might recognize the importance of their experiences and may even find a later use for what they had gained, but without facilitation, they may lose years of potential learning, growth, and change. But facilitation offers people a chance to share what they have learned and to recognize that they are supported, not alone, in their efforts.

People simply don't learn, grow, or change without reflection on their experiences; without evaluation of the good and bad; without analysis of mistakes, failures, or successes; without considering the impact of actions or decisions; without anticipating consequences or committing to new behaviors; and without understanding how they can use new learning, growth, and change. You can facilitate these gains by escorting people through the process and by accelerating it.

IMPORTANCE OF TRANSFER OF LEARNING

Transfer is a key concept in facilitation. It represents the integration of learning from the adventure program into the participant's real life. Adventure programs are typically characterized by small groups led by one or two leaders. Participants engage in challenging activities that inherently involve risks, forcing them to use personal competence. But clients may or may not be able to successfully apply what they learn in the adventure environment to other environments, such as on the job, within the family, or at school, because these other environments have characteristics that are very different from the adventure program. Still, our hope as adventure program leaders is that clients will transfer and apply the change and growth started in the adventure activity to the their real world situations. We may view transfer as successful if this occurs, making the new learning permanent.

Types of Learning Transfer

Gass (1985) has identified three types of transfer in adventure programming:

1. **Specific transfer** involves the learning of particular skills for use in a closely related situation. Learning to type (on a typewriter) for the purpose of operating a computer terminal is a common example of specific transfer. Here the skill learned is used in the same manner and in a similar situation to where it was learned. Applying knots from sailing to rock climbing is an adventure-related example of specific transfer, because the knots serve similar purposes, even though the activities are different.

2. **Nonspecific transfer** refers to the learning of more general principles or behaviors and applying them to a different situation. For example, mastering a new way to solve problems learned in a classroom situation potentially has use in other settings. In adventure programs, the general principle of "trust" developed during belaying to protect against physical injury can translate to trusting one another for support in other types of risk taking, such as sharing secrets, volunteering ideas, or lending money.

3. A third and specialized form of transfer is known as **metaphoric transfer**. As you know, a metaphor is an idea, object, or description used in place of a different idea, object, or description, in order to denote comparative similarity between the two. This case can occur quite often in adventure education, because the activities can have a strong similarity to actual life experiences.

Metaphoric transfer occurs when parallels exist between the two learning environments. For example, an individual engaged in a rappelling or abseilling activity, poised on the edge of a cliff, may see the parallel connection between the risky options in the activity and real life. The risks in the activity are the perceived physical risk of descending versus the perceived social risk of stepping back despite peer pressure, despite the best intentions of challenge by choice. In real life, the perceived mental risk may be not seeking psychiatric counseling versus the perceived financial risk of paying for it with time and money. Another of many metaphors in rappelling or abseilling is the gathering of internal strength in order to commit to the "first step" of the descent and gathering sufficient courage to begin many other endeavors in life, such as beginning a new job, starting a recovery program, or entering a new social situation.

The key to metaphoric transfer often lies in the power of the metaphoric connection between the adventure and actual life experience. The greater the strength of the parallels, the stronger the clarity of connection. And the clearer the connections appear between the two environments, the more likely a person is to carry over the new learning. Therefore, if an individual personally identifies the metaphors that link the adventure experience with daily living, the potential for transfer is enhanced. Your job is to use various facilitation techniques to strengthen such connections, thereby enhancing transfer.

EMPOWERING CLIENTS

To achieve the purposes of enhancing the quality of the learning experience, assisting clients in finding sources for functional change, and creating changes that are lasting and transferable, two policies must be present in adventure programming: "challenge by choice" and the "full value contract."

Challenge By Choice

Originated by Rohnke (1984), **challenge by choice** strives to empower clients by proactively informing them that they, not you as the outdoor leader, control a major part of determining the degree of challenge, risk, and competence with which they will engage in the adventure experience. This policy is more than simply not forcing people to be involved. The purpose of advising clients in this way is not to lead them to withdraw from the experience, but to provide them with opportunities to challenge themselves in the manner they wish, in the amount they would like, and with the type of support they want. In short, clients may select levels of participation, including, but not limited to, full or partial participation or observation in physical, social, and emotional events. Since, however, nonparticipation makes learning impossible due to the absence of a common experience, you should encourage clients to engage, but at whatever levels they desire.

Schoel, Prouty, and Radcliffe (1988) describe the challenge by choice concept as offering clients

- a chance to try a potentially difficult or frightening challenge in an atmosphere of support and caring,
- the opportunity to "back off" when performance pressures or self-doubt become too strong, knowing that an opportunity for a future attempt will always be available,
- a chance to try difficult tasks, recognizing that the attempt is more significant than performance results, and
- respect for individual ideas and choices (p. 131).

The challenge by choice concept also extends to participation in debriefings: clients have the right to pass at any point in a discussion.

Full Value Contract

We can trace the origins of the **full value contract** to Medrick's (1979) interpretations of Berne's (1961, 1964, 1972) "contracting" work in transactional analysis. The focus was to have participants agree to not discount themselves before beginning an adventure experience. This was done to allay any fears they might possess, to validate their reasons for being involved, to reduce client passivity, and to motivate participation. Let's examine one way in which you might introduce this concept to participants in the following sample presentation:

In response to our concern that every participant gets what they came for on our programs, we ask for two commitments. The first is what we call a "no-discount" or "passivity confrontation" contract. We ask you to agree to pay at-

tention to the information that we provide for your safety and satisfaction. We ask you to follow and support these guidelines to the best of your ability and judgment. When you have questions or are in disagreement with any of these, we ask you to make this known and to work with us to take care of your concerns. In addition, we ask each to agree to confront or be confronted if you observe others or are observed discounting information you have about the provisions taken for your safety and satisfaction (Medrick, 1979).

Building on this work and popularizing its use throughout the profession, Project Adventure reframed the "no-discount" concept to highlight the positives of a group focus with the term "full value." While described in a number of ways, Schoel, Prouty, and Radcliffe (1988, p. 95) described the three elements of the full value contract as an agreement to

1. work together as a group toward individual and group goals,
2. adhere to certain safety and group behavior guidelines, and
3. give and receive feedback, both positive and negative, and to work toward changing behavior when it is appropriate.

One method of presenting the full value contract, constructed similarly to Medrick's presentation for comparison, might go as follows:

In response to our concern that every participant get what they came for during our programs, we are asking each of you to agree to abide by what we call the "full value contract" while you are a member of this group. There are two parts to this contract, the first being that you agree to fully value, respect, and consider yourself during all of our activities as a group. This includes your reactions to all physical and emotional issues that may arise. Treat yourself as you want to be treated, and if this is not happening, we encourage you to not wait until the group picks up on this, but to let us know yourself.

The second part of the contract is to fully value, respect, and consider others during our activities as a group. For example, validating someone's efforts and letting them know that you think they can improve even more is a better example than calling people names or using "put-

Sidebar 14.1

FACILITATION ASSUMPTIONS

Knapp (1990) has identified four assumptions that underlie the facilitation process in adventure experiences.

- As an outdoor leader, assume that your **facilitator assistance** will benefit the insight and comprehension of clients and such benefits will further their efforts to grow toward reaching their goals. Moreover, assume that you possess the facilitation skills necessary to assist clients in achieving the functional changes they desire. Also assume that if you don't possess the facilitation skills necessary to assist clients in achieving the functional changes they desire, you will not become involved with this client as a leader.

- Most adventure experiences are conducted in a **controlled group setting** (see chapter 5). Assume that the use of a group and its associated influences, such as reciprocity and support, will also assist clients in obtaining their objectives through the facilitation process.

- Assume that clients' learning or changes that take place in the facilitation process have **application** and relevance to situations the clients will encounter outside of the adventure experience and in the real world.

- Assume that the stress and adaptive dissonance produced in an adventure experience (see chapters 4 and 11), combined with appropriate facilitation, can provide the necessary elements, stimulus, and **impetus for change**.

These are standard assumptions that exist is almost all adventure programs that are educational, developmental, or therapeutic in purpose. If any of these assumptions are invalid, adapt your style or approach to maintain the effectiveness of the facilitation process

downs." If you see another group member who may not be valued, agreeing to the full value contract also means that you will address this, rather than possibly thinking "Ooh, that's their issue" or "they can take care of themselves." Fully valuing yourself and others is a serious undertaking, but a condition that we've found to be extremely helpful in making sure our experience together is productive and valuable.

Is this contract clear to everyone? If this is, we'd like everyone to verbally agree that they are willing to work by these two principles while we are together. Okay?

During such presentations, you need to watch clients' reactions to the content and, if confusion appears present, encourage clients to ask questions. Once everyone understands the contract, ask them to verbally agree to participate under the full value contract or have them sign a written contract.

FACILITATION GUIDELINES

Beyond challenge by choice and the full value contract, you need to follow particular guidelines and make certain assumptions (see sidebar 14.1). But beyond making assumptions, it's important that you look for ways to refine your skills as a facilitator. Some of the fundamental ground rules that you can implement to help you become a better facilitator include 10 facilitation guidelines regarding group position, time, single speaking, nonviolence, participation, responsibility, commitment, role clarity, confidentiality, and other ethical issues (e.g., Hammel, 1986; Knapp, 1990, 1993; Nadler & Luckner, 1992; Schoel, Prouty, & Radcliffe, 1988).

1. **Group position** is important for effective communication. Group members need to be in a physical configuration that permits them to see

the things that are most relevant for the facilitation process, such as eye contact, facial expressions, and body language. You must provide a setting that allows for this, yet is also warm and relaxing to encourage discussion. For example, position clients in a circle where everyone can see each other but stay in shade so no one is blinded by the sun.

2. **Time** is critical. Schedule sufficient time to reflect on the experience. Match the length of debriefing time to the maturity, needs, and abilities of the clients. Unless working with children or people who are intellectually challenged, a rule of thumb is to spend equal amounts of time doing and discussing. But some may not be able to sit still even this long!

3. **Single speaking** is a sign of group respect. Having one person speak at a time ensures an opportunity for each person to be heard and for everyone to hear what is being said.

4. In keeping with the full value contract, **nonviolence** is a must; violence is never acceptable in any form, whether physical or emotional.

5. In accordance with challenge by choice, clients have the right to pass on **participation** in activities or discussions, selecting their own ways of getting involved in the experiences.

6. Let clients know that each is the only one who possesses the ultimate **responsibility** for her or his own behavior.

7. Place group members in situations in which they can offer **commitment** to the entire facilitation process and not in situations that prevent them from being committed, such as inclement weather or exhaustion.

8. Facilitating **role clarity** in the group process is important to clients. Proactively establishing your role and the group's responsibilities can alleviate potential confusion, such as clients asking the question "Why didn't you let us know we were going in the wrong direction five miles ago?!" You need to be clear about what you are there to do and what you're not there to do (see chapter 19).

9. Make sure that clients understand whether or not information can be shared outside the group. Promise **confidentiality** only when it can be maintained, understanding its limitations. For example, situations in which you may fall into the role of a mandated reporter in which you are dictated by law to report certain issues that may arise, such as abuse, override issues of confidentiality.

10. Beyond confidentiality, many **other ethical issues** exist. Considering how to handle these issues in advance is critical in your preparation. These could include, but may not be limited to, conflict of interests, sexual issues, value differences, client rights, environmental concerns, and individual needs versus group needs. Refer to chapter 23 for further details.

SIX GENERATIONS OF ADVENTURE FACILITATION

The evolution of facilitating adventure experiences has passed through several distinct stages of development with earlier styles fostering the growth of more recent ones (Bacon, 1987; Doughty, 1991; and Priest & Gass, 1993). From these stages several different styles of facilitation have emerged that are used in adventure programs today. We can categorize these styles in order of development and sophistication as follows:

1. Letting the experience speak for itself— learning and doing

2. Speaking for the experience—learning by telling

3. Debriefing the experience—learning through reflection

4. Directly frontloading the experience—direction with reflection

5. Framing the experience—reinforcement with reflection

6. Indirectly frontloading the experience—redirection before reflection

A major philosophical and evolutionary shift in the way leaders facilitate adventure experiences occurred between the third and fourth generations of approaches. The first three generations are used *after* the adventure activity to bring about change. The leaders are reactive to the experience, simply commenting on the group's learning. The last three generations are used *before* and *during* the adventure activity as well as *afterward* to bring about change. In these latter generations, the leaders are proactive, creating unique learning opportunities that enhance reflection later on.

Primarily, the philosophical shift between the former and latter generations has to do with where change takes place during the facilitating process. The difference lies in the belief that the

Sidebar 14.2

PHASES OF FACILITATION

The process of facilitating adventure experiences can be arranged into five phases: diagnosis, design, delivery, debriefing, and detachment. To diagnose, you seek information about the goals people have for the adventure program. In the design phase, you plan the best experiences to meet those goals. In the delivery phase, you present the experience in a safe, environmentally sensitive and educationally effective manner. In the debriefing phase, you guide a reflective discussion or analysis of the experience in order to help people get the most out of the adventure program. In the detachment phase, you provide follow-up and ongoing support to continue the benefits people obtained from participating in the adventure program.

These five phases can be presented in four sequential approaches: linear, cyclical, nested loops, and spiral as diagrammed in figure 14.1. The linear approach has the five phases arranged one after the other in a line. The cyclical approach has the five phases arranged into a circle with detachment leading back into diagnosis. The series of nested loops begins with diagnosis, followed by three phases repeated in small loops and terminated with detachment. The spiral approach has all five phases repeated like in a cycle but on a continual and integrated basis, especially diagnosis and detachment.

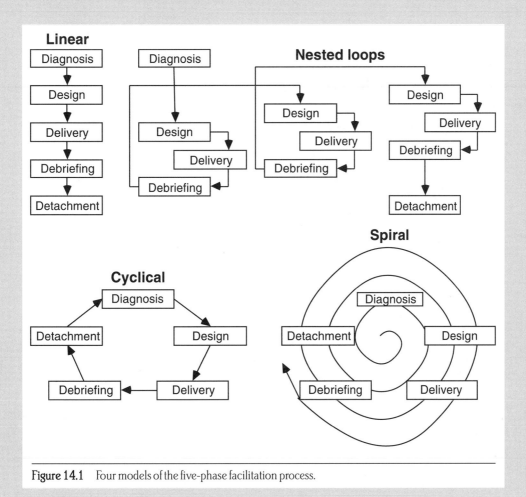

Figure 14.1   Four models of the five-phase facilitation process.

The model you should follow depends on your training as well as on the type of program. The linear model seems to work best with recreational adventure programs for which the usual purpose is to have fun, to learn a new skill, or to be entertained. For example, you might diagnose the goal as learning whitewater paddling skills. So you plan, execute, and evaluate a kayaking trip. Afterward, you provide a list of resources to help people practice and improve their new-found skills. The phases proceed in a straightforward manner.

The nested loops model seems to work best with educational adventure programs for which the purpose is to understand new concepts, to enrich the knowledge of old concepts, or to generate an awareness of the need for change. For example, you might diagnose the goal as being learning about risk taking and fear. So you plan and supervise a sequence of increasingly difficult rock climbs. You independently design, deliver, and debrief each climb, paying attention to the issues of risk taking and fear. At the end of the day, you discuss with the clients their strategies for applying what they have learned about risk taking and fear to their home, school, or work lives once they return.

The cyclical model seems to work best with developmental adventure programs for which the purpose is to improve functional behavior or to train new and different behaviors. For example, you might diagnose that the group goal is to enhance their teamwork skills. So you plan and present a problem-solving exercise that requires teamwork for its solution. After the exercise, you direct a discussion of what was learned and how this might be useful for people in the future. But during the exercise, you note that the group had poor communication. So you use this information as part of the diagnosis for the next cycle of designing, delivering, and debriefing a communication exercise. In this second exercise, you note a lack of trust among group members, and so the cycle repeats once again, the third time focusing on issues of trust. In all cycles, later phases provide information that feeds into earlier phases in the next cycle.

The spiral model seems to work best with therapeutic adventure programs for which the purpose is to reduce dysfunctional behavior or to condition less negative behaviors. For example, you might diagnose that the goal for a group is to manage their addictions to drugs. Addiction, however, is such a complex and personal behavior that you rarely will have the total diagnostic picture nor all the developmental answers for each individual. Therefore, diagnosis and detachment must be ongoing during the entire therapeutic experience. As you design, deliver, and debrief a series of activities, new information arises which helps you refine your diagnosis hypotheses and detachment strategies. As these hypotheses and strategies change, so do the designing, delivering, and debriefing approaches to subsequent activities. The relationships among all five phases are merged, integrated, and reciprocal in nature. The CHANGES model, which we'll discuss in chapter 17, is an example of a related and integrated spiral approach to diagnosis.

Often the design, delivery, and debriefing phases can form a small repeated cycle within one of the programming models we've already discussed. Shown in figure 14.2, this small repeated cycle can be particularly useful for group initiatives as well as other adventure activities (Priest, 1989). The diagram is based on the optical illusion of an "Eternal Staircase," designed by the Penroses in 1958 and popularized by Escher in his infinity artwork of the 1960s. "Eternal" suggests a cyclical sequence that repeats as necessary. "Staircase" indicates steps that may be skipped or taken in any reasonable order, allowing you to customize your presentations as desired. For example, information obtained during the delivery or debriefing phases can feed back into the diagnosis or design phases, helping you refine your original diagnosis of needs via the observation or assessment steps of the cycle.

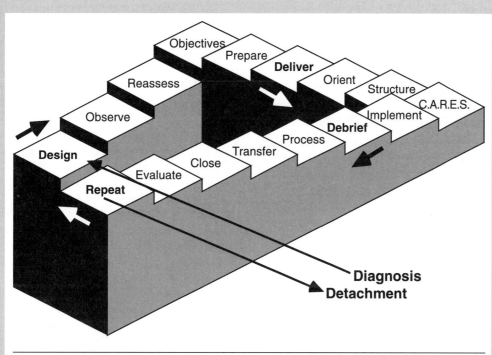

Figure 14.2   Design, deliver, debrief, and repeat the steps of facilitation.

Although the four models appear to fit the four types of adventure programming, with practice, you can easily mix and match approaches to suit the situation. But until you have plenty of background knowledge, facilitation expertise, and practice, you should stick to the simpler models. In reality, the linear model is the easiest to apply, while the spiral model is the most difficult with the cyclical and nested loop models representing intermediate variations of these extremes. Nevertheless, the content of each of the five phases remains relatively constant.

experience itself (not just reflection) can be a powerful medium for change. Therefore, you can facilitate changes before and during the experience as well as after the fact. Debriefing is used for discovery of learning in the first, second, and third generations. It remains a part of the fourth, fifth, and sixth generations, but leaders use it more often for reinforcement and redirection of prior learning, rather than for actual discovery.

The following are brief explanations of each generation with an example of how you might use each of these facilitation styles with the well-known adventure activity: the Spider's Web (Webster, 1989).

Letting the Experience Speak for Itself

The first generation experience, **letting the experience speak for itself**, is a method found in numerous adventure programs in which clients are left to sort out their own personal insights (Doughty, 1991). When properly sequenced and otherwise well-designed, the inherently enriching qualities of adventure activities serve to lead clients into their own insights and discoveries through "learning and doing." This approach is fine, as long as you're not concerned with achieving identified or prescriptive intrapersonal and interpersonal goals. Clients may well have a good time and possibly become proficient at new skills, but they are less likely to have learned anything about themselves, how they relate to others, or how to resolve certain issues confronting them in their lives.

In letting the experience speak for itself, you do not look to add any insights regarding the Spider's Web exercise when the experience was completed. If you make any comments, they might pertain to how much fun the experience was and then encourage the group to move on and try the next event: "That was great! Good job! Now let's try something new and different."

Speaking on Behalf of the Experience

In an effort to enhance programming efforts, several programs have implemented the second generation approach of **speaking on behalf of the experience**. Here you (often in the role of an expert) interpret the experience for the clients, informing them of what they have learned and how they should apply their new knowledge in the future.

In speaking for the experience, you provide the group with feedback about their general behaviors after the activity was completed: what they did well, what they need to work on, and what they learned from the exercise. Examples of such statements might include the following: "You've learned to cooperate by virtue of working together and succeeding. Your communication is poor, everyone is talking, and no one seems to be listening to anyone's ideas. The level of trust seems to be improving, since no one appeared to worry about being picked up by the others. You could have benefited from having a coordinator for this activity!"

"Learning by telling" can be appropriate in role-playing and simulations in which results are predictable and reproducible time and time again. In the adventure experience, however, groups bring unique behavioral history to bear on the way they act under stress. The results of these experiences also seem to be more unpredictable and unique. Due to this uncertainty, client learning is generally quite varied and personal. Telling individuals what they received from an experience can invalidate and alienate them, possibly disconnecting you from clients, thereby hampering future learning opportunities.

Debriefing the Experience

One solution to the problems arising from telling has been to encourage "learning through reflection" styles that enable clients to discover learning after the experience. As clients bring up issues to work on or state personal commitments to change, they are more likely to follow through if they possess ownership of such issues. By your asking questions, instead of telling, clients are much more likely to assume ownership. This idea has given rise to the third generation approach of **debriefing the experience**, popularized in North America as the "Outward Bound Plus" model (Bacon, 1987). Here you ask clients to reflect on each adventure activity, discussing points of learning that you believe took place. Obviously, if an experience is to have true meaning for clients or if they are going to make use of new learning, then they should have a vested interest in the experience and be prepared to bear responsibility for their actions or how they functioned during the experience. In this model, clients learn under the guidance of a questioning leader, who helps the group to discover their own learning. Although numerous methods of debriefing exist, the most common approach in North America is the group discussion. Some successful examples of other debriefing approaches include "funneling" (Priest & Naismith, 1993), portions of the "Adventure Wave" (Schoel, Prouty, & Radcliffe, 1988), and other methods based on cognitive hierarchies (Quinsland & Van Ginkel, 1984; Hammel, 1986).

In debriefing the experience, you facilitate a group discussion concerning the details, analysis, and evaluation of the group's behavior following activity completion. Sample questions of this style of facilitation might include the following: "What happened? What was the impact of this? How did that make you feel? What did you learn from this? What aspects of this activity were metaphors of your life? What will you do differently next time?"

Directly Frontloading the Experience

Since reflection is typically accomplished after the experience, a number of leaders have concluded directing the clients before the experience even begins may also be beneficial. This kind of thinking has led to the fourth generation approach of **directly frontloading the experience**. Frontloading is a term used for highlighting, or loading, the learning prior to, or in front of, the experience. In most adventure activities, you typically brief clients before the experience by explaining how the activity should work, including tasks, rules, or safety concerns, and then debrief them afterwards by guiding reflective discussions. In the fourth generation, however, you hold the frontloading session right before engaging in the adventure as a kind of extra "prebriefing" during which you emphasize several key points, such as the following:

1. **Revisit**: what behaviors or performances were promised and learned from the last activity
2. **Objectives**: aims of the activity and what can be learned or gained from this experience
3. **Motivations**: why experiencing the activity might be important and how it relates to life
4. **Function**: what behaviors will help bring about success and how to optimize these
5. **Dysfunction**: what behaviors will hinder success and how to overcome these barriers

In essence, in the frontloading style, you focus clients on certain distinct learning outcomes that you have ascertained as valuable. By loading the learning up front, debriefing simply becomes "direction with reflection," reemphasizing the learning rather than reacting to events as in earlier generations.

In frontloading the experience, you introduce the Spider's Web with the same logistical briefing as usual: group members should be passed through the opening in the web, from this side to that one, without touching the strands. Contact with a strand wakes the spider, who bites you, causing you to start over. A repeated contact sends your whole group back to the beginning. In addition to this, you add a series of questions to focus the learning before starting the activity: "What do you think this exercise might teach you? Why is learning this important? How might what you learn help you in the future? Do you recall from past exercises what each of you wanted to work on in situations like this?" Since this frontloaded prebriefing has already covered many of the topics you usually cover in debriefing, you can concentrate the concluding discussion on changes.

Isomorphically Framing the Experience

A fifth generation of facilitation involves **isomorphically framing the experience** and is still a relatively rare approach in adventure programming. Recall that metaphors are the analogous connections made by clients between the adventure experience and their real lives. **Isomorphs**

are the parallel structures added to the adventure experience by you to encourage clients to make certain metaphoric connections (Gass & Priest, 1993). For example, if you use the word "marriage" to describe a canoe, you may be creating an isomorph that links the skills of tandem paddling to the dynamics of living with a partner. Strong linkages, that is, those that are meaningful and relevant, increase client motivation and usually enhance transfer of learning. If you can "frame," or introduce, an activity with several isomorphs, painting a mirror image of reality for the clients, then any changes they express in the similar adventure experience may match the change desired for daily living. When this framing is successfully accomplished, transfer will also be effective, since the dynamics and processes of the two experiences will not be all that different. As with the frontloading style, you only need to lead a little debriefing afterward. Thus, debriefing becomes "reinforcement in reflection" since clients discuss the close similarities and immediately see the obvious connections for themselves. For example, clients think "If a strategy works here, it can work in real life, too."

So in isomorphic framing, you address the prebriefing in terms of the structures that are similar between the adventure and corresponding present-life experiences of the client. For example, with a group working in a company warehouse, the Spider's Web activity might be transformed into a distribution network (the web) through which goods and services (team members) are passed from the warehouse (one side) to the customer's many outlets (other side). Passage takes place along unique routings (openings), and contact with the network (brushing up against a strand) damages the goods and services, which means they need to be returned to the warehouse. If damaged goods and services are purposely passed on to the customer, then all shipments will be refused by the customer and returned to the warehouse to be fixed and shipped again! If this form of briefing is close to a mirror image of the workplace and current reality of this organization, then the debriefing need only focus on reinforcing the needs of the organization that were accomplished during the activity and on those that weren't achieved due to particular shortcomings.

One critical feature of framing adventure experiences of tremendous importance is that the basis for constructing appropriate frames lies within what the *client,* and not the facilitator, brings to the experience. Too often this form of facilitation has failed when facilitators have presented their own "favorite frame" of an adventure experience that makes sense to their reality and has little isomorphic connection to the clients' reality. Mack (1996) has termed this "imposed metaphors" and has called for the need to use "derived metaphors" from clients. As we shall see in chapter 16, frames are derived from what clients bring to the adventure experience yet are *co-created* by the client and the facilitator on the basis of what the clients need.

Indirectly Frontloading the Experience

The most rare generation of facilitation are instances involving **indirectly frontloading the experience**. Effective leaders generally use this style only as a last resort: when all other approaches have failed, only when it is in the clients' best interests, and for the purpose of addressing continuing problematic issues. For example, when the harder a client tries to eliminate an unwanted issue, the more it occurs, or the more a client tries to attain a desired result, the more elusive this result becomes, this approach may help. Indirect frontloading (i.e., the frontloading benefit indirectly addresses the client issue) can take several paradoxical forms: double binding (e.g., "win-win" frames), symptom prescription, symptom displacement, illusion of alternatives, and proactive reframing (Waltzlawick, 1978). (See chapter 16 for more information.)

ADVENTURE PROGRAMS AND FACILITATION STYLES

Because of the unique goals of each type of adventure program, certain styles of facilitation tend to be more appropriate or more commonly used with certain types of programs:

- In **recreational** adventure programs in which having fun, learning a new skill, and being entertained is the purpose, the first and second generations tend to be the most appropriate facilitation approaches.
- In **educational** adventure programs, in which understanding new concepts, enriching the knowledge of old concepts, and generating an awareness of the need for change is the purpose, the third generation

is the most commonly used method of facilitation.

- In **developmental** adventure programs, in which improving functional behavior and training new and different behaviors is the purpose, third, fourth, and fifth generations appear to fit best.
- In **therapeutic** adventure programs, in which reducing dysfunctional behavior and conditioning clients to use less negative behaviors are the main purposes, the fifth and sixth generations are the most effective techniques.

You have a responsibility to your adventure program, which provides a service, and to your clients, who consume that service, to be clear as to the level of facilitation you can and should provide. For example, the reputation and credibility of the profession suffers when a client requests therapy with the intent of getting specific prescriptive change, the program provides education with a more general focus, and the leader offers recreation with little or no facilitation! Thus, you have the responsibility to consider the types of programs you can offer, which generation is most appropriate for your program, and how the choice of approach will impact clients.

EFFECTIVE OUTDOOR LEADERS SHOULD

☞ Be able to implement challenge by choice and the full value contract policies with clients in their adventure programs.

☞ Be able to apply the 10 facilitation guidelines.

☞ Be able to comprehend the four facilitation assumptions.

☞ Know the difference between types of transfer, understanding when to use each type in an adventure program.

☞ Be capable of correctly applying the six generations of facilitation techniques to the four types of adventure programs.

☞ Be capable of determining the best facilitation process to use in each particular adventure program.

☞ Be capable of hypothesizing client's needs and goals from interviewing multiple sources.

Sidebar 14.3

TAKING CARE OF ONE ANOTHER: THE CARES MODEL

This model gives guidelines detailing the importance of acting safely toward self, others, and the environment when facing physical, social, emotional, or intellectual dangers. CARES can be an acronym for

Physical	Social	Emotional	Intellectual
C aution	**C** onsideration	**C** oncern	**C** ommitment
A lertness	**A** dmiration	**A** ppreciation	**A** wareness
R esponse	**R** ecognition	**R** espect	**R** easoning
E liminate	**E** ncouragement	**E** mpathy	**E** mpowerment
S afeguard	**S** ynergy	**S** haring	**S** upport

CARES is another way of expressing challenge by choice and the full value contract. Initially, you might choose to explain CARES guidelines and seek adherence. But if the group creates its own "operating principles" as it works through activities, then they are more likely to own and follow these guidelines and not to devalue themselves, others, or nature with words or actions. Examples of operating principles include celebrating and valuing diversity in the group, seeking input and ideas from everyone, making all criticism constructive, and protecting the environment. Examples of devaluing might include making fun of people using "zingers" or put-downs, ignoring belaying or spotting responsibilities for people at risk, fighting, or littering. A verbal or written contract, mutually created by you, your coleaders, and your group, can outline acceptable or unacceptable behaviors and the consequences for infractions.

☞ Be capable of observing behaviors, reassessing needs, setting objectives, and preparing activities to meet the objectives.

☞ Be capable of orienting, which involves briefing group objectives, structuring for individual objectives, discussing risks and responsibilities (CARES guidelines), and implementing the activity as referee and counselor.

☞ Be capable of guiding reflection by processing, transferring, closing, and evaluating the learning.

☞ Be capable of establishing support, planning for action, and following up.

SUMMARY

Facilitation is the collection of techniques you should choose from to optimize and enhance the learning and change which come from an adventure experience, based on a thorough needs assessment. Challenge by choice and the full value contract are two policies at the center of good facilitation. Challenge by choice puts the client, not you, in control of selecting how and when to participate in activities or discussions. The no-discount or full value contract suggests operating principles that govern how people should treat themselves and one another. Ten facilitation guidelines are concerned with group position, time, single speaking, nonviolence, participation, responsibility, commitment, role clarity, confidentiality, and other ethical issues. Four facilitation assumptions include facilitator assistance, controlled group setting, application, and impetus for change.

Transfer of learning is successful when changes noted in the adventure program show up and are retained in the clients' daily lives. Transfer can be specific through which particular skills are applied to similar situations, and nonspecific, through which more general principles are applied to a different situation. Metaphoric transfer refers to a special type of transfer that occurs when several elements of the adventure program appear—in the mind of the clients—similar to their everyday lives. Clients begin to think that if they can change in an activity that is very similar to their home, school, or work situations, then perhaps they can change in real life. The more metaphoric the connection, the greater the transfer.

Facilitation techniques in adventure programs have evolved through six generations. The first generation involves no debriefing at all. The second two generations are normally used in the debriefing phase, and change takes place after the activity. The fourth, fifth, and sixth generations are usually most effective when applied to the design or delivery phases, and change takes place before or during the activity, although reflective debriefing still plays an important role after the fact.

The first generation, letting the experience speak for itself, involves no debriefing. In the second generation, speaking on behalf of the experience, you tell the group what they learned. In the third generation, debriefing the experience, you guide reflection about the experience, typically by asking carefully sequenced questions. In the fourth generation, directly frontloading the experience, you emphasize key learning points in advance of the experience. In the fifth generation, isomorphically framing the experience, you introduce the activity with isomorphs (prescriptive metaphors) in a way that makes it uniquely meaningful and relevant to the client. In the sixth generation, indirectly frontloading the experience, you use paradox to create change in extremely difficult situations. These six generations are well suited to particular types of adventure programs, such as recreational, educational, developmental, or therapeutic. You have a responsibility to know which generation of facilitation techniques you can or should perform and what influence your chosen techniques will have on clients' needs and program types.

The process of facilitating adventure experiences can involve various arrangements of five phases: diagnosis, design, delivery, debriefing, and detachment. In the diagnostic phase, you assess the needs of the clients, determining the adventure program goals by interviewing as many sources as possible to create, confirm, or reject initial hypotheses about the group and its members. In the design phase, you observe the group and its members, reassess your original hypotheses, set your objectives, and prepare the best activity to meet those objectives. In the delivery phase, you orient the group to the task with a briefing of group objectives, structure the activity in order to meet individual objectives, discuss the risks and responsibilities of the activity by sharing CARES guidelines, and then implement the activity with attention to those guidelines, all while playing the roles of referee and counselor. In the debriefing phase, you guide the group through reflection about the experience by processing what was learned, which involves looking backward, by transferring this new learning, which involves looking forward, by closing the activity with feedback, and, finally, by evaluating whether or not the experience met the objectives. In the detachment phase, you establish support for the group and its members, planning practical strategies and follow-up procedures. These five phases can be presented in linear, cyclical, or spiral models, or in a series of nested loops. Each model is well suited to a particular type of adventure program: linear for recreation, nested loops for education, cyclical for development, and spiral for therapy.

QUESTIONS TO THINK ABOUT

1. Differentiate among the three types of transfer. From your own learning, give examples of each of the types in action.

2. Explain the rationales behind the challenge by choice and the full value contract policies.

3. Contrast the 10 facilitation guidelines with the four facilitation assumptions.

4. Differentiate among the six styles of the facilitation process. From outdoor activities you know, give examples of each of the phases in action.

5. Differentiate between the two different uses of the word "process" in this chapter.

REFERENCES

Bacon, S.B. (1987). *The evolution of the Outward Bound process*. Greenwich, CT: Outward Bound, USA. (ERIC Document Reproduction Service No. ED 295 780)

Berne, E. (1961). *Transactional analysis in psychotherapy.* New York: Grove Press.

Berne, E. (1964). *Games people play.* New York: Grove Press.

Berne, E. (1972). *What do you say after you say hello?* New York: Grove Press.

Doughty, S. (1991). Three generations of development training. *Journal of Adventure Education and Outdoor Leadership* 7(4), 7-9.

Gass, M.A. (1985). Programming the transfer of learning in adventure education. *Journal of Experiential Education,* 8(3), 18-24.

Gass, M.A. (1991). Enhancing metaphoric transfer in adventure therapy programs. *Journal of Experiential Education* 14(2), 6-13.

Gass, M.A. (Ed.). (1993). *Adventure therapy: Therapeutic applications of adventure programming in therapeutic settings.* Dubuque, IA: Kendall/Hunt.

Gass, M.A., & Dobkin, C. (1991). *Book of metaphors: Volume I.* Durham, NH: University of New Hampshire, Department of Kinesiology.

Gass, M.A., & Priest, S. (1993). Using metaphors and isomorphs to enhance the transfer of adventure learning. *Journal of Adventure Education and Outdoor Leadership* 10(4), 18-23.

Hammel, H. (1986). How to design a debriefing session. *Journal of Experiential Education* 9(3), 20-25.

Knapp, C. (1990). Processing experiences. In J.C. Miles & S. Priest (Eds.), *Adventure education* (pp. 189-198). State College, PA: Venture.

Knapp, C. (1993). Processing experiences. In Gass, M.A. *Adventure therapy: Therapeutic applications of adventure programming in therapeutic settings.* Dubuque, IA: Kendall/Hunt, 239-244.

Mack, H. (1996). Inside work, outdoors: Women, metaphor, and meaning. In K. Warren (Ed.). *Women's voices in experiential education.* Dubuque, IA: Kendall/Hunt Publishing Company, 24-31.

Medrick, R. (1979). *Confronting passive behavior through outdoor experience: A TA approach to experiential learning.* Denver: Outdoor Leadership Training Seminars.

Nadler, R., & Luckner, J. (1992). *Processing the adventure experience: Theory and practice.* Dubuque, IA: Kendall/Hunt.

Priest, S. (1989). A model of group initiative facilitation training: GIFT. *The Outdoor Communicator* 20(1), 8-13.

Priest, S., & Gass, M.A. (1993). Five generations of facilitated learning from adventure experiences. *Journal of Adventure Education and Outdoor Leadership* 10(3), 23-25.

Priest, S., & Naismith, M. (1993). A model for debriefing experiences. *Journal of Adventure Education and Outdoor Leadership* 10(3), 20-22.

Quinsland, L.K., & Van Ginkel, A. (1984). How to process experience. *Journal of Experiential Education* 7(2), 8-13.

Rohnke, K. (1984). *Silver bullets.* Hamilton, MA: Project Adventure.

Schoel, J., Prouty, D., & Radcliffe, P. (1988). *Islands of healing: A guide to adventure-based counseling.* Dubuque, IA: Kendall/Hunt.

Waltzlawick, P. (1978). *The language of change.* New York: Norton.

Webster, S. (1989). *Ropes course safety manual: An instructor's guide to initiatives, and low and high elements.* Dubuque, IA: Kendall/Hunt.

chapter

15

Basic Facilitation
Techniques

During a challenge course experience, two groups moved on to their next low element activity, the Spider's Web. With the groups facing the web, each outdoor leader went over the rules and safety procedures for the activity and asked if there were any questions. After clarifying these points, the leaders gave each group 25 minutes to complete the task.

After the first group had completed the experience, one leader led a lengthy group discussion concerning the details, analysis, and evaluation of the group's behavior during the activity. Sample questions the leader asked included "What happened? What was the impact of this? How did that make you feel? What did you learn from this? What aspects of this activity were metaphors of your life? What will you do differently next time?"

For the second group, the outdoor leader asked a series of questions to focus the learning *before* the activity: "What do you think this exercise might teach you? Why is learning this important? How might your learning help you in the future? Do you recall from past exercises what each of you wanted to work on in situations like this?" After the group completed the experience, the outdoor leader led a brief discussion summarizing the answers the group discovered during the activity.

The two scenarios may appear similar, but are quite different. The first is an example of debriefing the experience: the questions are asked afterward. The second is an example of frontloading the experience: the questions are asked beforehand. With debriefing, any client changes come after the debriefing and in the next activity. With frontloading, client changes come in the present activity. You should, however, reserve frontloading for those few times when learning needs to be primed in advance. In this chapter, we'll examine some of the basic approaches to facilitation, including discussion and nonverbal techniques, debriefing techniques, and the more recently developed technique of frontloading.

DISCUSSION TECHNIQUES

Discussion is an unstructured form of debriefing that permits clients to analyze past experience and to transfer learning from their adventures to their future lives. By verbalizing reactions to an adventure, clients may reinforce their own perceptions and see the situation from a fresh perspective. Furthermore, knowing that a discussion will follow the activities, many clients will be more attentive to what is going on during an experience and will exhibit a heightened awareness

of relationship dynamics, task product, and group processes. To accomplish these outcomes, you must guide the discussion, using a number of facilitation tips and tricks to make the discussion content and format valuable to clients. These same tips and tricks are equally applicable to the later generations of techniques found in the next two chapters, such as funneling, frontloading, and framing.

Remember, to begin a discussion, you should typically arrange clients in a circle. This allows them to more easily hear what everyone says and to see one another. Clients should be comfortable and ideally should all stand or all sit, but not both, so eye contact is possible. You should also be part of the circle, so as to guide discussion, read body language for signs of discomfort, and make eye contact but not enough to dominate or threaten anyone. If the sun is shining, you should be facing the sun, keeping it out of the clients' eyes.

Client investment in the group and willingness to change stems from existing in a safe and supportive atmosphere. Such an atmosphere is characterized by mutual trust, respect, equality, flexibility, freedom, empathy, acceptance, and anonymity. Physiological needs for food, water, shade, and shelter are met. Psychological safety is protected through fully valuing self and others, and through challenge by choice. With a supportive atmosphere in place, clients are able to take risks by experimenting with new thoughts, feelings, and behaviors. In this setting, they take personal responsibility for their own learning, and change comes more easily than when the atmosphere is competitive, harmful, fixed, controlled, or critical.

To create a supportive atmosphere, you must establish and expect clients to follow certain ground rules. Furthermore, you must guide the group in evolving their own operating principles. These may include, but are not necessarily limited to, speaking for oneself, single speaking; listening and talking in the here and now, instead of dwelling on past history; respecting self, others, and the environment; giving everyone the right to pass and not respond; welcoming all points of view; agreeing or disagreeing with the idea, not the person; avoiding put-downs; and maintaining the confidentiality of group members.

But you should never facilitate beyond your ability. If a client discloses a psychiatric concern, don't open that can of worms unless qualified in psychiatry; instead, refer the individual to appropriate professional counseling. You should do your homework by finding out about the client group in advance and assessing their needs and objectives for the adventure.

Before the discussion, you should explain the difference between a product and process orientation, adding that the discussions will center on group dynamics although clients may be tempted to talk about task outcomes. In addition, explain the concepts of transfer and metaphors in advance. Remind clients to search for metaphors throughout the program.

The ensuing discussion should progress from positive topics to dealing with negative issues, then end on a positive note. Ask open-ended questions (see sidebar 15.3) of the entire group and speak loudly so everyone can hear. Be sure that phrasing is clear and concise by avoiding complex wording. After asking one question at a time, provide plenty of time for clients to think about the question, to think about answers, and then about how they will respond within the group. Listen to clients' answers, then correctly paraphrase their responses in order to confirm and clarify the intent for others. Acknowledge and validate all responses with a verbal thank-you or a nonverbal signal, such as a nod of your head.

You must also act as a "gatekeeper" for discussion by giving everyone a chance to contribute. While recognizing that silence can be a form of contribution, you should be attentive to clients who are always quiet or speakers who are too dominant, run off on tangents, and talk forever.

Invite quiet clients to contribute by asking them by name, seemingly at random, but without putting them on the spot. Make gentle eye contact, lean forward, and smile invitingly. Be certain to provide a legitimate way out if the person chooses not to share by shifting your eyes to other clients and backing off.

Listen to overbearing speakers for expression of a useful statement. Once you hear such a comment, ask "What do others think of this point?" Ask the speaker to reemphasize the point if necessary, but clearly move on to others.

Redirect tangential speakers back to the topic of discussion without sounding critical or angry. You can ask them to relate their comments to the theme being discussed or you can note a time limitation, indicating the need to return to the main issue. Be supportive of the speakers' ideas, but put them on hold and return to them later. Avoid confronting the individual, thereby inhibiting future valuable comments from others.

Stop lengthy speakers with a polite interruption. When interrupting, excuse yourself and explain your reasons for doing so. If repeated interruptions become necessary and seem ineffective, you can introduce the burning match constraint. Each client is given the same number of matches and may only speak for as long as one match keeps burning.

Another technique is to use fishbowling, which splits the group in two, one half surrounding the other. The outer circle observes the inner circle's discussion and notes the frequency with which people speak, and what they say or do. The outer circle reports their findings to the inner circle, and then clients change places. Tossing a ball of string, with the tail unraveling from speaker to speaker, also enables the group to identify a pattern of dominant and recessive talkers among them.

Or have clients pass a talking stick or another inanimate object in one direction around the circle. Only the person with the stick may talk. These procedures can give quieter group members a chance to speak up and may be less intrusive than "picking on" the silent ones by name.

Sometimes private conversations within the discussion can interfere with client learning, and so you may need to deal with these. Calling attention to this potential problem before beginning the discussion may provide a nonthreatening, proactive way to deal with this problem. Initially, figure out why the conversations are taking place. One person may be clarifying a discussion point for another. Or the discussion may be so boring that two people are making small talk on the side. If the reason is appropriate, you can ask the two to share their thoughts with the whole group or you can break into small groups to encourage side discussions, then have small groups return to the big group. If the reason is inappropriate, you can comment on the distraction being counterproductive or you can even terminate the discussion and go to the next activity.

Occasionally, clients can get "stuck in a rut" during an activity. They may have promised change in the last discussion, but can't seem to get it together in this activity, or they have just fallen apart as a team, straying dangerously off-task. At times like these, you can call a time-out or freeze the action, then follow this with a single well–thought-out comment. This careful intervention and a brief interjection can get the clients out of the rut, putting the group back on track to positive change.

In the event of failure at a task, clients will frequently concentrate on how they could fix the product of their actions, that is, what physical things they could have done better. Instead, you should focus the discussion on the process of their actions: the human relationships and group dynamics used to solve the problem. But in the event that clients continually return to the task during the discussion, let them talk about this hang-up until they are satisfied enough with their product to be willing to talk about the process.

Create a balance in the topics of discussion. You shouldn't always examine mistakes, setbacks, failures, and other weaknesses. You should generally balance such negativity by discussing the strengths, such as success and achievement. Too many negatives can prolong agonies and lead to "paralysis by analysis," in which some clients become reluctant to discuss anything, freezing up in fear of constantly examining their shortcomings.

ALTERNATIVE REFLECTIONS AND NONVERBAL METHODS

Most of the tips and tricks we have discussed so far are for verbal forms of reflection. Certainly, verbal reflection is the most common form of debriefing conducted in North America. Not all clients are masterful at expressing their feelings through words, however, and a few may not even speak English or some may not be cognitively mature enough to benefit. Therefore, alternative ways to reflect for these people may prove more beneficial and less intimidating than verbal reflection. You should consider nonverbal methods of reflection, such as the use of art, drama, music, dance, poetry, writing, storytelling, photography, presentations, or even repeating the same activity (Greenaway, 1993). These methods should be appropriate for the age and culture of the clients. Be aware, however, that they can become routine, so use them in moderation, alternating methods often.

Art can take many forms: cartooning, making collages, drawing, graphing, painting, sculpting, or mapping. Cartoon balloons can convey true feelings. Clients can cut up old outdoor magazines to make collages that interpret their experiences. They can draw posters to represent their thoughts. They can graph their energy levels over time to infer shifting morale and motivations. They can paint murals to share their ideas. They can sculpt clay to illustrate emotions.

Realistic art is often the most difficult to create in limited time and is usually the least useful for generating discussion since it is too close to what actually transpired. Therefore, abstract and symbolic art provide the greatest opportunities for making metaphoric connections. For example, a trip down a river can be a journey metaphor for completing projects in daily life. By drawing on plastic over the trip map, adding key points during the journey, clients can link key points of the project by using a second plastic sheet or by overlaying the first plastic sheet on the project time line. Once linked in either manner, metaphoric connections become conspicuous.

Using drama may enable clients to act out what happened during the experience, what should have happened, but didn't, and what they expect will happen next time. This can be accomplished through fantasy skits, modeling group members as if they are clay, or reenacting the activity. Clients can perform in silence or by talking.

You can have clients use music for singing songs or playing instruments. Music also proves useful in solo reflection. Expressive dance or creative movement can enhance the music. Poetry can take the form of cinquains, couplets, haiku, or limericks. Writing can be analytical, as in preparing a newspaper article or completing quan-

Sidebar 15.1
DISCUSSION DOS AND DON'TS

Several dos and don'ts apply to the when and where of facilitating discussions.

DO:

· Take discussions seriously and schedule plenty of time for them. But if energy levels are falling, end the discussion early.

· Discuss often and immediately after each experience. If this is not possible, have a brief discussion afterward and save a lengthy discussion for later.

· With most populations, take an equivalent amount of time to discuss as was spent doing the activity. If on a multiday experience, then have periodic discussions throughout each day.

· Discuss in close proximity to the activity location unless noise from running water or blowing wind interferes with hearing. This permits clients to more readily visualize what took place and where and how it happened.

· Pick a special place, such as a rock by a lake or the darkness of a forest nearby, or a regular time, such as campfires or meals, to discuss during residential programs. This way, clients will know that they are to concentrate on discussing at the chosen time or place.

· Encourage clients to ask their own questions that fit the discussion theme. This permits self-discovery, freeing you from some of the responsibility for client learning.

· Remain alert for client metaphors, then incorporate them into the discussion using client language. For example, if a client says "I feel like a volcano," you might ask "What kinds of eruptions have you experienced lately?"

· Welcome client contributions with a relaxed posture, open facial expressions, and verbal appreciation. Observe body and verbal language, then communicate in return with the same kind of movements and words in a respectful manner.

DON'T:

· Lead clients by suggesting words for them to use in their responses or by finishing their sentences for them. Ask questions instead of offering answers.

· Compare clients with other groups that have gone before them or judge their actions as good or bad.

· Give false feedback. Instead, avoid giving insincere praise or unwarranted criticism.

· Assume what is best for clients, forcing them to change.

· Accept only one answer as correct, since this will create a situation reminiscent of the reward and punishment mentality of institutionalized schooling. If you do this, soon you will only receive one answer to every question, because clients will become afraid of being wrong.

titative and qualitative questionnaires, or be creative, as in keeping a journal and generating short stories. Fantasy storytelling by leaders and clients can be an effective way of imparting metaphoric messages by reading quotes, morals, fantasies, legends, parables, or fables.

Photography, slides, video, or still snapshots from instant film can be useful when reviewing an experience. As you replay videotapes or audiotapes with an occasional pause for discussion, people can remark on what they were feeling or thinking at the time. You can display slides and pictures on the wall for clients to comment on.

Presentations are formal showings from the adventure. As examples, clients can write a report on the trip, share photo albums with their families, give a slide show to the next group of incoming clients, or demonstrate new skills to the general public during an open house. In doing so, clients reexamine the experience from the viewpoint of an outsider. They must find a way to explain their personal and significant life-changing adventures to people who haven't yet experienced one for themselves.

Repeating the same activity a second time without debriefing the first time or frontloading can provide people with an opportunity to reflect by themselves, then improve what may not have worked well the first time. They may increase the product of their efforts, but they will more often enhance the process. In addition, you can have group members exchange roles. They may act differently in someone else's shoes.

To summarize, sometimes verbal debriefings may be limiting or inappropriate for producing functional change. Verbal debriefings may center on complicated and dynamic interactions, requiring you to deal with extremely complex issues. Alternatives that are less complex, less speech-dependent, less group-oriented, and less rigid, can be more effective than verbal debriefings (Smith, 1986). Moreover, alternatives may require less complex facilitation skills and therefore may be easier to implement for leaders with less experience. Some clients may find expressing their thoughts with speech to be incredibly difficult, provoking anxiety, withdrawal, defensiveness, or frustration. Alternative methods are often less threatening. Traditional debriefing procedures rely heavily on group processes, and some clients have a reluctance to interact and share in group settings. Many alternative techniques are oriented more toward the person; thus, individual clients may find these more meaningful and relevant. Alternative procedures may also provide a more beneficial structure than verbal debriefings for some clients, and this can often increase involvement from group members. Alternatives may be easier to schedule than debriefings that require the entire group's time, so you can implement them on an "as needed" basis. This may make the logistics of facilitation more flexible.

DEBRIEFING THE EXPERIENCE

As stated in chapter 14, as adventure programs grew in popularity during the 1960s in North America, more teachers, counselors, therapists, and other human service professionals became involved in conducting these experiences. Many of these individuals imported techniques from their professions to heighten the experience. One example of this was using debriefing techniques to discuss the experience afterward. While this alteration sometimes met with resistance from proponents of the "let the experience speak for itself" model, it changed the very foundation of adventure programming.

The initial thought behind debriefing was that if clients discussed issues and stated personal commitments to change, based on what they accomplished in their adventure experiences, then they would assume ownership of such issues, becoming more likely to follow through on change. The term "debriefing" was used because of its similarity in structure (but not content) to military debriefings that were familiar to some of the early Outward Bound instructors with military service backgrounds.

As a facilitator, your role in debriefing is usually to guide clients through reflective processes so they discover their own learning. You should not proclaim judgments about what you think your clients did; rather, you should guide clients in their learning by asking effective questions. In this way, you encourage clients to share their personal observations and own their behaviors or the consequences of their actions. Two successful examples of questioning are funneling (Priest & Naismith, 1993) and cognitive hierarchies (e.g., Quinsland & Van Ginkel, 1984; Hammel, 1986; also including the "Adventure Wave Plan" by Schoel, Prouty, & Radcliffe, 1988).

Funneling

One type of debriefing that is successfully used by a number of adventure programs is the **funneling approach**. In this process, you guide the group through a series of steps that funnel client attention from the experience toward making beneficial changes in their lives. These steps are an expansion of the classic three questions from Gestalt therapy: "What? So what? Now what?" (Borton, 1970).

Figure 15.1 illustrates the debriefing funnel used in this process. During the funnel process,

Sidebar 15.2

THE RELUCTANT GROUP

North Americans are generally more comfortable than many other cultures when it comes to speaking aloud, talking about themselves, or discussing in a group. Nevertheless, public speaking scares most people. Therefore, you can always expect to encounter people who may not be comfortable discussing issues because they are afraid of failing, those who may prefer to avoid negativity, those who may deny their problems, or a group who is reluctant to discuss issues in general. At these times, you can modify your approach in a number of ways to increase a client's willingness to enter into a discussion. Some of these modifications include nonverbal responses, closed questions, trigger questions, written responses, solo time, partnerships, trios, gift giving, reporting, and rounds.

You can encourage clients to use nonverbal responses to simple statements you make to generate discussion. They can give you a thumbs-up or thumbs-down or raise a number of fingers to express agreement on a scale from 0 to 10. They can also position themselves along a lineup, distributing themselves according to who contributed or listened to ideas from most to least. Or they can be "targeted" by positioning themselves near or far from an imaginary bull's-eye displayed on the ground to represent their level of whether certain statements are "right on" to believing that they "missed the mark."

You can ask the occasional closed question, but these should not comprise the whole discussion. Clients, able to respond with either a yes or a no, can get used to speaking up with short, easy answers before you ask probing questions. After warming up with closed questions, you can ask trigger questions. These evoke controversy, possibly motivating people to dissent and thus speak their minds. For example, "What is the role of competition in teamwork?" This question assumes competition has a role in teamwork, but some clients may disagree with this assumption.

Consider having clients write their responses before responding aloud. They can respond to questions you ask or statements you make; or they can finish sentences you start. By writing their ideas down first, clients can collect their thoughts, thereby reducing the chances of making mistakes while speaking. This approach ensures that quieter and more reluctant clients have as much time to respond as more eager clients.

Another way to allow clients to prepare for discussion is to give them a little solo time before any discussion. Clients can go off on their own to contemplate the topics of the upcoming discussion. Music, natural sounds, or silence can enhance introspection. Encourage controlled breathing, meditation, or relaxation exercises to "center" clients before asking them to contemplate your questions.

You can also divide clients into partners who discuss the topics in advance. Their mutual reinforcement of one another's ideas and comments can serve to strengthen the resolve to speak out. Making partners into trios can introduce the concept of interviewing with an observer. While two discuss the topics, the third observes, reporting after the partners are finished. In both these procedures, people may speak for themselves or can paraphrase and report their partner's responses. These approaches help because speaking on behalf of others is normally less stressful than talking for yourself.

You can build speaking practice into the discussion through gift giving and reporting. Physical gifts found outside or made from art supplies or inexpensive materials, or nonphysical gifts of words or mimed actions can be presented by clients to give one another feedback. Making gifts, whether physical or nonphysical, encourages clients who are more comfortable with or talented at nonverbal communication to participate more fully in verbal communication by bridging the gap between the two. To use the technique of reporting, you can select people to perform the roles of interaction observer or quality inspector. They observe process or product issues, then report their findings back to the group. Both gift giving and reporting encourage clients to speak out.

In rounds, clients take turns reviewing the activity one at a time. When one person forgets an occurrence or loses track of the order, the next person can chime in, and so on around the circle. Clients identify points from the experience that were positive or negative, good or bad, easy or difficult, and funny or interesting. Clients need only identify these topics and need not discuss them in any depth to begin with. In the ensuing discussions, you can probe only the positive topics until clients have loosened up to the point that you feel you can move on to any negative topics that need attention. Last, you can go first and disclose something very personal, then ask clients to follow the precedent you set.

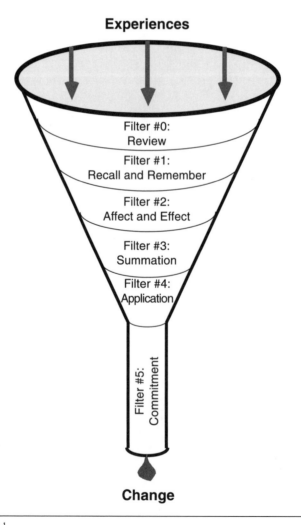

Figure 15.1   The debriefing funnel.

you pour experiences into a series of six "filters," or types of questions, that "distill" learning changes through client reflection on and answers to those questions. Each question filters out unwanted parts of the experience, narrowing clients' concentration toward discussing wanted changes. The six filters are review, recall and remember, affect and effect, summation, application, and commitment.

Before the funneling process for debriefing can take place, you must have a thorough and correct understanding of client needs. Without this knowledge, you can easily misdirect clients, no matter how well-meaning you are. Obtain this information by observing the group during the experience and keeping mental or written notes on what they say, how they behave, with whom they interact, or what incidents take place during the experience. The toughest choice for you may be in sorting out which issues and topics to debrief! Identifying specific learning objectives in advance, based on assessment of client needs can often help you make this decision (see chapter 17). Examples of topics to focus on when debriefing most adventure experiences include trust, cooperation, communication, teamwork, planning, problem solving, decision making, judgment, innovative thinking, self-confidence, commitment, risk taking, coping with fear, dealing with change, resolving conflicts, leadership, gender inequity, group split, and emotional disclosure. Of course, you can't focus on everything every time! But if you and your group miss an issue, it generally resurfaces in the next adventure activity or during its debriefing.

The review question (filter #0) focuses the group on the topic or issue of interest, based on client needs, your objectives for the program, and any incidents that took place in the activity. At this initial review stage, you can ask the group to replay the experience in their minds or to describe it aloud in order to refresh everyone's memories. In this way, you are getting the group to concentrate on a single topic to the exclusion of everything else that happened during the experience. If the topic of concern is obvious from the outcome of the experience, then this filter may not be necessary (hence filter #0). Once the group has agreed to center further discussion on this one topic, you can progress to the next level.

The recall and remember question (filter #1) gets the clients to identify the incident that took place during the experience. If you bring up the occurrence, the group may deny the incident or

perhaps feel confronted. Therefore, you should ask a question that gets the group to bring up the topic and issue, giving them ownership of the incident and control over the situation. If a group is reluctant to speak about a topic or issue, you still have a few choices. Pushing a confrontation will likely be the least productive, so you should leave the denied topic and start a funnel of questions about another issue, or design the next activity to more obviously highlight the point you'd like to make. We'll discuss techniques for dealing with denial further in chapter 16 "Advanced Facilitation Techniques."

The affect and effect question (filter #2) addresses emotions and causes. Once clients bring up and buy into a specific instance related to an issue, you can ask other questions designed to ascertain the impact of that occurrence. These questions examine how each individual felt and how the group was influenced by the event. The answers permit a group to recognize positive or negative impacts of their behaviors and to separate personal impacts from group impacts. At this level, discussion is about sharing feelings and noting concerns about what happened. Once again, you must get partial acceptance from the group about the validity of these questions before moving on to the next type of question.

The summation question (filter #3) helps highlight new learning. Once you have ascertained the impact of the event, you ask clients to summarize what they have learned about the issue. So far, they have identified an occurrence and discussed the influence that it has had on their task performance and group dynamics. Now they are talking about what they have distilled from all of this so far. When several clients' summaries of learning seem to be in accord with their objectives, you can move on to the next filter.

Once clients have identified new learning, you must help them apply it to real-life situations, thereby reinforcing new learning and helping solidify its transference. The application question (filter #4) helps to establish such linkages. At this level, you ask clients to make connections in the form of metaphors, or analogies between the adventure and reality. When a number of clients concur that the metaphoric links are accurate and understand how this experience is like real life, you can ask the final question.

The commitment question (filter #5) looks toward change. Once clients have noted the usefulness of the new learning and how they might apply it in their daily lives, you ask them to make

Table 15.1

FUNNEL GUIDE QUESTIONS

Review

Let's talk about (issue or topic). Can you review the last activity for me? On a five-point scale, hold up the number of fingers that indicate your level of performance with five being excellent.

Recall and Remember

Do you remember an example of excellent (or poor) (issue or topic)? Can you recall a particular time when (issue or topic) was good (or bad)?

Affect and Effect

What affect (emotion) did you experience? How did this make you feel? How did this emotion affect the group? What influence did it have on the task?

Summation

How does the moral of this story go? What did you learn from all of this? Can you sum up what you have gained from our discussions (reflections)?

Application

Do you see a connection between this learning and your life back at school? Can you apply this on the job? Do you see any parallels to your family?

Commitment

What will you do differently next time? Begin with the words "I will . . ." How can you commit to change? Who will help support you in upholding this pledge?

---

a pledge and plan for action. Here you should press for answers in the form of an "I statement" and get the group to buy in and support members who commit to doing things differently as a result of their guided reflection on the experience.

Too much to remember? Before debriefing, you may want to write a list of questions that you will likely ask clients. This list should focus on the original objectives for doing the experience and on some predictable topics that may arise. But if unexpected issues surface, you should remain flexible, tailoring your questions to address these. Nevertheless, to help you practice preparing debriefings, we have listed some sample questions in table 15.1 based on the funnel model.

Remember, for funneling you identify a topic for discussion (review), ask for examples of its occurrence (recall and remember), ask about its impact on clients, the group, or the task (affect and effect), then ask what clients learned from this impact (summation), how the learning pertains to real life (application), and what people pledge to change about that (commitment). For example, groups often communicate poorly in the early stages of an adventure program. Clients

may all speak at once, rarely listening to one another. This is a pattern common to many groups in a variety of different activities. Here is a sample "funnel" that you might follow to get the group to improve its communication.

To begin, you leader might ask "Can we talk about communication?" Unless someone objects, you can then ask the group to review their communication in the past activity and rate their performance by asking "What would you give yourselves for communication on a scale from 0 (low) to 10 (high)?" If the average of the ratings is low, you could add "Are you interested in improving your communication?" If the average of the ratings is high, you could ask "Are you interested in making your communication a 10 or better?" Either way, this readies the group for identifying where communication broke down and a question such as "Can you give me an example of communication that could be enhanced?" Make your questions more specific if clients can't recall or remember the instance you wish to focus on: "Can you relate an instance in which listening was not done well?" Next, you can ask about affect or effect: "How did that impact the group morale? How did you personally feel about that? How did that cause the task to be resolved?" Then, you can follow these questions with others about summation and application: "What have you learned from this? Does this ever happen back home?" Finally, the leader can seek commitment: "What will you do differently in the next activity? How are you going to change when you return home?"

Some groups may be reluctant to answer questions and to talk about things they did poorly. You can overcome this by running funnels on positive topics, asking questions about things the group did well. Once they are comfortable talking about themselves and their actions, you can begin to address some negative issues or areas for improvement. Again, once you have completed the debriefing, composed of positive and negative funnels on several topics, you may often offer a new experience that gives the group a chance to put their pledges into practice.

In the debriefing after this new experience, revisit a funnel on communication to see if client strategies have worked. This funnel might contain a few key questions such as the following: "On a 10-point scale, how was communication this time? Give me an example of where it was improved. What caused this improvement? What were the results of the improvement? What did you learn from these results? How can you use this learning back at home? How will things be different in the future?" Note that this abbreviated sequence of questions leaves room for you to probe for deeper answers with more complex questions or to confirm answers by paraphrasing client responses.

Debriefing experiences require that you remain flexible in the way you ask questions. You must use your best judgment in "customizing" questions. For this reason, "cookbook" approaches to debriefing rarely obtain 100 percent success; you will always have to modify any approach. Once you are comfortable with this model, we encourage you to adapt this approach to suit your own particular style and your clients' needs. Furthermore, we encourage you to remember to not allow yourself to be bound by a single view of debriefing as the only way to guide reflection.

Cognitive Hierarchy

Another type of debriefing that has been successfully used by a number of adventure programs is based on Bloom's (1956) taxonomy of cognitive objectives. Similar in form to the funneling type of debriefing, you lead the group through a series of questions designed to foster positive changes in clients' lives, stemming from the adventure experience. In this model, you follow a sequence that mirrors Bloom's six levels of cognitive thought: knowledge, comprehension, application, analysis, synthesis, and evaluation (Quinsland & Van Ginkel, 1984).

Following this model, you ask questions that progressively develop the cognitive knowledge about the adventure experience. Through this, clients are able to organize information at more concrete levels, that is, the knowledge, comprehension, and application levels, so they can answer debriefing questions at more abstract levels, that is, the analysis, synthesis, and evaluation levels. The questions you ask at the abstract level, particularly evaluation questions, focus on producing the positive and transferable changes clients will use in the future. Table 15.2 (Hammel, 1986) illustrates the cognitive thought levels, debriefing functions, and corresponding sample questions that fit this hierarchy.

Knowledge operates at a memory level and involves remembering information by recognition or recall. Comprehension operates at an understanding level and involves interpreting or explaining information in a descriptive or literal manner. Application operates at a usage level and involves using information correctly. Analysis operates at a relationship level and involves breaking information down into component parts and detecting relationships among them. Synthesis operates at a creative level and involves putting pieces of information together to form a whole in new and innovative ways. Evaluation operates at an opinion level and involves making judgments about the value of ideas, solutions, and events.

For example, a group of clients on the ropes course might be learning information about cooperation. A knowledge question might be "Step by step, what happened between you and your belayer?" Clients typically respond with examples of how they worked in partnership, then you follow with a comprehension question: "What were the times that exemplified cooperative behavior between you and your belayer?" Clients talk about the seriousness of trust or support, then you ask an application question: "What were you doing to make cooperation so successful?" Clients answer with examples of

Table 15.2

COGNITIVE HIERARCHY

Cognitive Thought	Debriefing Function	Corresponding Questions
CONCRETE LEVELS 　Knowledge (memory) 　Comprehension (understand) 　Application (usage)	Review and describe events, feelings, thoughts, and problems.	What did you do when . . . ? What happened when . . . ? How did you feel when . . . ? What did your group do when . . . ?
ABSTRACT LEVELS 　Analysis (relationships) 　Synthesis (creative) 　Evaluation (opinion)	Make comparisons. Relate to daily life. Propose solutions. Examine values.	What was the highlight for you? What was the most challenging? Does this remind you of anything? What have you learned today that may help you in the future? What have you learned about you?

From Hammel (1986).

listening better to partner's needs, then you ask an analysis question: "When do you think you were cooperating best?" Clients identify a specific time that was a highlight for them in cooperating with their belay partner, then you continue with a synthesis question: "How does this highlight compare with your regular way of working with others in daily life?" Clients discuss the similarities and differences, to which you add an evaluation question: "How do you think you will work together in the future?" Clients talk about changes they will make and strategies for transferring their learning.

An obvious weakness of this model, as with most verbal debriefings, is that expressing emotional experiences in words and thinking about feelings in cognitive terms is very difficult for most people, especially children. So you may wish to debrief with metaphoric stories or other alternatives.

FRONTLOADING THE EXPERIENCE

Recall that **frontloading** is a technique that constitutes the fourth generation of facilitated learning in adventure education (Priest & Gass, 1993). "Front" indicates that the facilitation takes place up front, or before the beginning of the experi-

ence. The "loading" portion of the word refers to the point that the learning is loaded together, or emphasized, in combination beforehand. In summary, frontloading means punctuating the key learning points in advance of the adventure experience, rather than reviewing or debriefing any learning after the fact.

Direct frontloading typically addresses one or more of the following five functions: revisiting, objectives, motivation, function, and dysfunction. The excitement of adventure activities can often help a group focus intensely on completing a task, distracting them from the changes they are there to accomplish. The revisiting question reminds the group of the behaviors they pledged to perform after the last activity. Just before the activity begins after you have explained the task, you can interrupt with a single question: "One more thing, what were the commitments that the group made last time?" This brief question brings previous answers to the "do things differently next time" question to the front of clients' minds. By doing this, clients are more likely to act on their revisited affirmations during the activity.

You can ask four other types of frontloading questions in combination or alone. Objective questions ask about the aims of the activity and what can be learned or gained from this experience. Motivation questions ask why experiencing the activity may be important and how this learning relates to daily life. Function questions ask what behaviors will help bring about success and how the group may optimize these. Dysfunction questions ask what behaviors will hinder success and how the group can avoid or overcome these. These five functions are very similar to those of the various filters of the funneling model; the difference is that you ask frontloading questions before instead of after the experience.

These five functions can be illustrated with "The Wall" group initiative. This activity includes a 12- to 14-foot structure with a platform ledge on the back side. The group is challenged to pass its members up the front side and over the top. One difficult aspect of getting the whole group over the wall is getting the first person up. Generally, the crux of the problem is getting the final person over the wall with no one remaining below to lift the last group member. In a typical briefing before the activity, you might introduce the problem by mentioning the group goal of getting everyone over the wall to the other side; task constraints, for example, you cannot hold onto the edges or use props other than resources with you; safety rules, including no more

than two people on the platform and no one held upside down; safety procedures, for example, you must remove jewelry and spot at all times; and time limit, such as 30 minutes, including planning. Many programs then give clients the right to pass and be challenged by choice; some programs may employ helmets and harnesses to prevent head injury or clothes tearing; and a few programs may include handicaps such as blindfolds or muting of clients. During the briefing, you could also add the frontloading questions outlined in table 15.3.

Frontloading can take place either before or after this type of logistical briefing. You may even occasionally include frontloading within the briefing. But we caution you about the impact of too much frontloading. The average person can juggle five to nine things in the mind at once. A typical adventure activity briefing has a half-dozen or so important points that must be retained by clients for reasons of safety and accuracy. Adding more than two or three extra points to the brief by frontloading can overload clients, possibly causing them to forget the key points you're teaching. Even so, when used in moderation, frontloading can be an effective teaching tool.

Table 15.3

FRONTLOADING FUNCTIONS AND CORRESPONDING QUESTIONS

Revisiting (commitments)

Our last event this morning concluded with some personal pledges about what we were going to do differently this afternoon and when we depart from this program. Would each of you care to share those commitments with the group one more time before we start?

Objectives (learning summation)

What do you think the group will get out of doing this activity? What do you think this exercise is designed to teach?

Motivation (application to reality)

Where might this learning be useful in your regular lives?

Function (positive actions)

What will the group need to do in order to succeed? What strategies does the group have for making sure these happen?

Dysfunction (negative actions)

What things has this group done in the past that may get in the way? What can the group do to ensure these don't occur?

Sidebar 15.3

SAMPLE QUESTIONS FOR DISCUSSIONS AND DEBRIEFINGS

Knapp (1990) has identified a series of questions associated with common adventure program topics that may prove useful to you as a guide to formulating funnels or frontloads. These topics include communication, feelings, evaluating others, listening, leadership, followership, decision making, cooperation, diversity, trust, and closure. Use these lists of questions as models for developing your own funnels and frontloads, making them your own so you can ask them in a natural manner tailored to specific client needs. Of course, remember you can't cover every topic in one discussion. Instead, pick one topic that may lead to another, stopping before clients become tired or restless.

Communication

1. Can anyone give an example of when you thought you communicated effectively?
2. How did you know that what you communicated was understood?
3. Who didn't understand someone's attempt to communicate?
4. What went wrong in the communication attempt?
5. What could the communicator do differently next time to give a clearer message?
6. What could the message receiver do differently next time to understand the message?
7. How many different ways were used by the group to communicate messages?
8. Which ways were the most effective? Why?
9. Did you learn something about communication that will be helpful later? If so, what?

Feelings

1. Can you name a feeling you had at any point in completing the activity?
2. Where in your body did you feel it most?
3. What personal beliefs were responsible for generating that feeling?
4. What was the main thought behind the feeling?
5. Is that feeling a common one in your life?
6. Did you express that feeling to others? If not, what did you do with the feeling?
7. Do you usually express feelings or suppress them?
8. Would you like to feel differently in a similar situation?
9. If so, how would you like to feel?
10. What beliefs would you need to have in order to feel differently in a similar situation?
11. Could you believe them?
12. How do you feel about the conflict that may result from expressing certain feelings?
13. How do you imagine others felt toward you at various times during the activity?
14. Were these feelings expressed?
15. What types of feelings are easiest to express? Most difficult?
16. Do you find it difficult to be aware of certain feelings at times? If so, which ones?
17. Are some feelings not appropriate to express to the group at times? If so, which ones?
18. What feelings were expressed nonverbally in the group?
19. Did expressing appropriate feelings help or hinder completing the initiative?

Evaluating others

1. Is it difficult for you to avoid judging others? Explain.
2. Can you think of examples when you judged others in the group today?
3. When didn't you judge others?
4. What were some advantages you gained by not judging others?
5. What were some advantages others gained when you didn't judge them?
6. How did judging and not judging others affect the completion of the activity?
7. Were some behaviors of others easy not to judge and other behaviors difficult?
8. Would deferring judgment be of some value in other situations? Explain.
9. Can you think of any disadvantages of not judging others in this situation?

Listening

1. Who made suggestions for completing the activity?
2. Were all of these suggestions heard? Explain.
3. Which suggestions were acted on?
4. Why were the other suggestions ignored?
5. How did it feel to be heard when you made a suggestion?
6. What interfered with your ability to listen to others?
7. How can you overcome this interference?
8. Did you prevent yourself from listening well? How?
9. Did you listen in the same way today as you generally do?
10. If not, what was different about today?

Leadership

1. Who assumed leadership roles during the activity?
2. What were the behaviors that showed leadership?
3. Can everyone agree that these behaviors are traits of leaders?
4. How did the group respond to these leadership behaviors?
5. Who followed the leader even if you weren't sure that the idea would work? Why?
6. Did the leadership role shift to other people during the activity?
7. Who thought they were taking the leadership role? How did you do it?
8. Was it difficult to assume a leadership role with this group?
9. Why didn't some of you take a leadership role with this group?
10. Is it easier to take leadership in other situations or with other group members? Explain.
11. Did anyone try to lead the group, but felt you were unsuccessful?
12. What were some possible reasons for this? How did it feel to be disregarded?

Followership

1. Who assumed a follower role at times throughout the activity? How did it feel?
2. How did it feel to follow different leaders?
3. Do you consider yourself a good follower?

4. Was this an important role in the group today? Explain.
5. How does refusal to follow affect the leadership role?
6. What are the traits of a good follower?
7. How can you improve your ability to follow in the future?

Decision making

1. How were group decisions made during the activity?
2. Were you satisfied with the ways decisions were made? Explain.
3. Did the group arrive at any decisions through group consensus?
4. Were decisions made by one or several individuals?
5. Did everyone in the group express an opinion when given a choice? If not, why not?
6. What is the best way for this group to make decisions? Explain.
7. Do you respond in similar ways in other groups?
8. What did you like about how the group made decisions? What didn't you like?

Cooperation

1. Can you think of specific examples of group cooperation? Explain.
2. How did it feel to cooperate?
3. Do you cooperate in most things you do?
4. How did you learn to cooperate?
5. What are the rewards of cooperating?
6. Are there any problems associated with cooperation?
7. How did cooperative behavior lead to successfully completing the activity?
8. How can you cooperate in other areas of your life?
9. Did you think anyone was blocking the group's efforts to cooperate? Explain.

Diversity

1. How are you different from some of the others in the group?
2. How do these differences strengthen the group as a whole?
3. When do differences in people keep a group from reaching certain objectives?
4. What would this group be like if there were very few differences in people?
5. How would you feel if this were so?
6. In what cases did being different help or hinder group members from reaching objectives?
7. How are you like some of the others in the group?
8. Were these common traits helpful to the group's approach to the task? Explain.
9. Did these common traits hinder the group's approach to the task? Explain.
10. Do you think you have other things in common with some of the group members?
11. How did this setting help you discover how you are similar to others?

Trust

1. Can you give examples of when you trusted someone in the group? Explain.
2. Is it easier to trust some people and not others? Explain.

3. Can you think of examples when trusting someone would not have been a good idea?

4. How do you increase your level of trust for someone?

5. On a scale of 1 to 10, rate how much trust you have in the group as a whole.

6. Can you explain your rating?

7. How does the amount of fear you feel affect your trust of others?

8. What did you do today that deserves the trust of others?

Closure

1. What did you learn about yourself?

2. What did you learn about others?

3. How do you feel about yourself and others?

4. What new questions do you have about yourself and others?

5. What did you do today of which you are particularly proud?

6. What skill are you working to improve?

7. Was your behavior today typical of the way you usually act in groups? Explain.

8. How can you use what you learned in other life situations?

9. What beliefs about yourself and others were reinforced today?

10. Would you do anything differently if you were starting the activity again?

11. What would you like to say to the group members?

EFFECTIVE OUTDOOR LEADERS SHOULD

☞ Be competent at facilitating verbal debriefing.

☞ Know how best to handle groups that are reluctant to enter into verbal debriefing.

☞ Be able to debrief experiences by reflective alternatives to the verbal debriefing.

☞ Be able to debrief experiences according to both the funneling and cognitive hierarchy models.

☞ Be able to frontload experiences by all five direct methods, using the technique in moderation.

SUMMARY

A basic level of facilitation involves discussion and alternative methods. Discussion is unstructured debriefing that allows analysis, sharing, and reinforcement of learning and change. Arranged in a circle and talking in a supportive atmosphere, created by accepted ground rules and operating principles, you guide the group's discussion by asking open-ended questions. You listen to their answers and then ask probing questions. By managing overbearing, tangential, and lengthy speakers and by using a toolkit of tips and tricks, you ensure input from all clients. Work with reluctant groups by encouraging nonverbal responses, by asking closed questions and trigger questions, by requiring written responses and reporting, and by arranging for solo time, partnerships, trios, gift giving, and rounds. Since verbal debriefings can put some clients at a disadvantage, provide for reflection through alternative methods such as art, drama, music, dance, poetry, writing, storytelling, photography, presentations, and repeating the same activity.

To verbally debrief an activity, ask questions after the experience. In frontloading, ask the questions beforehand. Each is a technique of reflection developed in North American adventure programs in the 1960s and 1970s, respectively. Debriefing can take any number of nonverbal forms, but is most commonly a verbal experience guided by you. You ask questions so that the clients discover their own learning. If you were to make statements, the clients might feel confronted and deny their necessary learning points. Funneling and cognitive hierarchy are two models for verbal debriefings.

Funneling is a series of six types of questions that successively filter out parts of the experience, thereby narrowing the clients' focus onto change. The six filters are review questions, recall and remember questions, affect and effect questions, summation questions, application questions, and commitment questions. You create this sequence of questions with a predetermined learning objective in mind, a topic that warrants discussion, or an issue that arises during the experience.

Debriefing by cognitive hierarchy is based on Bloom's taxonomy of learning, which includes six levels: knowledge, comprehension, application, analysis, synthesis, and evaluation. You ask questions at the lower, concrete thinking levels (knowledge, comprehension, and application) to have clients organize the learning, before progressing to the higher, more abstract thinking levels (analysis, synthesis, and evaluation), which help clients transfer the learning.

Frontloading stacks the learning before the activity by prebriefing instead of debriefing. You ask questions similar to those you ask in debriefing, but the difference is that you ask clients to anticipate the future rather than respond to the past. Direct frontloading has five forms: revisiting, objectives, motivation, function, and dysfunction. Too much frontloading can overload clients; thus, you must be careful to use the technique only occasionally and only when emphasizing key points of learning ahead of time is required or helpful.

QUESTIONS TO THINK ABOUT

1. Prepare a funnel by writing out six filter questions in sequence for use with an individual client (rather than a whole group) who has just experienced an adventure activity of your choice.

2. Ask a peer to role-play for that individual and ask her the questions. If needed, modify your questions, based on her answers, as you progress through the funnel.

3. Repeat the first two questions, using the cognitive hierarchy model.

4. Compare and contrast the funnel and cognitive hierarchy models. Which one do you prefer? Why? Are there times with certain groups that one model might work better than the other?

5. Prepare five questions using the frontloading model, then practice asking them of a peer.

REFERENCES

Bloom, B.S. (1956). *Taxonomy of educational objectives*. London, England: Longman Group.

Borton, T. (1970). *Reach, touch, and teach*. New York: McGraw-Hill.

Greenaway, R. (1993). *Playback: A guide to reviewing activities*. Edinburgh, Scotland: Callander Printers, The Duke of Edinburgh's Award, and Endeavour Scotland.

Hammel, H. (1986). How to design a debriefing session. *Journal of Experiential Education* 9(3), 20-25.

Knapp, C. (1990). Processing experiences. In J.C. Miles & S. Priest (Eds.), *Adventure education* (pp. 189-198). State College, PA: Venture.

Priest, S., & Gass, M.A. (1993). Five generations of facilitated learning from adventure education. *Journal of Adventure Education and Outdoor Leadership* 11(1), 18-24.

Priest, S., & Naismith, M. (1993). The debriefing funnel. *Journal of Adventure Education and Outdoor Leadership* 10(3), 20-22.

Quinsland, L.K., & Van Ginkel, A. (1984). How to process experience. *Journal of Experiential Education* 7(2), 8-13.

Schoel, J., Prouty, D., & Radcliffe, P. (1988). *Islands of healing: A guide to adventure-based counseling*. Dubuque, IA: Kendall/Hunt.

Smith, T.E. (1986). Alternative methodologies for processing the adventure experience. *The Bradford Papers Annual* 1, 29-38.

chapter

16

Advanced
Facilitation Techniques

Trust Fall

"Probably lots of you think that this exercise has something to do with trusting others, or with knowing that people will support you if you let them. And that's a fine meaning to get out of this activity. But our purpose in choosing this exercise is actually pretty different; we picked it because we feel there is an even more important lesson here. And that lesson concerns letting go of an old lifestyle. Let me tell you a bit more about what I mean.

Each of you will be getting up here and holding on to this tree before falling backwards. Before you fall, I'm going to ask you to close your eyes and imagine that the tree is that part of your personality—that piece of you—most responsible for your drinking and drugging. I don't want you to think of this as a tree anymore; I want you to think of it as the most powerful factor responsible for your using. And I want you to hug it like you love it—like it's all you've got.

Because after you hold on to it for awhile, for 30 seconds, I'm going to ask you to let go—to give up and let go of whatever it is that keeps you drinking and drugging. You'll just lie back and fall towards these people.

And don't be surprised if you feel a little nervous. All alcoholics/addicts have at least some love for their old lifestyle, no matter how much they really want to change it. And there's always some degree of hesitation towards committing to a drug-free life. Cause you don't know what it is like. So I'd be surprised if you didn't feel some kind of nervousness about falling."

—Bacon, 1991a, p. 11-12

Ropes Course

"I'm sure that many of you have heard descriptions of this next activity: the high ropes course. As you can see, it's a big jungle gym in the trees. But it's a jungle gym that tends to have a large impact on clients; many participants talk more about this than anything else in the program. They tend to talk about how scary it was.

From our point of view, the ropes course isn't included to practice courage or risk taking or anything like that. I mean, what good would that be? Does it really help your sobriety to be able to walk a narrow log between two trees? Does the fact that you can do that mean you won't take a drink? No, it doesn't!

But we think the ropes course does have something to do with sobriety. At some point on this ropes course, we expect that you'll feel some degree of challenge, risk, and maybe even fear. And we want you to feel that not because we want you to experience those things for their own sake—but for another reason. When we see that you are in the midst of a serious challenge, we're going to do a rather strange thing.

Before telling you exactly what that strange thing is, I need to diverge for a moment. Research has shown that many alcoholics return to drinking because they can't resist temptation. You know, like the temptation of having a friend or acquaintance invite you out for "just one," or whatever. So we've designed this particular ropes course activity with this temptation problem in mind.

I know you are all used to depending on staff for support for your sobriety and you have probably also gotten used to the idea that the Outward Bound instructors are on your side; but today, because we think it'll help your sobriety, we're going to reverse that. Out there in the real world, you're going to be tempted and when that happens, you're going to be all alone. It may be your best friend pushing alcohol on you just when you really want a drink.

So to help you with that situation, we've decided that we're going to let you have a little pre-temptation training. Just when it gets real hard on the ropes course and you're really tempted to quit, we—that is, the [Outward Bound] instructors—are going to try and talk you into quitting. That's right, instead of offering support or help we're going to try and get you to come down. You might hear us say, 'Hey, you've done enough.' Or, 'It's OK to come down; this doesn't really have to do with sobriety.' Or, 'You've already done as much as can be expected of you, given your fear of heights. Why don't you just come down now?'

What I'm saying is, you can't trust us on this one. Or maybe I'm saying that you need to trust your own ability to know what's right and do it no matter what others tell you. We want you to know that in reality, we all really hope that you'll complete the element. And I can tell you that right now in a very clear manner. It would please us all if every one of you had a total success. But we won't be acting like that in a few minutes. During the course, from time to time, you'll see and hear us trying our best to tempt you or your friends. You'll see us trying to talk you off of the ropes course. Of course, most of the time we'll just be helping out, just like we usually do, but when the crunch is on, you may notice that we've shifted into another perspective. Do all of you understand this? Do you know why we may be encouraging people to quit or take the easy way out?"

—Bacon, 1991b, pp. 9-10

As we outlined in chapter 14, facilitation styles in adventure programs have evolved through a generational process. Primarily influenced by the work of Milton Erickson and investigators of his work, Bacon (1983) published the book *The Conscious Use of Metaphor in Outward Bound*. One of the accomplishments of this book was the specific attention Bacon paid to the use of metaphors in facilitation processes in adventure programming. By focusing on metaphors as a cornerstone for creating future relevance from adventure experiences, the paradigm of how to facilitate adventure experiences evolved to include fifth and sixth generations of facilitation. Most of the examples in this chapter are for corporate and therapeutic situations, since most of the applications for these latter generations have been associated with these populations.

Bacon and Kimball (1989) identified three ways metaphors are used in adventure programming: spontaneous, analogous, and structured. With **spontaneous metaphoric transfer**, learners spontaneously discover important and relevant connections between the adventure experience and their lives without assistance from you, the outdoor leader. Spontaneous metaphoric transfer is often found in the first generation of "letting the experience speak for itself."

With **analogous metaphoric transfer**, you employ discussions and other debriefing techniques, such as verbal therapy and social learning techniques, to help clients understand the importance and relevance of what they learned in the adventure experience to their daily lives in a retrospective, or "after the fact," fashion. This approach is often characterized by your carefully choosing and asking questions after adventure experiences are completed. Typically, you can use analogous metaphoric transference in the second, third, and fourth generations of facilitation: speaking on behalf of, debriefing, and directly frontloading the experience.

With **structured metaphoric transfer**, you purposefully frame adventure experiences prior to client participation, often through a briefing that strengthens the metaphoric message. You do this in such a way that you increase the probability of the spontaneous discovery of metaphors or the analogous recognition of metaphors during the debriefing session. But you can also use structured metaphoric transference in the fifth and sixth generations of facilitation: isomorphically framing and indirectly frontloading the experience. In this chapter, we'll take a more detailed look at these two methods of facilitation.

ISOMORPHICALLY FRAMING THE EXPERIENCE

Of all of the critical features of utilizing metaphors in adventure experiences, probably most important is the concept of **isomorphism**, which literally means "equivalent structures." Highlighted by a number of professionals in the field (e.g., Bacon, 1983, 1987; Gass, 1985, 1991, 1993; Mack, 1996; Nadler & Luckner, 1992) as well as outside (e.g., de Shazer, 1982; Minuchin, 1981; Zeig, 1994), isomorphism explains how metaphors create current relevance as well as future importance for clients in adventure experiences. Once again, an isomorph is an idea, object, or description that is identical in form or structure—but not necessarily composition or function—to another idea, object, or description. For example, consider the isomorphs present in the two introductory vignettes. In the Trust Fall, the tree represented a personality component responsible for substance abuse. In this case, it served as an isomorphic relationship for this client. On the ropes course, several other isomorphs existed. In this case, the ropes course represented the challenges of life for this client; the leader's unusual behavior represented temptation; quitting and coming down represented succumbing to enticement and relapsing; and completing the course, despite the

temptations, represented maintaining sobriety in the face of seduction. When metaphors contain isomorphic connections to the client's goals, they offer powerful vehicles for producing functional change. Thus, isomorphism is central to the success of any fifth or sixth generation technique of facilitation.

Mack (1996) has criticized Bacon's example of the Trust Fall stated above, labeling it as "imposed" and representative of many of the expectations imposed on women in a patriarchal society. She is correct in her assumptions when such a framework makes little sense to a client's reality, that is, has little isomorphic connection to this particular client's issues. Her work reminds us that isomorphic frames must be derived from what clients bring to the adventure experience and then *co-created* by both the client and the facilitator on the basis of what the clients need. Such "co-creation" is necessary for functional change to occur, unless the metaphoric transfer occurs spontaneously as outlined earlier in the chapter.

As we introduced in chapter 14, the fifth generation of facilitation involves framing an experience in such a way that the adventure experience mirrors the client's issue. This includes the manner in which you structure the activity as well as using a facilitated introduction. Framing used in this manner differs from the way it has been described in some sources as briefing or orienting a group (e.g., Schoel, Prouty, & Radcliffe, 1988, pp. 90-92). **Isomorphic framing** focuses on matching a client's needs, mind-set, and objectives with an adventure experience in such a way that successful completion of the adventure experience mirrors successful resolution of the client's issue. This framing is done before the adventure experience, working to produce behavior change within the context of the adventure experience. This is in contrast to the process of creating analogies with reflective techniques after the experience as in discussion or debriefing.

To better understand this concept, look at the first introductory vignette. Here, clients with substance abuse issues are involved in a Trust Fall activity. But as stated in this isomorphic frame, the leader is not using this activity to address issues of "trust." Rather, the outdoor leader is focusing client attention on how this experience relates to "letting go of an old addictive lifestyle." This is accomplished by isomorphically relating the tree to this client's addictive personality. By framing this as something to "let go of," other isomorphs are created in the mind of the client.

These isomorphs also connect certain features of the adventure experience with client issues, thereby strengthening the overall metaphor and enhancing transfer. Some additional examples of the isomorphic connections created in this Trust Fall scenario include hugging the tree as a desperate "hanging on" to an addictive lifestyle; giving up and letting go of the tree as a commitment to give up and let go of forces sustaining addiction; nervousness in the adventure as anxiety or hesitation to commit to a drug-free lifestyle; fear of the unknown involved with falling backward as the terror of not knowing what it's going to be like to enter into a drug-free lifestyle; and being caught by the group as being supported by others while maintaining sobriety.

The most important point of isomorphic frameworks is the need for these frameworks to be relevant to the client and the structure of their issues. Illustrations like the vignettes provide wonderful examples of what introductory metaphoric frameworks may look like once they're completed. But unless the framework makes sense, is relevant, and is "owned" by the client through the use of isomorphic structures, its utility for the client will be lessened or even worthless. As identified by Gass (1993), the "most difficult tasks in creating metaphoric (isomorphic framing) transfer in adventure programs generally lie in (1) constructing therapeutic metaphors that are isomorphic to client needs, (2) framing experiences in such a manner that they can be interpreted and integrated into clients' perspectives, and (3) using appropriate debriefing techniques after the experience to reinforce change" (p. 249).

Developing Isomorphic Frames

How do you create **isomorphic frameworks** that are relevant to client issues? Gass (1991) outlined a process for creating appropriate overall metaphors by establishing multiple isomorphic connections. The seven steps in this process include assess, identify, and rank client goals; select the metaphoric adventure experience; identify successful resolution to the therapeutic issue; strengthen the isomorphic framework; review client motivation; conduct the experience with revisions; and debrief.

1. A thorough needs assessment is the first step to **assess, identify, and rank client goals**. Before you can develop isomorphic frameworks,

you must have an understanding of clients and their particular needs. To best accomplish this, you should list—and then rank in order of importance if possible—the attributes, needs, and objectives of the client group. These client attributes, needs, and objectives are typically the central features for creating the isomorphic framework of the adventure experience.

2. Next, you need to **select a metaphoric adventure experience** that already possesses a strong isomorphic relationship to meeting client needs. Experienced outdoor leaders are often able to do this by second nature, since they know which structures of adventure activities possess a strong affinity for matching particular client needs. You may find the process is made easier by listing attributes of an adventure activity, including goals, rules, equipment, facilities, settings, typical outcomes, and successful resolution of a problem, and then comparing and contrasting these with the group's needs and goals they have already identified in step one. It's your job to ensure that the adventure experience is a mirror image of each client's objectives with each matching attribute possessing the potential to become an isomorphic link, provided you can help the client implement a means to connect them. Note that these experiences are "co-created" with input from clients based on their particular needs and input from you based on your knowledge of how certain adventure experiences possess natural affinity for creating opportunities for client growth in particular areas.

3. Once you have created these isomorphic connections, you must **identify successful resolutions to the therapeutic issue**. Do this by hypothesizing how a successful ending or positive resolution in the adventure activity will correspond to a similar result in real-life experiences. Moreover, you should consider how a failure, setback, or negative outcome may mirror an inability to overcome dysfunctional behaviors that are already present in the group. In other words, if the group succeeds in their efforts, then the behaviors they use to succeed in the adventure should mirror resolutions for the group's identified needs. On the other hand, if the usual dysfunctional behaviors persist, then these should bring about failure in the activity, resulting in natural consequences, such as getting wet, falling to dangle on a rope, traveling extra distance, setting up camp in the dark, loss of credits accumulated during the program, or delayed meals.

4. Once you have developed these initial iso-morphic structures and resolutions, you must **strengthen the isomorphic framework**. Concentrate on adapting the client's metaphor and enhancing its presentation through symbolic language. The activity may benefit from a new iso-morphic title; for example, the Trust Fall becomes "Letting Go of Old Lifestyles." You must examine each matching connection for how it might fit into the context of the client's metaphor as well as how you should present each isomorph. In this step, it may be necessary to change the rules, facilities, props, or equipment to strengthen the framework. When you are satisfied with the framework, combine all the isomorphic links and alterations into a rich and descriptive introductory frame that is meaningfully presented in the client's jargon. The use of familiar language enhances symbolic meaning for clients as well as brings identity and relevance to the client's adventure. In doing so, the experience ceases to be an activity and becomes an analogous exercise in the client's reality. The isomorphic frame, coupled with the symbolism, creates a powerful metaphor that fosters clients' development of associations between the concepts and complexity of the experience and real life.

5. Before presenting the frame and conducting the activity, however, you need to **review client motivation** by double-checking that the structured metaphor is compelling enough to hold the clients' attention (i.e., with appropriate issues and language) without overwhelming them with anxiety or detail. In addition, you must also make sure that the isomorphs used to create the metaphor possess the appropriate content, whether positive or negative in focus, and that you have correctly linked relationships between the adventure and daily life situations.

6. Next, **conduct the experience with revisions**. Begin the adventure with an introduction consisting of the isomorphic framework and associated safety guidelines. As the clients listen to the framework, you may need to make adjustments in order to highlight the isomorphic connections. Clients may recognize links that you missed but can now emphasize. Occasionally, clients may miss or purposefully discount the metaphor by a negative interpretation of the framework. This may require you to offer an appropriate reframing of their interpretations in the form of a new perspective. For example, clients who state that the Trust Fall activity described

earlier has nothing to do with letting go of dysfunctional lifestyles may be failing to perceive the metaphor or choosing to obstruct the process. To help them see the connection more clearly, you might ask the group to discuss what links *they* see within the activity. An explanation by a peer often contains more appropriate symbols, permitting the unaware clients to grasp the metaphor or unmotivated ones to alter their obstructive behavior.

7. After the experience, reinforce positive changes, reframe negative changes, and guide the integration of functional changes into the client's lifestyle through a **debriefing**. As with most iso-morphically framed adventure activities, you can afford to concentrate more on application of the learning or commitment to change, than on events and impacts, in the debriefing. Other topics such as "what happened" or "what this meant" were already very obvious to clients within the initial frame. When conducted in this manner, debriefings tend to be concerned with "change by doing" as clients prove they can function effectively in situations that are similar to their daily lives and recognize that repeating their newly learned behaviors in their real world setting will result in reaching their goals.

Isomorphic Example

Gass (1991) describes the creation of a metaphor with several isomorphic connections for a substance abuse group. The listing and ranking of client needs and attributes resulted in three main points:

1. The ability to ask for help
2. The ability to set appropriate boundaries around issues of recovery to maintain abstinence
3. The elimination of dysfunctional behaviors that undermine the ability [of others] to maintain abstinence [and] placing the needs of others ahead of the [personal] need to stay sober (p. 8).

Other attributes of this group included those who were currently addicted, others who were inpatients in a recovery program, many having difficulty letting go of their abusive patterns and holding on to abstinence, and those who were involved with the initial steps of a 12-step recovery process.

The Maze activity was selected for its potential to meet these needs because it possessed a strong metaphoric relationship to the client's needs. The following attributes of the Maze activity were important for creating isomorphic links. The Maze is built from a length of rope strung between nearby trees at about waist height of the average client to create a random enclosure. One small opening is created between two trees. While blindfolded, clients are placed inside the Maze and are challenged to find their way out by locating the opening without getting lost. Rules exist for not crawling under or jumping over the rope, not letting go of the rope, and not removing blindfolds. When individuals successfully exit the Maze, they may reenter the Maze to assist others, but must remain blindfolded.

The outdoor leaders who designed this activity determined that a successful resolution would be if each client asked for help, choosing to place personal abstinence above others' needs. These behaviors were meant to mirror the initial steps to recovery. The outdoor leaders also considered a negative outcome to be rescuing others: an indication of placing the needs of others above personal sobriety. This behavior was seen as a parallel to the insidious and distracting nature of the clients' addictions.

The outdoor leaders matched many of the client and activity attributes, forming potential isomorphic links. The rope represents a pathway to recovery; the enclosure, the addiction process; and the opening, the reaching of sobriety. Blindfolds mirrored the limitations of addiction, symbolizing how the disease prevents clients from helping themselves and getting a true perspective on reality. Maintaining contact with the rope represented staying committed to the recovery process, while reentering the Maze represented placing the needs of others above maintaining sobriety. The designers ignored other attributes to ensure the design did not become too complicated or altered attributes to become more isomorphic, strengthening the metaphor.

Then the designers made several modifications in the Maze to make it mirror the reality of these clients. They changed the title of the activity to "Path to Recovery" in order to emphasize the clients' current reality. They sealed up the small opening physically and planned to create an isomorphic exit when clients asked for help from the outdoor leaders. The leaders also made minor rule changes, including having all clients put their blindfolds on before the brief-

ing began. After double-checking for clarity of the structure and reviewing client motivation, one outdoor leader presented the following introduction (Gass, 1991, p.8; and Gass & Priest, 1993, p. 22):

The next activity is called the "Path to Recovery." It's called that because a number of the obstacles you'll encounter are very similar to obstacles many of you are currently encountering in your addictions. Our addictions often blind us on our path to a substance-free lifestyle, and we often fail because we don't remember to live by principles that will allow us to free ourselves from abusive substances. After my description of this activity, we will place you on the [path] to recovery by putting your hand on a rope. This rope leads you along a path of indeterminable length. Along your journey to recovery, you will meet a variety of other people going in different directions. Some of these people will be in a great hurry, showing a lot of confidence. Others will be tentative, moving cautiously. Some will seem to know the right direction, whereas others will seem lost. Don't let go of the rope, because if you do you will lose the path. . . . The goal of your journey is to reach one of the exits to abstinence. There are several exits in this maze, and as you reach one of these exits, I'll be there to ask you an important choice. The choices will be (1) stepping out of the maze. If you make this decision, I'll ask you to remove your blindfold and sit quietly in the abstinence area until this initiative is over; or (2) you may choose to go back into the maze to help others. If you choose to go back into the maze, you run the risk that this particular exit may be shut when you return, forcing you to find another exit. If at any time during this activity you would like to receive help, all you need to do is ask for it and guidance will be provided. Otherwise we would like everyone not to speak throughout this initiative until it is completed.

As the activity progressed, the exits remained closed until each client asked for help. In that instance, the client was informed that asking for help had created a pathway from addiction to an area of abstinence. Next, clients were faced with a decision critical to maintaining their abstinence: stepping out of the Maze of addiction and removing their blindfolds or returning to the Maze blindfolded and possibly losing the exit to abstinence.

In the course of conducting this adventure experience, two clients became frustrated with the activity and ripped off their blindfolds, each stating "I'm not going to play this game any more!" After checking what each meant by their remarks, this incident provided the outdoor leader with a critical opportunity to make a framing revision that highlighted the initial isomorphs and addressed the different needs of each particular client.

For one individual, this display of frustration was reframed by the outdoor leader as a breakthrough. The outdoor leader reframed the frustration as a celebration, stating; "I'm struck by the way you recognized the futility in playing the 'game of addiction,' and I think this is wonderful! It's obvious to me that you are prepared to take positive action and not remain endlessly trapped in the maze of the addictive process." This first response reframes a negative interpretation of failure in a positive light: success was achieved by a different method. Note that the leader became aware of the "fit" or "correctness" of the intervention by observing its meaning for this particular client.

The other individual's behavior indicated to the outdoor leader an inability to accept personal responsibility for recovery. On the basis of this perception, the outdoor leader commented on the client's unwillingness to admit powerlessness and take the first step toward recovery. The outdoor leader reframed the situation by expressing the recognition of this to be valuable. This second response, while somewhat challenging for a client to hear, led to a stronger personal resolve to commit to a substance-free lifestyle.

For this activity, the therapeutic objectives focused on asking for help, making healthy choices for a functional recovery process, and avoiding behaviors that could undermine the recovery process or the ability of others to maintain abstinence. The first two objectives encompassed positive recovery behaviors, while the last one addressed avoiding a negative or dysfunctional one. The outdoor leaders' debriefing initially focused on these three objectives, but also dealt with other issues, including how asking for help assisted people, the decision made at exits, what "failing to hold on" to the rope represented, what abstainers felt while observing others "lost" in the maze of addiction, what struggling to get out was like, and what is necessary to stay on the straight path. Given the power of the metaphor in this activity, clients discussed their experiences in light of trying to reach or maintain sobriety. They elaborated on their choices, using words that indicated the activity was meaningful and realistic to them. More importantly, several demonstrated two positive behaviors of asking for help, particularly when feeling lost or "blinded" by their addictions, and of making positive choices to leave their addictions behind. Furthermore, others did not succumb to the temptation of relapse and avoided the risk of becoming permanently "lost" in the maze of addiction.

Bacon (1987) clarifies the differences between framing and other forms of facilitation: "The difference between the approaches is that [usually clients] do not realize the metaphoric nature of the event until the post-activity debriefing [when using earlier styles]. Conversely, [fifth] generation [clients] perceive the metaphoric qualities of the experience as they pass through it; their post-activity discussion focuses on how they reacted to the metaphor, not on how they reacted to the literal experience" (pp. 12-13). The strengths of this approach lies in the metaphoric briefing, rich in isomorphs, which enables clients to focus on the issues at-hand. Resolving the adventure experience becomes parallel to resolving real-life issues, using the experience to create lasting changes.

Drawbacks to Isomorphic Framing

While this approach to facilitating adventure experiences has obvious benefits to client groups with prescriptive needs, and although it is a powerful way to address these needs, it does have at least six drawbacks. If you choose to operate in the fifth generation, you ought to be aware of the following shortcomings.

1. This approach is far more complex than the previous four other facilitation styles. In addition to all the other tasks associated with facilitation, such as diagnosis, design, delivery, debriefing, direction, safety, and ethics, the structuring and framing tasks give you even more responsibility when conducting the experience. This complexity can limit the utility of this technique to those facilitators with advanced training and abilities. At the very minimum, it demands a strong sensitivity to a client's needs, an ability to co-create meaningful experiences with clients, and a deep understanding of how adventure experiences can provide successful resolution to client issues.

2. To help produce this type of change through framing, you must be more prescriptive in your

techniques. This often requires a greater breadth and depth of assessment of the needs of the client as well as an understanding of what change will mean to the client's life if it occurs. Without this information, this approach can be destructive and changes short-lived.

3. The efficacy of this approach depends on the ability of clients to see parallel structures. Metaphors and isomorphs are confusing things to the uninitiated. Confusion can easily lead to dismissal of the frame by clients, creating dissension among the group and therefore inhibiting learning. You must be able to adjust this approach to the capabilities of the group and in some cases teach clients to think metaphorically.

4. Presenting isomorphic frameworks also requires an ability to balance your introduction with the client's reality. Knowledge of each client's language and other symbols is important, but you cannot afford to underestimate the importance of properly comprehending each client's context and other related background issues. Truly effective framing requires much more than merely placing labels or images from the client's environment on to adventure activities.

5. No two members of a group are alike, so you must account for the individual differences among clients when working with groups. Creating frames that are open enough for each client to internalize personal perspectives will lead to a greater ability to produce individual change. Failure to do this by presenting closed or restrictive frames may hinder group development.

6. By narrowing the focus of a frame to a predetermined metaphoric message, you are dictating what will be learned in the activity. Even if you are on target with the frame, by prescribing the way the experience will be interpreted, other metaphors may not be available for the group to interpret. Since the power of transfer is closely linked to metaphoric connections, loss of other meaningful metaphors for some people may inhibit overall transfer.

INDIRECTLY FRONTLOADING THE EXPERIENCE

As you know, the fifth generation of facilitation involves directly framing an adventure experience in such a way that the experience mirrors the client's goals and needs for the activity. In this process, you and the client work in a deliberate and expected way toward reaching a specific objective; and generally speaking, the harder you work to "coconstruct" efforts to attain the client's objective, the greater the success of the experience.

For a number of reasons, a small percentage of the time such direct efforts fail. This often happens with groups or individuals labeled "dysfunctional," such as clients with therapeutic issues who want to resist changing or corporations with a long history of failures at trying to eliminate unwanted behaviors. Probably the easiest way to view behaviors that resist such direct efforts are either the more you and the client try to eliminate unwanted behaviors, the more the unwanted behaviors occur; or the more you and the client try to attain a desired result, the more elusive the result seems to become (Waltzlawick, 1978). In such cases, the answer for helping such clients may not lie so much in working harder to facilitate, but in working "easier" at doing something differently. Consider Bacon's (1987, adapted by Gass, 1993) facilitation dilemma in working with delinquent adolescents during a backpacking experience:

When [a leader] asks an adolescent to put on his pack and hike, this request potentially places the adolescent in a dilemma. If he complies with the [leader's] suggestion, he is obeying an adult order. Not only does the delinquent have many experiences that have taught him that following an adult's advice often leads to problems, he also has typical teenage developmental needs to defy adults in order to sustain his newly formed sense of individuation. In addition, he belongs to a peer culture where he gains status by resisting adult directives. If the delinquent complies with the request, he will feel as if he is betraying his individuality, losing status, and trusting problematic advice. However, if he defies the request, he will reap the [leader's] displeasure and is likely to become the recipient of a variety of negative consequences. In addition, he may lose the benefits of the Outward Bound course. The adolescent is in a lose-lose situation. Given the way he sees the world, he has no choices that lead to unambiguous success and satisfaction. He has succeeded at transforming a helpful, direct suggestion—put on your pack and participate in this program—into a non-therapeutic double bind. It is no wonder that such adolescents are marked by hostility, distrust, depression, labile affect, and other negative emotions and behaviors; their world view and the typical responses of others to that world view frequently double bind them into lose-lose situations. (Gass, 1993, p. 261)

As Bacon illustrates, the adolescent is placed in a **negative double bind** when given such a direct request. Such situations are inadvertently structured by well-meaning leaders, so that adolescents believe that no matter which action they choose, it will produce a negative outcome. In addressing such behaviors, the answer for you may lie in being less direct. This may be accomplished by supporting the adolescent's attempts at being functional by providing a situation in which both options lead to beneficial results. You must create a win-win situation: a **positive double bind**.

Say that in this same situation, several clients have demonstrated a number of consistently resistant behaviors, such as not putting on their packs after repeated requests from leaders. In this instance, Bacon offers an alternative approach to facilitating these behaviors:

At Outward Bound, especially after things start going well and people are getting more motivated, the pace of the course sometimes gets faster; the group hikes farther and more quickly, climbs more, and so on. This increase in pace tends to make folks nervous because some students start wondering if they are going to be able to keep up; they start worrying that they might be the ones who will mess up and slow the group down. In some groups, students solve this concern by having one or two students be the regular "screw-ups." These are the people who always get up late, or complain, or hike slowly, or forget something. On the surface, it may seem like these people are messing up badly, but actually they do a lot for the rest of the group. First of all, it reassures the other students to know that they aren't the worst group member—the screw-up has being in last place all locked up. In addition, the screw-up usually distracts everyone from their own problems; there's nothing like finding a scapegoat to blame for everything when you're feeling blue. At this point, the leader stops and asks a few questions about scapegoating to ensure that the clients understand these points. Following this brief discussion, the leader continues by pointing out that although the screw-up helps everybody else, he also tends to lose out pretty seriously. Most of the time, people are mad at him. So, while this group may choose to have

a scapegoat to gain the benefits, maybe the only fair thing to do is to be willing to share the screw-up role around equally—kind of like [chores are] shared. Everyone could take a turn. The [leader] wonders [aloud]: who would volunteer to be the first screw-up? (Bacon, in Gass, 1993, p. 262)

Such a statement by an outdoor leader is certainly not "direct." What type of empathetic, caring, concerned outdoor leader would ask clients already burdened by a "dysfunctional" label to purposefully "screw up?" By looking at the intention behind the outdoor leader's comments, however, an "indirect," yet truly empathetic method of assisting clients emerges. Let's see what Bacon has to say:

[After delivering such a request] the group can follow [such] directions—an atypical act—and cooperate by having a member function as the scapegoat, or it can defy the [leader] and refuse to allow any group member to assume that role. It is most probable that the [clients] will unite against the [leader] and his "crazy" request and refuse to allow anyone to volunteer to be the scapegoat. Even if someone does volunteer, their misbehaviors will be pseudo misbehaviors, not the real thing. The group is in a win-win situation; any choice it makes leads to success. If a [client] does begin to act out genuinely, the [leaders] can comment that someone has decided to volunteer to help the group by being the scapegoat after all. This reference brings some humor into a typically tense, confrontive situation and provides an easy way for the acting out [client] to apologize without losing much face. He can agree that, yes, he was just doing a bit of spontaneous volunteering. Finally, if the situation continues to escalate, the group can be asked to view the misbehavior from a different context. They can be questioned about whether they really need this [client] to help them in this way. The [clients] will probably respond in the negative and proceed to confront the misbehaving [client] about his unsolicited assistance and inappropriate behaviors. One of the significant benefits of using therapeutic double binds is that they are unusual and unexpected; it is unlikely that a person who has chronically maladaptive personality strategies has ever encountered this type of intervention. As mentioned above, such people do have sophisticated ways of resisting typical change strategies, but they are usually defenseless against the paradoxical qualities of

888

the double bind because they simply have never encountered it before. After all, how often is an adolescent asked to [voluntarily] act out? (Gass, 1993, p. 263)

Approaches like this indirectly work in the clients' best interests. In such cases, directly confronting client behavior often produces a high degree of resistance, and in a sense, makes it more difficult for the client to achieve her objective from the adventure experience. Such efforts, while much more difficult than all of the other techniques in other generations, may produce the best results for clients. Notice in this last example, and in the ropes course vignette given earlier, the leader's behavior is unusual and unexpected: a behavioral paradox. Paradoxical behavior is common in many forms of indirect frontloading.

You can find other examples of indirect frontloading, such as symptom displacements, illusion of alternatives, and proactive reframing, in other sources (e.g., Waltzlawick, 1978). We caution you, however, that these other techniques require a greater degree of psychotherapy training than the other five approaches. While important for all facilitation techniques, you should especially consider the ethical use of indirect approaches. Don't use such techniques as "power tactics" or "trickery"; instead only use them with empathy and the clients' best interests in mind. The ethical concept of "nonmaleficence," which means "above all else, do no harm to the client," is probably most true and appropriate in utilizing indirect approaches (see chapter 23 for more information). Indirect frontloading approaches work best when done truthfully. Contrived indirect frontloading procedures can often backfire on you, leading to client mistrust.

Let's look, now, at another situation involving double binds as well as a related technique called symptom prescriptions as further examples of indirect frontloading approaches.

Double Binds

In order for you to become a better leader, we are assigning you to be leader in this next activity.

As we have seen in the backpacking example with delinquent adolescents, one indirect intervention that can be implemented when direct approaches to frontloading fail to work is the use of **double binds**. Because it is so valuable, yet difficult to

apply artfully, this advanced technique deserves further discussion.

But what is a "bind?" A bind prevents or restrains a person from natural or customary behaviors. When you place a client in dilemma, or a situation that almost demands opposing behaviors, you are "binding" the client to a certain behavior. Remember, a bind may be positive (win-win) or negative (lose-lose) as it obligates a person to act in a new or unusual manner.

Another example of a positive double bind a corporate group has working on the Spider's Web task. This particular group has experienced an ongoing problem with gender equity, that is, the men tend to dominate. Furthermore, the group is in denial of this fact: some members are unaware, while others refuse to acknowledge it.

Let's look more closely at this example to further illustrate the ease with which a frontload may turn into a negative or positive double bind. Say that during the frontloading brief, a well-meaning male outdoor leader innocently comments that the women need to be more empowered and spontaneous in their group roles. While unintentional, this statement creates a negative double bind: a lose-lose situation. If the women in the group ignore the statement, they lose because they fail to achieve empowerment or spontaneity, remaining submissive or powerless within the group structure. If, however, they take charge of the Spider's Web situation in response to the outdoor leader's comment, they also lose because any perception of empowerment or spontaneity will be false: how can they be truly empowered or spontaneous if told to do so, particularly by a male? In other words, they have not earned the empowerment by themselves, because the "spontaneity" was generated and preplanned. With these remarks, the outdoor leader has lost a learning opportunity and negatively bound these clients into continuing their dysfunctional behaviors. This lose-lose double bind is similar in structure to the negative double bind statement at the beginning of this section: how can a person be a leader when they are assigned the leadership role?

The example, however, focuses on creating a positive double bind for clients. The outdoor leader offers this alternative frontload:

Most . . . groups who attempt the Spider's Web tend to do it in a particular way. At the beginning, they mill around a bit with lots of people offering their suggestions. After some time a couple of dominant males tend to start the group off. They get a few men to the other side of the web and then throw the women through like sacks of potatoes and often with embarrassing remarks about female anatomy disguised as humour. Then the same group of dominant males decides how to do the hardest part [of the task] which is getting the last few people through. Afterwards, during the discussion of the exercise, everyone agrees that the leadership was more-or-less sexist and there are various emotional reactions to that. There are other ways to do the Spider's Web . . . (Gass & Dobkin, 1991)

Stated in this way, the frontloaded double bind is positive, creating a win-win situation. If the group chooses to perform the task in a sexist manner, then they win because their true behaviors will become painfully obvious, and the awareness or denial of the group's sexist behavior will be heightened for the debriefing. If the group chooses to perform in a nonsexist and equitable manner, then they also win since they have clearly demonstrated that they can act differently and may continue to do so in the future. One way brings dysfunction to the forefront of discussion, while the other breaks old habits, leading to new learning. With this frontloading technique, the outdoor leader has positively bound this resistant client group, bringing them to a unique turning point opportunity.

A third example is the second introductory vignette at the beginning of this chapter in which the group of alcoholics deals with the issue of temptation. Here coming down from the ropes course is designed to represent a relapse, or a return to substance abuse. Offered in an appropriate atmosphere, this framework serves to enhance a client's motivation to complete the course and usually results in success: people accomplishing preset goals despite temptation not to. The fear of succumbing to temptation mirrors fears associated with heights or lack of strength. In the event someone does descend, the group may argue that temptation won out. Provided a supportive atmosphere exists for debriefing, the postactivity discussion provides a powerful opportunity for clients to talk about how they will deal with temptation once they leave treatment.

Remember that all indirect techniques must be: (1) offered with true sincerity and (2) presented with the best interests of the client in mind. To use them to negatively manipulate clients, as

some sort of "power struggle," or without regard for what the client needs, will lead to failure in the intervention, lose elements of trust and rapport that you may have developed between you and your client, and is contrary to the ethical guidelines of an adventure professional.

Paradoxical Symptom Prescriptions

Please, don't tell me anything that you don't want me to know until you're ready to talk about it.

A **paradox** is a piece of information that seems to contradict common sense or oppose the generally accepted opinion. From one perspective it may appear quite absurd, but in reality it may be quite true. At one time or another, you may encounter clients who are inhibited by certain dysfunctional behaviors with which direct techniques fail. At these times, remember that you may use techniques that address the issue in a more indirect manner to empower the client to change. We've examined double binds, now let's investigate another way to approach a client indirectly: paradoxical symptom prescriptions for which you prescribe the very issue that seems to be keeping the client from success.

One example of this technique is with clients who are anxious about participating in adventure activities. In some cases, their worries about upcoming activities, such as ropes courses, expeditions, or skit presentations, continually serve to "freeze" them with indecision and inaction. This paralysis can prevent them from learning. You might be tempted to continue to assist them with attempts at inspiring, supporting, reasoning, or confronting anxious clients by sharing stories of success by others, offering verbal comfort and reassurance, listing all the good that will come from the experience, or by stating that worrying won't make a bit of difference.

Unfortunately for some anxious clients, these direct responses may not work. Such clients often decide that they are different from others so success won't come to them, that they are less worthy or able, that they don't need the benefits, or that worrying makes them feel good. The more you press such clients with these direct responses in an effort to help, the more the clients will argue and resist. By resisting, the clients are actually receiving attention and partial acceptance in the form of reassurance from you, which makes them feel quite good. The more this occurs, the more inadequate they feel, negating the benefits of the adventure experience. As Bacon (1993) explains: "They are capable of becoming more helpless regardless of the amount, quality, and type of help offered. Everything leads them to assert their inadequacy: inspiration makes them feel weak, support causes them to claim they are not worth all the fuss that is being made over them, and confrontation generates tears plus an implicit or explicit counterattack accusing the confronter of a deficit in empathy" (p. 264). Their behavior is a paradox.

In such cases, you must recognize that anxiety is an involuntary emotion beyond human control, one that cannot be prevented by sheer willpower alone. In order to counteract the dysfunctional paradox that is keeping such clients from achieving the gains they want, you need to prescribe the actual "symptom" of anxiety. To do this, you actually encourage clients to experience anxiety at least once a day before the upcoming activity that has them so worried. You suggest that they contemplate their apprehensions, since fear is an important guard, preventing injury in outdoor pursuits. By consciously concentrating on their fears for a set period of time at the same time each day, they may be able to avoid danger when the activity day arrives. The connection between anxiety and danger avoidance is an important one because it reframes a negative occurrence in a positive light: it gives usefulness and meaning to something that the clients are troubled by.

In this manner, the clients find that experiencing true anxiety is extremely difficult for many and impossible for some. Bacon elaborates: "Since, by definition, anxiety is something which arises without solicitation—something that is neither invited nor welcomed—the consciously created anxiety generated through this assignment is not 'real' anxiety" (p. 265). In short, the clients will either experience pseudoanxiety from their daily contemplations or they will decide that your suggestion seems stupid and will put their efforts into resisting the suggestion to the point of excluding their previous worries. In this manner, the paradox has the appearance of being contradictory, but in reality, it's both a valid way to address dangers and an effective way to help clients deal with their anxieties.

Through such paradoxical suggestions, you encourage clients to view things from a new perspective that contradicted their usual reality. Either they will abandon the old view of reality in favor of a new one in which they no longer perceive anxiety, or they will retain the old view, but abandon the behavior that stemmed from it in favor of new behavior—pseudoanxiety instead of a genuine attack. The contradictory content of the paradox encourages clients to redefine their interpretations or perspectives of their problems, thereby enabling them to find new solutions.

Direct approaches to facilitating growth in adventure experiences work 90 to 95 percent of the time. The other 5 to 10 percent of the time, however, when certain client behaviors and goals make these approaches ineffective, actually leading clients toward becoming even more "stuck" in their self-defeating and limiting behaviors, explore indirect techniques to change unproductive dynamics.

Indirect approaches, such as double binds and paradoxical symptom prescriptions, work because they are unusual and unexpected. It's likely that dysfunctional individuals have never encountered these techniques before. As a result, when faced with a paradox or double bind, the clients' normal strategies to resist change fail, and they become obligated to make breakthrough discoveries as they attempt to resolve the discrepancies of the dilemma they find themselves in. The outcome can be especially therapeutic for resistant clients.

Again, paradox and double binding are extremely sophisticated techniques of frontloading that demand great care. They are beyond the scope of most outdoor leaders, especially those not properly trained in psychotherapy, and you should not use them without appropriate experience. We encourage you to practice the five points of direct frontloading (mentioned in chapters 14 and 15) and to reserve employing the paradox and double binding methods until you have proper training and practice under qualified supervision. Nevertheless, you can benefit from fully understanding these techniques, especially if you cofacilitate with a psychotherapist or other trained professional who might utilize these approaches.

EFFECTIVE OUTDOOR LEADERS SHOULD

☞ Understand the three types of metaphoric transfer and how they relate to the six generations of facilitation techniques.

☞ Be capable of creating isomorphic frameworks.

☞ Understand the drawbacks to isomorphic framing.

☞ Understand the indirect frontloading methods we have explained in this chapter and, rather than using them, be able to support a qualified psychotherapist's use of them.

SUMMARY

Metaphors are one key foundation of transferring change from adventure to daily life. Three types of metaphoric transfer and their corresponding generations of facilitation are spontaneous (first), analogous (second, third, or fourth), and structured (fifth or sixth). Fifth generation facilitation uses metaphors composed of multiple isomorphs to frame or introduce an experience so that it is meaningful and relevant to client needs. An isomorph, in which both items have the same form or structure, represents a specific link between the adventure and daily life. Several of these isomorphs in combination can create a general metaphor that matches client issues. Isomorphic framing before the adventure means that successful completion of the experience mirrors successful resolution of client issues.

You can create an effective isomorphic framework by following a seven-step process. Before an experience, you should assess, identify, and rank client goals; select metaphoric adventures; identify successful resolution to the issue; and strengthen the isomorphic framework. During and after an experience, you should review client motivation; conduct the experience with revisions; and debrief. But the use of fifth generation techniques has some drawbacks. These include greater complexity, the prescriptive nature, the needs to rely on parallel structures, to balance with client reality, and to account for personal differences and the potential loss of spontaneous metaphors.

On those rare occasions when all direct efforts at facilitation fail by causing increased resistance, you may need to use indirect methods. Two of many methods of indirect frontloading are the double bind and the paradoxical symptom prescription. A double bind channels behavior in a direction you prefer by giving the client two choices. When both choices are lose-lose, the double bind is negative. Negative binds are un-intentional, but unfortunately common in some situations in which outdoor leaders are controlling clients. When both choices are win-win, the double bind is positive. A positive bind is difficult to create, but works because it is unusual and unexpected. It lowers a client's resistance to being changed.

A paradox is seemingly contradictory to the expected, but for a good reason. To create one, you act in a way that clients are not used to. Symptom prescription refers to demanding the behavior that is preventing clients from changing. This method allows clients to see things from a fresh perspective that refutes their understanding of the situation. They redefine their interpretations and may find new ways of behaving.

You should use indirect frontloading methods with great caution and only for the right reasons. Never use these advanced techniques without appropriate psychotherapy training or without first practicing under supervision. Never try to gain power over or trick a group. Use these sophisticated techniques only with empathy and the group's best interests in mind. Always desire not to harm clients and to be truthful. While accumulating experience as an outdoor leader, stick to using the five direct frontloading techniques we discussed in chapter 15.

QUESTIONS TO THINK ABOUT

1. From your own experience in outdoor activities, give an example of a powerful metaphor you remember.

2. Remember a learning situation that was a metaphor of reality and describe what new strategy you transferred and how you did it.

3. Describe three ways that you might use metaphors in adventure programming. Outline which types of metaphors are found in which generations of facilitation.

4. Define the term "isomorphism." Why is isomorphism so critical in the use of metaphors in adventure experiences?

5. List the seven steps to developing isomorphic frameworks. Using this model, design an isomorphic framework for a specific population.

6. Give four examples of adventure experiences that embody a strong, preexisting metaphoric relationship to cooperation.

Give another four examples of adventure experiences that embody a strong, preexisting metaphoric relationship to decision making.

7. Outline the benefits and drawbacks of using isomorphic framing facilitation techniques.

8. Explain when you might want to implement indirect frontloading techniques.

9. List the ethical guidelines you should use when considering use of indirect frontloading.

10. Differentiate between the terms positive and negative double bind. Explain how the sentence "In order for you to become a better leader, we are assigning you to be leader in this next activity" is a positive or negative double bind.

11. Define the term "paradoxical symptom prescriptions." Explain how the sentence "Please don't tell me anything that you don't want me to know until you're ready to talk about it" is a paradoxical symptom prescription.

REFERENCES

Bacon, S.B. (1983). *The conscious use of metaphor in Outward Bound*. Greenwich, CT: Outward Bound, USA.

Bacon, S.B. (1987). *The evolution of the Outward Bound process*. Greenwich, CT: Outward Bound, USA. (ERIC Document Reproduction Service No. ED 295 780).

Bacon, S.B. (1991a). Using the ropes course to help alcoholics resist temptation. In M.A. Gass and C.H. Dobkin (Eds.), *Book of metaphors: Volume I* (pp. 11-12). Available from editors at University of New Hampshire, Durham, NH.

Bacon, S.B. (1991b). Using the ropes course to help alcoholics resist temptation. In M.A. Gass and C.H. Dobkin (Eds.), *Book of metaphors: Volume I* (pp. 9-10). Available from editors at University of New Hampshire, Durham, NH.

Bacon, S.B. (1993). Paradox and double binds in adventure-based education. In M.A. Gass (Ed.), *Adventure therapy: Therapeutic applications of adventure programming in mental health settings*. Boulder, CO: Association for Experiential Education, 259-282.

Bacon, S.B., & Kimball, R.O. (1989). The wilderness challenge model. In R.D. Lyman (Ed.), *Residential and inpatient treatment of children and adolescents* (pp. 115-144). New York: Plenum Press.

de Shazer, S. (1982). *Patterns of brief family therapy*. New York: Guildford Press.

Gass, M.A. (1985). Programming the transfer of learning in adventure education. *Journal of Experiential Education* 8(3), 18-24.

Gass, M.A. (1991). Enhancing metaphoric transfer in adventure therapy programs. *Journal of Experiential Education* 14(2), 6-13.

Gass, M.A. (1993). *Adventure therapy: Therapeutic applications of adventure programming in mental health settings*. Boulder, CO: Association for Experiential Education.

Gass, M.A., & Dobkin, C.H. (Eds.) (1991). *Book of metaphors: Volume I*. Durham, NH: University of New Hampshire, Department of Kinesiology.

Gass, M.A., & Priest, S. (1993). Using metaphors and isomorphs to enhance the transfer of learning in adventure education. *Journal of Adventure Education* 10(4), 18-24.

Mack, H. (1996). Inside work, outdoors: Women, metaphor, and meaning. In K. Warren (Ed.). *Women's voices in experiential education*. Dubuque, IA: Kendall/Hunt Publishing Company, 24-31.

Minuchin, S. (1981). *Family therapy techniques*. Cambridge, MA: Harvard University Press.

Nadler, R. & Luckner, J. (1992). *Processing the adventure experience*. Dubuque, IA: Kendall/Hunt Publishing Company.

Schoel, J., Prouty, D., & Radcliffe, P. (1988). *Islands of healing: A guide to adventure-based counseling*. Hamilton, MA: Project Adventure.

Waltzlawick, P. (1978). *The language of change*. New York: Norton.

Zeig, J. (Ed.). (1994). *Ericksonian methods: The essence of the story*. New York: Brunner/Mazel.

chapter
17

Facilitation Roles

It was a sunny yet breezy morning as the group completed its final approach to the rock climbing site. Some members of the group were eager to begin, while others were a bit nervous about the upcoming experience and various issues associated with the day's activity. Both coleaders knew the clients' purposes for rock climbing: to assist them in meeting their particular goals, for gains toward these goals to be integrated into their daily lives, and for those gains to have a lasting and meaningful influence for them. As the leaders finished setting up the climbs, they gathered the group in a circle to implement various facilitation processes designed for the clients. Later that same afternoon, the group was back in a circle with some members arguing over what had just occurred, blaming one another for mistakes that were made. Other group members had stopped listening and several others were retreating from the group's circle. Both leaders began to use facilitating strategies that emphasized the group's strengths as well as addressed this issue in the context of the clients' goals.

The instructor's role is one of facilitation, that is, making interventions as needed to stimulate and encourage the development of positive relationships among group members. By means of creating and structuring diverse opportunities for interaction, the instructor seeks to move a newly formed social unit from disarray to collective unity. Due to the nature of this objective, facilitation is not at all an easy task. It places constant demands on the instructor to be at once aware of himself [or herself], observant of the group, sensitive to changing needs, and resourceful in directing the process along educative paths. A degree of maturity as well as many helping skills are required to effectively guide people in such an intense program setting.

—Kalisch, 1979, pp. 83-84

What are your responsibilities in the facilitation roles and how can you provide these vital services to clients? While a number of roles exist, let's focus on seven:

A = Assess needs.
B = Be neutral.
C = Construct change processes.
D = Deal with resistance.
E = Exceptions produce solutions.
F = Feedback aids learning.
G = Good listening elicits useful questions.

ASSESS NEEDS

Effective facilitation depends on a thorough needs assessment or diagnosis (see the facilitation process in chapter 14). Remember, you must constantly examine and determine what clients need from an adventure program. Find what clients need through the process of **assessment**. Assessment is an ongoing procedure through which you acquire and evaluate information in order to help clients attain their objectives. Using assessment in this manner advances the idea of client-based programming. Adventure programs that believe "one type of experience fits all individuals" will fail to reach the true potential of an experience. Proper assessment, however, provides you with the knowledge and ability to customize programs to meet the unique needs of a particular client group. In this section, we'll examine two methods of assessing client needs in adventure programming and their interaction: the CHANGES and GRABBS models.

CHANGES Model

The **CHANGES model** (Gass & Gillis, 1995a) is organized into seven interactive steps, focusing on acquiring information for developing functional client change (see figure 17.1). These seven steps, which, not surprisingly, make up the acronym "CHANGES," include context, hypotheses, action, novelty, generating, evaluation, and solutions. One way to view these seven steps is in a time sequence. For the most part, the first pair of steps are accomplished before the adventure experience, the next three occur during the adventure, and the final pair take place after the experience.

In preparing for a therapeutic program, you must identify the **context** of an adventure experience and the client group. This includes gathering all that you know about the general client population, this specific client group, the adventure setting, any therapeutic issues, available resources, program purpose, and scheduling. You must draw on your judgment (see chapter 20), based on previous experiences with similar clients in similar places for similar reasons.

Questions that may provide contextual information include: Why has the client or client group entered into the adventure therapy experience? How long will they be involved? What are their stated goals as a group and as individuals? How does your level of training and competence with adventure activities and various client groups match up? How well do your goals, competencies, and past experiences match those needed and desired by the client group? Should you hold the sessions inside or outside? What equipment is available for the adventure experiences? How will the weather and physical surroundings determine which activities you can use?

From this context of past experiences, you should then begin to establish initial working **hypotheses** about group and client behavioral patterns by tracking what happens and in what order. Specifically, create these hypotheses from information collected in the forms of intake interviews, pencil and paper tests, and simple games conducted early in a program. Then supplement these working hypotheses with your knowledge of typical and unusual client behaviors and from informal sources, such as intuitive analysis of how the group feels about engaging in an activity, their physical ability levels, comments about where they are emotionally and socially, and what they expect will happen next. Once established, verify your working hypotheses by observing client behavior in the adventure experience.

Client responses to experiences with **action** will either confirm or contradict your hypotheses. By comparing observed behaviors with hypothesized ones, you can obtain additional information to further assess client needs and to reconstruct, reinforce, revise, or reject your hypotheses accordingly. Using adventure experiences in this manner adds to the validity and richness of assessment as well as provides additional context for developing possible interventions.

Activities that have **novelty** value and are unfamiliar cause clients to struggle with the spontaneity of an experience. As a result, they don't know how they are expected to behave socially. The need to act quickly prevents them from hiding behind a false self, forcing them to show their true behaviors. By seeing if these behaviors match your hypotheses, you can confirm or adapt them.

The intent of **generating** information about clients is to determine how and why client behaviors make "sense" to them. You may be able to generate information regarding issues of client values and belief systems, patterns of behavior, levels of intimacy, boundaries, roles, alliances, power, communication, feedback, language, and "walking their talk." Then use such information as a rich resource for diagnosing client needs, planning objectives and procedures, and evaluating treatment. By combining hypotheses validated in previous steps, you can reach a full and holistic understanding of this sense. Another way of making sense is to "track" behavior patterns: what happens and in what order over time during an adventure experience. The whole purpose of generating is the very motive for assessment: piecing together hypotheses validated by actual experience to obtain the true "stories" of clients' behavior. Finally, and most importantly, you must interpret the information you have gathered to get a clear picture of the clients' issues, which will, in turn, lead toward evaluation and solutions.

Thus, you must **evaluate** which hypotheses seem to be supported or refuted by client behavior. Here, you must integrate knowledge gathered in the previous steps and interpret this information to make decisions about diagnosing processes and symptoms, identifying client motivation, and determining possible interventions.

In conjunction with evaluation and with the aid of clients, you must then identify and construct potential **solutions** to client issues. Create solutions by examining exceptions to client problems: those

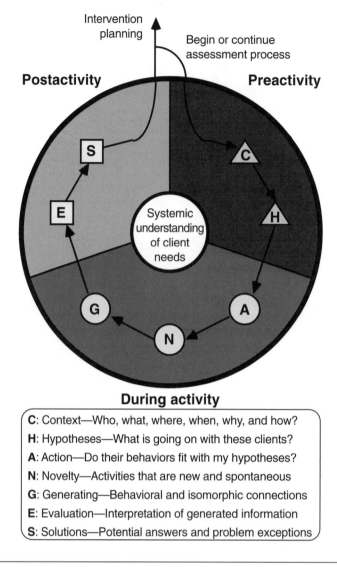

Figure 17.1   The CHANGES model (Gass & Gillis, 1995a).

times when their issues aren't present and their behaviors are functional. Finally, determine what strategies or solutions will be effective in working toward resolving the issues.

GRABBS Model

The **GRABBS model** (Schoel, Prouty, & Radcliffe, 1988) also provides a useful way to conduct ongoing client assessment. As with the CHANGES assessment model, apply the GRABBS model to acquire and evaluate client information in order to help them reach their objectives. GRABBS stands for Goals, Readiness, Affect, Behaviors, Bodies, and Stage. Ask questions such as "What are the **goals** of the experience—those of the group, its individual members, and of yourself?

What is the state of **readiness** of the group? Are they physically and psychologically safe for the activity? What is the level of feeling, or **affect**, among group members? What **behaviors** have clients shown toward the experience, each other, and you? Are group members treating each other's **bodies** respectfully? What **stage** of development is the group in: forming, norming, storming, performing, or adjourning?"

Combining the Models

While you can use each model independently, Gass and Gillis (1995a) have pointed out that you may use both models together to achieve a beneficial, interactive effect. In such a process, the GRABBS model can work within the context of the first five steps of the CHANGES model. You can use GRABBS as a sort of "scanning device," to search for and monitor the status of the six interests within CHANGES. The interaction of the models and the unique information they contribute to assessment help make the overall process more effective.

BE NEUTRAL

You will work best when you are able to align yourself with a variety of belief systems, realities, or client interpretations; and not as well when your perspective is aligned with only one opinion, especially your own. Maintaining a sense of **neutrality**, without being distant from clients, will tend to serve you best by making you more mobile in your facilitation processes. In other words, you'll be able to take on a variety of positions concerning a topic without taking sides. Certainly, you cannot afford to become sided, or fixed on a single path toward change.

One way to maintain neutrality and achieve mobility is to remember and act on the maxim: "As a facilitator, I am responsible 'to' you, but not 'for' you" (adapted from King, 1988; see chapter 11). This places clients in charge of what they gain from an experience and you in a flexible role that allows you to avoid getting caught up in the clients' issues. In this way, clients are free to direct their own facilitated experience.

Ironically, you can remain neutral if you know what issues you cannot remain neutral about. These are sometimes referred to as **nonnegotiable values**: those issues that are fixed for you as a leader. For example, several clients may begin to make a number of sexist comments. For many leaders, the depreciation of others based on their gender is not acceptable, especially under a full value contract. This behavior is clearly nonnegotiable, and you should proactively address it. If you inventory your nonnegotiable values before working with clients, you'll quickly know if you can remain neutral or not when problems arise. Moreover, you will be more prepared to deal with value-laden issues, which, we must warn you, constantly arise in adventure programming.

CONSTRUCT CHANGE PROCESSES

One of your primary roles as an outdoor leader is to provide mechanisms that can help clients create the functional changes they seek. Con-

ducted within the context of adventure programming, these mechanisms often take on the form of "problem-focused" or "solution-focused" facilitation approaches (Gass & Gillis, 1995b). As their names imply, the difference between the two approaches depends on what you center your attention on and the awareness of clients: is it on the problem or the solution?

When you apply a **problem-focused facilitation approach**, you attend to what is not working, putting energy into fixing what is out of order, that is, the dysfunctional action. Using this approach, you should seek to know as much as possible about the problem, so you can help the client correct the behavior. The more you understand the problem, the more helpful you can be in solving it. Therefore, as a problem-focused leader, ask questions such as "Why did the problem happen and what is causing it?"

When you use a **solution-focused facilitation approach**, you take another tack by identifying what is working, that is, the functional action, by holding this up as a model for change, and by integrating the positive behavior into the client's reality. Using this approach, you should seek to know as much as possible about exceptions to the problem. The more you identify and understand these exceptions, the more help you'll be to the client. Therefore, as a solution-focused leader, ask questions such as "When doesn't the problem happen and what takes place when the problem is absent?" Here, you are also gaining a more concrete perception of the problem, but only in light of how it pertains to possible solutions. This approach also emphasizes what clients are doing already that is useful, and this knowledge directs them to highlight, access, and build on their strengths.

You need to evaluate each approach, then select the one that makes the most sense for your particular clients at a particular time. But are you wondering how you'll apply these approaches in real life? Let's look at examples of each approach for activities conducted before, during, and after an adventure experience.

As you know, frontloading takes place prior to an adventure experience (see chapters 14, 15, and 16). Direct and indirect frontloading provide some of the most influential facilitation techniques you can use to help clients construct functional change. With these techniques, you allow clients to seek positive behaviors, often by asking them to consider possible growth areas in advance of an adventure experience.

As a problem-focused leader, you might frontload clients' attention on issues that have been somewhat problematic in the past. These may include how problems will hinder success, how the group will deal with these problems if they arise, and how the group will work together to overcome their problems. In this approach, clients center their attention on resolving these issues during the experience.

As a solution-focused leader, you might frontload the activity by asking the group to identify behaviors that might help bring about success, how to optimize these successful behaviors, and when they feel successful behaviors are most likely to happen during the adventure experience. You could also challenge each client to do something different in order to make other group members feel better about the group's ability to work together toward their objectives or encourage them to "have their antenna up" so as to figure out what the others did to support them (e.g., Kiser, Piercy, & Lipchik, 1993, p. 236).

In an adventure experience, you could use a **stop-action**, or **freeze**, technique to take advantage of a teachable or therapeutic moment. With this technique, you stop the action in order to analyze and learn from what is going on at that moment in time. For example, in the middle of an adventure experience, communication among group members can break down with everyone talking at once and no one listening. At an opportune moment, you or any client can call a time-out to discuss why things are going poorly. The group stops the experience at this time or as soon as possible after the call and discusses this issue until they feel ready to continue the action.

As a problem-focused leader, you might focus clients' attention on identifying, analyzing, and fixing those problematic elements that caused the group to have poor communication. The intent of this discussion would be to increase client's ability to improve their communication skills by better understanding how and why the dysfunction occurred.

As a solution-focused leader, you might ask the group to identify, analyze, and discuss times during the adventure experience when communication was good. If the group responds that no such times occurred, then you should ask them to consider and discuss what good communication might look like—as a hypothetical exception. To turn the clients' mind-set toward such solutions, you should also ask them to highlight and

concentrate on what they would do if they were communicating better, what they would be doing differently if they were communicating at their best, or how they would know if they were communicating well.

Scaling is a technique used to self-rate performance in regard to an issue, following the adventure experience. For example, you could ask a group to evaluate how they cooperated in an experience using a scale from 0 to 10, either by stating it aloud, holding up fingers, or writing it down. On this scale, 0 represents a total lack of cooperation and 10 is completely successful. Clients can use scaling to arrive at a quantifiable evaluation of the experience or to launch into a discussion of their performances. Let's assume this group rates their efforts with a mean of "five," which represents average cooperation.

As a problem-focused leader, you should center clients' attention on identifying, investigating, and eliminating those negative elements that prevented them from obtaining a higher mean score for cooperation. Then have the group focus on completing their next adventure experience by reducing these negative elements.

As a solution-focused leader, you should ask the group to consider the positive elements that made the score a five, keeping the score from being lower. This encourages the group to focus on building these positive elements in order to increase the score. You could also ask the group about the small things they will be doing differently when they obtain a higher score for cooperation in the future.

DEAL WITH RESISTANCE

People don't resist change, they resist being changed! As a result, clients can sometimes feel forced to grow, and so they will often resist. Applying further external "motivation" may simply cause greater internal resistance. Blocking (i.e., stopping the resistence from occuring) might prove fruitful at some times, but it often fails to address the underlying reasons of why such resistance occurs in the first place.

You can deal with such resistance by clarifying and reframing techniques. Both methods require you to view resistance as an effort on the part of clients to educate you as to how best to help them. Thus, you must learn to see resistance not as opposition from clients, but as their encouragement for you to understand their needs and issues (de Shazer, 1984). Therefore, don't block, disperse, diffuse, or deflect resistance: use it to better serve the clients.

In the **clarifying** method, you explain to the group that you are genuinely confused by what is happening and respectfully ask the group to help you understand the situation. In answering your honest and honorable inquiry, clients offer their own interpretations and expectations for the situation. In an open and honest manner, you are merely relating those parts of the experience which are truly confusing you. By responding to this lack of clarity, the clients become clearer about these same issues. Not surprisingly, however, this technique fails miserably when it is offered in a fraudulent or sarcastic manner. Consider this sincere use of clarifying:

Y'know, I've probably done over a hundred Spider's Webs before in my life as a professional, and I must admit that I've never seen anyone (any group) really act in this way. I don't know if it's just me or the day, but I can't get over how incredibly different this Spider's Web is. Usually groups come and (here, the leader discusses typical behaviors for the activity), but I just don't see this happening with this group. Did I give the wrong directions? Did I forget to tell you something at the beginning?

In the **reframing** method, you put forth new ways of looking at a situation. By offering new perspectives or alternative reasons for resistance, you attempt to see how the opposition to change can benefit clients; for example, you ask yourself "What function does resistance serve? Why do clients see it as useful?" Proposing new interpretations or helping clients to construct their own can redirect resistance, possibly enhancing efforts to change. You can reframe both the content or context of an experience.

With **content reframing**, you encourage clients to look for a new and more positive meaning of a behavior within the substance of the adventure. For example, a client comes off a climb having spent 60 minutes attempting to complete the final crux move. The client is very dejected because of an inability to succeed. In reframing the behavior, you may point out that a more valid thing to learn from the experience is the client's ability to persist for so long during the climb and how this may be of much more value for him than actually completing the climb.

With **contextual reframing**, you encourage the client to look for a new and more positive meaning of the behavior by applying an action to a different and more relevant circumstance. Using the same climbing example, you should downplay the shortcomings of the actual climbing by pointing out that the client could learn several lessons, such as learning when to stop when you are faced with a task you can't complete, learning what you need to do in the future to complete a task, and learning what your strengths and weaknesses are when really pushed to the limit. Then, you could say "We learn from our mistakes," helping the client apply the lessons learned to real life.

EXCEPTIONS PRODUCE SOLUTIONS

The answers to client questions and the solutions to their problems can often be found in the **exceptions** to their issues (de Shazer, 1985; Walter & Peller, 1992). This is the case when you ask clients to answer the question "When the problem is not happening, what is happening instead?"

For example, if one issue for a group is lack of trust, then you could focus on an exception to this lack: a time when clients were actually trusting well. If clients claim never to have been able to trust one another, then you can ask about speculative exceptions: an imagined time of trusting. You should ask questions such as "When this problem is not present, what are things like? What would happen if the group were trusting more? What would you be doing differently if you were trusting more? How would you know if you were trusting more?"

Questions about exceptions to client issues positively focus their minds on solutions and not problems. In answering these exceptional questions, clients highlight for themselves—as well as for you—what they should be doing differently. This gives them the ideas for how to act differently in the future.

Another way to find solutions is to foster expectations for success by posing the so-called **miracle** question (e.g., de Shazer, 1985). With this type of question, you ask clients to respond to a question that focuses the answer on what success would look like before the program even starts. Two formats for miracle questions might go as follows:

Say at the end of this course you're driving home with another participant. She turns to you and asks "What did you think of that experience?" What will have had to happen in this program for you to be able to truly respond: "That was incredibly valuable! It could not have gone any better"?

Imagine yourself after this course. You're back home discussing your experience with a friend or family member. How would you complete this one sentence: "That was the best (or worst) and most (or least) valuable program I've ever experienced, because I. . . ."

Responses to miracle questions indicate client's definitions and impressions of success; which, in turn, inform you as to what clients are looking for and hoping to gain from the program. These needs and desires can form the basis of upcoming learning and change.

Since clients often arrive at adventure programs feeling apprehensive about what will happen, dreading embarrassment, or feeling afraid of getting hurt, you can allay these concerns by implanting positive prospects at the outset of a program. Responses, gathered early in a program, can form the foundation for goal setting and may shed light on the values clients hold in high regard or the concerns they have for the future. Sharing anonymous answers aloud or posting written answers, focuses clients' energies on understanding one another and on successfully working for solutions, rather than failure caused by dwelling on problems.

FEEDBACK AIDS LEARNING

A critical feature of facilitation is the provision for **appropriate feedback** to clients from themselves, from other clients, and from you. Upcraft (1982, p. 80) defined feedback as the "exchange of verbal and non-verbal responses among group members based on commonly observed behavior" and identified eight characteristics associated with providing appropriate feedback between a sender and receiver (e.g., Upcraft, 1982, pp. 81-83; Nadler & Luckner, 1992, p. 34).

1. Appropriate feedback is **descriptive**, rather than evaluative. To give descriptive feedback, the sender offers observations of the event. But evaluative feedback assesses the value of what a person has done. Describing a behavior, rather than a personal reaction to it, allows recipients to use this information in a manner that works best for them. Moreover, avoiding evaluative language reduces the defensive posture of recipients.

2. Appropriate feedback is **specific**, rather than general. Learning what specifically caused a behavior lessens the possibility of misinterpretation. For example, being told an idea is "stupid" probably is not as valuable as being told "When we came to this point in the trail, I didn't understand why you decided to. . . ."

3. Appropriate feedback is **well intended**. You must keep the purpose of feedback in mind: to produce positive changes in an individual or to make the group more functional. When the motivations for presenting feedback shift to destructive intentions, such as to make another person feel bad or to feel powerful at the expense of another, you should look closely at why feedback is being given in this manner. In examining such motivations, take into account the needs of the recipient as well as the sender. Failure to meet both their needs can lessen the value and future integration of what is being presented.

4. Appropriate feedback is **directed toward change**: something the receiver can act on. Presenting constructive feedback about shortcomings the receiver has no control over can only increase frustration. For such issues, search for other solutions or better uses for such behaviors. For example, you might say "To me, it seems as if you don't have the background in this area; do you agree? Would it work better if you were put in another role?"

5. Appropriate feedback is **solicited**, rather than imposed. Feedback is most useful when clients are seeking it, rather than when it is thrust on them. Asking if the person would like to receive feedback on performance as well as the manner of and forum for reception (e.g., when, where, how, who) produces more constructive results.

6. Appropriate feedback is **well-timed**. Feedback that is presented immediately following experiences reduces confusion that can develop over a period of time. But some situations exist in which this is not possible or appropriate, for example, logistical constraints or the person is not ready to hear it.

7. Appropriate feedback is **checked out with the sender**. While giving feedback, check in with

the recipient periodically to increase the likelihood that the message and intentions you're sending are being received. Have the recipient repeat those portions of the feedback they are finding most valuable as a "reliability check" for the sender.

8. Appropriate feedback is **checked out with the group**. When appropriate and possible, invite other clients to provide a sounding board for the feedback. They can give further information on the reliability of the feedback and possibly offer other interpretations of what took place. Adding consistency or variation to the presented feedback can increase its richness and aid its reception. Be careful, however, to monitor group dynamics in order to ensure negative consequences don't result from such a process, such as the recipient feeling "ganged up on" or the introduction of inappropriate side issues.

Feedback brings learning and change. To this end, you should **implant circular feedback loops** in the group. This means getting members to observe one another, either covertly or overtly, and report back, either privately or publicly, their observations. Relationships in groups are recursive, that is, one person's actions positively or negatively influence the behaviors of others and their group's performance, and reciprocal, that is, the reverse is also true (i.e., the group's performance influences the individual's performance positively or negatively). Therefore, encouraging and monitoring these recursive and reciprocal interactions can further the development of most groups. Your introducing declared feedback loops places clients on alert for their behaviors, possibly making them more likely to experiment with changing negative ones.

GOOD LISTENING ELICITS USEFUL QUESTIONS

Good listening skills are fundamental to facilitation. If you don't hear or understand the answers to your questions, then facilitating change by asking questions is extremely difficult and possibly a waste of time. You must develop good listening skills, so let's look at a few key ideas as to how to do so (see also chapter 19).

Maintain eye contact with the speaker. Signal verbal and nonverbal attentiveness by saying "uh-huh" or "yeah" and by nodding your head. Don't initially express agreement or disagreement. Instead, simply indicate that you understood the message. Wait through pauses to encourage the speaker to resume talking. Don't rush to fill silences: be patient. Don't take the focus of the conversation away from the speaker by publicly disagreeing or by changing the subject. Use open-ended questions to encourage the speaker to elaborate. Summarize or restate the speaker's remarks from time to time to show comprehension of the ideas. Respond to the feelings that may lie behind the speaker's words. Show understanding of or empathy for how the speaker feels. Use a gentle tone of voice that expresses caring rather than judging. Lastly, seek feedback from other leaders about how to improve your listening skills.

Listen for action words. Active verbs depict a process rather than a product orientation. Clients can describe themselves and their issues in active terms, and by doing so, they become partially accountable for what might be happening. For example, instead of being depressed, clients can be depressing. Such an orientation can help them identify their issues and their sources. Once again, you listen for actions that are stated by the clients as unchangeable as well as those things that sound changeable. You need to know the difference and have the wisdom to act accordingly.

EFFECTIVE OUTDOOR LEADERS SHOULD

☞ Understand assessment processes involved in adventure experiences and know how to implement assessment information in order to best assist clients.

☞ Be capable of remaining neutral and mobile in regard to client issues.

☞ Be able to construct change processes from either a problem- or solution-focused perspective.

☞ Be able to deal with resistance through either the clarifying or reframing methods.

☞ Be able to help clients look for exceptions to their issues.

☞ Be capable of providing appropriate feedback and be able to elicit it from clients.

☞ Be good listeners, staying alert for active verbs.

SUMMARY

The seven facilitation roles are assess needs, be neutral, construct change processes, deal with resistance, exceptions produce solutions, feedback aids learning, and good listening elicits useful questions.

The CHANGES model is one way to assess client needs by using actual adventure activities as the measure, rather than the more traditional intake interviews, observation, or psychological diagnostic instruments (Kimball, 1993). When you facilitate adventure experiences in the correct manner, the information generated from them can help you assess client behaviors, and in many cases can provide an ongoing source richer than one-time, traditional procedures. Another advantage of this approach is the relationship of a continual feedback loop, in which adventure activities are both sources for assessment and interventions for change: a truly reciprocal process.

The GRABBS model stands for Goals, Readiness, Affect, Behaviors, Bodies, and Stage. Using this model, you ask questions about these topics in order to check client status throughout the assessment process. The CHANGES and GRABBS models can work together to contribute unique information for client needs assessment.

But you need to be neutral and remain mobile enough to adopt a variety of positions in response to client issues. You can accomplish this by determining for yourself which issues are flexible and which ones are nonnegotiable.

You can construct change processes from either a problem-focused or solution-focused facilitation approach. The former concentrates your and clients' efforts on solving the problem of dysfunctional behavior or changing negative actions. The latter concentrates your and clients' efforts on finding exceptions to the problem and emphasizing the times when behavior is functional, thereby reinforcing and enhancing positive behavior.

Resistance is the clients' way of telling you how to help them better. When you cannot deal with resistance by employing extra motivation or blocking opposition, the techniques of clarifying and reframing often prove fruitful. These methods cause clients to examine their issues from a fresh perspective, which may bring new change. Using the clarifying technique is the truthful and conscientious way to highlight your confusion. Using reframing helps clients examine the source of resistance by investigating it within the content or context of the experience.

Exceptions to client issues often hold the answers to their questions and the solutions to their problems. Frequently, you can encourage clients to identify exceptions to issues when the problem isn't present. When clients look for exceptions, they often find explanations for previously unexplained behaviors.

Appropriate feedback is descriptive, specific, well intended, directed toward change, solicited, well-timed, checked out with the sender, and checked out with the group. Implanting multiple opportunities to give and receive feedback in a group enables clients to learn and grow.

If you don't hear or understand client answers, then facilitating change by asking questions may be ineffective for you. Among many suggestions for attending to client's communication is listening for action words or verbs ending with "-ing." This attention can help you point out the sources of client issues.

QUESTIONS TO THINK ABOUT

1. Use the CHANGES model with a group and evaluate its effectiveness.

2. Explain how you would use the GRABBS model.

3. Identify your nonnegotiable values that you will not be able to remain neutral about.

4. Decide whether your approach to facilitation is problem- or solution-focused and explain the difference.

5. Differentiate between the clarifying and reframing methods of dealing with resistance.

6. What is the difference between content and context reframing? Give an example of each.

7. Describe how exceptions to problems can lead to solutions. Give an example.

8. Design a miracle question for your next group (actual or imagined).

9. Practice giving appropriate feedback to someone in a realistic situation. Ask that person or an observer to give you appropriate feedback on your performance.

10. Listen to a person in a realistic situation and practice attending to them. Ask a third

person acting as an observer to give you feedback on how effective your listening skills are.

11. Listen to another person speak about an experience. Identify all the action words and active verbs they use.

12. Explain how facilitation makes learning and change easier for clients.

REFERENCES

de Shazer, S. (1984). The death of resistance. *Family Process* 23, 11-21.

de Shazer, S. (1985). *Keys to solution in brief therapy*. New York: Guilford.

Gass, M.A., & Gillis, H.L. (1995a). CHANGES: An assessment model using adventure experiences. *Journal of Experiential Education* 18(1), 34-40.

Gass, M.A., & Gillis, H.L. (1995b). Constructing solutions in adventure therapy. *Journal of Experiential Education* 18(2), 63-69.

Kalisch, K. (1979). *The role of the instructor in the Outward Bound educational process*. Three Lakes, WI: Honey Rock Camp.

Kimball, R.O. (1993). The wilderness as therapy: The value of using adventure programs in therapeutic assessment. In M.A. Gass (Ed.). *Adventure therapy: Therapeutic applications of adventure programming* (pp. 153-160). Dubuque, IA: Kendall/Hunt Publishing Company.

King, K. (1988). The role of adventure in the experiential learning process. *Journal of Experiential Education* 11(2), 4-8.

Kiser, D.J., Piercy, F.P., & Lipchik, E. (1993). The integration of emotion in solution-focused therapy. *Journal of Marital and Family Therapy* 19(3), 235-244.

Nadler, R., & Luckner, J. (1992). *Processing the adventure experience: Theory and practice*. Dubuque, IA: Kendall/Hunt.

Schoel, J., Prouty, D., & Radcliffe, P. (1988). *Islands of healing: A guide to adventure-based counseling*. Dubuque, IA: Kendall/Hunt.

Upcraft, M.L. (1982). *Learning to be a resident assistant*. San Francisco: Jossey-Bass.

Walter, J., & Peller, J. (1992). *Becoming solution-focused in brief therapy*. New York: Brunner/Mazel.

PART
V

Metaskills
for
Outdoor
Leaders

Flexible
Leadership Style

One novice leader has marched a group of expert climbers up a long trail to an alpine meadow for the purpose of establishing a base camp for a week of climbing in California. The weather is clear, spirits are high, and plenty of low-impact campsites are available. Nevertheless, this novice leader begins telling the group members where they must put their tents. Arguments ensue, many of the climbers revolt, eventually the entire group mutinies, and a new leader is selected. The old leader isn't sure how things got so out of hand!

An expert leader has allowed a group of novice paddlers to find their way back to their camp after a full day of sea kayaking among a maze of islands off the coast of British Columbia. In fact, this school teacher has managed to relax during most of the afternoon as the students have done much of the work to successfully find their way back. Still an hour from camp, at the end of an open crossing, a stranger has been spotted waving frantically on the beach. In this case, the teacher simply paddles on by and asks the students to take care of the situation! The group investigates and finds that the man is injured. They are unsure of what to do next and so fall into arguing; one tired student begins to cry. The teacher returns an hour later and is surprised to see things much the same as when the group first arrived!

I n the two scenarios, both leaders made the same mistake. They simply failed to shift their styles to suit the conditions they encountered. Instead, they chose to implement the same style they had been using throughout the day and probably continued to use frequently when they led other trips. In each case, the leaders could have been far more effective had they expressed a more appropriate style for each situation. In this chapter, we'll discuss how and when to adapt, or "flex," leadership styles by presenting a model that will guide you when making these critical choices.

LEADERSHIP STYLES

Leadership styles are the ways in which you express your influence. We can categorize styles in many different ways. For example, as a leader, you can be seen as telling, selling, testing, consulting, joining, and delegating in your efforts to influence (Tannenbaum & Schmidt, 1973). Such styles are often portrayed as a range of approaches, based on how much authority you exercise and how free group members are to contribute to the situation.

With the telling style, you make the decision and demand action from the group members. With the selling style, you make the decision and convince the group members of its merit. When testing, you present the decision, but invite group members to modify the decision. When consulting, you present the problem and then seek input in making the decision. In joining, you outline the entire problem and let the group members formulate the entire decision. In delegating, you let the group members outline the problem for themselves and then come to their own decision.

We can group these styles together in three sets of pairs to define three outdoor leadership styles, based on a continuum of decision-making power: **autocratic** (telling or selling), **democratic** (testing or consulting), and **abdicratic** (joining or delegating). (See chapter 5 for how the three main styles relate to group development.) The autocratic style is characterized by an authoritarian approach in which you hold complete power over decision making and dictate the needed response. The democratic style involves shared decision making, with you and the group working together to solve problems. The abdicratic style is an outgrowth of the laissez-faire, or "leaving to do," approach (Lewin, Lippitt, & White, 1938), in which you abdicate all decision-making power directly to the group and agree to abide by their resolutions. True dictatorial, or all-leader power, and laissez-faire, or all-group power, have limited

Sidebar 18.1
LEADERSHIP POWER

Group members will not follow someone they perceive as powerless or not influential. But no matter what your level of experience leading, you possess some bases of power from which you can influence others. Leadership power has been categorized as coming from at least five sources: referent, legitimate, expert, reward, and coercive (French & Raven, 1960; Raven & Rubin, 1976).

- **Referent power** is the least obvious source, but is the most voluntarily accepted of the five. When as a leader you are admired, identified with, or valued by group members, they are more likely to agree with you, support your opinions, and follow you. We can say you have referent power if the group members gauge or mirror their personal actions in reference to your actions.

- **Legitimate power** refers to the authority given you when you are appointed by a controlling agency or elected by group members. The higher the appointment or election, the greater the legitimized power. Most group members are likely to follow you if you have been given the moral right or legal responsibility to make certain decisions on their behalf.

- **Expert power** is achieved through perceived competence. The more knowledge, skill, and experience you appear to have, the more likely group members will respect your expertise and the more likely they are to follow you. Often this power is founded on your expertise relative to one situation and is unlikely to generalize to other situations.

- **Reward power** is achieved by giving a reward for effort. As a rewarding leader, you influence group members by offering positive incentives, such as fewer chores or recognition for a job well done. This ploy only works if the rewards are valued by group members. This ploy fails, however, if group members find that they do not like the incentives.

- **Coercive power** involves the threat of punishment and usually follows the failure of reward power to influence people. As a coercive leader, you influence group members by threatening negative incentives such as decreased responsibility or carrying more weight on a trip. Ethically, this type of power has no part in outdoor situations, since forcing people to act in this manner ignores challenge by choice and has the potential to destroy the adventure experience or create barriers to learning.

application in outdoor leadership settings, since negotiated involvement by both parties is often a necessary part of adventure experiences, and effective leadership involves influence from both as well. Figure 18.1 presents a summary of the three outdoor leadership styles in relation to these last two aspects.

LEADERSHIP ORIENTATION

Historically, two dimensions have been identified by researchers in determining a leader's orientation to approaching leadership issues: task and relationship (Stogdill & Coons, 1957; Blake & Mouton, 1978; and Hersey & Blanchard, 1982). As mentioned in chapter 5, the type of leadership style that you choose to express, especially in difficult times, will depend on your orientation to the dimensions of tasks and relationships. We can think of the orientation to these two dimensions as the level of concern that you have for getting the job done or achieving the goal (task) and for looking after group interactions or maintaining a positive atmosphere among the

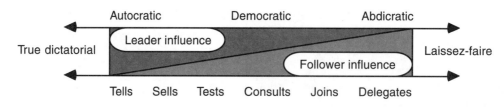

Figure 18.1   A continuum of outdoor leadership styles.

followers (relationship). Figure 18.2 shows these two orientations in a matrix.

These leadership orientations play an important role in determining the most appropriate style for you to express. If you want to get to the top of a peak at all costs, you may express an autocratic style to push people upward. Or as a laid-back leader, you may float down a river on a lazy day, preferring to engage people in conversation and so express an abdicratic style. Generally speaking, task-oriented leaders tend toward autocracy and relationship-oriented leaders tend toward abdicracy. But without the capability or willingness to flex your leadership style away from your preference, you will fail to be fully effective.

CONDITIONAL FAVORABILITY

The most influential orientation for you as an outdoor leader, however, is not task or relationship, but the favorability of conditions in which you find yourself working (Priest & Dixon, 1991). Conditional favorability for outdoor leadership is a mix of five factors (Fiedler, 1967; Benson, 1986; Ford, 1987).

1. **Environmental dangers**: weather, perils, hazards, and objective and subjective risks
2. **Individual competence**: experience, confidence, skill, attitude, behavior, and knowledge
3. **Group unity**: morale, maturity, cooperation, communication, trust, responsibility, and interest
4. **Leader proficiency**: credibility, judgment, level of stress, fatigue, and perceived capability
5. **Decision consequences**: clarity of the problem, sufficient solution time, available resources, expected ramifications, and degree of uncertainty or challenge

Figure 18.3 summarizes the favorability of conditions, expressed as a continuum from low to high.

CONDITIONAL OUTDOOR LEADERSHIP THEORY MODEL

Combining the information on leadership styles, leadership orientations, and conditional favorability creates the **conditional outdoor leadership theory** (COLT). Figure 18.4 illustrates this theory. Note that the orientations, concern for task and concern for relationships, are represented by the X and Y axes, respectively, and that conditional favorability is represented by the Z axis. With this graphic framework in place, the three outdoor leadership styles can be spread across the matrices created at each level of high, medium, and low favorability.

Conditions of **medium favorability** highlight the more typical outdoor settings in which the dangers are acceptable, the leader is proficient

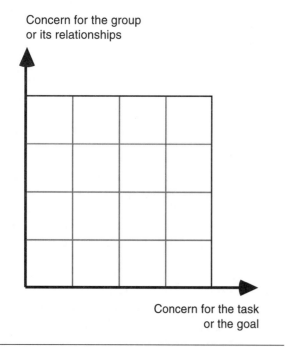

Figure 18.2   A matrix of outdoor leadership orientations.

CONDITIONAL FAVORABILITY

Low	Medium	High
Bad weather Many perils and hazards Mostly subjective risks not easily controlled	Environmental dangers	Good weather Few perils and hazards Mostly objective risks under human control
Disintegrated and divided Distrustful and competitive Immature and irresponsible	Group	Cohesive and unified Trusting and cooperative Mature and responsible
Novice members Incompetent, unskilled, unable Unsure, inexperienced, unknowledgeable	Individuals	Expert members Competent, skilled, able Confident, experienced, knowledgeable
Deficient and incapable Lacks power base for credibility Poor judgment, stressed out, fatigued	Leader	Proficient and capable Holds strong power base for credibility Sound judgment, in control, fit
Problem cloudy and uncertain Insufficient time and resources available Challenge high with unacceptable outcomes	Consequences of the decision	Problem clear and defined Sufficient time and resources available Challenge low with acceptable outcomes

Figure 18.3 A spectrum of conditional favorability.

enough, the individuals are reasonably responsible, the group gets along fairly well, and the consequences of decisions are mostly recoverable. Under moderately favorable conditions, if your orientation is toward relationships, you may prefer to express an abdicratic style, and if your orientation is toward tasks, you may prefer to express an autocratic style. If your orientation is balanced between both tasks and relationships, you may prefer to express a democratic style. The style expressed depends on the "pull" of the respective orientations under these conditions. A greater pull by a concern as well as your preferred orientation will cause you to favor one style over another.

Conditions of **high favorability** exemplify a more desirable outdoor setting in which the dangers are minimal, the leader is most proficient, the individuals are very competent, the group gets along extremely well, and the consequences of decisions are minor. Under highly favorable conditions, like many leaders, you may prefer to shift toward a relationship orientation, allowing an abdicratic style to prevail. Given a strong enough orientation toward the task, however, the expression of a democratic style, or perhaps even an autocratic style, can be appropriate. When things are good, like many leaders, you may pay more attention to the group and therefore transfer decision-making responsibility. Hence, if you

find yourself in this situation, you will likely employ an abdicratic style, delegating power to the group.

Conditions of **low favorability** hallmark the less desirable outdoor setting in which the dangers are extreme, the leader is deficient, the individuals are incompetent, the group gets along poorly, and the consequences of decisions are quite major. Under unfavorable conditions, like many leaders, you may prefer to shift toward a task orientation, favoring an autocratic style. But given a strong enough orientation toward relationships, the expression of a democratic style or perhaps even an abdicratic style can be appropriate. Still, when things are bad, you will probably tend to pay stricter attention to the task and therefore retain decision-making responsibility. Hence, if you find yourself in this situation, you will likely employ an autocratic style to authoritatively vest power in yourself.

Applying the Model

Let's look, now, at a real-life example by applying the COLT model to a backpacking adventure. Say at this point in the activity, you are responsible for teaching route-finding skills to five participants on the first day of a three-day backpacking trip near timberline during the summer in the Rocky Mountains.

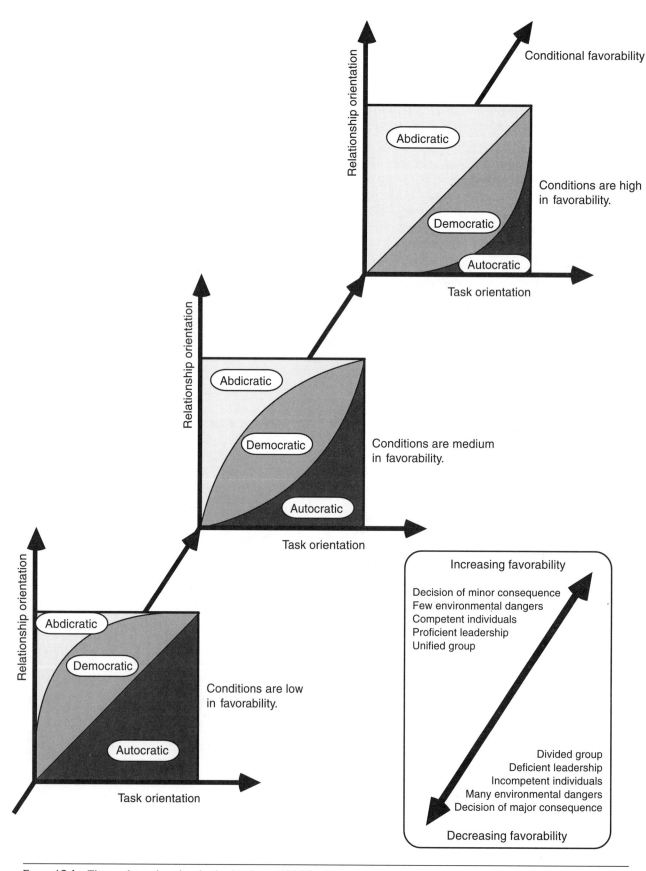

Figure 18.4   The conditional outdoor leadership theory (COLT).

At the trailhead, you inform the group that they are in charge of reading their maps, using their compasses, and finding their way to the campsite. In this situation, you have chosen an overall abdicratic style because conditions are high in favorability. The participants are skilled in navigation, their group spirits are high, you are a master orienteer, well within the proficiency requirements for this activity, the weather is clear with no apparent danger, and the consequences of the group getting lost are minor since they have plenty of daylight and all their overnight gear. Furthermore, at this time, your concern lies with relationships. Thus, you are giving group members a chance to learn for themselves as they work together as a team. Therefore, an abdicratic style is appropriate, leaving the group to learn from their own minor mistakes. If your attention shifts more toward the task and somewhat away from relationships, you would probably flex toward a more democratic or autocratic style.

As time goes on, conditions begin to deteriorate, and such a flex does indeed become necessary! It's several hours later, and group members are experiencing some confusion at a trail junction. The group has stopped discussing possible solutions and is now arguing over which path to choose: the left or the right. They all have strong opinions as to which direction to take, and tempers flare because people are tired and hungry. Confusion erodes group morale. To further depress the conditions, you are frustrated, becoming more concerned with the lack of teamwork displayed by the group. The weather is changing dramatically for the worse: snow begins to fall lightly as a few group members express a desire to hurry up and decide, because they are starting to get cold. You choose to enter into the decision-making process with a democratic style. The final decision rests with both the group and you, but you attempt to influence the group toward picking the correct path. In addition, under such conditions, which we can now label as medium favorability, you are prepared at any moment to flex autocratically if the concern of hypothermia arises; or abdicratically if the group is ready to work toward the correct decision on their own. In the former, you are concerned about the task of keeping everyone safe from cold exposure; and in the latter, you are concerned with rebuilding positive relationships in a dysfunctional group.

Let's say you remain flexible as conditions get worse. Now late in the day and at a much higher elevation, snow is falling steadily, the ground is slippery, and the group has lost sight of any trail they were following. The fog is rolling in, the map indicates intermittent cliff bands in the area, and a poor decision might mean an accident. Individuals are well fed, but tired. None are too cold yet, but one person is feeling ill from the altitude. The group is frustrated with what they perceive to be a failed exercise. At this point, you have the immediate concern of getting the group to a safe location to make camp before they become hypothermic or get lost in the fog. You move to an autocratic style because conditions are definitely low in favorability now. But if your attention focuses more on the opportunity for group members to get along better or less toward getting to camp because the group becomes a team or several camping options unexpectedly arise, then you could choose to flex toward a democratic or even abdicratic style.

By maintaining flexibility and by expressing the correct style for each circumstance, you will effectively influence the group, helping them to achieve their goals, which are to maintain their relationships and to deal with the variety of conditions they encountered. Use of an inappropriate style at any time in this scenario could have been devastating. Imagine the risks for a group in similarly unfavorable conditions if you were to express an abdicratic style, leaving the decisions entirely up to them! Also imagine the same group at the start of the trip if you were to apply an autocratic style, marching them up the trail in favorable conditions. In the former example, the incorrect style could have resulted in an accident. In the latter instance, the incorrect style would likely cause several group members to become immediately discouraged, frustrated, and unable to reach their goals. Thus, your choice of style can make all the difference in an adventure experience. Temper your choice at any given moment with careful consideration for task, relationship, and conditional favorability. But most of all, you must remain flexible in that choice.

EFFECTIVE OUTDOOR LEADERS SHOULD

☞ Understand the connections among influence, power, and style.

☞ Be capable of expressing all three outdoor leadership styles and remain aware of their levels of concern for task, relationship, and conditional favorability.

☞ Be able to flex style to match levels of concern accordingly and be able to switch style in concert with changing circumstances and conditions.

SUMMARY

Leadership is a process of influence based on power. Power in outdoor leadership circles comes in five different types: referent, legitimate, expert, rewarding, and coercive. Power refers to control over decision making and who has the control—the appointed leader or other group members—determines who is being most influential and who is, in turn, taking a leadership role.

The three dimensions of the conditional outdoor leadership theory (COLT) are represented by three axes. The horizontal axis (X) is task orientation, or the degree to which you, as the outdoor leader, are concerned about achieving the goal or getting the job done. The vertical axis (Y) is relationship orientation, or the degree to which you are concerned about interactions within the group and the group's ability to work together. The diagonal axis (Z) is conditional favorability, or the degree to which the conditions associated with the task at-hand and group relationships are favorable. These are the conditions under which you and your group must function to make decisions. They are derived from five factors: the respective levels of environmental dangers, individual competence, group unity, leader proficiency, and decision consequences.

You may employ a spectrum of styles from autocratic through democratic to abdicratic. The style you choose depends on how concerned you are about task, relationship, and favorability of the conditions at that moment in time. Autocratic styles are wise when you have a high concern for task and a low concern for relationships and are working under unfavorable conditions. Democratic styles are appropriate when your concern for task and relationship are balanced, or of medium favorability. Choose an abdicratic style when you have a low concern for task, a high concern for relationships, and are working under favorable conditions. We encourage you to analyze the flexibility of your style in relation

to these three variables, adjusting your choices to suit the particular circumstances.

QUESTIONS TO THINK ABOUT

1. Relate the words leadership style, power, and influence to one another in a single sentence.
2. Differentiate among the five types of power.
3. Compare and contrast the three outdoor leadership styles.
4. Discuss the effect that a leader's concern for task orientation, relationship orientation, and conditional favorability have on expressed leadership style.
5. List the five factors that contribute to overall favorability of conditions. Provide three examples of each factor that clearly explain what each factor indicates.
6. Describe two personal experiences in which you have used appropriate and inappropriate leadership styles. Analyze both experiences by using the COLT model to explain why one was effective and the other was not.

REFERENCES

Benson, L. (1986). *Changing your leadership style because of risk.* Unpublished manuscript.

Blake, R.R., & Mouton, J.S. (1978). *The new managerial grid.* Houston, TX: Gulf Publishing.

Fiedler, F.E. (1967). *A theory of leadership effectiveness.* New York: McGraw-Hill.

Ford, P.M. (1987). The responsible outdoor leader. *Journal of Outdoor Education* 22, 4-13.

French, J.R.P., Jr., & Raven, B. (1960). The bases of social power. In D. Cartwright & A. Zander (Eds.), *Group dynamics* (2nd ed.; pp. 259-269. Evanston, IL: Row Peterson.

Hersey, P., & Blanchard, K. (1982). *Management of organizational behavior: Utilizing human resources* (4th ed.). Englewood Cliffs, NJ: Prentice-Hall.

Lewin, K., Lippitt, R., & White, R.K. (1938). An experimental approach to the study of autocracy and democracy. *Sociometry* 1, 292.

Priest, S., & Chase, R. (1989). The conditional theory of outdoor leadership: An exercise in flexibility. *Journal of Adventure Education and Outdoor Leadership* 6(2), 10-17.

Priest, S., & Dixon, T. (1991). Toward a new theory of outdoor leadership. *Leisure Studies* 10(2), 163-170.

Raven, B.H. & Rubin, J.E. (1976). *Social Psychology: People in Groups*. John Wiley & Sons, New York.

Stogdill, R.M., & Coons, A.E. (1957). *Leadership behavior: Its description and measurement*. Columbus, OH: Ohio State University Press.

Tannenbaum, R., & Schmidt, W.H. (1973). How to choose a leadership pattern. *Harvard Business Review* 51(3), 162-175, 178-180.

Tead, O. (1935). *The art of leadership*. New York: Free Press.

chapter

19

Effective
Communication

A group of 10 novices and their two leaders were on a long weekend backpacking trip. The purpose of the trip was to teach the basic skills of backpacking experientially. During the first day, the leaders used effective communication to convince their group of what route to follow, where to camp, and what to cook for dinner. Acting as instructors, the leaders taught basic backpacking concepts, attitudes, and behaviors through communicating how to light a stove, how to respect the natural environment, and how to act socially in the wilderness. That first evening, the group gathered to debrief the day's events. In this discussion, members shared their perceptions and reflections by communicating what they had learned from their first-day experiences.

On the last day, the two leaders decided to split their group so that one subgroup could take a more challenging cross-country route; the other subgroup would follow the usual trail. The leader of the trail subgroup assumed the cross-country subgroup was headed straight for the parking area, but the cross-country leader was certain they had agreed to rejoin subgroups at another junction on the trail. As a result of this miscommunication, the two leaders were stuck waiting for one another in different locations. As nightfall fast approached, and as group members worried about getting home to family and being late for work the next day, these two leaders began hasty search procedures to find the "lost" subgroup. Hours later they met in the dark half-way between the parking area and trail junction. It was after midnight when everyone finally arrived home. Most people were tired, and the two leaders swore they wouldn't work together again!

The need for effective communication permeates virtually all facets of adventure programming, yet it is one of the skills often overlooked in leadership development programs (Swiderski, 1987). For example, communication serves as a catalyst for participants' growth by providing a medium for reflection on experience, making it an essential tool for the effective facilitation of learning (Cox, 1984).

Effective communication also helps establish leadership through the processes of persuasion and influence, enhances the socialization process by strengthening intrapersonal and interpersonal relationships, and empowers teaching by improved dissemination of information. Without effective communication, your potential for establishing these crucial processes is severely diminished. Indeed, miscommunication can undermine everything you work to achieve through adventure programming.

COMMUNICATION DEFINED

We can define **communication** as a process of information exchange, directed at conveying meaning and understanding between two or more people. **Effective communication** occurs when people receiving the information alter their performances or beliefs on the basis of what the senders meant to convey. In short, the process of communication involves sending a **message** along a **pathway**, so that it is received the way it was intended and is effective when behavioral change results. Behavioral change may be as simple as disagreeing with the sender or as complex as overcoming a major problem, such as addiction to an illegal substance.

A pathway of communication may contain up to three different **channels**: audio, visual, and tactile. The message may hold information in the form of ideas, actions, emotions, or a composite of all three. Typically, we convey **ideas** verbally, passed on an audio channel; hence the receiver needs to listen carefully to the sender. We generally convey **actions** nonverbally on either the visual or tactile channels; hence the receiver needs to carefully watch or otherwise be in contact with the sender. **Emotions** may be conveyed both verbally and nonverbally; hence the receiver needs to look and listen at the same time. Truly effective communication requires both sender and receiver to practice active listening and observation.

One-Way Communication

In order to better understand the process of information exchange, consider a simple linear sequence along which the message is being passed in one direction (see figure 19.1). The subsequent addition of feedback makes the model two-way, or fully transactional (Chase & Priest, 1990). But first, let's examine one-way communication.

One-way communication can be a nine-stage process.

1. The sender **generates** the concepts, feelings, or behaviors to be communicated. This is accomplished when the sender thinks about the concepts, feelings, and behaviors in the mind.

2. These thoughts are converted by the sender into an **encoded** message. In this message, cognitive concepts become verbal ideas, internal feelings are expressed as external emotions, and visualized behaviors are put into physical actions.

3. The sender establishes a link, or **connection**, between himself and the receiver by means of eye contact (visual), physical touch (tactile), or use of personal names (verbal). Failure to link prior to communi-

cating usually means that the receiver has a difficult time receiving the message.

4. The sender **sends** the encoded message of ideas, emotions, and actions to the receiver.

5. The message is **transmitted** along a combination of audio, visual, and tactile channels of the communication pathway.

6. The receiver **receives** the message from the sender.

7. The receiver **decodes** the verbalized ideas, externalized emotions, and physical actions. Verbal ideas become cognitive concepts again, external emotions convert to internal feelings, and physical actions are visualized as intended behaviors.

8. The receiver **interprets** the intent of these concepts, feelings, and behaviors in his mind.

9. Based on his perceptions of the communicated message, the receiver makes a positive or negative response to the message in the form of **changed** performance or beliefs.

For example, say you want a client to stop littering. Communication can be as direct and deliberate as touching the client on a shoulder, making eye contact, and using a first name, followed by a verbal request not to litter. Communication can also be as indirect and subtle as saying nothing, but picking up the litter in front of the client so no one else notices. Your choice of approach

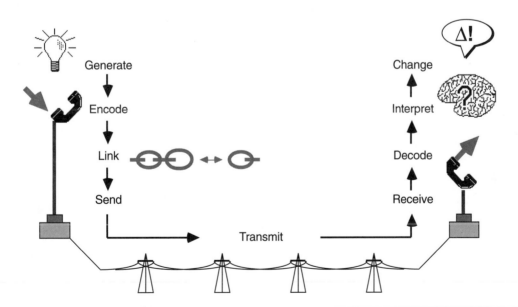

Figure 19.1   A one-way model of communication.

depends on many factors, not the least of which is the client's receptivity to change.

Noise

Noise can interfere with the communication process and may be classified as semantic, internal, or external. Figure 19.2 illustrates several examples of each noise classification as well as their location of interference.

Semantic noise impacts the encoding or decoding stages and refers to how words are used and defined. Technical jargon prevents understanding, and a language difference brings misunderstanding. For example, if you use words unfamiliar to clients, you may severely limit the effectiveness of your teaching. Jargon beyond the conceptual understanding of clients may reduce their motivation. Consider slang terms specific to a particular outdoor pursuit, like "dyno" and "pro" in rock climbing. You need to explain these terms to uninitiated clients, otherwise they may feel left out or spoken down to, possibly turning them off to the learning experience. The same word may have a different meaning in a field outside the adventure profession, like "being certified" in outdoor leadership and "being committed" in psychiatric hospitals. Clients may interpret the word in the context of their own cultures or experiences, possibly leading to an unfortu-

nate misunderstanding, which may inhibit their learning. But you can reduce these misunderstandings and increase learning by simply explaining any unusual terms you use during an adventure experience.

Internal noise influences the generating, interpreting, or changing stages. This form of interference is commonly the reason for client resistance. Internal noise refers to interference within the minds of the sender and receiver. Mental blocks prevent people from generating ideas, actions, or emotions. Much like a writer's block, senders sometimes can't think of what to say, feel, or do in certain situations. A kind of mental "short circuit" occurs, and they don't say what they mean or they say what they don't mean! Moreover, personal values temper the interpretation of messages, as receivers filter the message through their moral systems, determining what it means in relation to personal beliefs and ethical opinions. They may totally ignore the message when it opposes their values or may blindly accept the message when it happens to be similar to their values. Furthermore, social and environmental norms may occasionally prevent people from making changes in response to a communicated message.

The following are two examples of internal noise in the same experience. Say when working with a group of at-risk youth from two rival

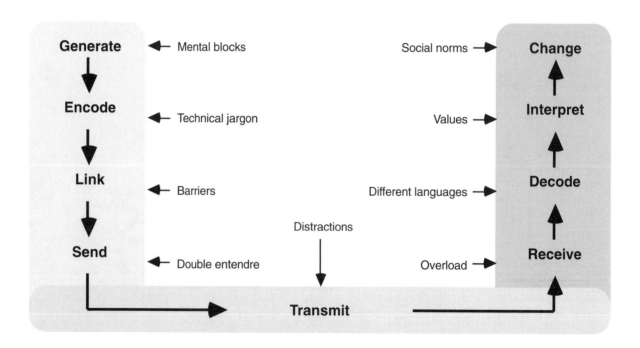

Figure 19.2   Locations of semantic, external, and internal noise interference.

gangs, one participant begins to experience a series of "breakthrough" realizations and positive changes through adventure activities. As this participant's behavior becomes more functional, for example, as she starts cooperating with adults, assisting rival gang members in the group, and asking about how she can change her life when she returns, the "noise" these changes makes exists in direct conflict with her past belief system, that is, the generating stage. As she offers assistance to rival gang members, they begin to wonder "Is this person for real?" The rival gang members develop internal noise in their interpretation stage of communication. They may think "This rival gang member appears to be sincere in helping me and wanting to be my friend. Is this truly sincere behavior or is she 'setting me up' like last time so she can take advantage of me?"

As we saw in these two examples, when existing environments are not conducive to change, behavior change becomes extremely difficult because of internal noise. Clients may remain resistant to change, causing you to be unsuccessful in facilitating change until the true messages can speak or be heard more loudly than the internal noise. This may require the client to change or alter her personal belief system and view of social structure.

External noise influences the linking, sending, receiving, or transmission stages, and refers to interference outside the minds of the sender and receiver. Barriers prevent links from being established. For example, in whitewater paddling, the roar of a rapid can prevent audio contact. In climbing, the distance between climbers can prevent tactile contact. In skiing, a snow blizzard can prevent visual contact. In all three cases, communication cannot even begin without an established link. Another communication involves the double entendre, which occurs when a message is sent with mixed meanings, for example, when information on one channel does not agree with information on another channel, like shaking the head "no" while saying "yes," or vice versa. This disagreement is confusing to receivers since two independent messages with opposing meanings are being interpreted as one communication.

Overload is caused by a rapid influx of information to the receiver. The human brain can convey information through the mouth about 10 times faster than the human ear can accept and transfer it back to the brain. When a sender chooses to speak this fast, the receiver commonly

suffers from information overload, and a state of overarousal ensues. Distractions can divert the attention of both sender and receiver during the transmission of a message, possibly disrupting the flow of information or breaking the communication link entirely. When people face a choice between attending to the communicated message or becoming diverted by a distraction, they usually base the decision on whether the message or distraction is most stimulating.

Several factors aid this process of selective perception: intensity, size or proximity, contrast, repetition, motion, and novelty. Stimuli that are extremely intense, for example, louder, brighter, tastier, smelly, or uniquely textured, tend to get people's attention more effectively than less intense stimuli. Larger sizes and proximal (closer) stimuli are more readily attended to by people than smaller objects located farther away. People also pay attention to stimuli that stand out from the immediate surroundings because of contrasting shade or color. Stimuli that are repeated are likely to get attention—a key reason for repeating important points when communicating. Moving stimuli are more readily attended to than stationary ones. Finally, people pay attention to stimuli that are novel or new in order to do away with the routine or the familiar and thus maintain a comfortable level of arousal.

These forms of noise may negatively impact the quality of communication. **Feedback** can provide one method of defense against ineffective communication.

Feedback and Two-Way Communication

Knowing that some of your message may be lost when noise is present, you can employ feedback techniques to increase the quality of your communication. By encouraging clients to give and gather feedback, you can double-check that interpretation by the receiver accurately matches generation by you, the sender. **Transactional feedback** comes in three general forms: paraphrasing, impression checking, and behavior description (see figure 19.3).

Paraphrase to confirm concepts and to determine if the receiver correctly understood the meaning of the sender's ideas. Paraphrasing is more than the mere repetition of a statement word for word: it is a more thorough reiterating of statements with different words. Use examples and

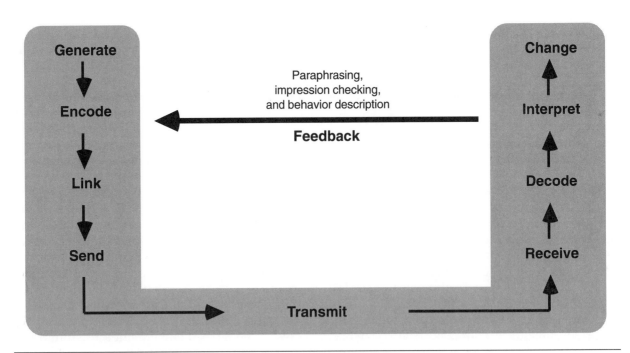

Figure 19.3   The role of feedback in making communication two-way, or fully transactional.

opposites to help make paraphrasing more effective.

Check impressions to double-check feelings and to determine if the receiver has correctly understood the sender's emotions. Read nonverbal clues, or body language, and then describe the perceptions and impressions of the underlying affective state.

Describe behavior to substantiate the observed actions and behaviors of a sender. The receiver makes a descriptive report of observations without evaluation or accusation and without the influence of personal biases toward the sender.

Feedback is most effective when it is dynamic, noncoercive, considerate, descriptive, accurate, and recent (Jung, Howard, Emory, & Pino, 1971). First, feedback should be dynamic, that is, about something the person can change. For example, discussing voice stuttering as a barrier to communication is both inappropriate and ineffective. Second, don't coerce or allow anyone else to coerce the person to make any changes. Telling even the least stubborn individual that they must do something will meet with opposition. Third, give and make sure others give feedback in a considerate manner, staying aware of the possible ramifications and possible consequences of change. In other words, you should consider what will happen if this person takes the advice. Fourth,

make the content of feedback descriptive by reporting observations without inference or implication. For example, gently mention the number of interruptions but not an apparent lack of politeness. Fifth, accuracy is important. Avoid the use of value-laden or biased statements: don't judge or prejudice others. Sixth, recency is vital. Give feedback immediately so that it has direct relevance to the present: Don't discuss "water under the bridge!"

Finally, feedback is more likely to be heard and accepted if it is delivered as "two apples and an onion." The apples represent positive feedback of a complimentary nature: it tastes good and people enjoy getting it. The onion represents the negative feedback of a critical nature: it doesn't taste so good, but is still edible. For example, when constructively critiquing a person's teaching presentation, mention the good parts first, add the bad bits that need working on, and end with a final positive comment. Although difficult to achieve in all critiques, this approach proves reliable, because two apples tend to soften the impact of an onion, yet permit the receiver to digest all the feedback and act on it later. To continue the analogy, this feedback must be digestible, otherwise the receiver may regurgitate the onion and the two apples as well. You can increase the digestibility by clarifying with examples and metaphors.

IMPROVING COMMUNICATION

The responsibility of improving communication lies in your being perceived as a trustworthy and credible sender and in your becoming an active listener and observant receiver. Indeed, a trustworthy and credible sender goes a long way to effectively communicating a message. Johnson (1986) cites several factors that may affect sender trustworthiness and credibility:

- Validity of the sender as a knowledgeable information source with expertise
- Openness of the sender in relation to motives, in other words, the sender has no hidden agendas
- Enthusiasm and friendliness of the sender toward other people, especially the receiver
- Majority opinion about placing trust and confidence in the sender

The hallmarks of an active listener and observer include watching the sender carefully for any decipherable body language, giving and gathering feedback to determine that the message received was indeed the message sent, and taking the time to absorb every piece of information and process these in relation to the context of the communication, even if this means a silent pause is necessary. While listening and observing actively may take much time and effort, your rewards will be great, and you will reduce the potential for costly miscommunications.

You may be able to further improve your listening and observational skills by trying to get a sense of sympathy or empathy for the sender by imagining what the situation must be like in the sender's shoes or how things must look from the sender's perspective. Other approaches you might train yourself to use include gaining an awareness of your personal biases that block active listening and observing skills, attending to communications among other people so as to identify some of the good and bad examples of active listening and observing skills, doing away with bad listening and observing habits by showing genuine interest and courtesy toward the sender, and practicing giving and receiving feedback (Johnson, 1986).

Poor listeners and observers can be identified by their frequent use of automatic conversation extenders, such as "okay, all right, uh huh, oh yeah, and yep," combined with a tendency to interrupt, to jump on key points without considering context, and to ignore body language. They hurry the sender by finishing off sentences, avoid eye contact or physical touch with the sender, and fail to provide the sender with feedback. Instead of listening to and observing the sender, these people are simply formulating their own response.

Take, for example, the following situation. In discussing a variety of options of which route to take to reach a summit, one group is presenting their idea. Say that another student, "Mike," has formulated his own idea about how to reach the summit that he believes is "obviously better." In the group's presentation, Mike tacitly responds by a few "okays, all rights, uh huhs, oh yeahs, and yeps" to give the social appearance that he is truly listening. But Mike is also looking at his own map, thinking how he can sway the group to his way of thinking without listening to and observing the sender. Effective listening requires that verbal as well as nonverbal focuses match.

EFFECTIVE OUTDOOR LEADERS SHOULD

☞ Clearly state ownership of messages by speaking for themselves, rather than for others, and by using first-person language such as "I" statements.

☞ Encode messages specifically by thinking carefully before phrasing concepts.

☞ Finish one message before starting another, avoiding sending multiple or mixed messages.

☞ Suit the message to the receiver by avoiding technical jargon and by speaking the same language.

☞ Be able to repeat messages by restating key points of their messages.

☞ Send messages on more than one channel, equalizing verbal and nonverbal messages by making sure that statements and body language agree.

☞ Disclose personal emotions and actions by using figures of speech, metaphors, and plenty of examples.

☞ Ask for feedback often, providing, in turn, appropriate feedback.

SUMMARY

Communication is a key metaskill for you to hone as an outdoor leader. Effective communication is a process of information exchange between two or more people that results in behavioral change. A sender transmits a message containing information in the form of ideas, actions, and emotions along audio, visual, and tactile pathways.

One-way communication is a nine-stage process: generating, encoding, linking, sending, transmitting, receiving, decoding, interpreting, and changing. Two-way, or transactional, communication involves the use of feedback to reduce the impact of noise, whether semantic, internal, or external, that can interfere with each of the nine stages, and to confirm that the message received was the same as the message sent. Feedback in the form of paraphrasing, checking impressions, and describing behavior should be dynamic, noncoercive, considerate, descriptive, accurate, and recent. Being perceived as a trustworthy and credible sender and becoming an active listener and observant receiver are the keys to improving communication.

QUESTIONS TO THINK ABOUT

1. Recall a time when you effectively communicated a piece of critically important information to someone. Describe this process using the nine steps in the one-way model of communication.

2. Recall a time when your attempts at communication were interfered with by noise. Describe the occurrence in terms of the types of noise, discussed in terms of the one-way model of communication.

3. Recall a time when you miscommunicated with someone. Describe how you might have used a type of feedback in the two-way model of communication to prevent the error. Detail how you should have done this by considering the six criteria of effective feedback.

4. As an outdoor leader, what can you do to become a more effective communicator?

REFERENCES

Chase, R., & Priest, S. (1990). Effective communication for the reflective leader. *Journal of Adventure Education and Outdoor Leadership* 7(1), 7-12.

Cox, M. (1984). Leadership training and development. *Peak Viewing* 19, 6-12.

Johnson, D. (1986). *Reaching out: Interpersonal effectiveness and self-actualization*. Englewood Cliffs, New Jersey: Prentice Hall.

Jung, C., Howard, R., Emory, R., & Pino, R. (1971). *Interpersonal communications: Participant material*. Portland, OR. Northwest Regional Education Laboratory.

Swiderski, M. (1987). Soft and conceptual skills: The often overlooked components of outdoor leadership. *Bradford Papers Annual* 2, 29-36.

chapter

20

Experience-Based
Judgment

In estimating the time of arrival at a distant camp, two leaders base their predictions on past experience and reasoning. From a previous mastery of map-reading skills, they are capable of knowing the direct distance by map scale, the elevation change according to contours, and the expected vegetation or terrain they'll encounter from the colors and symbols on the map.

But they also know from experience that maps are not always correct. Each leader can recall past incidents in which a map failed to show changes in a trail system, incorrectly interpreted the lay of the land from data gathered by aerial photographs, or was simply out of date regarding recent logging and mining operations. Nevertheless, they need to determine the time it may take their group to reach the camp.

They base their first estimate on the past experience of backpacking on similar trails with groups of this size, age range, competence, and fitness. They expect a pace of about 5 kilometers per hour on the flats. Then they refine this estimate because the trail may change elevation frequently and travel through dense forest, so they figure on 3 kilometers per hour, since this is the lower end of what they feel the group is capable of doing. Last, one leader recalls a recent experience in which a group member became exhausted on the previous trip and is concerned that this may happen again. The leaders finally decide to allow fours hours to travel the estimated 10 kilometers to camp.

On the way, they encounter unexpected deviations from the map and are not moving as fast as they had expected as group members become tired. They reassess their calculations and update the estimated time of arrival every hour or so. As they gain new experience from their earlier estimation errors, their subsequent predictions become more accurate.

Remember, adventures are defined by the presence of an uncertain outcome. The uncertainty is created by the fact that important information is missing, vague, or unknown. Consider these examples:

1. Uncertain fragility of a rock climbing hold
2. Absence of key knowledge on the avalanche stability of a snow slope
3. Vague obstacles downstream on a new river during high water
4. Unknown reactions to risk by group members

In all these situations in which you need information, but you cannot easily obtain it, problem-solving or decision-making processes become difficult or may even stall temporarily until this critical information becomes available. In order for you to solve the problem or make the decision in such cases, use the indispensable tool of judgment for estimating the uncertainty, substituting for the missing, guessing about the vague, and predicting in place of the unknown. With this "newly created" information, you can continue with the problem-solving or decision-making process (Priest, 1988).

But you only need to use your judgment when uncertainty is present. Interestingly enough, this is all the time in the case of adventures! Since you operate under uncertain circumstances most of the time, you cannot possibly anticipate when a problem or decision may come along. Furthermore, adventure program administrators cannot prepare standard responses to all situations, because each one is unique in its uncertainty. Therefore, to be an effective outdoor leader, your forte must lie in your ability to effectively solve many problems and frequently make accurate decisions in these uncommon situations. Such effectiveness and accuracy depend on the use of sound judgment (Petzoldt, 1984, p. 42).

THE JUDGMENT CYCLE

We can view judgment as a cycle of three reflective processes: inductive, deductive, and evaluative. Let's look at each closely in turn.

Inductive reflection is used to create general concepts from specific experiences. For example, show children specific pictures of various birds and fish, and they will form general concepts about fish and birds. The more pictures they see and the more information people tell the children, the more accurate their concepts become.

Deductive reflection is used to make specific predictions based on general concepts. For example, show the same children a picture of a penguin, asking them to identify it as a bird or a fish, and they will make a prediction based on what they believe to be the truth about penguins.

We use **evaluative reflection** to analyze the accuracy of the prediction, and then we use this analysis as a new specific experience to help us define the general concept or refine the base of experience. For example, if the prediction of the children is incorrect (fish), then they need to identify why they were wrong (swims in water) and to use that evaluation to modify their concepts of birds and fish to include this exception to the rule. Similarly, if the prediction of the children is correct (bird), then they need to identify why they were right (has a beak and feathers) and to use this fact to reinforce what they already know about birds and fish.

Consider the judgment cycle diagrammed in figure 20.1 and the outdoor leadership example of backcountry navigation.

As you know, backcountry navigation has a great deal of uncertainty associated with it, giving us the perfect example to explain how this reflection cycle develops sound judgment in outdoor leaders. Consider all the information you receive when first learning navigation: how to read a map, how to use a compass, and how to orienteer off trail. These specific experiences are input to the human brain for processing by inductive reflection. The result is numerous general concepts stored in your memory for future use, including, for example, interpreting contour lines, adjusting for magnetic declination, and purposefully "aiming-off."

When faced with the task of navigating from a ridge top down to a camp by a river, you can retrieve these general concepts from memory and output them to deductively reflect and create a specific course of action. Perhaps you will decide to walk along the ridge to a low saddle, following the contours, drop down into the woods on a magnetic-adjusted bearing, and head for a point deliberately upstream of the camp by aiming-off only to follow the river downstream after reaching it. After arriving at camp, you can evaluate the relative success of the exercise and reflect on how you may have been done things differently.

But suppose you did not reach the river in the correct place and walked downstream to arrive at a lake instead of the camp. Analysis of this error may show you that your interpretation of contours, your adjustment of bearings, your technique of aiming-off, or a combination of these three, may have caused the error. By reflecting on the outcome of this experience and based on this new information, you can enhance any general concepts held in your memory so that you navigate better next time.

Thus, you can benefit from gathering a breadth and depth of experience from as many sources as possible, not only first-hand experience but also vicarious experience, gained through observation and discussion. While gathering experience is important, this alone does not guarantee that you will have sound judgment. Certainly, experience without reflection cannot result in learning.

The process of inductive reflection creates a "base" of intensive and extensive experiences. You hold this base in long-term memory as a complex map of general concepts. The map contains facts, confirmed through repeated judgment cycles; beliefs, partially supported by experience; and hypotheses, as yet untested, arranged in relation to one another by many common connections, such as the same topic, similar outcomes, and so on. When uncertainty is present and information may be missing, vague, or unknown, you access the memory map of general concepts, retrieving those facts, beliefs, and hypotheses you deem to be most relevant to the circumstances. Then you subject these to deductive reflection, composing specific predictions to fill in for the uncertainties. Finally, you should hone your judgment skills and broaden your base of experience by evaluating and analyzing the effectiveness and accuracy of your predictions.

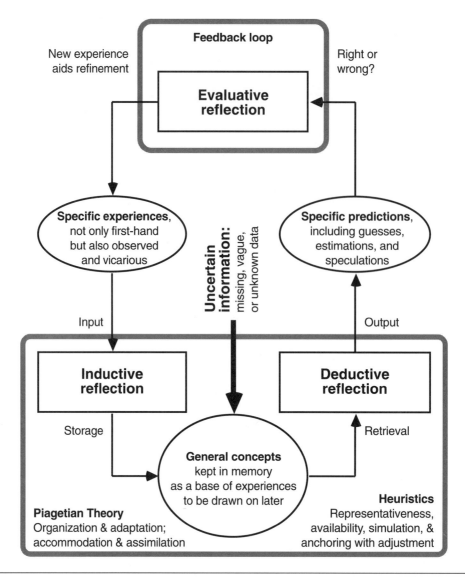

Figure 20.1   The cycle of experience-based judgment.
Adapted from Priest, 1990.

THE ROLE OF PIAGETIAN THEORY

The processes of input, induction, and storage of experiences are guided by the theories of Piaget. Piaget studied the cognitive development of children and asserted that such development took place in phases and at distinct ages. Although many modern researchers dispute Piaget's sequencing and precise partitioning of ages, most accept his original equilibrium theories of organization, adaptation, assimilation, and accommodation. These four have formed the basis of current research on logical and moral reasoning and

are useful for understanding judgment for our purposes.

Piaget believed that the functions of humans were organized and adapted. **Organization** refers to the fact that these functions are arranged into distinct and coherent systems. For example, we tend to follow an organized system of reasoning. For the most part, we handle information in a sequential manner. This sequencing influences the way information is organized or mapped into memory as well as the way bits of information are arranged on a memory map and connected by relationship to other bits of information and to other memory maps.

We also have an exact scheme for every unit of learning. As children grow, they develop many more schemes and become increasingly complex in their organization of these schemes. **Adaptation** refers to the fact that these schemes, or systems, would not function properly had they not evolved to meet the needs of a changing environment. For example, the human reasoning system can learn to think by different and new methods, such as logically or creatively. We can implement techniques for weighing multiple options while decision making or we can apply a nonevaluative form of brainstorming to problem solving. Simply put, if we couldn't adapt by finding new ways to learn or think, then this inability to function would likely lead to our ultimate demise as a species.

The two complementary processes by which humans adapt schemes involve assimilating and accommodating. **Assimilation** refers to fitting new and similar information into an existing scheme. **Accommodation** refers to modifying an existing scheme to incorporate new but different information. For example, consider clients learning to route-find in difficult terrain without map or compass. The clients are learning to induce general concepts from specific experiences. This induction may be as simple as "sidestepping on inclined embankments prevents slipping," or as complex as the belief that, "due to the slope of the land and underlying geological strata, the trail will always be found on the summit side of creeks." These two general concepts have come about from repeated specific experiences. Every time the clients employed sidestepping, they no longer slipped. When the trail was found near a creek, it was always on the summit side with a particular slope and strata present.

But then they note exceptions to these rules. Someone learns that digging the boot heels into the slope also prevents slipping, and someone else discovers the trail on the valley side of the creek at least once with the usual slope and strata present. The use of boot heels represents new and similar information requiring assimilation into the slipping prevention scheme. The unusual trail discovery appears to be an exception to the rule, for which the group needs to accommodate new but different information into a revised trail location scheme. In both instances, the group assimilates or adapts the schemes, updating their induced general concepts. Then, they keep these in their memories as bases of experience to be drawn on later.

This example illustrates how evaluative reflection can be valuable to you as an outdoor leader. By analyzing the belief that a trail will be found on the summit side of all creeks, you may reject the reasons of slope and strata and perhaps find other reasons, such as soil moisture content, or may confirm and retain those reasons by finding some exception to explain the unexpected occurrence, such as an exposed cliff bank in this case only.

ROLE OF HEURISTICS

Recall that deduction and output are guided by **heuristics**, which are simple principles or rules of thumb. Kahneman, Slovic, and Tversky (1982) outline several heuristics that influence judgment: representativeness, availability-simulation, and anchoring with adjustment. They are useful in reducing the complexity of a judgment by identifying similarities, recent information, and starting points relative to your memory maps of general concepts and your base of past experience.

Representativeness

Representativeness is the extent to which information from a past situation represents or matches information needed for the current situation. When you are called on to make judgments, you search your memory map for instances that are identical to or at least as similar as possible to your present predicament. Consider a whitewater paddling trip during high runoff. You and your coleaders compare and assess each piece of information retrieved from memory in regard to how well it represents the actual river you are on. Past trips on rivers of similar difficulty and on rivers during high runoff are likely to be the memory maps you use most heavily for deductive reflection about what to expect on this river. Obviously, everyone stands to benefit from having had sufficient intensive experiences, conducted under stressful conditions, and extensive experiences, encompassing a variety of situations, environments, and clients, to enable you to accurately generate a diverse variety of memory maps.

Availability

Availability is the ease with which you can bring specific information to mind. In making a judgment, you are more likely to be swayed by information that is recently available to you or that has had a lasting impact on you than things you heard a long time ago or that had little bearing on your life. For example, your perception of avalanche probability is likely to be influenced by media reports of avalanche fatalities of well-known skiers or by recent good weather reports from the local ski resort. But you may not assign an accurate level of importance to such influences. For example, recent negative information may lead to an overperception, and recent positive information may lead to an underperception of avalanche probabilities. This is where simulation can come in to guide your judgment in a more appropriate manner.

Simulation

Simulation refers to the related ability of imagining or constructing scenarios from retrieved information. Consider the risks involved in expeditioning. These are often determined by "imagining contingencies with which the expedition is not equipped to cope. If many such difficulties are vividly portrayed, the expedition can be made to appear exceedingly dangerous, although the ease with which disasters are imagined need not reflect their actual likelihood. Conversely, the risk involved in an undertaking may be grossly underestimated if some possible dangers are either difficult to conceive of, or simply do not come to mind" (Kahneman, Slovic, & Tversky, 1982, p. 13). The degree to which simulation is possible depends on your access to information in memory maps and your ability to combine, compare, and contrast that information. In this case, lack of information or experience can compromise the availability-simulation heuristic and, in turn, lead to poor judgment.

Anchoring With Adjustment

Anchoring with adjustment is the weighing of information's importance in relation to the time it was obtained and the interpretation of late information in light of early or already obtained information. First impressions are an excellent example of this heuristic. In estimating a person's expectations of and reaction to an adventure, you are likely to put a lot of faith in your first observation of an individual and then temper your opinion with further observations. If the individual initially appears confident, it is highly likely that you will continue to see the person in

that light, regardless of subsequent deviations, unless the departures are blatant. This is desirable, because a reference point is available from which to judge and refine judgments; but of course, the jeopardy may lie in the first impression being false.

DEVELOPING JUDGMENT

Sound judgment is a lot like memory capacity. It cannot be taught, but it can be developed and improved to an optimal level for any outdoor leader. Everyone has an absolute level of judgmental capacity, just as many have maximum memory capacities. However, contrary to judgment, most people develop their maximum memory capacities in the early years of their lives, with a few being able to push their limits later on in life. The trick to judgment lies not in regurgitating facts memorized for tests, but in the power of reasoning. Unfortunately, instead of asking people to think for themselves and to reason through the reflective processes in the judgment cycle, most educational institutions ask people to commit information to memory and reproduce it verbatim on paper for a test! This is a prime example of the fact that society is information-rich, but individuals are experience-poor. As an outdoor leader, you must break out of this trap and concentrate on information processing, rather than on information memorizing. You must discard the system of memorization in favor of three-way reflection: induction, deduction, and, especially, evaluation.

All too often, outdoor leaders forget to evaluate successful resolutions and choose instead to analyze only those actions that have failed. While analyzing failure aids learning, not evaluating success can be an equal opportunity lost forever. Furthermore, the belief that people learn best from their mistakes is frequently touted as the rationale for allowing clients or leadership candidates to make plenty of errors. But this approach concerns us because it is founded on the obvious ease of figuring out what went wrong versus the difficulty associated with determining why something worked so well. No matter what happens, spend plenty of time reflecting on negative and positive outcomes alike. You can learn just as much from either.

Strive to develop and improve your capacity for making good judgments to the optimal level possible. Try these suggestions to help hone your judgment:

- Listen to the rules and the exceptions to those rules.
- Gather as much information as possible from lectures, historical case studies, and the "horror stories" of other leaders.
- Observe other leaders and how they use judgment.
- Develop a questioning attitude and inquire about the predictions others make.
- Recall personal near misses and share them openly with others.
- Consider the analyses of personal mistakes made by others.
- React, either verbally or in writing, to uncertain situations posed by other leaders.
- Keep a logbook of experiences and a judgment journal, reflecting on those experiences.
- Get experience at every opportunity: never turn down any reasonable chance to lead.
- Take a group of peers on an expedition and ask for their honest feedback often.
- Undertake practical internships with several programs, always asking for someone to observe and give advice.
- Become an apprentice to an expert leader and have this mentor guide and pass on responsibility in a gradual manner.

Above all, evaluate and thoroughly reflect on every experience.

EFFECTIVE OUTDOOR LEADERS SHOULD

☞ Understand the cycle of judgment, using it to follow their reasoning as they further develop their judgment.

☞ Seek a variety of experiences that are both intensive and extensive, then inductively reflect on these experiences.

☞ Practice making predictions (initially under appropriate supervision) by deductively reflecting on their bases of experience.

☞ Evaluate the outcomes of their predictions, examining both the successes and failures associated with their judgment.

☞ Be open to reviewing and discussing their own judgments with others, thereby improving their future judgment.

SUMMARY

A common thought is that "good judgment comes from experience—usually experience which was the result of poor judgment." In other words, you can learn from your mistakes and from everything you ever experience. But simply getting a lot of experience will not ensure that you will learn what you need to know to make sound judgments. Judgment and learning are more than experience alone: each requires plenty of reflection.

Judgment is an experience-based application of the human brain's ability to reason in a cycle of three reflections. The input data are a collection of specific experiences, which are first-hand, observed, or vicarious. Inductive reflection on these experiences creates a map of the connected general concepts, which you then store in your memory as a base of experience from which to draw later. When the information you need for problem solving or decision making is uncertain, missing, vague, or unknown, you search this collection of memory maps for relevant general concepts. Then you recall these concepts and those connected with them for deductive reflection. The final output occurs when you make an estimation, substitution, guess, or prediction. Last, you evaluate whether the prediction was accurate or effective, providing new data for future cycled reflection.

Deduction and output are often guided by heuristics, or simple principles or rules of thumb. Several heuristics that influence judgment are representativeness, availability-simulation, and anchoring with adjustment. Representativeness is the extent to which information from a past situation represents or matches information you need for the current situation. Availability is the ease with which you can bring specific information to mind. Simulation refers to the related ability of imagining or constructing scenarios from retrieved information. Anchoring with adjustment refers to weighing the importance of information in relation to the time you obtained it and the interpretation of late information in light of early or already obtained information.

Sound judgment is a lot like memory capacity. It cannot be taught, but it can be developed and improved to the optimal level possible for any outdoor leader. How? Listen to the rules and the exceptions to those rules, gather as much information as possible from accounts of other leaders, observe other leaders and how they use judgment, develop a questioning attitude, share personal experiences with others and consider their analyses, keep a logbook of experiences and a judgment journal, reflecting on those experiences, gain more experience and learn from it, get honest feedback from peers and supervisors, undertake practical internships with several programs, asking for someone to observe and give advice, and become an apprentice to an expert leader, having this mentor guide and pass on responsibility in a gradual manner. Above all, evaluate and thoroughly reflect on every leadership experience.

QUESTIONS TO THINK ABOUT

1. Differentiate among the three types of reflection. Give examples of applying each type in an outdoor leadership setting.

2. Discuss the differences among Piaget's equilibrium theories.

3. Describe the roles that various heuristics play in deductive reasoning.

4. Identify key components of the judgment cycle in the introductory vignette.

5. Outline the steps you are taking to develop your judgment as an outdoor leader.

REFERENCES

Kahneman, D., Slovic, P., & Tversky, A. (1982). *Judgment under uncertainty: Heuristics and biases*. New York: Cambridge University Press.

Petzoldt, P. (1984). *The new wilderness handbook*. New York: Norton.

Priest, S. (1988). The role of judgment, decision making, and problem solving for outdoor leaders. *Journal of Experiential Education* 11(3), 19-26.

Problem Solving

The leader had a problem to solve: what would be the best way to portage a heavy load of two packs and a canoe on a long rocky trail around a class V rapid in Big Canyon? His solution was initially to prop the canoe at an angle against a tree, then to put the first pack on his front with the straps over his back, and then to put the second pack on in the usual fashion. Last, with both packs on, he stepped underneath the canoe and stood up with the canoe supported on the packs and the canoe's weight, plus the weight of both packs, transferred to his body by the packs' suspension systems.

This solution worked really well until he became tired and wanted to rest. While trying to reverse the "dressing" process, he knelt down and propped the canoe at an angle against a large rock. While standing up from beneath the canoe, he caught one pack on the canoe. The canoe slipped from the rock onto the leader. As he struggled under the weight of two heavy packs to avoid getting hit by the canoe, he stumbled off the trail, rolled down a hill, and struck his head on a small rock. When the next group member found him, he was unconscious and bleeding heavily.

The assistant leader provided correct first aid and then put a group member in charge of monitoring the unconscious leader's vital signs. The group still had one day to paddle before they could get out of the steep-walled Big Canyon to a helicopter landing site. The assistant leader sent two of the strongest paddlers ahead to get help sent to the helicopter landing site, and now she had a problem to solve: What would be the best way to evacuate this victim by water?

Sometimes the solution to a little problem can create bigger problems. Although the leader's solution to the initial problem was appropriate, his solution to the subsequent problem of needing to rest was not.

Problem solving is the process of finding answers to both simple and complex questions. In its purest mathematical form, problem solving is the act of determining what needs to be done to one side of an equation to make it equal the other side. You accomplish this by finding out the value of missing variables and calculating the operations on either side to make them equate.

When faced with a problem, such as being lost with your group, you must figure out what to do with the present situation to make it "equal" the way you would like things to turn out. You can achieve this outcome by substituting for missing information with judgment. How? By guessing trails, predicting directions, estimating distances, based on experience, then combining this with information available to you, for example, with what you can see on the map and in the field, and putting your ideas into action to reach a successful end result, in this case, correctly finding your way again.

Problem solving is closely related to decision making and judgment. **Decision making** is choosing between options: should we do this *or* that? In the problem-solving process, decision making is useful in deciding what the problem is, which is one side of the equation, picking the desired outcome, which is the other side of the equation, choosing possible solutions, and selecting the most probable one (see chapter 22). Remember, **judgment** is a process of logical reasoning used to reflect on past experience and substitute for the missing information (see chapter 20). In problem solving and decision making, judgment is useful to restart the processes when these temporarily stall due to the uncertainty of key pieces of information (Priest, 1988).

MULTIPHASE PROBLEM SOLVING

The flowchart in figure 21.1 diagrams a **multiphase model for solving problems**. The three phases are assessment, analytical, and creative. The analytical phase is scientific and seg-

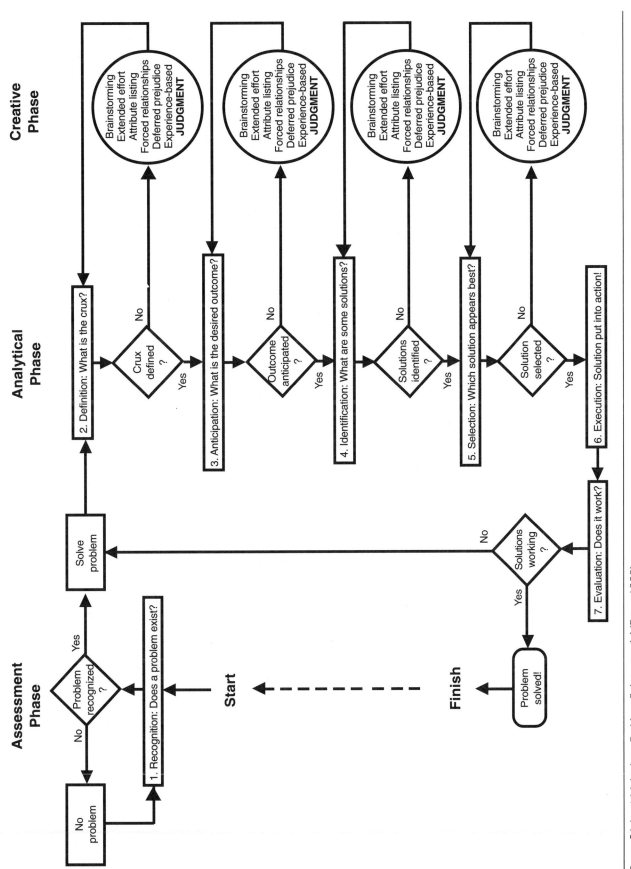

Figure 21.1   A Multiphase Problem-Solving model (Priest, 1988).

Adapted from Priest, 1988.

mented into several steps. It fits the rational, left side of the brain. The creative phase is holistic and an artistic synergy perspective (i.e., it possesses a comprehensive, systemic, and interactive nature) of many techniques. It appeals to the brain's right hemisphere. Like most people, you may have a preference for solving problems, yet you may benefit from mixing both methods.

In the **assessment phase**, you question the problem's reality. If at any given moment you don't recognize a problem, then we encourage you to stay on the alert for problems. If, indeed, you do recognize a problem, then you are obliged to enter into the analytical phase of the model.

In the **analytical phase,** you look to define the crux of the problem, anticipate the outcome to be used in later evaluation, identify several possible solutions, select the most probable one, and put it into action.

If you have trouble answering affirmatively when at any one of the analytical procedures, you generally use some of the techniques from the **creative phase**. Creative techniques include brainstorming, extended effort, attribute listing, forced relationships, deferred prejudice, and experience-based judgment. Indeed, sound judgment can also have a role in the analytical phase and in decision making.

Once you have executed a solution, you have the final responsibility of evaluating whether the solution is working. If not, then you must repeat the cycle.

Analytical Procedures

The analytical phase consists of five steps represented by questions: definition, anticipation, identification, selection, and execution. If you can answer a question affirmatively, then you proceed to the next step. If you answer any question negatively, then you should consider using creative techniques to generate a more positive and informed response.

The initial question places emphasis on **defining the crux** of the problem, or that part that is going to be the most difficult to overcome. Most problems are composed of several little problems. The trick for you is figuring out which one to focus on first. The next question **anticipates a desired outcome** to success. Then you can use your assessment of outcome as criteria for evaluating the impact of the solution when you put it to use at a later time. Once the problem and end result are clearer, you **identify solutions** to the prob-

lem. Listing the known facts and uncertain information can help you identify possible options. Near the end of the analytical phase, you **select the probable solution** and execute it.

Throughout this sequence, you make decisions at every step of the analytical phase by diverging and converging a range of options. But we'll look at decision making as a separate metaskill in chapter 22.

Creative Techniques

The creative phase becomes necessary when answers to questions in the analytical phase are negative or when problem solving stalls temporarily. These six techniques may prove useful:

1. **Brainstorming** involves the open expression of any idea that comes to mind without fear of criticism by other group members. By creating a receptive atmosphere, people are free to share suggestions no matter how unusual or weird the ideas may seem and without anyone else putting them down. The uninhibited sharing of ideas can spark creative new ideas in others. During brainstorming the generation of ideas is usually slow at first, reaches peak production, and then tends to taper off.

2. **Extended effort** refers to encouraging group members not to give up too quickly on the process. By waiting through any pauses or dry spells, groups usually find that ideas generated later in the process often prove to be the most creative and, occasionally, the most useful.

3. **Attribute listing** involves making an inventory of the characteristics that might be associated with any idea or piece of the problem. Listing attributes, such as abilities, limitations, strengths, weaknesses, or required resources, all help to draw connections and to formulate relationships among the ideas generated. People may possibly be able to combine these characteristics to generate new ideas.

4. **Forced relationships** relate to the comparison and contrast of ideas with an eye to creating new ideas by altering old ones. Often it is a forced substitution, combination, adaptation, modification, enlargement, reduction, reversal, or rearrangement that leads to these new ideas.

5. **Deferred prejudice** requires that people remain open to the generation of new ideas, not settling their minds on the first one that sounds good to them. By providing ample time and freedom from bias, you provide opportunities to enlarge the pool of generated ideas. This allows you to make better choices from a larger number of ideas.

6. **Judgment**, as we discussed in chapter 20, is very necessary when the act of delaying the process due to lack of information might result in compounding the problem further. In other words, you must balance the need to generate creative ideas with the time restrictions dictated by the problem.

SOLVING PROBLEMS USING THE MULTIPHASE MODEL

Because adventure experiences are situationally, individually, and chronologically specific due to features such as changing risks, competence, time variables, and the like, so is problem solving. You should recognize that no two problems are exactly alike—at least one variable will always be different—suggesting the need to avoid becoming complacent regarding possible solutions. Remember the portaging accident in which the leader incorrectly reversed the dressing solution to the undressing problem without considering that getting out from under the canoe would be different from getting under it? The problem changed in some small way that made an incredible difference.

The complexity of problems can range from simple for which you know all variables to complex for which you must deal with several unknown variables. Since adventures are full of uncertainty, you will rarely come across a problem for which you'll have all the information; most have some missing piece to the puzzle. Solving a simple problem for which everything appears known is a relatively straightforward process when applying a short form of the multiphase model, that is, using only the analytical phase. Solving a complex problem with several unknowns is much more difficult, requiring you to apply sound judgment to substitute for missing information. This requires using a long form of the multiphase model, including creative techniques. Of course, you need to know the kind of problem you are attempting to solve to correctly apply this model.

You can use the model combining analytical procedures and creative techniques in its long and short forms. Figure 21.2 lists a few criteria for determining what form to apply to a problem. You should consider which of these criteria are most important to your preferred choice of form. To help you see what we mean, we'll demonstrate the short and long forms of the model shortly. Of course, for some problems, elements of one model may be necessary to assist the other. For example, you may need to use creative techniques at any step in the short model process if an answer proves to be not readily available. Thus in essence, you might end up using both forms. So be flexible!

Short Form for Simple Problems

The short form of the model is appropriate when answers to questions in the analytical phase come easily and positively: you simply proceed through the sequence. Although judgment does not play a formal role in this process, naturally you cannot afford to abandon judgment at any time while solving a problem.

The dressing problem on the Big Canyon canoe trip is a good example of the short form in action. The leader recognized that a simple problem existed: he had to portage a canoe and two packs from the takeout across the rocky trail to the put-in. The left-hand side of the equation was complete: a collection of equipment was in an unfavorable place.

The leader defined the problem as finding a way to carry all the equipment from the takeout to the put-in without wasting time. If he had defined the problem differently, perhaps including a concern for carrying the equipment in a way that would permit easy resting, his injury might not have occurred. Instead, however, this leader chose time as the important criteria for evaluating success.

The leader anticipated the desired outcome to be the canoe and two packs located at the end of the rocky trail. The right-hand, or final, side of the equation was complete: the collection of equipment needed to be in a favorable place. The leader now had to actually move the equipment in order to equate the two sides, and as the crux suggests, he believed his real problem was finding a way to do this without wasting time.

If . . .

crux is known,

problem is simple,

desired outcome is clear,

key information is available,

consequences are expected,

range of options is complete,

time to consider is limited,

decision is *not* life-threatening,

group resources are sufficient, or

success is predictable,

. . . use the short form!

If . . .

crux is unknown,

problem is complex,

desired outcome is vague,

key information is missing,

consequences are unexpected,

range of options is incomplete,

time to consider is ample,

decision is life-threatening,

group resources are lacking, or

success is uncertain,

. . . use the long form!

Figure 21.2 Comparison of when to use the short and long forms of the multiphasic model.

The leader had at least six possible solutions from which to choose:

1. Carrying the two packs and the canoes separately, thus making a total of five trips (three outgoing and two return). This first solution had the advantage of not carrying heavy loads, but had the disadvantage of covering five times the distance in triple the time of one portage.

2. Initially carrying one pack in order to become familiar with the trail and then returning for the canoe and remaining pack together, thus making three trips (two outgoing and one return). This second solution had the advantage of one heavy load and one light one, but had the disadvantage of covering three times the distance in double the portage time.

3. Initially carrying the canoe and a pack together in order to carry the difficult load before becoming tired and then returning for the last pack, thus making three trips (two outgoing and one return). Like the second, this third solution had the advantage of one heavy load and one light one, but had the disadvantage of covering three times the distance in double the portage time.

4. Carrying the two packs together first and the canoe second, thus making three trips (two outgoing and one return). This fourth solution had the advantage of equal loads, but still had the disadvantage of covering three times the distance in double the portage time.

5. Carrying the canoe first and then returning for both packs together, thus making three trips (two outgoing and one return). Like the fourth, this fifth solution had the advantage of equal loads, but still had the disadvantage of covering three times the distance in double the portage time.

6. Carrying all the equipment in one trip. This sixth solution had the advantage of covering the distance once with the time of a single portage, but had the disadvantage of an extremely heavy load, which may take longer to carry due to rest breaks.

While selecting the best solution, two new alternatives arose. The seventh and eighth solutions came out of the first solution when the leader recognized he could carry the packs and canoe separately, yet in different orders (canoe, then pack A, then pack B; pack A, then canoe, then pack B; or pack B, then pack A, then canoe). In the mind of the leader, the advantages and disadvantages did not change with the order of portage, so he decided to ignore these newly evolved options and stick with considering the single option of carrying the items independently.

After considering the alternatives, he might have determined that the second and third solutions were close to identical, as were the fourth and fifth ones, since these two pairs had similar advantages and disadvantages. By collapsing these pairs, the leader narrowed the choice of solutions to four: carry the equipment one piece at a time (five trips in triple time), carry the packs together and the canoe by itself (three trips in double time), carry one pack alone and the other pack with the canoe (three trips in double time), or carry all the equipment together (one trip in single time).

Since the leader held time as an important criteria in solving this problem, he preferred the sixth solution of taking everything at once, because it afforded the least number of trips and the least time consumed. Had the leader defined the problem in terms of safety, light loads, or a balance of weight and time, these criteria might have led him to put a different solution into action.

Before executing the solution of carrying everything in one trip, the leader considered a contingency plan that helped reinforce the chosen solution. If he got tired during the portage, he could rest and if the load was too much for him to carry all at once, he could drop everything and reconsider one of the other solutions. This reconsideration was possible only with the solution he had chosen. Exercising any other solution would have limited the number of other solutions that he could consider after starting to portage because they would have meant that the equipment pieces were separated on the portage trail.

In this scenario, an accident intervened and evaluation was limited strictly to the execution. Until the accident, the leader believed the solution was working and did not need modification. If the solution had been completed, then the leader could have compared the arrival of the equipment at the trail's end with the desired outcome. He would have determined that the two sides of the equation were equaled and the problem was solved.

Naturally, this entire problem-solving process took place in less time than we can describe it, but maybe if the leader had slowed down and thought things through more, the outcome might have been better! But not necessarily, as the short form fits simple problems—if you take the time to define the most important problem, which in this case was safety, not time.

Long Form for Complex Problems

Use the long form when answers to questions in the analytical phase are negative or if those answers do not come easily. You stand to benefit from including several creative techniques to get a positive response or at least to be certain you have exhausted all opportunities to find an answer. Of course, judgment also plays a large role in this form of the problem-solving model.

The evacuation problem facing the assistant leader on the Big Canyon canoe trip is a good example of the long form in action. Let's join the group now on the trail and see how they solve the problem. First, the assistant leader has to define the crux. To her the crux is not immediately obvious, but after some discussion with the group, they determine that the crux will be transporting the unconscious leader inside a canoe so that he is secure but will not drown if the canoe capsizes.

Second, the desired outcome is more obvious. They agree that a successful resolution will involve transporting the leader to the helicopter landing site without placing anyone in further jeopardy. This requires that they portage all major rapids, ensure that group members get adequate rest when needed, and find an acceptable method of transporting the injured leader by canoe that does not violate the first two provisions.

Third, identifying possible solutions may prove difficult for the leader and her group, since no quick and easy answers are available. The group begins brainstorming, facilitated and recorded by the assistant leader. Avoiding establishing boundaries, they present some wild and crazy ideas about how to transport the leader. The assistant leader fosters the generation of ideas by preventing members from assessing any of the ideas when presented, by encouraging members to think harder when the stream of ideas dwindles, and by deferring their prejudices to keep them from jumping on the first good idea that comes up. Once all the ideas are out, the assistant leader helps the group list the attributes of each idea, then guides them through combinations of these attributes to create new ideas through forced relationships. The creative phase generates well over one hundred ideas and, after careful consideration of each one, the assistant leader retains nine ideas. Note that some build on others and that a few are the result of combining other ideas.

Idea one suggested that the unconscious leader be lashed into a canoe with a lightweight person in the bow to monitor his vital signs during the trip and the strongest paddler in the stern to propel the canoe. Idea two suggested a pair of strong paddlers for extra speed during the evacuation, but no extra person to monitor vital signs due to insufficient room in the canoe. Idea three suggested rafting two canoes side by side with three paddlers in the two canoes and plenty of room left over for the leader and an attendant, but with increased canoe drag and decreased maneuverability of the raft. Idea four suggested testing any rigging before going ahead with the arrangements. Idea five suggested using the frame from a backpack to build a partial stretcher to carry the leader and to tie the stretcher across the canoe thwarts. Idea six suggested removing the central thwart to lay the stretcher on the canoe floor, thereby improving the craft's stability. Idea seven suggested the leader not be tied into the stretcher nor the stretcher be tied to the canoe. Idea eight suggested putting two personal flotation devices (PFDs) on the injured leader. Idea nine suggested attaching an extra PFD to the leader's head in order to keep it above water in the unlikely event of a capsize.

At the conclusion of this step, three solutions seemed possible (although many more could have been generated and reduced by the divergence and convergence process we will explain in chapter 22). All three solutions included having the unconscious leader wearing two PFDs with a third acting as a headrest. Solution A had the unconscious leader tied on a backpack frame stretcher lashed across the canoe thwarts with one attendant and one paddler on board. Solution B also had the leader lying on the canoe floor, without a central thwart or any lashing, and with two paddlers, but no attendant on board—the stern paddler would monitor vital signs. Solution C had the leader tied to a stretcher lashed across the thwarts of two canoes with three paddlers and an attendant on board.

Fourth, selecting the best probable solution from these three possibilities is a matter of eliminating one possible solution at a time by applying key criteria. In this case, the assistant leader applies the safety-related criteria of craft stability and speed. She recommends that solution A be dropped after testing craft stability and finding that the canoe became top-heavy and capsized easily with a volunteer on the stretcher while solutions B and C passed this test. She then eliminates solution C after a speed test determined that the raft design was slow and clumsy to propel, even with the attendant working part-time as a fourth paddler while solution B passed the speed test.

The assistant leader subjects the remaining "best" solution to all of the important criteria as a double-check for its probability of success. The assistant leader checks solution B against other criteria such as victim's safety, victim's comfort, group safety, group comfort, and ease of monitoring vital signs. It passes all tests except two:

victim's comfort and monitoring vital signs. After regaining consciousness, the leader complains that the bottom of the canoe was a very cold place to lie for an extended period. The stern paddler finds dividing attention between paddling, steering, and monitoring an extremely difficult task to perform. Therefore, they modify solution B before putting it into action. Two extra sleeping pads are inserted between the leader and the canoe for added insulation. A second canoe is paddled in close and parallel so as to keep a continual watch over the injured leader.

At this point in our story, you may be feeling anxious about the time this process is taking, considering the leader's injury and lack of consciousness. But remember, it was rushing to make a decision that got the leader in trouble in the first place! Far more time will be lost if the assistant leader acts in haste as well, setting the group up for another accident. So while a group member monitors the injured leader's vital signs, let's see how our story ends.

Fifth, executing the solution involves clearly communicating group members' roles. We cannot emphasize enough that effective communication (chapter 19) is a critical metaskill for outdoor leaders. Before the evacuation, the assistant leader consults the map and guidebook, only to remark about the presence of several major rapids that they will need to portage. During the evacuation, she assigns roles to the group members and places the finishing touches on the canoe and PFD arrangements. As the evacuation proceeds, the assistant leader keeps a careful watch on the group and the injured leader, remaining alert for new problems that might crop up.

Along the way her judgment proves useful when important information turns out to be vague, missing, unknown, or otherwise uncertain. For example, she used her judgment about people to assign an appropriate attendant for the injured leader. She used her judgment about canoe travel at night to select a stretch of river that could be safely completed in darkness, thus permitting a very early morning start to the day-long evacuation. She used her judgment and experience with previous rapids to extrapolate what subsequent rapids might be like, thus allowing her to choose which ones to portage and which ones to save time by paddling—if she correctly predicted these to be washed out by the present river levels and flow rates.

Sixth, evaluating the executed solution completes the circuit. In this case, the group emerges from Big Canyon and arrives successfully at the landing site, where a helicopter is waiting to fly the injured leader to the hospital. The problem is solved!

Common Breakdowns

As you might expect, the problem-solving process is prone to breakdowns. A few common sources of breakdowns in this process may include stress, haste, misinformation, miscommunication, and perceived boundaries.

Stress is a primary factor influencing the breakdown of the problem-solving process. Information may bombard you at a rate that exceeds your capacity to make wise choices. At such stressful times, rushed decisions or unsound judgments may interfere with problem solving. In contrast, in situations in which opportunities are eustressful, or pleasant, such as the perfect challenge, you are more likely to enhance your actions and perform at your best because you are optimally aroused (see chapter 4). But in situations in which opportunities are distressful, or unpleasant, such as working against adversity, you are more likely to feel rushed, and your performance may drop off correspondingly because you are overaroused.

Often emergency situations are limited by time constraints, which can rush you to respond. But remember "Haste makes waste." For example, you may miss a good possible solution in the identification step or may jump on the first likely crux that comes to mind in the definition step. When time is short, be sure you don't choose to avoid looking for alternatives, blindly adhere to your original plan, and regress to following established procedures. But don't fall into the trap of choosing to change your plans no matter what the cost either, searching endlessly for alternatives until time runs out. Neither scenario is desirable, so given insufficient time, to be an effective outdoor leader, you must seek to balance time consumption with idea generation. Take the time to seek out diversity in resources and information by considering everyone's ideas. Avoid premature decisions or searching to exhaustion for that one "perfect" solution.

In the selection step, you must select a probable solution from a collection of possible ones by comparing strengths and weaknesses, testing solutions against important criteria, and analyzing their consequences. If the information you use for comparing, testing, or analyzing is flawed, your selection may fail to solve the problem. Thus, misinformation can cause the process to break down. Use your judgment to reinforce and recheck information, attempting to reduce errors in selection. Don't let your judgment be colored by a tendency to exaggerate, procrastinate, or avoid responsibility under pressure, or by attempts to maintain self-respect, become accepted by peers, profit personally, or allow others to benefit. Therefore, as an effective outdoor leader, you should remain as neutral as possible while solving problems.

During the execution step, ineffective outdoor leaders may miscommunicate a selected solution to their groups. When it is put into action, the solution may fail because some members were unclear or unaware of their own roles or the roles of others. Miscommunication can also interfere with the quality of information, perhaps leading to misinformation as we have discussed. Don't let this happen to you! Work on effective communication techniques at all times so that when the crunch is on, you'll be ready.

Breakdowns in the creative phase are often the result of perceived boundaries. Thinking creatively requires you to suspend your perceptions of limited resources or capabilities, even if in reality these are truly limited. If you believe something won't work, it probably won't! Remaining boundless in mind and spirit directly contradicts the premise of the analytical phase in which you must set parameters at all steps in order to evaluate success. Because of this, resolving the paradox between thinking analytically "in boxes" and creatively "outside the boxes" is one of the toughest tasks facing you when you use multiphase problem solving. The only answer to this quandary is to gain practice in actual situations, including intensive and extensive experience in solving actual problems under the guidance of an established mentor. The mentor's role is to guide you as you strive to develop sound judgment, decision making, and analytical and creative problem solving.

EFFECTIVE OUTDOOR LEADERS SHOULD

☞ Understand the relationships among problem solving, decision making, and experience-based judgment.

☞ Be able to recognize problems and know when to use the short or long forms of the multiphase model to solve them.

☞ Be able to follow and utilize the five steps in the analytical phase of problem solving.

☞ Be able to name and apply the six techniques in the creative phase of problem solving.

☞ Be aware of the ways in which the problem-solving process commonly breaks down and do all that they can to prevent such breakdowns.

SUMMARY

Problem solving is the process of finding answers to questions by determining a strategy applied to a situation to make it turn out the way you desire. This process includes making decisions about the nature of the problem, using judgment to speculate on the value of unknowns, and combining these predictions with known information to create effective solutions. Decision making is choosing between options at central steps embedded within the problem-solving process. Judgment is reasoning logically from past experience and substituting for information that is missing, vague, unknown, or uncertain. All three skills are closely related, but distinctive.

Multiphase problem solving has three phases: assessment, analytic, and creative. The assessment phase involves recognizing and evaluating whether a problem exists before or after the solving process. The analytical phase contains a sequence of five steps (definition, anticipation, identification, selection, and execution), which you should usually follow in sequence to solve a problem. The creative phase includes six techniques (brainstorming, extended effort, attribute listing, forced relationships, deferred prejudice,

and experience-based judgment); creativity proves useful when the process stalls at one of the analytical steps. Combining the phases helps you be more effective in your problem solving than you might be with just one approach.

Problem complexity ranges from simple problems for which everything appears known to complex ones for which you must deal with several unknowns. Apply the short form of the multiphase model when solving simple problems and the long form when solving complex problems. But remember, you must grasp the complexity of the problem accurately, so you can apply the correct form.

Stress, haste, misinformation, miscommunication, and perceived boundaries can obstruct the problem-solving process. With practice and sound judgment, you can overcome these potential breakdowns and be a more effective outdoor leader.

QUESTIONS TO THINK ABOUT

1. Use the short form of the model to solve a simple problem, then describe how well the model worked or didn't work for you.

2. Use the long form of the model to solve a complex problem, then describe how well the model worked or didn't work for you.

3. Identify examples of common breakdowns in problem solving you have experienced in outdoor situations. Explain how these were overcome.

REFERENCE

Priest, S. (1988). The role of judgment, decision making, and problem solving for outdoor leaders. *Journal of Experiential Education* 11(3), 19-26.

Decision Making

The avalanche that had buried a student was small in comparison to some of those the head leader had seen in ten years of ski patrol experience. Nonetheless, there was absolutely no sign of the student anywhere. Four hours earlier, the head leader's group of three novices had left the remaining 12 students of the skiing class with two other leaders. The two subgroups (4 and 14, respectively) were making their way to a common meeting place by different routes. With four hours of daylight left, the head leader's group of four was about two hours from the road head when the avalanche struck. The head leader began recalling the events immediately leading up to the accident.

The group of four had been traveling on the ridge top and was descending a leeward slope to reach and follow the valley floor below. The leader had "pit tested" the snow slope's substructure and determined it to be stable. Although they were above treeline, no old slide paths or running cracks had been noticed. Before descending, they had taken all the necessary precautions. Each had removed their straps on skis, poles, and packs to prevent these items from dragging them under in the event of an avalanche. All had zipped up their layers of clothing, and put their hats and mittens on to keep themselves warm. Each had placed covering handkerchiefs across their mouths and nostrils to prevent possible snow inhalation. So as not to expose more than one person to danger at any time, they moved across individually and planned to rest only at points of relative security. The leader had gone first, planning a careful path from safety point to safety point. Given the beginning nature of the ski touring class, no one had been issued avalanche cords or radio beacons (these were rare and expensive years ago when this accident happened).

Whump! The small slab avalanche had suddenly let loose under the student's feet and thundered down the slope past the leader. The other two skiers saw the student discard a pack and attempt to swim "ferrystyle" to one side of the avalanche, but powerfully it turned the student over and over again, progressing downhill forcibly. Once the snow had settled there was nothing but pristine silence. From a distance the other skiers could not discern the fate of their friend. From their viewpoints, no one could see any visual clues that might lead them closer to the buried skier. They could only hope that as the avalanche had slowed, the student had made a last ditch effort to gain the surface or at least make an air pocket in front of his face.

The leader surveyed the slope for further danger and then assembled the remaining two students above the debris area at the last spot they had clearly seen the student. After briefly pondering the problem, the leader explained that speed and accuracy were of the utmost importance: the longer the student remained buried the lesser the chances of recovering the student alive! The leader realized the obvious problem was to how best to find the student ALIVE and thus faced making a series of very difficult decisions.

—Priest, 1988

Decision making is the process of choosing the most probable option from a collection of possible ones. The process involves **diverging** or building up a range of several options and then **converging** or narrowing down that range to select the best option. Making decisions is necessary at several steps of the problem-solving process. Recall from chapter 21 that the analytical phase of the multiphase problem-solving model contained these central steps: definition (What is the crux?), anticipation (What is the desired outcome?), identification (What are some possible solutions?), and selection (What solution appears best?). These four steps require you to pick the best crux, best outcome, best possible solutions, and best probable solution from a wide range of options.

DIVERGENCE

The wider the range of options generated through **divergence**, the better. As you know, the creative phase of the multiphasic model contains several techniques that are most effective at diverging options: brainstorming, or expressing ideas without evaluation or criticism; extended effort, or carrying the expression of ideas through pauses; attribute listing, or inventorying problems and solutions; forced relationships, or combining, comparing, and contrasting new ideas; and deferred prejudice, or refraining from jumping on the first good idea.

For the avalanche example, the leader has identified at least seven options. Two options involve outside help: first, seek a professional search and rescue team (120 minutes to road head plus 60 minutes to phone plus 60 minutes return with SAR team plus 30 minutes for dogs to find student equals 270 minutes) or second, meet up with the other subgroup to gain their assistance (120 minutes to find the other subgroup plus 180 minutes to return to accident site plus 45 minutes to carefully search with new and enlarged group equals 345 minutes). The third through fifth options involve the small subgroup and its own resources. Third, perform a hasty search with the two remaining students (5 minutes); fourth, perform a coarse probe search, for example, move forward 70 centimeters, probe once, two meters deep with ski poles (30 minutes); and fifth, perform a fine probe search, for example, move 30 centimeters forward, probe three times, two meters deep (120 minutes). Still other options

exist. Sixth, wait for help to find them once they become overdue (several days) or seventh, split the subgroup further, sending one student for help, while the leader and other student search (unpredictable time limits). Given ample time to apply divergence methods—not very possible in an avalanche situation—a group could easily enlarge the list of options to a much greater number.

CONVERGENCE

Convergence is generally the most difficult part of the decision-making process. Here you must discriminate the best option from many options. Five methods exist to narrow the field: gathering, weeding out, organizing, weighting, and choosing.

Gathering

Gathering involves collecting all pertinent information that supports or refutes the merit of a particular option, then categorizing that information under three headings: facts, which are what you know as true; assumptions, which are what you have judged to be true; and constraints, which are possible barriers to success.

For the avalanche example, here are three facts that you could gather in the avalanche scenario. Hasty searches find victims 30 percent of the time. Rescue dogs have a success rate of 90 percent for finding a victim, but due to the long time required to summon them to an accident scene, the find is rarely a live one; and the half-life period for remaining alive after being caught in an avalanche is about 30 minutes. This means that if a victim survives the initial impact of an avalanche and is buried alive, then after 30 minutes the probability of the victim still being alive is half what it was at the time of the avalanche; after 60 minutes of burial this probability decreases to one-quarter, and then to one-eighth after 90 minutes.

Here are four assumptions that you might make in this avalanche scenario. Using sound judgment, based on extensive and intensive ski patrol experience, the leader in our scenario estimated the chance of the student being killed outright by the impact of this avalanche as 36 percent. If a dog search was employed as a last resort, several hours after the accident, the student's chances of being alive would be very slim, maybe 1 percent. Since they would be probing with ski poles and the two remaining students had limited practice with this technique, the leader expected that the buried student would not be "hit" by a probe if buried deeper than five feet. Given that the avalanche debris area was small and not too deep, the leader estimated the chances of locating the student at 40 percent for a coarse probe search and 80 percent for a fine probe search.

Here are five constraints that you might consider in this avalanche scenario: time of day, weather, group dynamics, group member's experience, and available resources. Time is clearly of the essence since prolonged burial may lead to suffocation, but also because nightfall is a few hours away and the leader has a duty to care for the other two students. A storm is expected within 24 hours, and fresh snow could increase the danger of further avalanches and could camouflage this accident site. The leader in our scenario also considered several group dynamics, including arguments, fears, loyalties, and desires as well as how these might influence the situation. The leader had already factored into the last pair of assumptions the limitations of having inexperienced students and only ski poles for probing. Furthermore, the leader considered other related concerns, including how the students' inexperience might cause them to react in a crisis and the availability of other survival resources, such as food, water, oxygen, shelter, and warmth for the subgroup.

Weeding Out

Weeding out involves removing those options that are clearly inappropriate considerations. Often a large field of seven or more options is too much for most leaders to truly consider. Reducing this number to three or four options becomes more manageable. How? Reduce the options you are considering, based on how plausible the information you have gathered is. For example, evaluate the cost of exercising the option, the consequences of putting that option into action, and so on.

In the avalanche example, the leader immediately dismissed the second, sixth, and seventh options. The second option of meeting up with the other subgroup to gain their assistance would take 345 minutes, and finding the buried student may have still not been possible; getting a SAR team—an option with less time and higher chance of success—was clearly a better option than the second one, based on these two variables alone, especially since the leader might meet the other subgroup on the way out as a bonus. Either way,

darkness would fall before help of any kind could return. The sixth option of waiting for help to find the group a few days later would certainly result in not finding the student alive. The seventh option of further splitting the subgroup and sending one student for help, while the leader and other student searched, would put the single student at risk due to ongoing avalanche danger and the unfamiliar new route they were following: they should stick together regardless of the decision made.

A word of caution, however: don't be tempted to automatically weed out ideas during the divergent process because this could inhibit the generation of subsequent ideas. Weeding out is a useful step for shortening the decision-making process when certain conditions become limitations, such as time, weather conditions, etc. When time is ample and you take that time and are competent at juggling alternatives, you can consider all options, consequences, or other information.

Organizing

Organizing involves ranking the three or four remaining options, arranging them in a decision tree. The decision tree is a simple drawing that details the possible choices you may make in solving a problem and the probable chance events that might occur in the course of a solution. You can draw each decision and chance event as branching forks on the tree that divide into separate paths on the basis of choices made. The advantage of a decision tree is that all options are paired to create choices between two options at a time rather than all options at once. The fewer options in the choice dilemma, the easier and more efficient the process of choosing becomes for you. Ordering enables you to examine any situation from the level of its component decisions, making the overall situation more manageable.

With the avalanche example, the leader arranged the options into two categories: go for help or search without help. The leader further ordered the "search without help" options from quickest to slowest: a hasty search to a slow, fine probe. In this instance, the decision tree contained three choices: go for help or hasty search without help, then go for help or coarse probe search without help, and then go for help or fine probe search without help. But you also have to consider the flexibility, alternatives, and contingencies for each decision tree so that you don't get locked into a dangerous, irreversible direction. In this case, you could also stop searching at any time and elect to seek outside help; and if searching was futile, then getting help would be the final option.

Figure 22.1 summarizes the decision tree for the avalanche vignette with three decision forks (black squares) and a dozen chance event forks (white circles). Chance event forks represent the various probabilities of success and failure for each of the two options as determined during the gathering of information.

Look at figure 22.1 and picture yourself as the leader in this scenario. The first decision has two options: go for help and return with a dog search team or perform a hasty search. If you elect the former option, then the search team will take over,

and you will have no further decisions to make. If you elect the latter option, then either the student will be found or not found. If not found by hasty search, then the need for a second decision arises.

The second decision also has two options: go for help and return with a dog search team or perform a coarse probe search. If you elect the former option, then again the search team will take over. If you elect the latter option, then either the student will be found or not found. If you do not find the student by coarse probing, then the need for a third decision arises.

Like the others, the third decision has two options: go for help and return with a dog search team or perform a fine probe search. If you elect the former option, then the search team will take

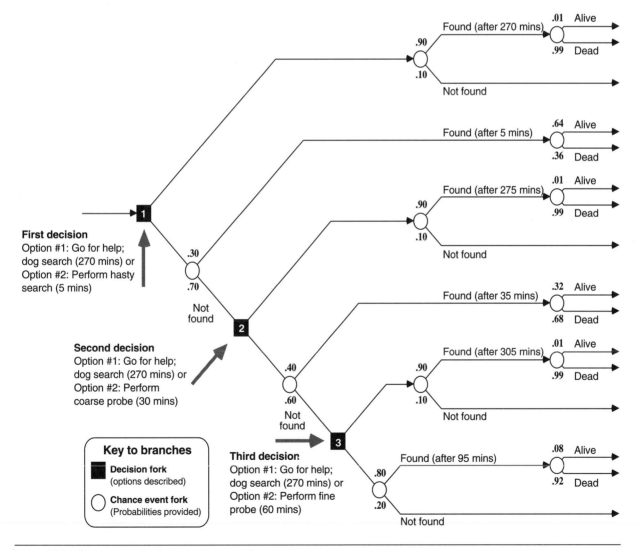

Figure 22.1   Decision tree for the avalanche example.
Adapted from Priest, 1988.

over. If you elect the latter option, then the student will be either found or not found. If you do not locate the student by fine probing, then you should seek professional assistance as nightfall fast approaches.

Weighting

Weighting involves considering the positive, neutral, and negative aspects of each option at each decision point in the decision tree. For the avalanche example, this means including the probabilities of finding the student by each search method and the probabilities that the student will be alive, given the time that has elapsed when the student is finally found.

Going for help and returning with a dog search team has a 90 percent chance of finding the student and a 10 percent chance of not. The hasty search has a 30 percent chance of finding the student and a 70 percent chance of not. The coarse probe search has a 40 percent chance of finding the student and a 60 percent chance of not. The fine probe search has an 80 percent chance of finding the student and a 20 percent chance of not.

Since the half-life period for remaining alive after being caught in an avalanche is about one-half hour, and since the estimated chance of the student being killed outright by the impact of this avalanche was 36 percent, you can calculate the probabilities of live finds from the cumulative duration of the searches. After an immediate hasty search, the student has a 64 percent chance of being alive (100 percent − 36 percent). After a coarse probe search, the student has a 32 percent chance of being alive (since half an hour has passed, the probability of success has been cut in half [64 ÷ 2 = 32]). After a fine probe search, the student has only an 8 percent chance of being alive because another two half-hour periods have expired, cutting the probability in half twice more (32 ÷ 2 = 16; 16 ÷ 2 = 8). Due to the length of time needed to secure a dog search, the student has less than a 1 percent chance of being alive after 270 or more minutes.

Choosing

Choosing involves selecting a path through the decision tree by picking the preferred option at each decision point. The preferred option is the one with the best overall probability of success. In a situation in which several factors are at play, overall probability is the product of all probabilities multiplied by one another. For the avalanche

example, this means multiplying the probability of finding the student with the probability of a live find.

In the first choice, going for help and returning with a dog search team has an overall success probability of 0.9 percent, which is based on a 90 percent chance of finding the student, but with a less than 1 percent chance of being alive (90 × .01 = 0.9); while the hasty search has an overall success probability of 19.2 percent, which is based on a 30 percent chance of finding the student but with a 64 percent chance of being alive (30 × .64 = 19.2). The better, first decision clearly is to perform a hasty search. In the second choice, getting help still has an overall success probability of 0.9 percent; while the coarse probe search has an overall success probability of 12.8 percent, which is based on a 40 percent chance of finding the student, but with a 32 percent chance of being alive (40 × .32 = 12.8). Clearly, the better second decision is to perform a coarse probe search. In the third choice, going for help still has an overall success probability of 0.9 percent; while the fine probe search has an overall success probability of 6.4 percent, which is based on an 80 percent chance of finding the student, but with an 8 percent chance of being alive (80 × .08 = 6.4). Clearly, the better third decision is to perform a fine probe search. Although the option for getting help is the last resort here, and is never the first preference due to poor probability that the victim will be found alive, these values could change given closer proximity to a professional SAR team. The lengthy response times make success unlikely for this scenario, but, remember, every decision-making situation is unique.

Overwhelmed with numbers in the weighting and choosing phases? In this example, we have used a **quantitative** method of weighting that is difficult for leaders who are not mathematically inclined or who are unable to juggle and balance several numbers in their heads. We'll look at a **qualitative** method of weighting in the next section.

QUALITATIVE MODIFICATIONS TO THE PROCESS

Of course, you can't break every decision down into quantifiable probabilities. In fact, you will be able to deal with the majority of decisions you'll face by effectively considering the "qualities" of the information you gather for any option. Picture yourself as the bicycle trip leader with a choice of six different routes to take between campsites as mapped in figure 22.2. Driving there or staying put are two other options available to you. The problem facing you is how best to balance safety with biking pleasure.

By interpreting the map and using judgment, you should gather the facts and assumptions of the six routes. Route #1 (15 miles) is a straight line along a major divided highway with a very high volume of traffic, no shoulder, and gentle grades. Route #2 (50 miles) follows beside and crosses a creek on a scenic winding route on hard-packed paths along old railway grades. Route #3 (30 miles) has light traffic on a hilly gravel back road, part of which follows a flat railway cut with a section of road missing, and you think walking the bikes along the side of the tracks might be

possible here. Route #4 (20 miles) follows minor highways with heavy traffic, which parallels the major highway and cuts underneath it at one point. Route #5 (35 miles) duplicates #3, except that it crosses the railway instead of following it and climbs over a steep mountain pass with nice views on dirt back roads. Route #6 (40 miles) rambles along paved farm roads with moderate traffic, crossing the same scenic creek as #2, but by a less direct route of straight segments and right-angled turns. Finally, remember, you could just drive to the next campsite or hang around the same campsite all day.

Because you are seeking a balance of safety and enjoyment, you should probably drop the two options of driving to the campsite or staying put for the day during the weeding out process. Certainly, driving or hanging around all day doesn't

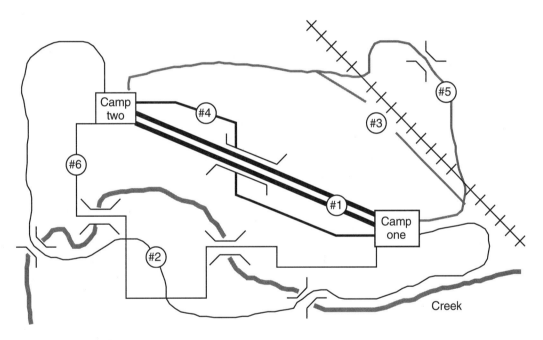

Qualities	Route #1	Route #2	Route #3	Route #4	Route #5	Route #6
Dangers	No shoulder	Bridges	Walk by rail	Underpass	Rail crossings	Bridges
Concerns	Straight	Winding	Missing bit	Straight	Steep hill	Straight
Road type	Highway	Bike path	Back road	Highway	Back road	Farm road
Traffic	Extreme	None	Light	Heavy	Light	Moderate
Terrain	Gentle grade	Flat	Hilly & flat	Gentle grade	Mtn. pass	Flat
Surface	Paved	Hard-packed	Gravel	Paved	Dirt	Paved
Distance	15 miles	50 miles	30 miles	20 miles	35 miles	40 miles
Key points of interest	None	Scenic	None	None	Nice views	Scenic

Figure 22.2   Tabulated summary of qualities associated with the six bike routes.

let anyone enjoy bicycling. Once you have weeded out the superfluous options, the six routes remain. This is a large number to subject to the next step, but you could reduce it by applying some additional criteria, such as avoiding vehicle fumes or hills and seeking paved surfaces or scenery.

Organizing the six routes into a qualitative comparative table, as in figure 22.2, replaces the quantitative decision tree. The figure is a simple way to compare and contrast the pros and cons of the available options. We have listed qualities worth considering in the decision in order of importance, and then have entered sample responses to each quality for all six options.

Qualities are typically organized around the three themes of positive, such as alternatives, benefits, contingencies or points of interest; neutral, such as costs, distances, terrain, road type, or surface; and negative, such as traffic and other dangers, concerns, or possible consequences. You don't necessarily have to include all themes in such a comparative table, but to be the most effective, you should consider all the available information and evaluation criteria. For example, alternatives and contingencies are often overlooked variable options to any consequences that might result if you select an option and put it into action. You should take into account any contingency plan that might make an option more desirable and prepare an alternative plan in case the option you select falls short of expectations.

When following a qualitative approach to weighting the content of these tables, you may prefer to avoid the use of numerical quantities. While the mathematical leader might correctly state that negatives are half the concern, positives are a third, and neutrals are the remaining sixth (or a similar weighting), this approach is not in keeping with qualitative modifications. Instead, you may prefer to mentally cross out the entries that are equivalent options, recognizing that entries higher on the list carry more weight of importance in the decision.

For example, you can view entire options and entries between options or within the same option as "six of one and half a dozen of another." Exposure to extreme traffic for 15 miles without a shoulder on route #1 may be equivalent to 20 miles of exposure to heavy traffic with an underpass to negotiate on route #4. In another light, the bridge crossings on routes #2 or #4 may be equal to the railway walk on route #3. For route

#5, the extra energy expended for the hill climb may well be worth the benefits obtained from the nice views.

For the purpose of choosing, identification of these equal entries removes many of the more moderate qualities. Those few extremes that remain may allow the best option to stand out. Thus, once you have accounted for equivalencies, the reduced number of entries permit you to more effectively choose the option that appears to have the strongest chance of success.

APPLICATION TO PROBLEM SOLVING

Whether the approach you use is quantitative or qualitative in nature, the same five divergent steps and five convergent steps can be an effective method for decision making. Figure 22.3 summarizes the divergent and convergent processes of making decisions.

Returning to the multiphase problem solving model of chapter 21, the process of divergence and convergence fits in at the definition, antici-

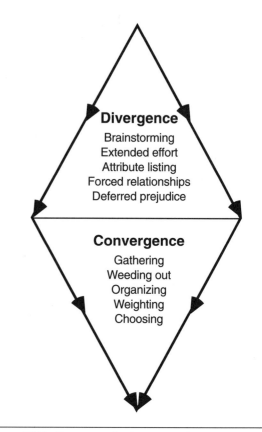

Figure 22.3 Ten steps in the divergent and convergent decision-making process.

pation, identification, and selection steps. Remember, the problem-solving sequence can stall due to a lack of necessary information, including knowing the crux, desired outcome, and possible solutions, and selecting the best solution. When this happens, the creative techniques, which are also part of divergence, help to come up with a crux, a desired outcome, a list of possible solutions, or a best solution, thus allowing the problem-solving process to continue.

The difference between using these creative techniques in restarting problem solving and in generating ideas for the building up half of decision making lies in whether you are simply trying to find one option or choosing from a range of several options. Sometimes when all the information is present for problem solving, only creative techniques may be necessary to confirm that the one crux or desired outcome is the right one since no others are apparent. At other times when uncertainty is present, which is, of course, common to all adventures, you should use creative techniques to generate as many options as possible. In this instance, narrowing down these options to provide the desired outcome is necessary: the full decision-making process is appropriate.

DECISION MAKING AND LEADERSHIP STYLES

Recall from chapter 18, "Flexible Leadership Style," and chapter 5, "Group Development and Dynamics," decision-making power can reside solely with you as the leader (autocratic), with the group (abdicratic), or shared between you and your group (democratic). Likewise, the divergent and convergent process can be used solely by you or your group or by a combination of both. Remember, however, that some situations, such as emergencies, demand that you alone make the decision, while other decisions can be the group's responsibility only, such as what to have for dinner. The fewer people involved in making a decision, the better, because many varied opinions are difficult to resolve. Sometimes the group is going to want involvement, especially for decisions where much is at stake or where they believe they have expertise to share. You must make clear to everyone your decision on who is part of the process, who is not, and why you have made these decisions to include or exclude group members.

EFFECTIVE OUTDOOR LEADERS SHOULD

☞ Know when to apply creative techniques and how much to use them in a divergent process before beginning a convergent process.

☞ Be able to gather and categorize information as fact, assumption, or constraint.

☞ Know the maximum number of options they are capable of managing in a decision-making situation, weeding out those options that are clearly inappropriate in order to reduce that number to the maximum limit.

☞ Be able to organize the remaining options by either quantitative or qualitative approaches and know how to construct a decision tree or a comparative table, depending on their preferred approach.

☞ Be able to weight options, using the relevant information they have gathered.

☞ Be able to choose the option with the greatest chance of success for resolving the situation by weighting the options.

☞ Be able to develop reasonable alternative and contingency plans, considering these alternatives and contingencies in their choice of best option.

☞ Be able to determine who should be included in or excluded from the decision-making process, clearly communicating that determination using the appropriate leadership style (autocratic, democratic, or abdicratic), depending on the situation.

SUMMARY

Decision making is choosing the most probable option from a collection of possible ones. The process involves diverging, or building up, a range of several options and then converging, or narrowing down, that range to select the best option. The divergent process of decision making utilizes the same creative techniques as found in multiphase problem solving to build up a field of options: brainstorming, extended effort, attribute listing, forced relationships, and deferred prejudice. Such creativity should lead to many more ideas in decision making than in problem solving. The convergent process of decision making uses five methods to narrow the field of options: gathering, weeding out, organizing, weighting, and choosing.

Gathering involves collecting all pertinent information that supports or refutes the merit of a particular option. Weeding out involves removing those options that are clearly inappropriate considerations, based on how plausible you evaluate them to be. Organizing involves ordering the three or four remaining options and arranging them into a decision tree for the quantitative approach or into a comparative table for the qualitative approach. Weighting involves considering the positive, neutral, and negative aspects of each option. Choosing involves selecting the preferred option with the best chance of success on the basis of having the most positives and least negatives.

QUESTIONS TO THINK ABOUT

1. You are leading a hiking trip with a dozen 11- and 12-year-old students and one other coleader. You stop at a trail junction to count heads and realize one student is missing. List all of the factors that would be important pieces of information. Based on this information, make a decision using the divergence and convergence model as to what you would do as a leader.

2. Choose another situation to make a decision using the divergence and convergence model, then discuss which aspects of the model worked well and which ones didn't.

3. Now make two similar decisions using the quantitative and qualitative approaches (one for each decision), then compare or contrast the strengths and weaknesses of each approach.

REFERENCE

Priest, S. (1988). AVALANCHE! Decision analysis: One way to solve problems. *Journal of Adventure Education and Outdoor Leadership* 5(3), 14-16.

Professional Ethics

A group of students on a wilderness-based experiential education course were having a hard time learning the fundamentals of emergency first aid. They were not taking the lessons seriously and wanted to go climbing instead, claiming that first aid was not very important or [was] boring to learn. The instructor of the group had the assistant instructor sneak into the woods where she feigned a severe accident. Cosmetic devices were used to give the injury the look of an actual accident. Hearing her screams, the students ran over and were confronted by a scene of trauma that shocked many group members and impelled them into action. Several minutes later, the group realized that the accident was staged. The instructors debriefed the group on the importance of first aid and several group members expressed their appreciation of the feigned accident. One member of the group was extremely angry that she had been deceived by the instructors.

—Hunt, 1990, pp. 53-54

Sue was an experienced and capable wilderness-based experiential educator. She was 28 years old and unmarried. During one of her courses, she had a student named Al, who was 30 years old, single, and interested in the possibility of pursuing an outdoor career. As the course went on, Sue and Al began to have long talks together when time permitted. The course was going exceptionally well and Sue and Al began to anticipate their time together alone. It became clear to both of them that there was a romantic attraction. Being mature adults, Sue and Al sat down one evening and discussed their emerging feelings for one another. They decided that they better be very careful about the emerging romance, but they also felt they could handle sexual expressions of their feelings during those rare moments when they were alone.

—Hunt, 1990, p. 79

Hearing from a corporate friend in California on the positive value of adventure experiences for building teamwork in organizations, the ABC Corporation (located in Boston) contacted a service provider in California (called California Adventure Training, Inc.) to provide training for them. After going over several logistical details, the California Adventure Training contacted several of the listed facilities close to Boston to ask if they could use their ropes course for part of a five-day training. One of these facilities was Boston Adventures, Inc., which happened to be located near the ABC Corporation. In fact, several of the human resource professionals from the ABC Corporation had heard of the locally based Boston Adventures, Inc. program and contacted them a few days later to find out what corporate adventure training actually entailed, how the ABC Corporation could maximize working with the California Adventure Training, Inc. program, and how good California Adventure Training, Inc. was at providing such services. In speaking with the Corporation, Boston Adventures, Inc. stated they could provide better services for the ABC Corporation and actively pursued the contract. They did not inform California Adventure Training, Inc. that they were stating this information to the ABC Corporation or that they were now negotiating for the contract that California Adventure Training, Inc. had contacted them for in order to use their ropes course. Given this information, the ABC Corporation contacted California Adventure Training, Inc. to let them know that they were no longer interested in using them for these training services and would be signing a contract with a more locally based service provider, who they had been told knows their needs better.

—Gass & Wurdinger, 1993, p. 43

As with most disciplines, certain professional actions are more appropriate than others. When these actions pertain to moral decisions and conduct, they are usually identified as ethical issues. **Ethical decision making** involves determining which behaviors in such issues are morally "right." As we have seen in the three scenarios opening this chapter, issues of ethical concern might arise when a conflict or disagreement over what is the best course of action to follow occurs. Such conflicts raise ethical questions, such as "Is it appropriate for a leader to deceive clients in order to enhance learning, or is it inappropriate to use such means to achieve the goal of having the clients take their learning seriously? Is sexual intimacy between a leader and client appropriate under certain conditions, or is it inappropriate since it could interfere with group learning processes? Is "attracting" a customer away from a competitor good business practice, or could it produce professional dynamics that limit the growth of the industry?" While these questions only touch a few of the potential ethical situations and their dynamics, they do illustrate some of the reasons why ethical decision making should be a major concern for you as an outdoor leader.

PRINCIPLE AND VIRTUE ETHICS

How does a professional go about determining ethical conduct, particularly when ethical considerations conflict with one another? While several writers have evolved models for ethical decision making in outdoor leadership (e.g., Hunt, 1990; Mitten, 1994), we can group most approaches used for making ethical decisions into one of two approaches: **principle ethics** and **virtue ethics.**

Principle ethics are guided by a proactively determined set of impartial rules, often determined by a governing professional organization or by the current professional standards of behavior if no such guidelines exist. Outdoor leaders following principle ethics examine their actions and choices, looking to answer the questions of "What shall I do?" and "Is this situation unethical?" (Jordan & Meara, 1990, p. 108). Principle ethics are also based on the belief that issues being examined are somewhat similar in context and can be connected to other situations.

Virtue ethicists, however, believe that you must examine the particular factors and influences of each act, asserting that "correct behavior" is defined in each specific situation and that you cannot link any decisions made in other situations. Virtue ethics are also guided by the particular virtues associated with being a moral outdoor leader rather than the principles of being ethical. Specifically, virtue ethics are concerned with professional character traits, focusing on the questions of "Who shall I be?" and "Am I doing the best for my client?" (Jordan & Meara, 1990, p. 108).

The strengths of each approach are the very weaknesses of the other. Principle ethics are *independent* of the situation. Professional behavior, ethical for a general situation, therefore becomes the rule for all specific situations. Say, for example, you notice that a group has made a navigational error and is heading the wrong way into a fragile ecosystem (Hunt, 1990). Should you tell the clients that they have made a mistake, or should you let them find out for themselves? At least three principles are in play here: client learning, client comfort, and environmental protection. Ask yourself "Will clients learn the lesson by being told or should they experience the consequences? How far do they have to travel off-route to learn? Will they damage the place they are headed into?" In deciding whether clients have a right to be informed about their error, you should order all principles by importance and simply make an ethical decision on the basis of the guiding order. For a principle ethicist, this order would remain the same in every similar situation.

In contrast, virtue ethics are *dependent* on the situation. Professional behavior is contextual or subjective and may vary from one set of circumstances to another. For the navigational example, several virtues are in play: honesty, caring, and sensitivity. As a virtue ethicist, you should ask yourself questions like "What would an honest person do about informing the clients? What would a caring person do about allowing them to travel out of their way? What would a sensitive person do to protect nature?" Instead of deciding what to do, you are concerned with the type of person to be and the greatest benefit for the client and environment. Therefore, for a virtue ethicist, this decision may differ from or agree with that of the principle ethicist, but it will also be different in any other slightly different dilemma.

While principle ethics ask you to look outside the situation to maintain a degree of objectivity in determining ethical behavior, virtue ethics ask you to step inside the dilemma to better ascertain what your professional actions mean. Several authors (e.g., Gass & Wurdinger, 1993) have suggested that the idea of using principle or virtue ethics should not be an "either-or" decision: you need to consider both. One model in which you may use either or both elements is an adaptation of Kitchener's (1984) model of ethical decision making.

KITCHENER'S MODEL OF ETHICAL DECISION MAKING

Kitchener's model consists of multiple steps in a process of ethical reasoning, examining issues in a progressive sequence. If you can't make a well-founded ethical decision at one step, you advance to the next one, which is usually more general and abstract in its approach to the issue. Specifically, the five steps of this ethical decision making model are intuition, option listing, ethical rules, ethical principles, and ethical theory.

Intuition

Ethical responses in the **intuition** level come from prereflective or "gut reactions" to the question "What feels right?" The ethical beliefs associated with these decisions are so well established the answer is obtained through "ordinary moral sense." Little need to even consider the decision exists since the ordinary moral sense process has already been predetermined, usually based on your "individual experience, ethical knowledge, and level of ethical development" (Zygmond & Boorhem, 1989, p. 271). For example, almost all outdoor leaders would intuitively claim that damaging the environment in a survival situation is acceptable. In order to save lives, they would gladly light signal fires with green wood or build stretchers by cutting down trees.

Option Listing

When you are unable to resolve ethical decisions at the intuition level, **option listing** and the evaluation of these options, their outcomes, and potential ramifications need to occur. This serves as a foundation for the ethical decision-making process in whichever of the three remaining steps you use. For example, you could list these two options for the example: damage a fragile environment and increase the chances of group safety or protect the environment and run the outside chance of someone becoming seriously injured.

Ethical Rules

Ethical rules are generally externally established codes of conduct, like the guidelines created by the psychological, medical, and legal professions. Probably the closest example of ethical rules in adventure programming are the guidelines published by the Therapeutic Adventure Professional Group (AEE, 1992; Gass, 1993) and the ethical criteria established in their *Manual of Program Accreditation Standards for Adventure Programs*, published by the Association for Experiential Education (Williamson & Gass, 1993). Principles like these are established by a profession to maintain a certain level of ethical behavior, and their creation is generally considered to be a developmental benchmark in the quest for professionalism. One example of an ethical rule is that adventure programs discriminating on the basis of gender, race, or sexual orientation cannot become accredited by AEE, and accredited programs found to discriminate in this manner will lose their accreditation status.

Ethical Principles

Ethical principles are "enduring beliefs about specific modes of conduct or end-states of existence that, when acted upon, protect the interests and welfare of all of the people involved" (Zygmond & Boorhem, 1989, p. 273). More general in nature than ethical rules, the five principles identified by Kitchener (1984) as being the most critical for members in the "helping professions" include autonomy, "nonmaleficence," beneficence, fidelity, and justice. In **autonomy,** individuals have the right to freedom of action and choice as long as their behavior does not infringe on the rights of others. **Nonmaleficence** means that, above all else, no harm will be done to people. **Beneficence** means that the focus of an outdoor leader's actions is to contribute to the health and welfare of others. **Fidelity** means be faithful, keep promises, and be loyal and respectful of people's rights. **Justice** means individuals will be treated as equals and implies a concept of "fairness." For example, Rohnke's axiom of challenge by choice (see chapter 14), in which people are not coerced to participate in an adventure, illustrates all five of these ethical principles.

Ethical Theories

When intuitive thought, ethical codes, and ethical principles fail to resolve ethical issues, implement **ethical theories**. This helps you determine which factors are relevant to the situation and should take precedent. Two principles used in this process are balancing and universalizability. With **balancing**, you compare options, trying to pick the one that brings the least amount of avoidable harm to all parties involved. This is similar to the consequential theory of ethics, which suggests that the action is ethically correct only if it produces the greatest happiness for the greatest number (Mill, 1985). With **universalizability**, you seek to institute and generalize the same ethical actions across similar situations (e.g., if it would be ethical to act one way in this situation, then seek to act that way in another similar situation). This is similar to the nonconsequentialist theory of ethics based on the "categorical imperative," stating that actions should only be taken when the processes used can be fairly and broadly applied as a universal law to all similar cases (Kant, 1964). For the survival and environment example, you should balance the two options against the measure of a human life versus others. In some cases, the cost in terms of money and risk to rescuers in a highly inaccessible environment might dictate not sponsoring government efforts to save human life as in the concept of rescue-free wil-

derness, or areas for which the government assumes no responsibility for rescuing people from designated wilderness areas (McAvoy, 1990). If the option not to rescue was chosen, perhaps because not entering the wilderness with a search team might save more lives in the long run, then a universal application of this option would also have to hold true in all such wilderness areas.

Applying Kitchener's Model

Recall that if you are unable to resolve a situation by determining professional or appropriate action at one level, you should move to the next step. But in the Kitchener model, one step is not better than another, only more appropriate for providing professional guidance when making an ethical decision. One advantage of this model is that it creates conditions under which you may continually evolve at all levels of your ethical development. Remember, the more experience you gain making certain ethical decisions, the more likely your decisions will become intuitive level decisions. In other words, as you become more experienced in making ethical decisions, it is more likely that you will be able to resolve dilemmas at this lowest level, using your intuition. Hence, you should practice resolving ethical dilemmas. To give you some more vicarious experience, let's examine the third scenario in regard to the Kitchener model, involving adventure organizations competing for corporate customers.

The first step in the model is to examine the practice of attracting customers away from other organizations as an intuitive ethical decision. Based on professional experience and the belief that ethical behavior is important, you should ask yourself if it makes "ordinary moral sense" to follow such behavior or that such behavior is unethical in all cases. You may determine that this type of behavior could lead to a wide variety of negative implications for individual programs as well as for the field and so choose not to involve yourself in this practice. You may, however, determine that this practice is ethically acceptable because the program appropriately attracted customers away on the basis of safety standards or actual competence, since the staff of Boston Adventures actually did know ABC Corporation's business better than California Adventure Training. If, however, you determine that this issue is not easily resolved due to conflicting ideas, elements, principles, or virtues, then you must move to the next level of the model and list possible options of competing behavior and the consequences of such actions.

In the second step, you make a list of possible options that you could take and the strengths and weaknesses of each. Four options are possible for the scenario, and, in this case, we might call them **prohibitive**, prohibiting "stealing" since it is unethical; **open market**, allowing competition since it is ethical; **objective conditional**, attracting customers is okay under certain conditions; and **subjective discretional**, attracting customers at your own discretion. If you believe in the absoluteness of the first two options, then these are easy choices, made at an intuitive level. In the prohibitive option, stealing is wrong at all times and would not be ethically permissible under any circumstances. In the open market option, competition is right in all cases and would be ethically expected under any circumstances. The remaining two options are full of conflict, leading to an ethical dilemma. You would need to more closely examine these options along with their respective strengths and weaknesses.

The objective conditional option includes establishing a proactive and objective set of standards that outline criteria as to when providers could not attract customers away from other providers. Some of these set conditions might be possession of a current contract or in negotiation to contract and a waiting period of a few months after an initial contact ended. At these times, other providers could not approach the customers of these contracted providers. A series of clearly identified conditions in place before a competitive situation arose seeks to prevent some problems. And this option does have its strengths. It establishes objective conditions for you to follow while eliminating potential negative exploitation of professional interaction. It provides some degree of "freedom of choice" among customers wishing to switch providers. It fosters the belief that outdoor leaders and adventure programs may freely interact to provide quality programs without fear of losing customers. It proactively identifies the rules of professional interaction as well as competition for customers. It encourages a climate of professional collaboration with the advance knowledge that losing customers in such a manner will not occur. This option has several weaknesses as well. It does not remove the possibility that stealing customers still could occur after the objective conditions were met. It limits, to the degree of the conditions, the customers' freedom to choose another service provider.

The subjective discretional option recognizes that there are times when attracting customers away from other businesses would be unethical and inappropriate. But it would be up to individual outdoor leaders to use their own belief systems to determine when this would or wouldn't be appropriate on a case by case basis. The strengths of this position are that it establishes subjective conditions for you to follow, trying to eliminate potential negative exploitation, and it provides for greater autonomy for providers and customers, given that the rights of others are not being infringed on. The weaknesses of the position are that it does not remove the possibility that negative exploitation still could occur after the subjective condition is met (e.g., beliefs by outdoor leaders that customers were "stolen"), and it does not promote the positive development of professional collaboration without fear of losing customers.

Once you outline the strengths and weaknesses of various positions, you should then look to the third, fourth, and fifth steps for guidance in deciding between both options. In the third step, you should examine the ethical rules of the profession. (A code of conduct for outdoor leaders is described in the next section of this chapter.) If you see the central issue to be one of competence in which the California program truly did not possess the competence to conduct the program, but the Boston program did, then you can make your choice based on this ethical rule. If, however, competence is not at the heart of the issue, this step is of little use to you, and you should look at the next one.

In the fourth step, you should evaluate the major advantages and disadvantages of both options, comparing them to the ethical principles of autonomy, "nonmaleficence," beneficence, fidelity, and justice. The objective conditional option (OC) establishes an impartial set of rules regarding contracts and waiting periods that blocks other providers from attracting customers away from the program. The subjective discretional option (SD) recognizes that the choice of attracting customers should be made by you, based on the situation and considering your personal values.

Autonomy seems to be lower for both providers and customers in the OC option, because their rights to choose and their freedom to interact outside the contract are restricted by these rules. Autonomy is higher for both providers and customers in the SD option, because each are free to choose in a way that does not significantly infringe on the rights of other providers.

Nonmaleficence appears to be higher for providers and moderate for customers in the OC option, because providers are protected by the rules, and customers could be harmed by being unable to change their minds if stuck with a poor program. Nonmaleficence is lower for providers and moderate for customers in the SD option, because providers are open to "attack" from other providers, and customers could be harmed by the possible lack of program quality.

Beneficence seems to be moderate for providers, depending on whether they gain or lose customers in the OC option, because collaboration can occur and may bring increased quality or decreased motivation to improve. It is also lower for customers in the OC option, because they lose the chance to benefit from an open selection process that encourages the best program to come to the forefront. Beneficence is moderate for providers, again depending on whether they lose or gain customers in the SD option, because competition can bring increased quality and decreased sharing of information. It is also higher for customers in the SD option, because they benefit from a wide variety of providers and quality programs to choose from.

Fidelity appears to be high for providers and customers in the OC option, because customers remain faithful or loyal to providers, keep written promises, and respect a collaborative environment. Fidelity is low for providers and customers in the SD option, because customers switch providers, break verbal contracts, and respect only the programs' rights to compete.

Justice seems to be moderate for providers and customers in both options. In the OC option, everyone has equal knowledge of the operating rules in advance and has a fair chance to begin trusting one another in collaboration. In the SD option, everyone has fair access to discuss contracts with one another as they operate in a competitive market with equal opportunity.

In this case, if you believed that one of these two options took the highest ethical stance for addressing the issue of attracting customers away from other programs, then you could follow either the OC or SD option, completing the ethical decision-making process. But if you were unable to determine the ethical decision based on these principles, you should advance to the final step of the ethical theories of balancing and universalizability to determine the appropriate ethical action.

Balancing considers both options and chooses the stance that produces the greatest benefit for the greatest number of people. Everyone would be indirectly inconvenienced, including the customer, by including rules, and the only direct benefit would go to the program with a contract in the OC option. The only one inconvenienced would be the program who loses a customer to another provider; all others, including the customer, would benefit in the SD option. Therefore, the SD option seems to be the clear preference for balancing.

Remember, universalizability refers to how well the option applies to all similar cases. The OC option is the clear preference for universal generalizability: its rules suit any situation. The SD option has no universalizability, because each situation is decided on its own merits. Since one option is favored by one theory and the other by another, in this final step, you will have to decide which of these two theories you hold in higher regard.

In following such a model, principle and virtue ethicists would tend to focus on different features. As highlighted earlier, principle ethicists would strive to remain objective and impartial in following the model, focusing on what you should do to end up following the most ethical practice. Virtue ethicists, however, would examine the particular factors and influences of this particular action, attempting to interpret the intentions of Boston Adventures in the dilemma to better ascertain the reasons for their actions.

We encourage you to use both the principle and virtue approaches when possible to achieve a well-balanced view of any ethical decision. While at certain times these approaches come into conflict with one another, a combined "objective-subjective" approach will give you a balanced perspective.

ETHICAL GUIDELINES FOR OUTDOOR LEADERS

Probably one of the brightest developments of ethical decision making for outdoor leadership is the formulation of ethical guidelines by the Association of Experiential Education's Therapeutic Adventure Professional Group (AEE, 1992). You can find another version of these guidelines in the ethics section of the program accreditation standards identified in the *Manual of Program Accreditation Standards for Adventure Programs* (Williamson & Gass, 1993). These guidelines were created with the support of the

American Psychological Association (APA), the American Alliance of Marriage and Family Therapists (AAMFT), Council on Outdoor Education for the American Alliance of Health, Physical Education & Dance (COE/AAHPERD), Council of Accreditation of Services for Families and Children (CASFC), and the Worldwide Outfitters and Guides Association (WOGA). While these guidelines were not established as an ethical code or as rules professionals must follow or be censured from practice, they do show that the outdoor leadership field is on record for supporting certain practices. Specifically, the seven guidelines relate to competence, integrity, responsibility, respect, concern, recognition, and objectivity. Although developed for therapists, we will paraphrase these seven guidelines for your review.

While these seven guidelines represent a critical and invaluable step in advancing the outdoor leadership profession, you should recognize that following such guidelines does not release you from the need to apply ethical judgment. As you should not blindly follow safety protocols for a technical skill without considering the changing elements of an outdoor setting, you should not forgo the need to constantly examine your behavior in professional endeavors.

Indeed, ethical standards have limitations. Ethical guidelines may conflict with the framework of certain cultures, requiring you to adapt them in such instances. Or you may find yourself in a situation in which a conflict exists among legal, organizational, and ethical guidelines. Conflict between ethical guidelines and their interpretation will likely arise and lead to dilemmas for you to resolve as best you can. No matter what the course of action you select, the *summum bonum* (i.e., do no harm) ethic you as a professional follow to resolve dilemmas should be guided by empathy for the client. With this in mind, let's look closely at each of the seven guideline areas.

Competence

Professionals conduct experiences with an appropriate level of **competence**. As an outdoor leader, promote and conduct activities within your level of competence. Provide services within the boundaries of your education, training, supervision, experience, and practice. Take reasonable steps to ensure the competence of your work. Avoid situations in which personal problems or conflicts will impair your performance or judg-

ment. Stay abreast of current information in the field. Participate in ongoing professional efforts to maintain your knowledge, practice, and skills.

Integrity

Professionals conduct experiences with **integrity**. Conduct activities with honesty, fairness, and respect in interactions with both clients and peers. Avoid false, misleading, or deceptive statements when describing or reporting qualifications, services, products, or fees. Be aware of how your personal belief system, values, needs, and limitations affect clients.

Responsibility

Professionals conduct experiences with **responsibility**. Uphold the ethical principles of your work. Be clear with clients as to what everyone's roles and obligations are. Accept responsibility for your behavior and decisions. Adapt methods to the needs of different populations. Ensure that you possess an adequate basis for professional judgments. Do not offer services when the constraints of limited contact will not benefit client needs (e.g., promising a single day adventure experience will resolve a deep issue for a therapeutic or corporate population). Continue services only so long as it is reasonably clear that clients will benefit. Conduct experiences in a manner that results in minimal impact or temporary damage to the environment.

Respect

Professionals conduct experiences with **respect** for the rights and dignity of clients. Respect the fundamental rights, dignity, and worth of all people. Respect clients' rights to privacy, confidentiality, and self-determination within the limits of the law. Strive to be sensitive to cultural and individual differences, including those due to age, gender, race, ethnicity, national origin, religion, sexual orientation, disability, and socioeconomic status. Do not engage in sexual or other harassment or exploitation of clients. Respect clients' rights to make decisions as well as help them understand the consequences of their choices. Provide clients with appropriate information about the nature of services and their rights, risks, and responsibilities. Offer an opportunity to discuss the results, interpretations, and conclusions of the adventure experience with clients. Respect clients' rights to refuse consent to services and activities. Obtain informed consent from clients and, when appropriate, their parents or guardians before beginning services. Accurately represent your competence, training, education, and experience relevant to the program you are delivering.

Concern

Professionals conduct experiences with **concern** for the well-being of clients. Be sensitive to client needs and well-being. Provide for the appropriate physical needs of clients, including necessary water, nutrition, clothing, shelter, rest, or other essentials. Monitor the appropriate use of emotional and physical risk in adventure experiences. Assist in obtaining other services if the program cannot for appropriate reasons provide the professional help clients may need. Plan experiences with the clients' best interests in mind both during and after the program. Respect clients' rights to decide the extent to which confidential material can be made public, except under extreme conditions as required by law to prevent a clear and immediate danger to a person or persons.

Recognition

Professionals conduct experiences with **recognition** for their level of social responsibility. Be aware of your responsibilities to community and society. Appropriately encourage the development of standards and policies that serve your clients' interests as well as those of the public. Respect the property of others.

Objectivity

Professionals conduct experiences with **objectivity** by avoiding dual relationships with clients that impair professional judgment. Do not exploit or mislead clients or other leaders during and after professional relationships. This includes, but is not limited to, business relationships, close personal friendships, family relationships, sexual relations, and otherwise inappropriate physical contact.

EFFECTIVE OUTDOOR LEADERS SHOULD

☞ Above all else, do no harm to the client.

☞ Understand that no governing body, other than the AEE program accreditation, holds outdoor professionals to a standard of ethical conduct.

☞ Make sure that facilitation efforts are done with the clients' best interests in mind.

☞ Ensure that the focus of the interventions are to serve the clients, not the leader.

☞ Be certain that a purpose and reason exist for using a particular technique.

☞ Know when to use intuitive and rationale approaches for ethical decision making (e.g., listing as in Kitchener's model).

☞ Be willing to stand up in front of other colleagues and say that they used this technique and state why.

☞ Understand the guidelines put forth by the AEE for ethical behavior and implement them when appropriate.

☞ Remind themselves that the experience possesses the resources to be more powerful than their best efforts.

☞ When in doubt, *do no harm*!

SUMMARY

Ethical decision making is usually based on principle ethics or virtue ethics. Principle ethics are independent of the ethical situation and are guided by a proactively determined set of impartial principles focused on actions and choices. Virtue ethics are dependent on the uniqueness of every situation and are guided by desired virtues and character traits.

Kitchener's model of ethical decision making is composed of five steps: intuition, option listing, ethical rules, ethical principles, and ethical theory. The intuitive first level is a gut reaction to what feels morally correct. The second step lists options, with strengths and weaknesses, that serve as considerations for the next three steps. Ethical rules are generally codes of conduct established by external professions. Ethical principles are ways of acting that protect others, including five concerns: autonomy, nonmaleficence, beneficence, fidelity, and justice. Ethical theories are balancing, considering the greatest gain for greatest number and least harm for least number, and universalizability, or that which can be generalized to the deepest and widest universal application.

The Association for Experiential Education has developed a series of seven guidelines related to competence, integrity, responsibility, respect, concern, recognition, and objectivity.

Competence refers to not working beyond your capability. Integrity refers to honesty, fairness, and respect with regard to client interactions and peer relations. Responsibility refers to caring for the clients' well-being as well as the environment's. Respect refers to the fundamental rights, dignity, and worth of clients and peers. Concern refers to clients' physiological and psychological needs and well-being. Recognition refers to social responsibility toward the community and society's needs. Objectivity refers to not establishing relationships with clients beyond the roles of leader and client. These seven guidelines do not necessarily substitute for ethical decision making; they merely shepherd you through the process of resolving ethical conflicts or dilemmas.

QUESTIONS TO THINK ABOUT

1. Which of the two options (OC and SD) in the attracting corporate customers scenario do you prefer and why?

2. At which step in Kitchener's model had you made up your mind?

3. Using Kitchener's model, determine your ethical decisions for each of the remaining two scenarios at the beginning of this chapter.

4. Outline the process you went through to arrive at your decisions and argue your logic with a partner.

REFERENCES

Association for Experiential Education. (1992). *Ethical guidelines of the Therapeutic Adventure Professional Group* (TAPG). Boulder, CO: Association for Experiential Education.

Gass, M.A. (1993). *Adventure therapy: Therapeutic applications of adventure programming in mental health settings.* Boulder, CO: Association for Experiential Education.

Gass, M.A., & Wurdinger, S. (1993). Ethical decisions in experience-based training and development programs. *Journal of Experiential Education* 16(2), 41-47.

Hunt, J. (1990). *Ethics in experiential education.* Boulder, CO: Association for Experiential Education.

Jordan, A. E. & Meara, N.M. (1990). Ethics and the professional practices of psychologists: The role of virtues and principles. *Professional Psychology: Research and Practice.* 21(2), 107-114.

Kant, I. (1964). *Groundwork of the metaphysic of morals.* New York: Harper and Row.

Kitchener, K.S. (1984). Intuition, critical evaluation, and ethical principles: The foundation for ethical decisions in counseling psychology. *The Counseling Psychologist* 12(3), 43-55.

McAvoy, L. (1990). Rescue-free wilderness areas. In J.C. Miles & S. Priest (Eds.), *Adventure education* (pp. 329-334). State College, PA: Venture.

Mill, J.S. (1959). *On Liberty.* New York: Penguin Classics.

Mitten, D. (1994). Ethical considerations in adventure therapy: A feminist critique. In E., Cole; E. Erdman; & E.D. Rothblum. (Eds.) *Wilderness therapy for women: The power of adventure.* NY: Harrington Park Press.

Williamson, J., & Gass, M.A. (1993). *Manual of program accreditation standards for adventure programs.* Boulder, CO: Association for Experiential Education.

Zygmond, M.J. & Boorhem, H. (1989). Ethical decision making in family therapy. *Family Process* 28, 269-280.

chapter
24

Trends and Issues

> Around the turn of the last century, not one of the futurists predicting our prospective lives mentioned anything remotely connected with the computer.
>
> —John Sculley, former CEO of Apple Computer

Predicting the future can be a very difficult and dangerous undertaking for any profession. Nevertheless, in this chapter, we'll outline six key trends and issues associated with adventure programming and outdoor leadership: growth, the environment, technology, burnout, professionalism, and research. To better understand these trends and issues, let's first examine some of the factors at work in them as well as some of the resulting growth areas.

FACTORS AT WORK

Ewert (1989) and Miles (1990) have identified several social trends and changes in global and local issues that have implications for the future of adventure programming. One is that an increasing number of people are seeking the outdoors. This change is placing the natural environment under increasing stress and will result in more nonrecoverable damage to the resource base. In short, more people are currently in the process of loving the outdoors to death!

At the same time, the world is shrinking due to continually developing communication and transportation technologies. The ability to instantaneously store, retrieve, and deliver a rapidly expanding information base may mean that the dominant global culture will move in the direction of being more empirical, rational, utilitarian, and manipulative. As a result, global markets for goods, services, or ideas will become easier to access, yet heavily competitive for customers and resources. The global economy is currently in the process of shifting from an industrial to a service-oriented society with lower worker pay and longer work hours.

Many factors are changing, affecting both the workplace and the home. More dual-income families as both parents work and more single-parent families are translating into increasing numbers of "latch-key" children spending less time with their families. The status and roles of women in society are continuing to change. The average age of the population will continue to increase. More people will switch careers in their working lifetimes.

What does it all mean? Society may become more consumptive, dominant, and manipulative and less moral, conservative, or compassionate. People are seeming to increase their levels of debt, "mortgaging" their futures in order to sustain their affluence. Growing levels of intellectual, cultural, and ethical anomie, or unrest, among young people may result in more drug abuse, crime, and teenage suicide. Among all of this, litigious attitudes will prevail, and lawyers will play a more influential role in determining what takes place in adventure programming. Two questions that need to be asked given these societal trends are (1) will adventure programming be able to continue to thrive in such conditions and (2) can the field possibly even change some of these societal trends?

GROWTH

In a summary of his speech presented at the 1996 Outdoor Industry CEO Roundtable Breakfast, Jim Lyons [Under Secretary of the Head of the US Department of Agriculture who oversees the US Forest Service] noted that growing recreation demands are failing to be met by the current [Federal] budget. He noted that in terms of recreation facilities, the Forest Service was underfunded by $818 million. Attendees were informed that outdoor recreation only receives 21 percent of the monies allocated to the total 1996 National Forest Service budget. On the other hand, when analyzing gross domestic products resulting from Forest Service functions, outdoor recreation contributes 74.8 percent with mining and foresting [on US Forest Service lands] being less than 25 percent.... Lyons stated, "If we don't provide a high quality natural environment, people won't come back to the lands, and you won't sell your products."

—Mentuck, 1996, p. 3

▲▲▲▲▲▲▲▲▲▲▲▲▲▲▲▲▲▲▲▲▲▲▲▲▲▲

As a result of the factors Ewert and Miles identified, several trends and growth areas seem to be probable. Adventure programs and activities will continue to grow in popularity. Some increases will probably be due to the need for greater leisure opportunities, and others may result from the need to use adventure experiences to address societal problems. This trend is already obvious from the increasing numbers of participants in, and revenues from, the outdoor recreation participation. For example, five of the top fastest growing sports are adventurous: board sailing, board surfing, mountain and rock climbing, horseback riding, and sailing (Ewert, 1989). Other growth factors include the following predictions:

The size and number of professional organizations will increase. Since the origin of the first Association for Experiential Education (AEE) Conference in 1974, for which 130 individuals preregistered (Garvey, 1990), this organization, seen by many individuals as the leading agency concerned with adventure programming, now has over 2,000 members in 20 countries. AEE has professional and special interest groups in the subject areas of experience-based training and development, schools and colleges, therapeutic adventure, and universal programming. Their organizational structure and intent has been replicated in several nations around the world, and numerous member and spin-off organizations have been created. Examples include the International Conference on Outdoor Recreation (ICOR), Association of Challenge Course Technology (ACCT), Coalition for Education Outdoors (CEO), International Conference on Experiential Learning (ICEL), National Society for Experiential Education (NSEE), and Council for Adult and Experiential Learning (CAEL). Other organizations include the Bradford Institute on Americans Outdoors (BIAO), Institute for Earth Education (IEE), Adventuresports Institute (ASI) Wilderness Education Association (WEA), Project Adventure (PA), American Mountain Guides Association (AMGA), National Outdoor Leadership School (NOLS), and Outward Bound International (OBI).

The profession will expand and diversify. For example, the latest version of the AEE's *Directory of Experiential Therapy and Adventure-Based Counseling Programs* (Gerstein, 1992) lists over 257 organizations that utilize adventure experiences for therapy. Within this listing are programs for clients who are at-risk youth, in adult corrections, families, psychiatric inpatients, addicts, terminally ill patients, in juvenile corrections, sexual victims, sexual perpetrators, and developmentally disabled. We can also expect a number of other client types in the adventure profession, including corporations and schools.

Adventure will be more often adopted by the schools. Classroom settings will slowly incorporate the concepts and methods of adventure programming into their conventional schooling. For example, the utilization of "wilderness learning," or the Outward Bound approach, has already met with success in the physical education curriculum through Project Adventure. Other curricula will be likely to benefit from the inclusion of adventure programming, for example, expeditionary learning.

Programs will be brought to the learner, rather than vice versa. With the interaction of the issues of shrinking wilderness, accessibility, fiscal restraints, and efforts to make concepts more applicable to clients' real lives, a number of professionals have called for adventure programs to center efforts more around the learner and the "adventures" in their own environments. One example of this is the growth of urban adventure programming (Proudman, 1990). Urban adventure has several potential advantages over more wilderness-based programming, which may include greater accessibility to a larger number of clients, clients who can directly benefit from adventure, such as 10- to 15-year-old youth from disadvantaged backgrounds, environments with cultural diversity, immediacy of human problems and solutions, availability of differing resources, continuing support systems, greater transferability to clients' futures, and a wide range of learning environments and programming options, such as cultural events and information sources.

Program operations will be more regulated and complex. Less governmental funding and more injuries to humans and damage to the environment all bring increasing regulation from resource managers. Concerned with their liability and visitor safety, these managers set policies and procedures to moderate resource use. Resource management agencies, such as the National Park and Forest Service, have introduced guidelines governing permit use, program licensing, and access fees. On some public lands, adventure programs must obtain permission via a lottery, be accredited by the AEE (Association for Experiential Education) or AMGA (American Mountain Guides Association), and pay a fee for the use of those lands. These measures have been implemented, in part, to cover shrinking bureaucratic support and increased use.

Artificial adventure environments will begin to dominate program settings. To some extent this is already the case. Group initiative tasks and ropes and challenge courses have all but replaced the classic outdoor pursuits with corporate clientele. A proliferation of ropes course builders has led to the creation of the Association for Challenge Course Technology (ACCT) to standardize construction methods and safety inspections for the thousands of American courses in use today. These numbers are expected to grow exponentially in the future with similar patterns to follow in other countries. The shrinking of natural outdoor settings coupled with the cost and danger of transporting clients (the most dangerous part of most programs) will necessitate that alternatives be found. Some alternatives might include the already popular climbing walls, ski slopes, kayak roll tanks, and whitewater canoe chutes. Others have yet to be invented.

The profession will slowly mature through self-examination. By formulating ways to investigate and theorize about the processes of adventure programming, the profession will grow to be more professional. One important step toward this is the development of a unique body of knowledge. This has already been accomplished in part by the creation of professional safety guidelines (Priest & Dixon, 1990) and the construction of program accreditation standards (Williamson & Gass, 1993). These publications highlight the profession's ability to identify, document, and refine the expression of practices to practitioners and consumers alike. Moreover, we

can see other such evolutionary benchmarks in written works about how adventure programming applies to specific populations; for example, Schoel, Prouty, and Radcliffe (1988), Gass (1993a, 1993b), Davis-Berman and Berman (1994), and Cole, Erdman, and Rothblum (1994) have all published books on the therapeutic applications of adventure.

ENVIRONMENT

Rock climbing activity has increased dramatically at Acadia National Park (ANP) over the past 10 to 15 years. The effects of climbing use in ANP are most evident at Otter Cliffs. Significant erosion is occurring around belay trees. Many of them are close to dying and may not be available as anchors within a few years. The proliferation of social trails are largely the result of climbers seeking privacy while "answering the call of nature." Human waste is an aesthetic problem, a possible health hazard, and an ecological concern.

The use of Otter Cliffs by organized groups is contributing to this resource damage. We estimate one-fourth of all climbing use at Otter Cliffs in 1994 was from groups. In addition, the presence of large groups may affect the climbing experience by causing crowding and congestion. It has also caused other climbers to seek new locations to climb in the park.

In order to protect these resources from further damage and to preserve the unique sea cliff climbing experience, ANP will begin to regulate use of Otter Cliffs beginning in 1996. This is the first of several actions which we intend to take at Otter Cliffs and throughout the park to accomplish protection of resources and the visitor experience.

Regulation of group use at Otter Cliffs will likely include a group size limit of twelve, including instructors, and a limit on the number of groups allowed per day at the site. Twelve is the group size we are currently using for commercial operations. Reservations would be required in advance.

We want to remind you that any groups charging a fee for climbing services or for any program must have a commercial use license even if they are a nonprofit group. The fee for commercial use licenses is $50, and special conditions are attached to the permit regarding the time and location of climbing activity, safety equipment, or other conditions as needed.

—Letter from P. Haertel, Superintendent, Acadia National Park, June 23, 1995

Many recognize that climbing is a very high-impact activity. We are on the "radar screens" of decision makers and their fingers are on the "buttons" of regulations. Make no mistake about it: climbing will be managed and regulated in the future. It is no longer a question of choosing between self-regulation or external regulation. It's too late for that. The Access Fund, American Alpine Club, and other national and local groups are working aggressively to preserve as much freedom as possible for climbers, but we must accommodate the competing values of other outdoor users, impacts on wildlife, soil, and vegetation, and members of our own community, who often climb for very different reasons. In short, we need to promote a new environmental ethic in climbing.

—Lenard, 1995, p. 200

No question about it, the environment is "reeling" from the actions of many untrained people. Their increasing numbers have led to degradation of wilderness and other natural areas, so much so that access is being restricted by resource managers. Their carelessness has led to constraints, such as licensing, permits, and fees, on the very freedom they seek to enjoy.

In 1995, the administration agencies for Joshua Tree (southern California) and Red Rocks (Nevada) National Parks have decided that only those adventure programs accredited by the AMGA or the AEE will be permitted to conduct rock climbing programs in these areas. While

such requirements only exist in these two areas, we can expect many others to follow. If such efforts do expand throughout North America, this could greatly influence the manner in which adventure programs use rock climbing or other outdoor pursuits to conduct their services.

Furthermore, the popularizing of wilderness areas has also produced several other changes in adventure experiences, including wilderness areas becoming less "remote" or "wild." People turning to the wilderness for solitude and "opportunities for self-sufficiency" (McAvoy & Dustin, 1981) often encounter crowded conditions that hamper or eliminate many of the reasons why they go there. Increasing management by governmental agencies, often heavily influenced by advances in wilderness rescue technology and a growing litigious society, have also reduced many of the advantages and attractions of going to the wilderness.

One solution advanced by McAvoy and Dustin (1981, 1983) is the proposal of **rescue-free** wilderness areas. "In these zones, the wilderness users would be completely responsible for their own safety. The government agencies managing these rescue-free zones would be absolved, indeed prohibited, from conducting or sponsoring any search and rescue operations for wilderness users in the area. The managing agency would be responsible for informing users of the principle risks in the area and . . . no government rescue services would be available for a recreationist there. . . . [This] is not a proposal championed by insensitive people. Rather, it is an attempt to preserve a few places to experience what wilderness was intended to be, the untrammelled experience full of opportunities for self-reliance, risk, challenge, and growth" (McAvoy, 1990, p. 329, 333).

TECHNOLOGY

Recently, a friend and his partner overtook another party high on the Bastille Crack in Eldorado Canyon, Colorado. Noticing that the belayer hadn't fastened the waist belt on his harness properly—like most buckled harnesses, this one required that the tail end of the webbing be doubled back through the buckle—my friend immediately pointed out the grave potential danger of the situation. Offended, the belayer replied that he had been climbing for almost two years, had always buckled his harness with a single pass, and that how he buckled his harness wasn't anyone else's business in any case. Taken aback, my friend—a product manager for a large outdoor firm—pointed out that his company had tested the same harness, buckled in an identical manner, and found that the webbing started slipping through the buckle under as little as 250 pounds of force. The response was chilling. The belayer turned and very clearly explained, "But I only weigh 170 pounds!"

Nothing came of this incident, but let's get out the crystal ball and take a somewhat pessimistic look at where climbing might be in the year 2000. With liability a major concern, all but a few retailers have stopped selling climbing equipment. Insurance, when it's available, costs far more than any potential profit, and only the largest shops can sell enough gear to justify the expense. Retail prices are astronomical. A carabiner is $50, a harness $300, and a rope $750, as manufacturers pass on the costs of insurance and safety features to the consumer. Every item of climbing gear sold comes with a detailed technical manual and extensive warning label, both mandated by law. So much redundancy is built into climbing equipment that the average carabiner (locking models only are available) weighs 8 ounces and fails at 20,000 pounds; harnesses and ropes are similarly heavy, foolproof, and complex.

Since the federal ban on all forms of individually-placed protection in 1995, initiated by the newly-formed American Climbing Club (ACC) and the Department of the Interior, all of the country's routes have been equipped to an acceptable standard: glued-in 1/2 inch bolts, at least 6 inches long, 10,000-pound test hangers, and triple-bolt anchors with chains and descending rings at all belays. Protection bolts are no more than one body length apart, and pitch lengths on longer routes have been standardized at 60 feet to allow easy top roping and rappels with a single rope. Hexes, stoppers, Rocks,

Friends, TCU's, and RP's are museum pieces; the fine for anyone actually caught using this antiquated gear is $2000 for the first offense, double that for the second.

—Kennedy, 1989, p. 6

Technology is changing more quickly than people can get a handle on it. Note the need to constantly upgrade computer hardware and software as new designs are released. Witness the recent advances in climbing protection and belaying devices. Are these driven by a concern for safety, efficiency, litigation, or other forces?

What are the environmental impacts of technology? Battery-powered electric drills have made bolting widespread. Bolting is the practice of drilling holes in the rock face and hammering expansion bolts into the hole to make foolproof or "bombproof" anchor points. A proliferation of bolts is offensive to some climbers and the constant noise of the drills is disturbing to others, not to mention the deteriorating aesthetic values and damage to nature. Consider this illustration:

In early October, bolting was banned in the Boulder Mountain Park system, which includes such popular areas as the Flatirons and Flagstaff Mountain. Park officials are also looking at ways of removing existing bolted routes from formations under its jurisdiction. Park officials have seemingly been loathe to compromise either, taking the unilateral position that "bolting, all fixed hardware, and the use of rock drills are strictly prohibited in Mountain Parks." Although they hope to obtain compliance through education and self-regulation by the climbing community, they can (and apparently will) issue summonses to offenders, with fines of up to $300 and/or 90 days in jail (Kennedy, 1990, p. 10).

As an outdoor leader, you should be aware of changing technology, particularly if it relates to safety. Failure to use readily available technology could lead to a lawsuit. Consider the recent availability of cellular phones and global positioning (satellite) systems (GPS). GPS is a locating device that scans for the location of at least 3 of 24 satellites in orbit around the planet, using their locations to triangulate its location on the map pinpointed by a six-digit grid reference accurate to within a few meters.

At the time of publication, these devices were available for a few hundred dollars each. What would be the result if a group was lost and injured without either piece of technology present? What would be the loss of wilderness atmosphere if both were brought along on a trip? How do you balance these costs and benefits?

Technological improvements and equipment advances may actually undermine adventure programming by hindering or limiting the ability of clients to achieve their goals (Browne, 1986; Gass, 1993b). By using gear that is more convenient or comfortable and less difficult or complex, clients learn to rely on the technology instead of themselves.

For instance, ultralight and super convenient backpacks may allow for clients to load their pack "any old way," losing out on valuable dynamics and natural consequences that lead to discussions of more important life issues. "Top of the line" tents may not make as much group sharing and learning, creativity, and problem solving necessary when figuring out as a group how to rig a tarp shelter with a variety of different knots.

While state-of-the-art equipment is designed to maximize safety in high-risk environments and under adverse weather conditions, it is often very expensive. Having the best gear may predispose people to venture into situations that they might not normally choose. Furthermore, clients may not always treat expensive gear with the care and respect it demands. For example, they may be better off with inexpensive rubberized rainsuits rather than expensive Gore-Tex ones. In short, the best money can buy is of no value if the client has lost, broken, or refused to use it.

Although those operating an adventure program would not want to compromise the safety of clients by using negligent or substandard equipment, you may find unexpected benefits from returning to older designs. Clients can learn to make and fix equipment and to live with the ramifications of their craftsmanship. Rather than simply adding water to dehydrated meals, clients can learn to bake from scratch in a group, thereby gaining important life skills in cooking, teamwork, cooperation, and interdependence all at the same time. Clients who demonstrate the ability to care for older equipment may be given the responsibility of caring for newer equipment. Last, damage to equipment can often indicate that

clients are having trouble coping with the demands of the adventure experience. "When clients end a course with the equipment neatly organized and accounted for, their spirits and sense of accomplishment and responsibility are high" (Browne, 1986, p. 19).

BURNOUT

Often I encounter people who are largely ignorant of the outdoor education field and who conjure up images of scaling peaks, running white water, living out of doors and incredibly, making money to boot! What they don't see is the extent to which I envy them in their stable 9 to 5 lives with predictable parameters when the not-so-romantic aspects of my job press upon me. I have become an outdoor educator by profession and although the rewards of the life make it worthwhile, the romantic sheen of the profession has certainly become tarnished to a more realistic hue. I find myself from time to time weighing the pros and cons, totaling up the balance sheet, and seeking out the issues and conflicts that confront me in this profession.

—Kesselheim, 1981, p. 20

Leading outdoor experiences can be a very enriching experience, but at the same time, the profession can be extremely draining. Gass (1993a) identified this paradox by pointing out that the very features that often attract individuals to becoming outdoor leaders often lead to professional burnout when not properly addressed. We can define **burnout** as a "state of physical, emotional, and mental exhaustion [that is] caused by long term involvement [with] demands most often caused by a combination of very high expectations and chronic situational stresses" (Pines, Ayala, & Aronson, 1988, p. 9).

Indicators of burnout are both subjective and objective. Subjective factors may include loss of self-esteem, resulting from feelings of professional incompetence or job dissatisfaction; physical depletion without an identifiable origin; feelings of helplessness and hopelessness; the development of disillusionment; exhibition of negative attitudes toward work, coworkers, or life itself; and problems with concentration, irritability, or negativism. Objective factors often involve a significant decrease in work performance as measured by lower quality, decreasing effectiveness, absenteeism, and a general loss of interest in work-related issues (Schaufeli, Maslach, & Marek, 1993). These subjective and objective factors may vary in intensity, duration, frequency, and consequences as well as from one individual to another. Several features that make outdoor leaders particularly susceptible to experiencing professional burnout are commitment, independence, lifestyle, experience base, and hopes and dreams (Gass, 1993a).

Generally speaking, most of us have strong commitments to our work, serving in a very altruistic manner that requires us to give certain levels of self-sacrifice and service to others. Such a high level of commitment can produce a great deal of energy, empowerment, and positive results for clients, but can also prove expensive to us personally. Long hours, physically exhausting work, and working with clients on emotionally charged issues are laborious. As outdoor leaders, we often pour so much effort into others that we neglect to take care of ourselves. We fall into the trap of expecting coleaders to have the energy to accomplish tasks that we would never ask clients to consider doing.

In comparison with other professions, we as leaders are quite independent and self-sufficient. Such independence often allows us the flexibility to meet a wide variety of needs for a broad range of populations. But such independence also leads us to overlook the strength and advantages of being connected with mainstream issues. MacArthur (1987) probably best described this quality with the term "mainstream fringe":

> We hang around the edge of the mainstream, putting up with the problems of interpreting why we do what we do, hoping that others will see the light. We are not really willing to make the full commitment to mainstream ways. As a survival technique, this probably makes a lot of sense. However, this may also mean that we are not committed enough to change politically. We are too transient in life to commit to one community, too concerned about our own freedom to invest in one place or one group of people for very long. Hence, we cannot sustain the momentum for significant change in our communities. (pp. 6-7)

One of the advantages of adventure programming is that it allows you to combine your avocations, which include hobbies or life interests, with your vocation: it is a lifestyle investment for most outdoor leaders. This often makes tasks intrinsically rewarding, yet can give the appearance that you are always on "vacation." However, this "blurring" of the boundaries between work and play can be depleting rather than replenishing. Interpersonal relationships, business relationships, maintaining appropriate ethical behavior, and the need to regenerate yourself can become complicated, leading to burnout when your work becomes so closely associated with your life outside of adventure programming.

As you well know, experience-based learning lies at the heart of most adventure programming. While we have already identified many advantages and disadvantages of experiential learning, some additional concerns contribute to professional burnout. One is that a possession that solely focuses on experience can lead to personal imbalances, particularly if you ignore the wealth of educational theory inside and outside the field. If you choose to live only by your own experiences, then the extent of what "exists" for you will become only the length of your lifetime.

Most outdoor leaders hope that adventure programs will make difficult situations better. Change processes often center on empowering clients in dysfunctional situations to attain healthier goals and lifestyles. Performing such work and living up to such expectations can be draining, especially when you don't reach such goals or expectations. Holding high expectations can lead to programming excellence, but it can also cost you a great deal, resulting in burnout.

To prevent and combat professional burnout, Gass (1993a) proposed a model based on the interconnected qualities of security, success, appropriate financial support, and balance. This model stresses that adventure programs need to position themselves in such a manner that these qualities are accessible to leaders. Security means that a program places you in positions with the potential to grow, receive constructive feedback, and regenerate your professional efforts. Success allows you to appropriately expect and achieve a sense of quality in what you do. This includes establishing appropriate boundaries, often by identifying nonnegotiable values, that is, those values that you are not willing to forsake to achieve client goals. Appropriate financial support addresses the idea that you must be paid in concert with the quality of work you do and the function you perform. As with other professionals, if educating, then be paid as educators; and if providing therapy, then be paid as therapists. Balance refers to your receiving the means to acquire and possess the necessary time, resources, support, and perspective to maintain appropriate professional quality.

PROFESSIONALISM

In the summer of 1990, two incidents occurred involving deaths of adolescents in private wilderness programs, which spurred regulatory activity in Utah and other western states. On May 9, 1990, fifteen-year-old Michelle Sutton died of dehydration and exposure while hiking in the Summit Quest program. The program was based in Utah, but the death occurred on a program expedition in Arizona. On June 27, 1990, sixteen-year-old Kristin Chase died of heat stroke while hiking in the Challenger program in Utah. Both incidents led to criminal investigations, and the founder of the Challenger program now faces criminal charges. The parents of both adolescents, who placed their children in the programs because of behavior problems, have brought wrongful death actions.

Even before the Challenger and Summit Quest incidents, Utah's child protective agency had removed several children from the Challenger program due to allegations of maltreatment. The deaths, however, prompted the Utah legislature to enact legislation enabling the state's Department of Human Services to adopt and enforce licensing standards for wilderness programs. The new standards were developed and implemented in the fall of 1990 (Utah Code, 1990). In addition to general standards applicable to all residential facilities, the standards governing staffing, equipment, admission and screening, nutrition, First Aid and general safety, transportation, and environmental precautions were developed. They do not, however, include safety rules for specific outdoor activities. Since that time,

Utah's Office of Licensing has granted licenses to 13 wilderness programs, suspended the licenses of two programs, and denied licenses to two new applicants.

—Mathews, 1991

This was written about incidents that occurred in 1990, regarding programs not following many of the standards present at that time. Unfortunately, in 1994, a similar tragedy occurred. Aaron Bacon died while participating in the North Star program, also in Utah. While the factors that resulted in these three deaths are rare in genuine adventure therapy programs following professional standards, it does call into question the concept of professionalism in adventure programming.

Ewert (1989) and Gass (1993b) have compiled lists of several characteristics that are used to determine the viability of a profession: the establishment and utilization of a unique body of knowledge, supported by a theoretical structure; integrity, dictated by an ethical code of conduct, including moral standards; the organization and representation of the field by professional organizations; skills that require extensive training; and the fulfillment of an indispensable social need particularly pertaining to client health and welfare.

As you know, we have already addressed each of these components to some degree in this text, summarizing a portion of the broad base of unique knowledge that exists concerning adventure programming. We have described in detail ethical principles addressing an appropriate level of competence, integrity, and client and social responsibility as well as respect for the rights, well-being, and dignity of clients. A number of professional organizations, most notably the Association for Experiential Education in North America with some international connections, the National Association for Outdoor Education in Britain, the Comenius Institute in Europe, and the Australian Outdoor Education Council, have been organized to further enhance these perspectives. Moreover, we have identified the skills and training necessary to conduct appropriate and effective adventure experiences. The intent and the outcomes of adventure programs are clearly directed toward the needs and welfare of the clients served. Adventure programming is a profession by definition, yet the question remains "Is it professional?"

Consider the recent and rapid growth of corporate adventure programs. Many operators have begun to work with this clientele for the large amounts of money that can be generated. While some may use these profits to offset the cost of running a youth camp or to subsidize hospital outreach efforts, many more are drawn simply by the opportunity to make a decent living for a change. As a result, a number of programs claiming to be "corporate" are poorly facilitated. These operators simply repeat the same programs they might conduct for their regular clients without adjusting the program to suit the corporation's needs or the participants' abilities. As a result, the programs become ineffective in the long run. To use a "fast food" analogy, these programs fill clients up, but they soon become hungry again.

Not only does this affect the prognosis for the adventure operator's survival, it also can adversely impact the entire profession's image since customers have difficulty differentiating good providers from bad. So, for example, a corporation looking for a developmental team-building program receives a recreational fun and games program instead. The transfer is absent and so the corporation remarks, "All this adventure stuff doesn't work!" The entire industry gets a negative reputation as evidenced by recent columns in the popular press, for example, the New York Times and Wall Street Journal, suggesting adventure training is a waste of money.

Yet how does a consumer differentiate "good" programs from "bad" ones—or at least those that profess to conduct valuable experiences from those that are inadequate? Program accreditation can be one indicator that the provider has met certain criteria for safety, ethics, and experientiality. Beyond this, Priest (1991) has suggested a list of 10 hallmarks for such corporate programs: safe, confidential, personalized, flexible, fast and efficient, enjoyable, educationally transferable, ethical, effective, and evaluative.

All adventure programs must be more clear about the level of programming they can supply. And consumers must understand the type of programming they need: recreational, educational, developmental, or therapeutic. This also requires you as an outdoor leader to be clear about the level at which you can capably facilitate and the techniques you can effectively use, such as funneling, frontloading, and framing. Until we are all open and honest about our strengths and weaknesses and have sufficient research or evaluation to counter the arguments against adventure programming, the profession will continue to suffer from this credibility crisis.

RESEARCH

In the late 1970s "Endeavor Enterprise" (not a real name) was generally acknowledged by many professionals as an effective and innovative adventure program. Sponsored by its local government and funded by tax dollars, EE received court-referred young people, who were at risk of imprisonment if they continued their behavior. For two decades, EE changed the lives of countless youth, putting them on the road to becoming productive members of society.

In the early 1990s, financial cutbacks brought an end to this top-rated program. Despite numerous protests from the staff and participants of EE, the powers that be canceled the program and refused to fund any similar programs that provided wilderness "holidays for criminals." While EE claimed to make an important difference and many experts agreed they did, EE could not present evidence of their impact. They could not prove that their recidivism rate was lower than other programs or that their program cost less than prison and other treatment alternatives.

This program had not bothered to conduct any program research or evaluation. So like many other programs, it suffered a very real end to its prosperity. Indeed, the lack of research and evaluation often leaves the profession "on the fringe," unable to claim its effectiveness when seriously challenged. Thus, more programs are being terminated due to decreases in subsidized (e.g., governmental) funding. More research and evaluation would help to further establish the field's credibility by demonstrating its effectiveness; more evaluation would enhance its current practices and methodologies. In other words, research can prove how and why adventure works and evaluation can improve the way programming works.

Specifically, as a profession, we need to do more research and evaluation to provide evidence that adventure programming is more than just fun and games and that it can serve as a powerful impetus for change when appropriately used. In order to accomplish this, several specific areas of study are necessary, including examining the elements of adventure programming and the means by which these elements bring about change and examining how change transfers effectively to the client's real life and how to sustain such change in the face of an unsupportive environment. In other words, ask "What transfers from the experience, how much of it, for how long, and because of what program elements or barriers?" We must organize studies that examine these program elements: duration, that is, one versus multiday programs; content, including activity numbers, lengths, types, and debriefings; location, that is, indoor or outdoor; setting, whether urban, rural, or wilderness; follow-up, including transfer strategies, reflection, and integration; clients, including types, ideal numbers, and gender segregation or mixing; and leadership, including facilitation techniques, teaching styles, and gender.

With an understanding of the need for and the methods of research and evaluation, you can contribute to its production and consumption. As a producer, you can conduct projects or assist others with their studies. Learn how to be a researcher or an evaluator by taking a course in research or evaluation. Get help from university faculty and support the efforts of students doing studies in order to graduate. As a consumer, you can read and critique existing published research and evaluation. When reading a study, check to see that the flow is logical and organized, that the intent of the study (purpose, questions, or hypothesis) is connected to the outcomes (findings, discussion, or conclusions), and that the study is easily understood (well-written, clear tables, or reasonable recommendations). When critiquing a study ask yourself two questions: "Does this make sense? Can I apply its findings to my program?" The first question refers to validity and reliability: Can the outcomes be explained by some other sensible explanation? The second question refers to generalizability: How are the outcomes and their context the same as or different from my adventure program? You don't have to be a research and evaluation expert in order to examine and comment on such studies, common sense is often sufficient.

Nevertheless, researchers and evaluators are likely to encounter a few routine difficulties when investigating adventure programming (Priest, Attarian, & Schubert, 1993). First, remember that credible adventure programs operate under the ethic of "challenge by choice" (see chapter 4), which means subjects are typically always **voluntary** and sampling can never be truly random because the participants are all at least somewhat ready to take risks. This lack of skeptics and timid or fearful participants may limit the study's application to all people. Second, small groups of 8 to 12 people, typical of adventure programming, means that distributions are more likely to be abnormal, requiring nonparametric (distribution-free) tests. Nonparametric statistics are generally less well-accepted by scholars than parametric procedures. Third, you cannot overcome this sample size concern by combining several groups with the exact same adventure, because truly effective programs customize the activities to best meet the clients' needs. If the program gets modified to suit the study, then the program suffers; and if the reverse is done, then the study suffers. Fourth, obtaining control groups (those not engaged in a program) is extremely difficult, because the experimental groups (those involved with the adventure) can often "contaminate" the purity of the controls by sharing experiences outside the study. Since the best controls are selected from the same situation as the experimentals, you can expect them to interact at home, school, work, or play and thus change the way the others respond to the study. Fifth, the phenomena studied in adventure programs are mostly human qualities, which are not easily measured in a quantitative manner. Since few valid and reliable instruments exist, the use of qualitative methods to measure qualities appears most logical. Sixth, some adventure programs and their clients simply do not want to be studied in case an inquirer discovers that they are ineffective in some way. Furthermore, research and evaluation can interfere with running a smooth program by interrupting processes or preventing people from concentrating.

Last, good research and evaluation follow some basic tenets of ethical behavior. First, informed consent is expected, except in cases in which deception or concealment are both justified and necessary for the intent of the study (i.e., participant observation). You must obtain the approval of an ethical human subjects committee of your organization or its equivalent before conducting this kind of study. Informed consent means that subjects must have the risks and responsibilities of the study explained to them verbally or in writing, and they should provide signed consent. Verbal agreement to participate is acceptable in general public surveys, but not in experiments in which subjects are assigned to treatment or control groups. Second, you must guarantee confidentiality by stating that individual responses will not be named, but instead will be reported in aggregate or averaged forms. Real names will be changed to protect subjects, and the names of organizations (clients or programs) will be withheld for reasons of privacy. Third, as a researcher and evaluator, you should resist the temptation to overgeneralize. Lack of random sampling techniques, often not possible due to the predetermined client group composition, may mean that you cannot generalize results beyond the groups or clients studied. Generalization is frequently limited to a particular program or training treatment. The perfect study is rare, as most research or evaluation is limited and flawed to some extent. People who fail to acknowledge these flaws in their studies are claiming credibility of research and evaluation that simply does not exist and may be misrepresenting the authenticity of their work. Fourth, research and evaluation should be given a peer review or refereeing process as in scholarly or academic journals. Here other researchers and evaluators critique the work, drawing attention to the possible flaws. This can either improve marginal studies or prevent poor studies from being disseminated to consumers. Therefore, releasing research or evaluation in prepublished manuscript form to anyone other fellow researchers and evaluators is unwise.

EFFECTIVE OUTDOOR LEADERS SHOULD

☞ Be aware of the trends, issues, contributing factors, and growth areas of adventure programming to be ready for the future.

☞ Be careful to use technological improvements and equipment advances to enhance program quality, not undermine it.

☞ Know how burnout arises and how to avoid it.

☞ Understand their roles in maintaining a professional image.

☞ Comprehend how to help the research and evaluation process.

SUMMARY

A number of trends and issues in the field of adventure programming are influenced by global and social factors, including increased population, increased environmental damage, improved communication and transportation technology, worldwide economic competition, decreased family association, decreased discretionary moneys, decreased work time, and decreased conservation and compassion.

These factors suggest that adventure programs will continue to grow in popularity and that the size and number of professional organizations will also increase as the profession expands, diversifies, and matures through self-examination. Adventure programs will find their ways into schools and urban centers as greater use is made of artificial adventure environments and as the natural environments become more regulated or complexly managed. Programs will see greater restrictions on their use of natural resources through outdoor licenses, use permits, and access fees. Wilderness will become even more popular and controlled, causing some to use rescue-free zones for greater challenge.

Technology will also impact the environment and the feeling of wilderness through such inventions as battery-powered electric drills, cellular phones, and GPS units. Equipment advances may work against program intents, and you will need to be careful that these do not undermine the adventure experience.

Burnout will continue to be common among staff due to a number of subjective and objective factors remaining to be addressed relating to loss of self-esteem, feelings of incompetence or dissatisfaction, physical depletion without identifiable origin, feelings of helplessness or hopelessness, the development of disillusionment, exhibition of negative attitudes toward work, coworkers, or life itself, problems with concentration, irritability, or negativism, and decreases in work performance, quality, effectiveness, attendance, and interest. You may remain susceptible to burnout due to your commitment, independence, lifestyle, experience base, and hopes and dreams. You can reverse burnout by working for programs which espouse security, success, appropriate financial support, and balance.

Recent deaths in programs lacking credible practices yet licensed by the state of Utah have highlighted the need for greater professionalism in adventure programming. Specifically, a profession has a unique body of knowledge and ethical integrity, is represented by governing organizations, uses skills that require extensive training, and fulfills indispensable social needs. Although adventure programming may qualify as a profession by definition, it does fall short on a few professional behaviors. Most notable is its systemic inability to "deliver the goods" once in a while. As a result, its professional image becomes tarnished by the popular press claiming that adventure programming is a waste of time and money. Program accreditation and 10 hallmarks may help consumers to distinguish the effective providers from the ineffective ones. To prevent further repetition of this concern, we encourage programs to be clear about their range of programming competence, and we caution you not to facilitate for a program purpose that is beyond your abilities.

Research and evaluation help establish professional credibility as well as demonstrate effectiveness. While research proves how and why adventure programming works, evaluation improves the way it works. Future research and evaluation ought to focus on answering several questions: What transfers? How much of it? For how long? Which program elements or barriers affect outcomes? Participation in research and evaluation should be voluntary with small groups in customized programs, compared to a control group if possible. As a profession, we must use more qualitative, as opposed to quantitative, methods to get a better understanding of the quality of the experience. Moreover, we must follow certain guidelines for ethical research and evaluation: informed consent, confidentiality, avoiding overgeneralization, and obtaining a peer review or refereed critique of the study.

QUESTIONS TO THINK ABOUT

1. Identify the factors and growth areas that are global and those that are local from this chapter. Add any new ones you come up with.

2. Which of these factors and growth areas influence each of the six trends and issues mentioned in this chapter?

3. In the role of program coordinator, write a response to the statements of the ANP superintendent in the first vignette of the "Environment" section in this chapter.

4. A very real threat is posed by increased mountain bike use in wilderness environments. After doing a background search of what the issues are in regard to mountain biking in your region, debate this issue with a colleague or class. Be sure to cover the real potential in most areas to have trails closed to mountain bike use.

5. Describe your attitudes toward technology. Can you think of another technological improvement that has had a major effect on the outdoor experience, either positive or negative?

6. Describe a time when you felt burned out. What did you do about it?

7. What can you do to contribute to the adventure programming profession?

8. How can you help enable research and evaluation of adventure programming?

REFERENCES

Browne, D. (1986). How to use equipment therapeutically. *Journal of Experiential Education* 9(3), 16-19.

Cole, E., Erdman, E., Rothblum, E.D. (Eds.). (1994). *Wilderness therapy for women*. NY: Harrington Park Press.

Davis-Berman, J. & Berman, D. S. (1994). *Wilderness therapy: Foundations, theory, & research*. Dubuque, IA: Kendall/Hunt Publishing Company.

Ewert, A. (1989). *Outdoor adventure pursuits*. Columbus, OH: Publishing Horizons.

Garvey, D. (1990). A history of AEE. In J.C. Miles & S. Priest (Eds.), *Adventure education* (75-82). State College, PA: Venture.

Gass, M.A. (1993a). Enhancing career development in adventure programming. In M.A. Gass (Ed.), *Adventure therapy: Therapeutic application of adventure programming in mental health settings* (417-426). Dubuque, IA: Kendall/Hunt.

Gass, M.A. (1993b). The future of the profession of adventure therapy. In M.A. Gass (Ed.). *Adventure therapy: Therapeutic application of adventure programming in mental health settings* (411-416). Dubuque, IA: Kendall/Hunt.

Gerstein, J. (1992). *Directory of experiential therapy and adventure-based counseling programs*. Boulder, CO: Association for Experiential Education.

Kennedy, M. (1989). Money talks, nobody walks. *Climbing* 114, 6.

Kennedy, M. (1990). Trouble in paradise. *Climbing* 118, 10.

Kesselheim, A. (1981). A look at the life of an outdoor educator. *Journal of Experiential Education* 4(1), 39-41.

Lenard, M. (1995). Toward a new climbing culture. *Climbing* 150, 200.

MacArthur, B. (1987). Habits of the heart. *Journal of Experiential Education* 10(1), 5-11.

Mathews, M. (1993). Wilderness programs offer promising alternatives for some youth: More regulation likely. In M.A. Gass (Ed.), *Adventure therapy: Therapeutic application of adventure programming in mental health setting* (pp. 441-450). Dubuque, IA: Kendall/Hunt.

McAvoy, L. (1990). Rescue-free wilderness areas. In J.C. Miles & S. Priest (Eds.), *Adventure education* (pp. 335-343). State College, PA: Venture.

McAvoy, L., & Dustin, D. (1981). The right to risk in wilderness. *Journal of Forestry* 79(3), 150-152.

McAvoy, L., & Dustin, D. (1983). In search of balance: A no-rescue wilderness proposal. *Western Wildlands* 9(2), 2-5.

Mentuck, A. (1996, August 18). Lyons speaks to industry leaders. *Outdoor Retailer Daily Exposure*, p. 3.

Miles, J. (1990). The future of adventure education. In J.C. Miles & S. Priest (Eds.), *Adventure education* (pp. 467-471). State College, PA: Venture.

Pines, B., Ayala, L., & Aronson, E. (1988). *Career burnout: Causes and cures*. NY: Free Press.

Priest, S. (1991). Shopping for a corporate adventure training program. *Personnel: Journal of the American Management Association* 68(7), 15-16.

Priest, S., Attarian, A., & Schubert, S. (1993). Conducting research in experienced-based training and development programs: Pass keys to locked doors. *Journal of Experiential Education* 16(2), 11-20.

Priest, S., & Dixon, T. (1990). *Safety practices in adventure programming*. Boulder, CO: Association for Experiential Education.

Proudman, S. (1990). Urban adventure. In J.C. Miles & S. Priest (Eds.), *Adventure education* (pp. 335-343). State College, PA: Venture.

Schaufeli, W., Maslach, C., & Marek, T. (Eds.). (1993). *Professional burnout: Recent developments in theory and research*. Washington, DC: Taylor and Francis.

Schoel, J., Prouty, D., & Radcliffe, P. (1988). *Islands of healing: A guide to adventure-based counseling*. Hamilton, MA: Project Adventure.

Utah licensing standards for wilderness programs. (1990). In Mathews, M. (1993). Wilderness programs offer promising alternatives for some youth: More regulation likely. In M.A. Gass (Ed.). *Adventure therapy: Therapeutic application of adventure programming in mental health settings* (pp. 441-450). Dubuque, IA: Kendall/Hunt.

Williamson, J., & Gass, M.A. (1993). *Manual of program accreditation standards for adventure programs*. Boulder, CO: Association for Experiential Education.

Williamson, J., & Gass, M.A. (1995). *Manual of accreditation standards for adventure programs*. (2nd ed.). Boulder, CO: Association for Experiential Education.

Author Index

Ford, P.M., 240, 244
Furlong, L., 122, 132
Fyffe, A., 85

G

Garvey, D., 30, 39, 295, 305
Gass, M.A., 13, 23, 26, 37, 38, 39, 40, 51, 59, 63,
    68, 71, 77, 84, 136, 138, 148, 174, 175, 178,
    183, 187, 200, 206, 210, 211-216, 217, 218,
    221, 225-228, 233, 284-285, 286, 289-291,
    292, 296, 299, 300-301, 305, 306
Gerstein, J., 295, 305
Gibbons, M., 140, 143-144, 148
Gilchrist, J., 85
Gillette, N., 85
Gillis, H. L., 138, 148, 225-228, 233
Goffman, E., 44, 59
Golins, G., 20-22, 26, 47, 59, 138-139, 140-141, 148
Gould, D., 48, 59
Gray, D., 35, 37, 39
Graydon, D., 85
Green, P.J., 3, 4, 7, 36, 37, 39
Greenaway, R., 192, 206
Grube, G.M., 136, 148
Gullion, L., 85

H

Hale, A., 89, 102
Halliday, W.R., 85
Hammel, H., 177, 182, 187, 194, 199, 200, 206
Hammerman, D.R., 151-153, 159
Hammerman, E.L., 152-153, 159
Hammerman, W.M., 152-153, 159
Hart, J., 85
Harter, S., 53, 59
Hersey, P., 239, 244
Higgins, L., 122, 132
Hopkins, D., 140, 143-144, 148
Howard, R., 252, 254
Hunt, J.S., 13, 17, 26, 35, 39, 284, 285, 292

I

International Mountain Bike Association, 85

J

Jackson, J., 31, 39
James, W., 14, 26, 29, 39

Jensen, M.A., 63, 70, 71
Jillings, A., 122, 132
Johnson, D., 253, 254
Jones, J.E., 140, 144-145, 148
Joplin, L., 16, 26, 137, 140, 142, 148
Jordan, A.E., 285, 292
Jung, C., 252, 254

K

Kahneman, D., 259, 262
Kalisch, K., 224, 233
Kant, I., 287, 292
Katzell, R., 48, 51, 59
Kennedy, M., 298, 306
Kerr, P.J., 63, 68, 71
Kesselheim, A., 299, 306
Kiewa, J., 141, 148
Kimball, R.O., 139, 148, 209, 221, 232, 233
King, K., 12, 26, 136, 148, 227, 233
Kiser, D.J., 228, 233
Kitchener, K.S., 286-289, 291, 292
Kjellstrom, B., 85
Klint, K., 54, 141, 148
Knapp, C., 177, 187, 202-205, 206
Kolb, D.A., 140, 144, 148
Kraft, R.J., 14, 16, 17, 26

L

LaFollette, J., 35, 37, 39
Langmuir, E., 31, 32, 39
LaRhette, M., 122, 132
Leave No Trace, 104, 105, 106-107, 108
Lee, J., 85
Lenard, M., 297, 306
Leopold, A., 105, 108
Lerman, D., 52, 60
Lewin, K., 238, 244
Lingard, 33
Lipchik, E., 228, 233
Lippitt, R., 238, 244
Long, J., 85
Loughman, M., 85
Lowe, J., 85
Lowry, R., 85
Loynes, C., 33, 39
Luckner, J., 174, 177, 187, 210, 221, 230, 233
Lupton, F., 30, 40

Subject Index

About the Authors

Simon Priest is an adjunct professor at several American universities and has been a visiting and guest professor at a number of universities around the world. He is also a retired full professor from Brock University in Canada, and the founding director of the Corporate Adventure Training Institute, a research center at Brock University. A member of the Association for Experiential Education since 1983, he is the director of their research task force and the chair of their student research grants committee.

Dr. Priest's contributions to the field of adventure programming have had a international impact. He has been a scholar in residence and has been awarded visiting professorships in Australia, New Zealand, England, and other European nations. He has also studied and taught about outdoor leadership in more than two dozen countries around the world.

Dr. Priest has researched and written extensively on the topic of adventure programming. He has authored or edited several books and book chapters, and his articles have appeared in publications such as the *Journal of Adventure Education and Outdoor Leadership*, the *Journal of Experiential Education*, *Leisure Studies*, and the *Journal of Physical Education, Recreation and Dance*. Dr. Priest received his doctorate from the University of Oregon in 1986.

Michael Gass is a professor and coordinator of the outdoor education program in the Department of Kinesiology at the University of New Hampshire (UNH). He is the creator of the Browne Center, a program development and research center on adventure learning that serves more than 5,000 clients a year. He also serves as a professional-in-residence at the UNH Marriage and Family Therapy Center.

Dr. Gass has helped to produce three books for the Association for Experiential Education (AEE). He authored *Book of Metaphors: Volume II*, edited *Adventure Therapy: Therapeutic Applications of Adventure Programming*, and coedited *Program Accreditation Standards for Adventure Programs* with Jed Williamson. His writing has also appeared in several professional journals.

Dr. Gass served as president of AEE in 1990 and was the chair of AEE's Therapeutic Adventure Professional Group in 1992–93 and 1995–96. He also was the chair of American Alliance for Health, Physical Education, Recreation and Dance's Council for Outdoor Education in 1994. Currently he serves on the advisory board for the Journal of Experiential Education and is the chair of AEE's Program Accreditation Council.

Dr. Gass received his PhD in experiential education from the University of Colorado at Boulder and completed postdoctoral studies in marriage and family therapy.

You'll find
other outstanding
educational resources at

www.humankinetics.com

In the U.S. call

1-800-747-4457

Australia 08 8277 1555
Canada 800-465-7301
Europe .... +44 (0) 113 278 1708
New Zealand 09-309-1890

HUMAN KINETICS
The Information Leader in Physical Activity
P.O. Box 5076 • Champaign, IL 61825-5076 USA